Law *and the* Company We Keep

Aviam Soifer

Harvard University Press
Cambridge, Massachusetts
London, England   1995

For Marlene, Raphael, and Amira

Copyright © 1995 by the President and Fellows of Harvard College
All rights reserved
Printed in the United States of America

This book is printed on acid-free paper, and its binding
materials have been chosen for strength and durability.

Library of Congress Cataloging-in-Publication Data
Soifer, Aviam.
    Law and the company we keep / Aviam Soifer.
        p.   cm.
    Includes bibliographical references and index.
    ISBN 0-674-51298-7 (acid-free paper)
    1. Collective settlements—Law and legislation—United States.
    2. Freedom of association—United States.   3. Culture and law.
    4. Group identity—United States.   I. Title.
KF1390.C6S67   1995
302.3—dc20
94-46602
        CIP

Contents

Preface

In a fine, sad novel about the Vietnam war, a veteran explains, "Stories are for joining the past to the future. Stories are for those late hours in the night when you can't remember how you got from where you were to where you are. Stories are for eternity, when memory is erased, when there is nothing to remember except the story."[1] Significant aspects of law also involve such stories. Remembrance, and the differences between history and tradition, are vital yet often ignored factors in judicial discourse. But it is the desire to mention those who have helped me most that leads me to tell a story from my own past.

All of my life, year in and year out, I have spent at least a small part of each summer at a tiny community called Raananah, which in Hebrew means fresh or green. Raananah was founded as a collective colony in 1937 by a group of urban Jewish immigrants who purchased an abandoned Catholic summer camp on a hill a few miles above the village of Highland Mills, New York, near Bear Mountain Park. Raananah then seemed to be way out in "the country." Today it is surrounded by subdivisions, and now many local residents commute daily over an hour each way to New York City.

Raananah's founders were Labor Zionists—that is, secularists and socialists. In fact, they bought their 64 acres on Yom Kippur, the most somber of Jewish holidays, when such an action is strictly forbidden by religious law. Raananah's small band vehemently opposed both religious Jews and Communists, with whom they often worked and argued incessantly.

I remember struggling not to fall asleep as I listened, night after night, lying out on an uninsulated porch, to the katydids, the wind, and the vigorous arguments about the news, politics, and what was good for the Jews, for the United States, and for Israel. Before television invaded this tiny community of thirty-nine families, the nightly entertainment was fierce debate—often bouncing back and forth from English to Yiddish and occasionally to Hebrew or Russian—about what the radio news had reported and the stories in the *Herald Tribune* or *New York Times* that morning, the *Post* in the afternoon, as well as the *Yiddish Forward* or *Der Tag*. (Much was revealed by which papers you read—and the blatant unreliability of a competing source for news was a constant refrain.)

A simple story about Raananah and its leader, Joseph "Yushka" Furman, has become a crucial tale of origin for me. It tells much about the place and the people there, whose influence on me I acknowledge with pride and deep affection. The relevant events took place in 1948, when it was already clear despite some initial hopes that Raananah would not become a kibbutz-like, year-round settlement. Furman had helped to start a Jewish agricultural commune decades earlier in Utah, and he and at least some of the other founders of Raananah envisioned a similar collective experiment for this small corner of New York State. (Some of Raananah's people were quite involved in the worldwide Labor Zionist movement. When luminaries such as David Ben-Gurion and Golda Meir came to the United States, they sometimes stopped in Raananah to relax and to argue a bit.)

As the High Holy Days approached in 1948—the year in which Israel had declared its independence and had to fight for it—a few Raananah members decided that it would be both fitting and convenient to celebrate Rosh Hashanah and Yom Kippur in the settlement, surrounded by the countryside's early fall beauty. Furman, however, had refused to enter a synagogue since his Bar Mitzvah. He was vociferously antireligious and opposed this proposal vigorously. Yushka was immensely charismatic, and his argument held additional force because he was a father still grieving for his youngest son, who had died when his plane crashed during World War II. But Furman lost this fierce Raananah battle. On the first evening of Rosh Hashannah, he was nevertheless the first person to show up for services. He explained his appearance to the surprised—some of them mocking—fellow members of Raananah, as follows: "If the people of Raananah are here, this is where I belong." This ineffable sense of commitment to community is surely familiar to most readers, no matter how radically different their particular experiences.

I have missed few Rosh Hashanah services in Raananah. My grandfather, Harry Woll, no longer pounds the table to establish a moment of quiet; my grandmother, Rivka Seldin Woll, no longer matches him combatively and critically, whether the subject was Jewish texts, current events, or the community's fervent internal disputes. My father, Samuel Soifer, is hardly the natural at table-pounding that his father-in-law was. Yet now it is my father who presides over the services in his gentle, good-natured way. My cousin Diana Woll Zurer—Yushka Furman's granddaughter—sings beautifully as the primary cantor, an unthinkable role for any woman even in Raananah until a few years ago. Sisters and cousins and aunts seem to be omnipresent on these festive occasions.

By now, it is a tradition that my mother, Ahuva Woll Soifer, reads the Haftorah that recalls Rachel weeping for her son, Ephraim, and there are tears of remembrance throughout the crowded, overheated social hall converted into a synagogue for this occasion. This is also a time of celebration, amid the noise of children playing underfoot or, more often, outdoors. I cannot sing as well as most of the others, nor do I know as much as many. But they have taught me to appreciate the memories and the sense of renewal and change I feel when I see my wife, Marlene Booth, and our children, Raphael and Amira, both in Raananah and far away from it as well.

The flavor of the place is captured in a wonderful documentary film, *Raananah: A World of Our Own* (1981), made by Marlene Booth. But my brief story of this tiny community and its memories, battles, and tough reconciliations helps to explain some of my own sense of the vital importance of community, of intermediate groups, and of tolerance even when it is rooted in combativeness. In Raananah, nothing is settled for good or even for long.

It is also important not to be carried away by warm thoughts and mushy feelings about peaceable kingdoms. Kiryas Joel, a settlement of the fiercely separatist, intolerant Satmar Hasidic Jews, sprang up less than a mile from Raananah. The ultraorthodox Jews in Kiryas Joel deny the existence of the State of Israel, and they frequently beat up other Hasidim and, on occasion, internal dissenters. These Satmar Hasidim repeatedly have litigated over the constitutional limits of state entanglement with their fundamentalist religious beliefs.[2] The Jews in the tight little islands of Kiryas Joel and Raananah have nothing to do with each other beyond occasional gawking and great mutual suspicion. In fact, each group defines itself in part through negation and exclusion of the other. Group identity often is forged through differentiation, suspicion, and even overt conflict. Yet our myriad, conflicting group identities are so essential and so inescapable that they cannot be ignored, no matter how assimilationist, integrationist, or universalist one seeks to be.

The personal is political—and familial, social, intellectual, and economic, too. In all these matters. I have been very lucky indeed. I owe this book and more that is much more important to my parents, Ahuva and Samuel. They are Jewish educators and community social workers by training, and community builders and family sustainers through constant attention and abiding, loving concern. My siblings, Carmi, Naira, and Eldon—respectively poet, lawyer, and philosopher—also are all teachers as well as exemplars of ways that commitment to others can coexist with great care in dealing with words and thoughts. They, too, have helped greatly to make me who I am and this book what it is. As we near the end of what often has been a horrific century, it seems fitting to dedicate this book to the future and to communities still in formation: to Amira, Raphael, and Marlene, whose love and laughter make me truly blessed.

Law and the Company We Keep

Introduction

Collectively is the smudgiest word in the English language.

Frederic W. Maitland

Our collective problem lies not in any one word but in ourselves. As individuals, we are largely defined by our groups. Associations—whether voluntary or imposed—constitute inescapable elements of identity. Yet the American legal system lacks any theory to handle groups. The dominant legal paradigm in American law is the relationship between individual and state. The company we keep is presumed to be each person's own business, beyond the notice of the law.

This book directly faces the "smudginess" of collectivity. It is a sustained account of the presence and importance of groups throughout our legal culture. It also steps outside legal doctrine to confront central questions about the multiple roles of culture and symbol in defining our groups and, through them, our lives. This book thus connects with the widespread debate about groups and communitarian values today in many fields. Accepting law as within the humanities, this book challenges the glaring omission of groups from dominant legal theory, while also challenging the overly abstract and general terms of debate about groups in the humanities.

The central argument draws upon many disciplines. History adds perspective and color to the virtually omnipresent issues of pluralism. Literature illuminates the variegated ways in which a whole may be more than the sum of its parts. As we search for coherence in discussing the contexts of groups as groups, sociology, anthropology, and political theory supplement traditional, pinched definitions of what constitutes law.

Yet the book's main focus remains legal discourse—particularly the opinions of leading judges who struggle with group claims. I explain and criticize the limits of the dominant intellectual topography. My purpose is to give substance to the pluralism that Americans delight to celebrate, but do not wish to think about much. In the process, readers will encounter a claim for an independent group right: a constitutional right to freedom of association. Although this right is not absolute, it is substantial. A discussion of specific contemporary controversies illustrates how such a right would and should make a practical legal difference.

It is not my goal to catch, pin down, and classify associations like so many butterflies in a glass case. Nor will I make much use of the anthropologist's zoom lens or the sociologist's wide-angle focus. Instead, I invite readers to consider how multiple associations connect with law. I hope readers will do so at a level somewhere between noticing the beating of a single butterfly's wings and theorizing about the cumulative causal effects of that butterfly, along with countless other variables, on next month's weather half a world away.[1]

Oddly, the very concept of group identity is opaque. Perhaps the more important something is, the more difficult it becomes to define. Group identities may still be studiously ignored in legal discourse, yet we will see that the rights and roles of groups are crucial issues in law today. It is daunting to attempt to describe what happens when people form, join, or try to leave a myriad of associations, collectivities, groups, and communities. In the beginning, however, there still must be the word. The absence of appropriate legal language for groups is part of the problem this book addresses.[2]

Recent presidential campaigns underscore the appealing imprecision of "community." In 1988, for example, George Bush and Michael Dukakis each used "community" at a pivotal point in his acceptance speech. Dukakis declared his faith in "an idea as powerful as any in human history . . . the idea of community." He invoked John Winthrop, the first governor of Massachusetts Bay Colony, who said before he landed in the New World in 1630, "We must love one another with pure heart fervently. We must delight in each other, make each other's condition our own, rejoice together, mourn together, and suffer together. We must . . . be knit together as one."[3]

Several weeks later, George Bush declared that "the differences between the two candidates are as deep and wide as they have ever been in our long history." Nevertheless, Bush also cloaked himself in "the idea of community—a beautiful word with a big meaning." Bush attacked Democrats for thinking of community as "a limited cluster of interest groups." In contrast, Bush rhapsodized, "we are a nation of communities, of thousands and tens of thousands of ethnic, religious,

social, business, labor union, neighborhood, regional and other organizations, all of them varied, voluntary and unique." Indeed, it was
these communities that Bush visualized, glimmering "like a thousand
points of light in a broad and peaceful sky."[4]

Celebrating his victory on Election Night in 1992, President-Elect
Bill Clinton similarly proclaimed, "If we have no sense of community,
the American dream will continue to wither." Clinton's theme was
that "we need a new spirit of community, a sense that we're all in this
together . . . and we will rise or fall together."[5]

It is surely to be hoped that nobody actually relies on the rhetoric of
American presidential candidates. Yet such overlapping celebrations
of "community" do merit attention. Here, after a decade exceptional
in its celebration of untrammeled individual initiative, the presidential
candidates of the two major political parties and their entourages
decided that an appeal to the idea of community in prime time would
be likely to touch the voting public.

Community and the values of voluntary associations seem to appeal
greatly to Americans today, but the concepts to describe and distinguish among such groups remain virtually beyond the ken of legal
discourse. This legal gap is particularly striking today, when the quest
for community has become fashionable across numerous academic
fields. In the world of academic discourse it is virtually impossible to
escape discussion of interpretive communities, neo-republican virtues,
and dialogic processes. As far back as the 1950s, "an enterprising
American sociologist had uncovered more than 90 discrete definitions" of the term "community" in the social sciences alone.[6] The term
"community" often functions as a palimpsest, and the idea of voluntary or private or nonprofit associations or lifestyle enclaves can
become an all-purpose container, to be stuffed with vague longings
and undifferentiated nostalgia.

The kind of desperate search for community we recognize in the
United States is hardly unique to our shores. With the dramatic crum-
bling of barriers and boundaries in Europe and Asia, for example, an
unstable admixture of centripetal and centrifugal forces proclaiming
community values is spreading across the globe. Technology has
moved global villagers closer together, and we have begun to learn
how loud, violent, and protracted the quarrels of our neighbors can be.
In fact, many seem to defend their longstanding group identities primarily through feuds with other groups. Similarly, the revival of religious communities is a crucial phenomenon around the world. Even

within relatively sophisticated legal systems, moreover, there are remarkably diverse responses to the problem of the appropriate role for groups.[7]

One of the historical continuities is a strong tendency to long for a golden age that never was. A fallacy about the "conservation of historical energy"[8] is commonplace: the mistaken belief that any increase in individualism must be at the expense of community values, and vice versa. The world would be more manageable if some reliable principle could demonstrate that caring, face-to-face communities tragically, but inevitably, must give way to self-centered, atomistic individualism. It is enticing to rely upon a notion of a clear-cut division between communitarianism and individualism. When we confront the remarkable tangle of intertwining group identities, however, we can begin to understand that "negative capability"[9]—the ability to hold conflicting generalizations in mind at the same time—is indispensable.

Only in this way is it possible to grapple successfully with a basic paradox in American social life. Americans express vehement commitment to individualism and deep faith that individuals can and should be let alone, but we also continue to join more, and more diverse, groups than do people in other countries. We rely on such groups for some of the most essential things in life—even if we are not very good at doing things together.

Our individualistic principles have never caught up with our practices. Surveying the sweep of American history, the legal historian Willard Hurst emphasized both the American tendency to join groups and the consequences of our failure to adjust our ideas to that reality. As Hurst put it, "Since our thinking did not keep pace with the increasing group emphasis in our life, it was not surprising that shrewd men could warp individualistic symbols of the constitutional ideal to sanction unchecked organized power."[10] We retain the individualistic ideology even when it masks group reality. To paraphrase Thomas Jefferson: We are all individualists, we are all joiners.

This crucial American paradox intensifies when we consider how Americans learn law. When logic and reason defy intuition or a widely shared sense of justice, it is common in law to pretend that the solution has been reasoned out earlier, by someone else. Alternatively, lawyers often resort to claims that benevolent results will follow in the long run if we deny benevolent or just principles in the short run.[11] And most lawyers and judges continue to miss a key point Arthur Bentley made at the beginning of the century: "The most insignificant suit between two parties over a contract is dealt with socially on the basis of great group interests which have established the conditions and the bounds for it."[12]

In the adversarial legal system of the United States, legal encounters are portrayed generally as either/or battles with clearcut individual losers and winners. Despite extensive contradictory evidence, we still follow what Karl Llewellyn, the leading legal realist, identified as a "vicious heritage of regularly viewing parties . . . as single individuals."[13] This allows us to ignore the multiple relationships, the complex institutional arrangements, the web of parties involved directly in the actual context of the dispute. A scrim of the individual ideal hides the mess.

Americans are reminded, through our faith in the secular religion of law and our ongoing celebration of constitutionalism, of stark alternatives to individual liberty and the rule of law. Just beyond are said to lie either tyranny or chaos. Accordingly, individual plaintiffs and defendants generally are assigned all the paradigmatic roles of individual and state actors. They litigate against each other in dramatic fashion, resolving their disputes in an isolated process presumed to be fair, evenhanded, and constitutional. Silence surrounds all their group affiliations and commitments.

If the apotheosis of law helps create a benign façade, a significant darker side must be noted as well. At the most basic level, litigants seek to invoke the state's legal sanction to inflict pain on others. To view law as legalized violence is simply to recast the paradox. This perspective moves beyond simple faith in contests between individuals. It underscores how extensively legal claims are grounded in human association.

The central tradition of individual adversaries and the set theatrical piece of the courtroom confrontation has a strong hold—perhaps a stranglehold—on how Americans think about law. Yet it hardly captures reality. It also fails to include communal ideals that anchor law. Robert Cover put it well when he claimed that law is a bridge, perhaps *the* bridge, between what we are and what we might become.[14] Legal words and legal force can form the springboard for a better life through committed social behavior. The words of the judges we will consider in the pages that follow suggest how difficult any significant legal innovation turns out to be, yet they also underscore how important it is both to remember the past and to try to change the future.

*   *   *

Combining law and the humanities, this book offers an American Studies type of approach to a series of important legal problems. Although there is some case analysis and legal doctrine crunching, this book differs from other books about law. My central concern is not with the rights of dissenting members of groups. There is considerable literature already about whether and how to protect the rights of those with the courage to rebel.[15] Nor does the book concentrate on the role of religious groups, though it touches on religious identification and the overlapping, much-debated issue of how we ought to interpret constitutional protection for the free exercise of religion. Instead, the focus here is on the boundaries between secular groups and governments. The book begins by exploring issues of law and reciprocal power that overlap uncannily in *The Tempest* and in Plymouth Plantation; it ends by probing some dilemmas of detached judging today.

As part of the effort to give substance to pluralism, some chapters delve into history and literature extensively, while others more selectively utilize these and other disciplines such as anthropology and sociology. Frequently, I offer normative critiques of contemporary decisions and suggest how a rebuttable presumption in favor of a constitutional associational right would make a difference in people's lives. In pursuit of practical suggestions for meaningful law reform, I try to move beyond the crabbed categories into which legal doctrine traditionally pigeonholes groups—if they are noticed at all.

Finding our places within a multitude of groups gets all of us where we live. Try as many do to escape, group identity is still at the core of law and judging, and of individual identity. A person's groups inevitably constitute part of any contemplative life. We think and therefore, willy-nilly, we must interpret and make judgments rooted in and largely bounded by a multitude of overlapping groups.

1   Authority and Freedom

The Tempest seems a peculiar text for the beginning of a discussion about law and groups in America. *The Merchant of Venice, Measure for Measure,* and even *The Second Part of King Henry VI* ("The first thing we do, let's kill all the lawyers") surely appear more appropriate for anyone who seeks the panache of Shakespeare to develop points about law and letters. Moreover, *The Tempest* is so mythic that even though most people never read the play, many believe they know it well. A new interpretation might therefore look obscure to some readers and redundant to the rest. Yet, I argue, *The Tempest* suggests—brilliantly and subversively—some crucial ways in which competing notions of community and freedom intertwine. For all its inherent difficulty, *The Tempest* illuminates the problem of limitations on freedom by authority. It beautifully clarifies the paradox of individual identity within various group contexts.

The Tempest will not oblige the familiar habit of categorizing something as comedy or tragedy, celebration or jeremiad. When first performed, the play offered a commentary on contests over foundational issues of politics and religion that simmered and occasionally erupted during the reign of James I. Within a few decades, of course, these basic disagreements produced Civil War and regicide. It was an era when "things English came to matter with a special intensity both because England itself mattered more than it had and because other sources of identity and cultural authority mattered less."[1]

Undoubtedly, *The Tempest* also looked outward. The play directly echoed reports from the New World. It spoke wisely and well about the problem of how to govern or be governed. The social contract, bruited about a good deal during the seventeenth century, does not permeate Prospero's island. We will see, however, that the social contract is *not* not there.[2] The metes and bounds of any social contract, explicit or implicit, constituted a vital question in seventeenth century

England. So did the quest for feasible alternative ways to organize and sustain human communities. *The Tempest* encapsulates and highlights this crucial contest. The play's setting is outside the context of time and space. Yet *The Tempest* wrestles directly with the challenge of the New World. As John Locke put it later in the century, "Thus in the beginning, all the World was *America*."[3]

In the early 1600s the claim that legitimate authority could be derived from "time immemorial"—in other words, that legitimacy could be "traceable to no original act of foundation"—was the subject of a deepening controversy.[4] Intrigue and ceaseless disputation about what gave anyone legitimate authority to claim to be in charge pervaded life among the first colonists in Virginia and New England. Continuous anxiety about sovereignty helps explain the trend to commit basic matters of governance to Compacts and Fundamental Orders and to delimit fundamental law in formal written documents.

This was only one of many responses we will encounter to an uncertainty about legitimate authority stretching across religious, national, political, and social realms. The difficulty is illustrated, for example, within one of the most famous Anglo-American judicial decisions: Lord Coke's famous effort in *Calvin's Case* (1608)[5] to thread several needles simultaneously early in the troubled realm of James I. That case was a fabricated inquiry about whether one Calvin, born in Scotland before James I ascended the throne, remained an alien, thereby not entitled to bring either real or personal legal actions for lands he claimed in England. Lord Coke's response had vital implications for the subsequent law of the English colonies. The most significant aspect was Coke's distinction between territory that England acquired by conquest from a Christian king, and territory acquired from infidels, who were presumed to be perpetual enemies. In the case of infidels, according to Coke, all laws were abrogated and the Crown governed under principles of natural equity until the laws of England were specifically introduced. In North America, therefore, legalistic necessity induced specific charters, widely considered essential for sovereignty and law. Yet experience often directly challenged and frequently undermined the entire repertoire of legalistic notions of power and governance, duties and rights that the early white settlers brought with and within themselves. The colonists learned from stark reality how contingent the circumstances were that determined whether they flourished or foundered.

The first white settlers of New England practiced a kind of clinical political science. Directly and pragmatically, they anticipated in practice the theoretical clash between Hobbes and Locke later in the century. Of necessity, these settlers played out fundamental ideas about individuals, community, and governance within the rocky reality of their new settlements. At the edge of a vast wilderness, they had to form and rewrite real society. Group realities proved sometimes synergistic, sometimes impossible to tolerate. Through it all, these settlers learned that they needed to associate to survive. Therefore, they had to wrestle repeatedly with basic issues of what constraints on individual and group desires were legitimate.

We begin with a brief account of what happened after the storm-tossed *Sea Venture* hit a reef and sank in 1609—a year after *Calvin's Case*—in a place *The Tempest* calls the "still-vexed Bermoothes." We will see that the specifics of history connect vividly to the gripping mysteriousness of a play that floats freely within some mystical dimensions. In particular, the subsequent history of one of the survivors of the *Sea Venture* will help us understand how *The Tempest* was both deeply embedded in, and yet prescient about, its era's bitter ambivalence about sovereignty. As we follow Stephen Hopkins aboard the *Mayflower* and pursue his legal and other entanglements in the founding period of Plymouth Plantation, we see how a timeless literary work and timebound history combine to clarify perennial issues of freedom and authority, individual and group.

These classic dichotomies, however, truly are false dichotomies. The irony becomes particularly significant as we discover moments when our perpetual yearning for the certainty of crisp choices does more damage than merely muddling thinking. As we will see repeatedly throughout this book, reliance on binary choices can betray the very quest for justice.

After the Wreck: "Freed from the Government of Any Man"

The Adventures of the Sea Venture

In June 1609, the largest flotilla ever assembled in Europe for colonizing purposes sailed from Plymouth, England, to relieve the new colony established by the Virginia Company at Jamestown. Sir Thomas Gates, the newly appointed lieutenant governor of Virginia, and Sir George Somers, admiral of the fleet, set sail together aboard the huge flag ship, the *Sea Venture,* in part to avoid disputes about who was legitimately in charge. We have two eyewitness accounts about the terrible Atlantic storm that drove the *Sea Venture* away from the other ships in the flotilla and onto a coral reef within the dreaded "Devils' Isles."[6]

When the *Sea Venture* castaways struggled ashore, they discovered wild hogs and other evidence of earlier shipwrecks. They also found an island blessed with remarkable abundance, with sea birds that could be caught by hand, plentiful fish, tortoises, crabs, oysters, and even adequate fresh water. They even were able to salvage supplies from the wreck and to make shelters from the cedar and palm trees they found on the island.

Lieutenant Governor Gates insisted, however, that the shipwrecked band resume their mission to Virginia. Gates's efforts to keep the men at work rebuilding a ship capable of taking the party to Virginia soon produced murmuring, and worse. The Lieutenant Governor would not leave the shipbuilding to the skilled craftsmen—he imposed himself into "every meane labour"—yet he could not get the men to work as hard as he thought they should. The slackers were not limited to the "lower sorts." Indeed, the actions of some of the "better sorts" seemed to suggest "affections and passions," and even possible "dangerous and secret discontents" (19 Hakluytus at 28).

When the men at work on the pinnace sought to convince others to go off to a nearby island until they were provided with better allowances, Gates accused them of a criminal conspiracy and banished them. Stephen Hopkins, about whom it was said that he knew and could reason well about the Scriptures, then became entangled in a dispute. He was accused of irreligious and seditious views that might "shake the foundation" (30) of the island community. The most threatening of Hopkins's recorded remarks was his argument that "it was no breach of honesty, conscience, nor Religion to decline from the obedience of the Governour or refuse to goe any further led by his authority except it so pleased themselves" (30–31). Hopkins proclaimed that Gates might have authority in Virginia, but not in the Bermudas. Now, he declared, the castaway community was "freed from the government of any man" (31). The duty of each was only to his own conscience, "to provide for himselfe and his owne family" (31).

Hopkins faced sedition charges before the entire congregation, and Gates quickly condemned the rebel to death for being "the Captaine and the follower" (31) of his own mutinous scheme. Somehow, Hopkins begged for mercy so effectively that he managed to save his skin. When Gates's men apprehended a gentleman named Henry Paine stealing weapons rather than serving his watch, Paine responded that the governor had no authority "and therefore let the Governour (said hee) kisse, etc." (34). Paine turned out to be more principled and less lucky than Hopkins. His plea, as a gentleman, to be spared hanging was honored. Instead, Paine faced a firing squad, and "towards the evening he had his desire, the Sunne and his life setting together" (34). When Sir George Somers and his men heard of Paine's execution, they absconded to the woods and sought to remain there, to avoid possible punishment for conspiring with Paine and to escape Gates's rule altogether. Soon, however, a compromise evolved. Somers and most of his group returned, having been given amnesty and the promise that, upon reaching Virginia, they need not stay there and would be free to return to Bermuda.

Gates and Somers, aboard new ships they christened respectively *Deliverance* and *Patience,* eventually cleared the treacherous coral reefs around the island. They and most of their passengers finally reached Virginia, only to find a colony so near extinction as to leave the settlers no choice but to abandon their settlement. The *Sea Venture* survivors, now accompanied by the decimated band of settlers, left Jamestown behind and began to make their way downriver. There they encountered Lord De La Warr and a relief fleet from England. Only this stroke of exquisite timing allowed the colony to survive. Somers returned to Bermuda aboard his *Patience* to fetch additional relief supplies. After his ship had been readied for the return voyage, however, Somers died in the aftermath of a sumptuous farewell feast. His men forced the ship to return to England rather than to Virginia, as Somers had promised.

In Virginia Gates ruled under martial law "of most dispatch and terror," which granted the governor "full and absolute power" (30) to govern and rule all subjects. Yet even when the struggling settlement faced starvation, the remarkably harsh punishments under Gates's laws could not force the settlers to work. The conduct of these first settlers at Jamestown during its first decade was so clearly counterproductive as to seem suicidal. As the historian Edmund Morgan put it, "they seem to have made nearly every possible mistake and some that seem almost impossible." For example, "the English, unable or unwilling to feed themselves, continually demanding corn from the Indians, take pains to destroy both the Indians and their corn." Their extremely self-destructive conduct, "their conditioned laziness . . . and disastrous alienation of the Indians," is explainable in part by a glaring lack of leadership despite Gates's iron rule.

Problems about legitimate authority in Virginia had begun with the initial decision by the Virginia Company to keep secret (even from the councilors themselves) the names of the councilors appointed by the king until the initial settlers arrived in Virginia and opened a locked box that contained the names of their leaders. This process was not conducive to building consensus, particularly when John Smith, who had stirred considerable enmity among his fellow passengers during the voyage, turned up on the list. Matters grew even worse after 1609, when the Virginia Company obtained a new charter granting it full control and, in turn, giving absolute power to the person selected as governor. The governors proved to be "ruthless," and their conduct toward the Indians grew "increasingly hideous." Still the settlers, a disproportionate number of whom were gentlemen, could not be made to work even when starvation was the obvious consequence of their idleness. Neither the initial communal production of food nor the later assignment of private gardens succeeded. Only a combination of for-tuitous circumstances—Rolfe's experiment with tobacco; a successful struggle by James I against some of his principal opponents, who led a faction within the Virginia Company; and the introduction of slavery—made Virginia begin to look like a going enterprise.[7] The dire early days and even the colony's paradoxical later "success" under-score the interdependence of ruler and ruled, individual and group, and even master and slave.

The historical tale of the beginnings of Virginia is fascinating in itself. It also deepens and darkens understanding of *The Tempest* and the contested social negotiations the play suggests. Conversely, *The Tempest* itself underscores the crucial intertwining of authority and group values. This is so even with Prospero, whose magical powers make him seem the sole and undisputed lord of all he surveys.

The Tempest: Thin Description

The Tempest[8] opens with the dramatic tumult of a storm at sea. The scene is a truncated lesson in interdependence. While there is a wealth of meanings in the exchanges between the boatswain and the passen-gers from the courts of Naples and Milan, there is little subtlety in the boatswain's message to his meddlesome and rank-conscious noble pas-sengers: "What cares these roarers for the name of king?" (I.i.16–17). When Gonzalo, a good-hearted but nattering old counselor, reminds the boatswain of "whom thou hast aboard" (I.i.19), the sailor replies: "None that I more love than myself" (I.i.20).

In the midst of the storm—one of the play's few dramatic scenes— the crisis leads to direct questioning of authority. The natural order is disrupted. Gonzalo is a bothersome fool; the ship's master is absent when he is most needed; and the nobles, Sebastian, the brother of Alonso, King of Naples, and Antonio, the usurping Duke of Milan, debate whether to sink with the King or to abandon him. At least Gonzalo argues for doing something, even if it is only to assist the King and Prince at prayers, "for our case is as theirs" (I.i.54). Although Gonzalo seems not to perceive that communal reciprocity should apply also to the boatswain and sailors, this first scene indicates that any hope of survival, if not of salvation, lies exclusively in the crew's seamanship and surely not in the bluster of their betters. It is also our first intimation of Gonzalo as a key figure in the play who focuses the play's basic tension between taking care of oneself and seeing "our case" as "theirs."

At the same time, it is worth pondering how this first scene's direct assault on hierarchy might have played on All Hallows Eve, 1611, when *The Tempest* was first performed before the always insecure James I and his court. From start to finish, the play seems to undermine authority. Prospero, seemingly the undisputed ruler of the island, renounces his magic and decides to return to Milan. In the Epilogue he says:

> Now I want
> Spirits to enforce, Art to enchant;
> And my ending is despair,
> Unless I be reliev'd by prayer,
> Which pierces so, that it assaults
> Mercy itself, and frees all faults.
> As you from crimes would pardon'd be,
> Let your indulgence set me free.   (Epilogue 13–20)

To be sure, this is in large measure a plea for tumultuous applause. But it is much more. Prospero has been the absolute ruler of an island that floats beyond time and space; he has used his powers for revenge, romance, and an assault on the past. Yet here Prospero describes his own vulnerability. He now recognizes that he must rely on the indulgence of his fellow human beings. Thus this speech, and indeed the entire play, directly address deep anxieties about what the appropriate boundaries of authority ought to be. We confront head on the mutual needs of authority and community. *The Tempest* combines optimism with fallibility; its hard-eyed realism about limits coexists with descriptions of the need for leaps of group faith. The Epilogue echoes and encapsulates crucial tensions throughout the play that make it a subversive examination of the pitfalls of power and the follies of freedom alike.

Most of the plot is described through reports of previous action. The bulk of this history is stuffed into Act I, Scene 2. The scene-setting begins with an empathetic speech by Miranda, who rues her lack of power to intervene to stop the storm or to save those on the ship. Prospero, her father, reassures Miranda that "There's no harm done" (I.ii.15). In fact, extreme paternalist that Prospero surely is, he tells her that "I have done nothing but in care of thee" (I.ii.16). At last he believes it is time for Miranda to hear the story of what occurred "in the dark backward and abysm of time" (I.ii.50). He tells his teenage daughter that she, after all, "Art ignorant of what thou art; nought knowing / Of whence I am" (I.ii.18–19).

Prospero's egocentrism, evident throughout the play, is near its peak here. Not only does Miranda's father define her entirely in terms of lineage (of "whence I am"), but he takes full credit, in the unexplained absence of Miranda's mother, for using his art to create Miranda's compassion. Proclaiming himself to be Miranda's "schoolmaster" (I.ii.172) as well as her father, Prospero now tells her what occurred a dozen years earlier. In the good old days—a time Miranda recalls but vaguely,—Prospero was "A prince of power" (I.ii.55) in Milan, while, with obvious double-entendre, her mother was "a piece of virtue" (I.ii.56). And what happened then?

It is a cautionary tale. Prospero explains the dangers of too much study, particularly the study of "the liberal Arts" (I.ii.73). While he studied, Prospero entrusted the government of the dukedom to his brother, Antonio, who "perfected how to grant suits, / How to deny them, who t'advance, and who / To trash for over-topping" (I.ii.79–81). With such Machiavellian skills, Antonio, like ivy, was able to hide and attack Prospero's "princely trunk" (I.ii.86). Antonio could do this because his brother neglected worldly ends and overprized popular support. Prospero's excessive trust, "confidence sans bound" (I.ii.97), gave Antonio his opening to turn Milan over to its enemy, Naples, and to exile Prospero and Miranda.

Prospero draws a parental analogy that is central to the play's basic themes: the complexity and contrariness of nature and nurture; what is taught and what is inherited; what is settled by the past and what can be changed. Prospero recalls: "my trust, / Like a good parent, did beget of him / A falsehood in its contrary, as great / As my trust was; which had indeed no limit" (I.ii.93–96).

Any parent—and, for that matter, anyone who remembers having been a child—ought to be able to relate to the need for limits (as the modern commonplace would have it). Shakespeare further sharpens the point. Not only does trust have limits, but Antonio remained unaware that he had gone wrong. Prospero recalls that Antonio, "having unto truth, by telling of it, / Made such a sinner of his memory, / To credit his own lie, he did believe / He was indeed the duke; out o' th' substitution, / And executing th' outward face of royalty, / With all prerogative" (I.ii.100–105).

Here we have a direct assault on pretensions of royalty. By undermining loyalty and royalty, moreover, this sobering lesson about the need to probe beneath appearances seems to confront directly the fiction of the divine right of kings, a fiction first advanced wholeheartedly by James I. The fiction was an integral part of the effort "to insure . . . a king who not only could do no wrong but would do no wrong."[9]

This subversive point is reiterated by Miranda. If her uncle, Antonio, could be so bad, she wonders, what is she to think of her grandmother? She concludes: "Good wombs have borne bad sons" (I.ii.120). Prospero avoids this issue and proceeds to explain that Antonio and Alonso, fearing popular outrage if they had executed their victims outright, put "me and thy crying self" (I.ii.132) aboard an ill-fitted boat several leagues at sea. Somehow, "noble Neapolitan Gonzalo" (I.ii.161) provided food and water and "volumes that / I prize above my dukedom" (I.ii.167–68). At this point Prospero still seems wedded to his books and his magic, and quite sure of himself as father, teacher, and ruler. He informs Miranda that she has benefited from their shared isolation, for "here / Have I, thy schoolmaster, made thee more profit / Than other princess' can, that have more time / For vainer hours, and tutors not so careful" (I.ii.171–74).

Miranda dutifully thanks heavens for that, and then wonders why Prospero raised the storm at sea. He answers vaguely that Fortune brought his enemies to the shore of their island home, and tells her not to ask any more questions but to sleep, for "'tis a good dulness, / And give it way: I know thou canst not choose" (I.ii.185–86). This clearly frames the questions of what constitutes a good tutor, a good parent, and a good ruler. Throughout the play, we encounter the nagging issue of how much control Prospero actually has over the other characters and himself, and whether it is through his magic or his personality, his nature or his studies. Much of the time his power seems akin to a version of "divinity" which, as Edmund Morgan points out, "when assumed by mortals (or imposed upon them), can prove more constricting than subjection."[10]

In the scene introducing Ariel, Prospero betrays little sense of the limitations of his power. To the contrary, he is terribly possessive of "my Ariel" (I.ii.188). Prospero turns belligerent when Ariel dares remind him of an erstwhile promise of liberty. Prospero threatens to return Ariel to a tree—this time an oak and not the softer cloven pine from which Prospero rescued the airy spirit—and he insists upon the full measure of two additional days of service that Ariel owes him according to their contract. Ariel has done wonders in carrying out Prospero's complicated plans for the storm and the safe separation of those on board the ship. When Ariel mentions liberty, however, Prospero excoriates his indentured servant as "my slave" (I.ii.270).

Prospero is even nastier to Caliban, this "freckled whelp hag-born" (I.ii.283) whom Prospero considers a natural slave, "A devil, a born devil, on whose nature / Nurture can never stick" (IV.i.188–89). The island was originally inhabited only by Caliban and Caliban's mother, Sycorax, who had been brought there pregnant and was abandoned by sailors. We hardly get a sympathetic portrait of this single parent, however; for example, her temper was too earthy for a delicate spirit such as Ariel, whom she imprisoned in that painful pine.

Now Prospero has taken the island from Caliban, though Caliban first loved Prospero and taught him how to make use of the island's natural abundance. As Caliban picks up this narrative strand, we learn that Prospero initially charmed the creature and taught him the power of naming. Now, Caliban claims, his only benefit from knowledge of language is the ability to curse Prospero. Miranda too has been carefully taught to demean Caliban, whose service is absolutely necessary, but who is an "Abhorred slave, / Which any print of goodness wilt not take, / Being capable of all ill!" (I.ii.353–55).

Caliban's character,[11] his relationship to the other characters, and his special, lyrical command of language have intrigued playgoers, readers, and critics for centuries. Indeed, a general impression of reactions to Caliban suggests that he continually serves as a palimpsest. At first, the dominant critical view was that the beauty of Caliban's speeches in combination with his savage status suggested that he had invented his own language. Dr. Samuel Johnson answered that Caliban's language was nothing more than what a creature like Caliban, in his situation, realistically would be expected to sound like.[12] Within the past fifty years, in an analysis that now seems distressingly racist, the distinguished critic Mark Van Doren still wrote of Caliban as the lowest creature in the natural order.[13]

Caliban may be a noble savage or a vicious cannibal, a being punished either wrongly or rightly for his attempt to follow his natural sexual urges toward Miranda. When he explores the possibility of rebellion, Caliban is eloquent about the yoke of the tyrant and the attractiveness of freedom; yet he is also immediately servile toward foolish would-be rebels, Trinculo and Stephano, at least so long as Caliban can consider any object of his worship "valiant" (III.ii.23). The play's final scene is fraught with interpretive possibilities. Prospero here refers to Caliban as "this demi-devil—/ For he's a bastard one" (V.i.272–73). To the masters of Stephano and Trinculo, Prospero says: "Two of these fellows you / Must know and own," and, he adds, "this thing of darkness I / Acknowledge mine" (V.i.274–76). To claim control is to acknowledge responsibility. On several levels, the character of Prospero suggests that to possess another is also to be possessed, to have control is also to surrender some freedom.

The play's romantic, comedic ending leaves such matters unresolved. Is Prospero merely reclaiming ownership of a slave cursed at birth with immutable traits, or has the magician learned empathy in the course of the play? Will Prospero be a better Duke when he returns to rule Milan, though "Every third thought shall be my grave" (V.i.311) despite, or because of, his decision to renounce his powerful magic? Will Caliban have his island back and be less of what he himself describes as a "thrice-double ass" (V.i.295) after the final applause?

This is not the place to pursue, and certainly not to answer, these questions. They can never be resolved, of course, which helps explain why *The Tempest* continues to hold us. Much of its force lies in its open-ended complexity and the multitude of challenges in its moral equipoise. Even forgetful Prospero might now think it time to return to the plot.

Ferdinand, the son of Alonso, King of Naples, is separated from the other castaways, and Ariel initially lies to him about his father's fate:

> Full fathom five thy father lies;
> Of his bones are coral made;
> Those are pearls that were his eyes;

> Nothing of him that doth fade
> But doth suffer a sea-change
> Into something rich and strange.
> Sea-nymphs hourly ring his knell:
> Ding-dong.
> Hark! now I hear them—Ding-dong, bell.   (I.ii.399–407)

But Ferdinand quickly becomes oblivious to his father's presumed fate as he and Miranda find love at first sight of each other. Indeed, reassured that Miranda is a virgin, Ferdinand willingly undergoes imprisonment, torture, and even the meaningless drudgery of slavery imposed by Prospero, since he now cares for nothing but Miranda. Unlike Caliban, who rails and raves against his loss of freedom, Ferdinand is charmed into becoming an enthusiastic, voluntary slave for virtuous love.

When Miranda dares to intervene on her lover's behalf, Prospero turns on her with, "What! I say, / My foot my tutor?" (I.ii.471–72). He commands her to silence and suggests that he may come to hate her if she utters another word. Prospero, as teacher, father, and self-proclaimed artistic creator of Miranda's virtue of empathy, remains the command-and-control type.[14] A Freudian might speculate that Miranda's feeling for Ferdinand, "the third man that e'er I saw; the first/ That e'er I sigh'd for" (I.ii.448–49), is what excluded Prospero and thus enraged him. Yet this hardly excuses Prospero's lack of self-control.

Through Prospero's insistent manipulation, Ferdinand and Miranda remain a content, albeit treacly, pair. Under Prospero's voyeuristic gaze, Ferdinand is soon proclaiming that the ends obviously justify the means, that "some kinds of baseness / Are nobly undergone; and most poor matters / Point to rich ends" (III.i.2–4). When Miranda proposes marriage to this smitten optimist, Ferdinand ecstatically agrees. In a kind of homage to delayed gratification and the Protestant ethic, the pair then go about their assigned tasks and happily await the formalization of their vows, with Ferdinand proclaiming his wish to live forever where "So rare a wonder'd father and a wise / Makes this place Paradise" (IV.i.123–24).

With few exceptions, the rest of the play is schematic and hardly dramatic. The villains, Sebastian and Antonio, plot more evil. Antonio, drawing on his evil experience, instructs that "what's past is prologue, what to come, / In yours and my discharge" (II.i.248–49). Antonio may have historical precedent, but this time Prospero's magic clearly takes precedence to foil both the bloody usurpation plotted by Antonio and Sebastian and the clumsy uprising discussed by Stephano, Trinculo, and Caliban. An elaborate wedding masque highlights the possibilities of "foison plenty" (IV.i.110)—plentiful harvest yielded by nature under cultivation, an image apparently already dear to English hearts—but it ends abruptly when absentminded Prospero recalls that he ought to intervene against the scheme by Caliban and his new masters to steal Prospero's books and thereby overthrow his rule.

Once Prospero is reminded by Ariel of the forgiveness he would practice "were I human" (V.i.20), the magician decides that "the rarer action is / In virtue than in vengeance" (V.i.27–28). This scene figures prominently in interpretations of Prospero as a direct surrogate for Shakespeare toward the end of his life. In the end, Prospero decides to break his staff and drown his book "deeper than did ever plummet sound" (V.i.56). He forgives everyone under his power on the island, even his brother Antonio, "Unnatural though thou art" (V.i.79), although Antonio may or may not accept the gesture. It is Gonzalo whom Prospero embraces first, in the play's final, grand reconciliation scene. Gonzalo is a man "whose honour cannot / Be measur'd or con-fin'd" (V.i.121–22). It also is Gonzalo who merits further discussion.

Throughout the play Gonzalo seems foolishly optimistic, as well as committed to doing good. He is aptly described as "this lord of weak remembrance" (II.i.232). In fact, though D. J. Palmer noted that Caliban "might even be claimed as the only American in Shakespeare,"[15] Gonzalo actually may be closer to an American archetype. True, Gonzalo is a representative of the court in Naples, a community clearly symbolizing decadence and evil machinations. Nevertheless, he repeatedly emphasizes two benevolent themes: first, the belief that even a bad situation will somehow improve if people only believe it will; second, that "we are all in this mess together" and therefore must help one another. By paying attention to Gonzalo, and to the way his ahistorical optimism is both celebrated and undercut throughout the play, we will begin to grasp *The Tempest*'s subtlety concerning human nature and the sources of varied ideas of community.

Recall the play's opening, when Gonzalo provokes the boatswain but also recognizes that "our case is theirs" (I.i.54), while all about him are losing their heads in their individualistic ways. Gonzalo begins Act II by urging his fellow shipwrecked passengers to be merry, reminding them that they are luckier than most people and that "Our hint of woe / Is common" (II.i.3–4). As was characteristic in initial reports describing the New World to English readers,[16] Gonzalo notes, "Here is everything advantageous to life" (II.i.48). Though the others all mock him, Gonzalo sees the grass as "lush and lusty" (I.i.51) and remarkably green. His fellows may rue their trip and mutually recriminate, but Gonzalo begins to describe his utopian scheme "had I plantation of this isle . . . and were the King on't" (II.i.139–41).

What follows is a wonderful, yet undercutting, summary of utopianism generally and of the optimism and celebration of what is "natural" in particular, inspired by Montaigne's essay "Of the Cannibales." Gonzalo describes a commonwealth in which "I would by contraries / Execute all things" (II.i.143–44). There will be no law. He envisions a world without magistrate, contract, succession, feudalism, or private property. All men will be idle, all women idle, but also innocent and pure. In sum, Gonzalo says, there will be "no sovereignty" (II.i.152).

Sebastian immediately punctures the dream: "Yet he would be King on't" (II.i.152). Then Antonio adds a classic criticism of reformers and dreamers: "The latter end of his commonwealth forgets the / beginning" (II.i.153–54). Shakespeare thereby captures, and pulverizes, a familiar strain of "after the revolution" rhetoric, as well as the psychology of some proponents of such fantasies. Yet while it is foolish for Gonzalo to believe in a world without sovereignty, in which nature surely will provide "all foison, all abundance, / To feed my innocent people" (II.i.159–60), it may be still more foolish, and significantly more blameworthy, to ridicule the old man who still manages to be visionary. Not only do Sebastian and Antonio mock Gonzalo's scheme for a commonwealth without sovereignty, but they immediately begin a direct assault against sovereignty by plotting to kill the King.

In several direct ways, then, Shakespeare seems to question authority quite effectively. To be sure, he does so subtly and cautiously, but his veiled social criticism is a crucial element of the play. In neither the tempest scene nor the byplay about Gonzalo's commonwealth is the problem of how to rule with justice resolved, nor does Shakespeare offer much instruction about how to wrestle with this issue. It is instructive to compare Prospero's manipulative use of power, coupled with his keen sense of the hold of the dark past, with Gonzalo's utopianism. What emerges is a subtle, subversive commentary that underscores "the paradoxical practices of an authority deeply complicit in undermining its own legitimacy."[17]

That James I would have *The Tempest* performed a second time, in

1613, to celebrate the marriage of his daughter, Elizabeth, might well suggest that my reading overstates the play's subversive qualities. Yet if anyone in England during the reign of James I was capable of missing effective but subtle critical commentary, it was precisely that "most educated fool in the world," James I himself. It is easy to surmise that the monarch remained unaware of "the half-hidden cultural transactions through which great works of art are empowered."[18] The play's lessons about "How to live at all in a groundless world"[19] are made particularly vivid through its lack of grounding in time and space.

Gonzalo is the play's only character—with the possible exception of Miranda, whose "O brave New World" naiveté is attributable almost exclusively to her innocence—who betrays any awareness of the wonder of the new world and its magic. Moreover, Gonzalo expresses awareness of radically changed perceptions within his own long lifetime; he even recognizes the illumination that travelers' tales cast on a reality assumed to be unchangeable.[20] Finally, it is left to Gonzalo to summarize the play's apparent happy resolution. He does this, significantly, by way of contrasts:

> Was Milan thrust from Milan, that his issue
> Should become kings of Naples? . . .
> And Ferdinand . . . found a wife
> Where he himself was lost; Prospero his dukedom
> In a poor isle, and *all of us ourselves*
> *When no man was his own.*   (V.i.205–13) (emphasis added)

At the very least, this notion of self-discovery while one is lost resonates with the suspension of disbelief during a successful theatrical production. It also evokes the commonplace sense of being lost, then found, in religious experience. But to encounter a time "when no man was his own" may have broader implications, when we recognize that "We are such stuff / As dreams are made on" (IV.i.156–57). It could be argued that Gonzalo's point encapsulates the essence of the present vogue for defining individuals in terms of our own social constructions of reality.[21] It also seems to encompass an affirmative conception of communitarianism, utopian or otherwise. Finally, it may relate to the theme of servitude discussed above, suggesting that there is no such thing as individual freedom, that we all experience various encumbrances on our liberty.

Of course, we must not get carried away. Gonzalo does not cut through the play's many quandaries. For example, only a few lines after his speech, Caliban, Stephano, and Trinculo enter the final scene and announce a strikingly similar benchmark for the drunken, absurd new world they seek to create out of the "misery" that "acquaints a man with strange bedfellows" (II.ii.40–41). Stephano proclaims: "Every man shift for all the rest, and let no man take / Care for himself; for all is but fortune" (V.i.256–57).

And yet, if we may properly celebrate Shakespeare as a master of paradox and a magician of challenging equipoise, this comic mirroring by the clownish trio emphasizes Gonzalo's point. The old man himself is clearly both a silly, cockeyed optimist and an honorable and perceptive observer. Both he and these ridiculous would-be rebels offer a prescription for what to do when sovereignty is undone.

The Mayflower Compact and the Strange Career of Stephen Hopkins: "For None Had Power to Command Them"

When the *Mayflower* reached Cape Cod in November 1620, as William Bradford tells the tale, some aboard murmured and proclaimed that "when they came ashore, they would use their own liberty, for none had power to command them."[22] Unfortunately, Bradford does not name names. Yet in one of those ironies that make history so entertaining, if not necessarily edifying, the outspoken Stephen Hopkins, reprieved from his Bermuda death sentence, was aboard the *Mayflower*. He had returned to London and become a gentleman. Then Hopkins, along with his pregnant second wife, three children, and several servants, joined the Pilgrims in their New World venture. Indeed, his second son, Oceanus, was the famous baby born during the *Mayflower* voyage.

Almost surely, we will never know whether Hopkins had anything to do with the murmuring that led to the formulation of the Mayflower Compact. But once safely on dry land at Plymouth, Hopkins quickly assumed a role as a leading figure in the tiny community. When Samoset first appeared, for example, and amazed his hosts with his knowledge of English and English ways,[23] it was Hopkins's house the settlers selected to lodge their important guest. Governor Bradford chose Hopkins to travel with Edward Winslow and Squanto on a sensitive mission to spy upon and treat with Massasoit, the greatest Indian chieftain.

The account of that trip can be read as a fine introduction to the still-fashionable motif of the ugly American tourist. When Massasoit and his wife shared their bed with the travelers, for example, Hopkins and Winslow complained that it was crowded "so that we were worse weary of our lodging, than of our journey." Though Massasoit fed them exceptionally fine fish he had shot with a bow and arrow, and importuned them to stay, the Pilgrims begged off, claiming that they desired to keep the Sabbath at home. The next sentence of their account reveals, however, that they had additional reasons: "For what with bad lodging; the savages' barbarous singing, for they use to sing themselves asleep; lice and fleas within doors; and musketoes without: we could hardly sleep all the time of our being there." In fact, on their journey home, Hopkins and his mates even managed to get into a dispute over whether to leave a tip. One Indian, they report, "marvelled we gave him nothing; and told us, what he had done for us. We also told him of some discourtesies he offered us, whereby he deserved nothing." And so the story ends: "Yet we gave him a small trifle. Whereupon he offered us tobacco."[24]

Stephen Hopkins and the Law: "Every Son of Adam His Brother's Keeper and Avenger"

Although Hopkins became the leading tavern-keeper in town and served four terms on the Governor's Council, he was not immune from scrapes with the law. He was fined for serving drinks after hours to servants, for charging more than the fixed price, and even for assaulting John Tisdale (which Hopkins did while he was still a magistrate). He also engaged in occasional contract disputes. One story that most directly echoes the themes I have tried to coax from *The Tempest* involved Hopkins's remarkable obstinacy concerning the plight of one of his maidservants.

It begins with a ne'er-do-well named Arthur Peach, who arrived in Virginia in 1635. He traveled north and allegedly fought bravely in the genocidal Pequot War of 1637, but soon thereafter he was "out of means and loth to work." Peach sought to evade his creditors by fleeing Plymouth to Manhattan. He enticed three servants and apprentices to accompany him. Near the present site of Pawtucket, however, Peach and his fellows persuaded a lone Indian they met on the path to smoke a pipe with them, only to rob and stab the man. Roger Williams aided what he took to be destitute men with food and rum, hospitality, and a canoe to continue their journey, but in the meantime the wounded Indian crawled back to the path and was brought to Providence.

Though (or perhaps because) two surgeons tried to save him, the Indian died after telling his story. Williams had the culprits intercepted. One escaped, but Williams turned Peach and his followers over to John Winthrop with the statement that every "son of Adam is his brother's keeper or avenger." They were quickly found guilty and executed, though they confessed and professed great penitence.[25]

The impact of Peach's grievously impeachable behavior continued, however, and soon produced what one commentator called "virtuous barbarity." Dorothy Temple, maidservant to the Hopkins family, had fallen victim to the man's wiles: soon it was apparent that she was pregnant. After she gave birth, Hopkins refused to shelter or provide for Dorothy and her infant son. The Plymouth magistrates determined that the maidservant's indentures had two more years to run. They decided, therefore, "that, as Hopkins was entitled to her service for that time, he must also clothe and board her in his family or elsewhere." When Hopkins refused to have anything to do with her, he was held in contempt and actually served four days in confinement before he agreed to support his maidservant and her child for two years. Dorothy Temple did not escape punishment entirely. She was sentenced to be whipped twice publicly; the remainder of the penalty was remitted, however, after she fainted during the first whipping.[26]

Hopkins, who died a wealthy and much-respected citizen in 1644, was considered unusually "stubborn and argumentative." He was often in trouble with the authorities, though he was himself one of the leaders of the colony. Hopkins may have been like *The Tempest*'s Prospero in his stubbornness and tempestuousness in relation to Dorothy Temple; he also behaved like the sailors who abandoned Sycorax, pregnant with Caliban, on the island over which Prospero later reigned. Most of all, however, Stephen Hopkins's career demonstrates the malleability of the categories of authority when unsettled English ways confronted an even more unsettling New World.[27]

"The Dark Backward and Abysm of Time"

Time, Sovereignty, and the Law

Sovereignty always was uncertain in early New England. Yet perhaps the most striking aspect of the intriguing tale of Peach, Dorothy Temple, and Stephen Hopkins is that men in power apparently applied the

law even against others in power. It is not surprising to discover that
the authorities whipped an unmarried servant girl who bore a child.
Even the outpouring of revisionist history that portrays Puritan life
and law as relatively tolerant concedes a strong moralistic strain
enforced by law. Perhaps it is more surprising to learn that Peach and
two other white men were executed for the murder of a single Indian.
(Some settlers did argue that it was inequitable that all three should
die.) But if this judgment is an anomaly, it surely can be explained in
terms of the heinous nature of the crime, Peach's "bad apple" character, and the sensitivity of white-Indian relationships in the years immediately after the Pequot War.

These two legal episodes are also quite suggestive in terms of broader
themes. They emphasize limits to *The Tempest*'s concluding message
of achieving, or even exceeding, "mercy itself [that] . . . frees all faults"
(Epilogue 18), at least in the context of the struggle for survival in the
first years of the New World colonies. They also underscore the symbolic and real violence within the use of law. These legal incidents
helped to define communal norms in the first decades of the New
England settlements. This was particularly important because, as
David Hall demonstrates, "fluidity of power" characterized the cultural politics of seventeenth-century New England.[28]

It is the punishment of Hopkins that is most interesting. For one
thing, his case was not one of those well-studied conflicts situated at
the junction of Puritan criminal law and morality. Rather, it fell into
the category of civil cases which, as Bruce Mann suggested in his fine
study of colonial Connecticut, may illuminate best how "people
defined and attempted to assure what they valued as a society—what
behavior was permissible, how people should act toward one another,
how people could resolve their differences without resort to violence,
and . . . what property was and what rights attached to it."[29]

In Plymouth, when Hopkins tried to treat Dorothy Temple as the
Bible says Abraham treated Hagar, such behavior was unacceptable.
Two wrongs would not make a right. To be sure, this episode requires
additional details. Even in stark outline, however, it illustrates a type
of foundational group morality that could prevail over the clout that
Hopkins clearly enjoyed in Plymouth's little commonwealth. Law
joins politics and religion to provide the foundation and scaffolding
for such group faith. If we now reconsider *The Tempest,* we may better
perceive several of its implications about community, law, sovereignty,
and freedom.

Communities and The Tempest: *What Is Natural?*[30]

Consideration of the tension between art and nature is a commonplace in critical commentaries about *The Tempest,* but determining what is natural remains a fundamental conundrum in the play. The complexity of the issue is magnified once we consider the range of human groupings the play suggests. As Ralph Waldo Emerson, in many ways a quintessential American, once remarked, differing views of nature "determine all . . . institutions."[31] The ecological images in the play, for example, range from confrontation with the uncontrollable storm to the bounty freely provided by uncultivated nature, so long as you know "the best springs" (II.ii.160), as Caliban does, and "how to snare the nimble marmazet" (II.ii.170). The plot revolves around the consequences of the idea that "good wombs have borne bad sons" (I.ii.120). The possibility that the opposite may also be true—that bad wombs could bear good sons, for example, in the case of Sycorax and Caliban—looms as an important, subversive thought.

The play's outlook is quite skeptical, judging by the depiction of its varied communities. The world of deference to the better sort crumbles in the teeth of the opening gale; Gonzalo's paternalistic commonwealth cannot withstand the villains' simple ends/means critique. The exultation and release in the comic government of Caliban and his rebellious cohorts contrasts directly with Ferdinand's silly certainty that "some kinds of baseness / Are nobly undergone; and most poor matters / Point to rich ends" (III.i.2–4). His relationship with Miranda is a triumph of inhibition, a paean to contractual obligations and delayed gratification; it is soppily romantic, yet it also suggests a popular vision of the best of all possible worlds.

The masque scene reflects the Ferdinand/Miranda relationship writ large, here domesticated to produce full, plentiful, but controlled "foison plenty" (IV.i.110). Yet there must be a Fall, even in this idealized version of agricultural England. Prospero cannot be satisfied and interrupts the masque, though Ferdinand and Miranda would settle for this misty vision and for Prospero's wisdom, which "makes this place Paradise" (IV.i.124).

The early history of Plymouth suggests parallel perils in its quest for a natural paradise. The first settlers aspired to live up to the message preached to them by their spiritual leader in the old country, Reverend John Robinson, before they set sail. Robinson had admonished, however, that their "House of God which you are and are to be, be not shaken with unnecessarie novelties or other oppositions at the first setling thereof." These settlers so quickly faced such serious oppositions amongst themselves, however, that they felt it necessary to innovate and to craft the Mayflower Compact even before they landed. And there was still more dissent in the New World. The Pilgrims could not agree about who might be an appropriate minister to replace Robinson, who refused to join them, and considerable intrigue ensued.

Plymouth confronted serious internal economic conflict as well. Communal ownership of property did not seem to be working. By 1623, moreover, William Bradford had to defend the colony against rumors reaching England that Plymouth was so alarmingly democratic as to allow women and children to vote. That same year, the planter-investors in England tried to convince Bradford that efficiency would be greatly increased if he allowed the men of Plymouth to work for themselves but pay a tax to the plantation. The English planters conceded that all assets might still be held in common and that no property could be passed by inheritance. Within four years, however, the Plymouth settlers decided to divide the plantation's assets into 58 shares and the colony generally found itself loosening the religious and social bonds of trust with which this "House of God" first sought earthly paradise on the harsh soil of New England.[32]

Free The Tempest *20!*

Bitter experience teaches Prospero that trust begets danger. According to "good old lord, Gonzalo" (V.i.15), however, danger should beget trust. Further compounding the societal fissures subtly elaborated in the play is the sense that no sympathetic character seems self-reliant or even free. We have already noted the indentured servitude of Ariel; the harsher, apparently innate slavery of Caliban; and the voluntary servitude of Ferdinand and, to a degree, of Miranda as well. But it is Prospero whose lack of freedom is most complex, most significant, and most memorable.

The issue of Prospero's old world authority in his new world is deeply problematic. Like the first white settlers in America, Prospero derives his power from books. Also like them, however, both the source and the reach of his authority are dubious at best. Because the Plymouth settlers landed well outside the area designated for their adventure, they knew they were, in essence, simply squatters. If the origin of Prospero's authority also remains mysterious, it nonetheless seems greater and more authentic than does Alonso's hierarchical claim, although Alonso can invoke "the name of king" (I.i.17). Nor does Antonio's practical, functional success legitimate his rule. Alonso mourns that "the best is past" (III.iii.51), and Antonio believes, in service of his evil plot, that "what's past is prologue" (II.i.248). Yet neither passivity nor activity, neither being bound by nor free from the past, can establish sovereignty.

The Tempest thus may be read as a series of elaborations on a linked set of highly contentious issues involving law, religion, and politics in Stuart England. These contests were not settled for years, and then only after considerable bloodshed. Controversy about what was the relevant, legitimizing tale of communal origins was at the core of the debate. As J. G. A. Pocock says of the time when *The Tempest* was first performed, "the idea of the immemorial . . . took on an absolute colouring, which is one of the key facts in Stuart historico-political thought." Pocock asserts that the notion of immemorial rights, ultimately invoked against the sovereignty of the king, was derived from custom, which had no traceable historical basis. This move, in turn, supported strongly nationalistic claims about the timeless origins of the English common law and the ancient constitution. There was not, and by logic could not be, any actual historical basis for faith in a mythical "process without a beginning." Yet the belief that all rule must conform to ancient law was, according to Pocock, "one of the deepest-seated preconceptions of the medieval mind," and it flowed as "a powerful stream" into the seventeenth century when it became a central, contested issue.

Even more than their English counterparts, Americans tended to "recur, if not to a state of nature, in which all must be equal, at least to the condition prevailing immediately after a state of nature, that is, to the community or society that a contract among individuals supposedly produced just prior to their creation of government."[33] The fiction of binding, written communal consent at some earlier but unspecifiable time has become an indispensable element of popular American constitutionalism.

Shakespeare conjures up a brilliant interweaving of mirrored images and half-hidden dark responses to bright hopes. After the coup, Prospero's life was saved because he had the support of the people, yet popular perceptions could not be trusted. Shakespeare compels us to consider both the multifaceted states of nature and the problematic nature of individuals. It may be this submerged but resilient skeptical quality that George Orwell saw—as usual, before most others—when he wrote that Shakespeare is "noticeably cautious, not to say cowardly, in his manner of uttering unpopular opinions . . . Throughout his plays the acute social critics, the people who are not taken in by accepted fallacies, are buffoons, villains, lunatics, or persons who are shamming insanity or are in a state of violent hysteria."[34] Although Shakespeare used subterfuges, he commented upon almost everything and often did so with biting criticism.

In essence, *The Tempest* may be read as a profound exploration of why people allow other people authority. Shakespeare emphasizes the role of history even as he places the play beyond the limits of time and place. Yet I have tried to contextualize *The Tempest*: this approach helps explain why *The Tempest*'s disconcerting qualities were particularly apt in times of widespread legal, religious, and political unrest, such as in England under James I, as well as at the birth of new communities, rife with the possibilities and dangers of new beginnings, such as in the nascent colonies Stephen Hopkins encountered in Virginia and Plymouth.

Perhaps I exaggerate when I hear echoes of Gonzalo, Stephano, and even Prospero—at least the diminished but more appealing Prospero at the play's end—in John Winthrop's *Arbella* speech. I refer neither to Winthrop's "city on a hill" phrase, one of the favorite misquotations by one of the favorite speech writers for the favorite former First Actor in the United States, nor to Michael Dukakis's use of the same speech in his 1988 acceptance speech, quoted in the Introduction. Rather, I mean Winthrop's recognition that the only way to "avoyde . . . shipwracke and to provide for our posterity" would be to follow the counsel of the prophet Micah. In practical terms, "wee must be knitt together in this worke as one man, wee must entertaine each other in brotherly Affeccion, wee must be willing to abridge ourselves of our superfluities, for the supply of others necessities."[35]

Stephen Hopkins was an oldtimer in the New World by the time the *Arbella* arrived in 1630. A few years later, a schism over communal norms and authority led Thomas Hooker and his band to head west from Massachusetts Bay to the Connecticut frontier. There, these squatters produced Connecticut's Fundamental Orders in 1639. It may not have been an entirely original idea, but they provided a theory and the outline of a practical governmental structure for a brave new world—at least for those who could live in isolation and put in lots of evenings. Theirs was a new response to finding themselves in what often seemed a nowhereland, perched between the state of nature and the creation of political community. And even silly old Gonzalo had not imagined the wild idea these hardy souls announced. They proclaimed that government ought to rest on "the free consent of people."[36]

Can we dream today of a real community, or a conglomeration of different communities, that rest on the free consent of people? Is it still possible in an interdependent, multinational world full of obvious suffering and bloody conflict to try to welcome "the homeless, tempest-tost"—the world's "wretched refuse" and "huddled masses yearning to breathe free?"[37] History is sobering, to say the least, and suggests that these ideas have been largely, perhaps hopelessly, utopian. Yet *The Tempest* whispers that there may be hope for the "tempest-tost."

Prospero must learn—it is a lesson the Epilogue underscores, though it remains unclear whether Prospero has absorbed it fully—that to grant indulgence is neither superfluous nor easy. *The Tempest* hints that individual wisdom always must be other-wise. It takes unusual courage to move beyond revenge; even the condescension of mercy may not suffice. Nobody, not even a commanding figure such as Prospero, is free until he can connect to the groupings of others. To avoid despair we must have mutuality. Reciprocal indulgence is required both for freedom of association and for individual fulfillment. Tolerance surely is difficult, if not impossible, to sustain. And we are too familiar with those who are good in the worst ways. Yet *The Tempest* warns that if we cannot give and receive indulgences together, no one even has a prayer.

2 The Right to Form and Join Associations

Americans of all ages, all stations in life, and all types of disposition are forever forming associations.

Alexis de Tocqueville[1]

The quest for community is very much in vogue today, across many academic fields. The contemporary search for past and present transformations of historical proportions tends to rely heavily on dichotomizing ideal types. There is a mix of pop sociology and mystical primitive anthropology in much contemporary fashionable thinking about "community," "groups," and associations.[2]

The individual in tension with the community is a trite tale. Even the sophisticated ironies that individuals need others and that hell is other people seem unexceptional. In fact, the idea that we each need others is so trite as to fall directly into the trap of simplistic binary reasoning. The fundamental paradox cannot be resolved. Yet enhanced individualism can coexist with enhanced community identification, just as atomization can accompany a decreased community sense. Neither individual nor community makes much sense as an end in itself. Exclusive reverence for either breeds idolatry. Paradoxically, both concepts are indispensable—as means for each and all of us.

The dominant tendency in American legal thinking to divide the world into binary boxes may help explain why bedrock legal assumptions about individualism seem to combine readily with a nostalgic belief in some mythical golden age of small but not confining organic communities.[3] Legal education itself may be largely responsible. Every few decades there is a new, dominant wave of assertions by judges, legislators, and lawyers that the rights of single individuals must remain the essential units of all legal discourse.[4] Recent examples abound.[5] First-rate studies of markedly diverse legal realms remind us, however, that legal thought about groups has a long, complex, and provocative past.⁶ We will consider some of that important factual and doctrinal history, but this chapter concentrates on constitutional theory. It examines whether there is, or ought to be, an independent First Amendment right to form or join an association.

Tocqueville and the Inalienable Natural Right of Association

It is *de rigeur* to begin any serious discussion of the role of groups in America with Alexis de Tocqueville's observation that, "Better use has been made of association and this powerful instrument of action has been applied to more varied aims in America than anywhere else in the world."⁷ Unfortunately, despite the current explosion of communitarian rhetoric, there is usually no further development of Tocqueville's ideas and little consideration of the context in which he wrote.⁸ Even Tocqueville's emphasis on the multitude of group functions in America tends to be overlooked as scholars choose sides and wield abstractions about communal versus individualistic values. Any "principle of association" remains hidden in the dark of appealing ambiguities.

Tocqueville's approach to groups is surprisingly detailed. His ideas seem to contrast with those of his contemporary, Ralph Waldo Emerson, famous for his faith in American self-reliance. This comparison illuminates the work of another Emerson, Thomas I. Emerson, who almost surely was among the nation's greatest First Amendment scholars. Finally, several recent Supreme Court decisions illustrate the differences to both individuals and groups that a better theoretical approach to freedom of association would make.

Tocqueville's Functional Approach

Though Tocqueville focused on political associations, he noted, in the 1830s, that "associations are formed to combat exclusively moral troubles: intemperance is fought in common. Public security, trade and industry, and morals and religion all provide the aims for associations in the United States. There is no end which the human will despairs of attaining by the free action of the collective power of individuals."⁹ Tocqueville did not suggest that the "natural right" of association, which he considered "by nature almost as inalienable as individual liberty,"¹⁰ could or should be confined to political associations. Instead, he linked freedom of association to freedom of the press in their vital role of checking the abuse of power by public officials.

It is hardly surprising that a French aristocrat, victimized directly by the attempt, in the wake of the French Revolution, to follow Rousseau and to eliminate the corporate form entirely, was particularly sensitive to the importance of groups in the United States.[11] Nevertheless, Tocqueville's perceptivity and prescience are remarkable. His insights about groups also underscore how crucial and controversial the role of groups already had become as the generation that followed the founding of the United States sought to make practical sense of their national and constitutional heritage.

Associations educate Americans to look beyond self-interest, Tocqueville observed, and thereby they serve as an incomparable check against tyranny. Indeed, associations help teach people crucial lessons about how to live as individuals. In summarizing his insight about the vital psychological and sociological impact of associations, Tocqueville said: "Feelings and ideas are renewed, the heart enlarged, and the understanding developed only by the reciprocal action of men one upon another."[12] He added, "Nothing . . . more deserves attention than the intellectual and moral associations in America."[13] Yet he anticipated that some crucial associations would be commonly overlooked: "American political and industrial associations easily catch our eyes, but the others tend not to be noticed."[14]

If Tocqueville's perspective was unique, his recognition of the importance of groups was not. There are countless references to the virtues of associations both in the prerevolutionary era and throughout our history as a nation. By the mid-1700s, for example, associations formed for local civic purposes had gained considerable prominence, and their role increased after independence.[15] In the 1820s William Ellery Channing regarded associations as the "most powerful springs" of social action and found "the energy [of] . . . the principle of combination, or of action by joint forces" to be one of the most remarkable features of his times.[16] We will return to Tocqueville's emphasis on the importance of differentiating groups by their greatly varied forms and functions. First, though, we must identify an important paradox. Electing to join groups has long been, and remains, as American as celebrating our rugged individualism. Yet our most basic myths tend to follow the beliefs of Ralph Waldo Emerson, whose transcendental faith in the individual left nothing between that individual and the cosmos.

Ralph Waldo Emerson: A Representative,
Self-Reliant American Scholar?

Within a few years of the publication of Tocqueville's *Democracy in America*, Ralph Waldo Emerson had fully developed his "long trumpeted theory, and the instinct which spoke from it, that one man is a counterpoise to a city . . . [and] that his solitude is more prevalent and beneficent than the concert of crowds."[17] Later, as Emerson's friends and some of his closest followers joined the Brook Farm collective experiment, Emerson wrote in his diary, "Concert, men think, is more powerful than isolated effort and think to prove it arithmetically with slate and pencil; but concert is neither better nor worse[,] neither more nor less potent than individual force."[18] As R. Jackson Wilson put it, "What was most nearly new about the Emersonian assertion and its dozens of echoes in American literature and philosophy was the unqualified claim that society was an obstacle to the alignment of the individual with cosmic order."[19]

Emerson's uncompromising individualism may be viewed as a powerful antidote to the remarkable outpouring of communal ventures in the 1830s and 1840s. The "communitarian wave" included a vast range of religious revivals and zealous reform movements. Undoubtedly—albeit also unquantifiably—this antebellum burst of new associations was triggered by a percolating blend of rapid industrialization and economic booms and severe busts, along with new mass technology, a revolution in popular culture, and the political upheaval generally associated with the Jacksonian era.[20]

By the 1850s, the nation's preoccupation with slavery and the concomitant triumph of free labor ideology provided fertile, if bloody, ground for laissez-faire ideology.[21] Yet the Civil War also "opened the door to bold experiments in voluntary association for public ends."[22] It is hardly surprising, therefore, that James Bryce, the foremost foreign observer of post-Civil War America, echoed antebellum observers when he noted the pervasive American "habit of forming associations" and remarked that "associations are created, extended and worked in the United States more quickly and effectively than in any other country."[23] Even within legal thought, it is easy to perceive a cyclical pattern in romanticizing either radical individualism or cozy communitarianism. Contemporary critical legal studies pundits, for example, might be surprised to find that they share with Herbert Hoover the idea that "voluntary associations constitute self-government by the people outside of government."[24] Similarly, it was somewhat odd to find members of the Bohemian Club and the Century Club evoking Proudhon's advice to "multiply your associations and be free."[25]

Surely there was and still is strength in numbers. It must be added that there is also aid and comfort in identifying oneself by distinguishing the groups to which one belongs from groups of other people. Moreover, guilt by association can never be separated entirely from freedom of association. We *are* known by the company we keep; we do define our friends by identifying common enemies.[26] As Shakespeare put it: "Misery acquaints a man with strange bedfellows."[27] Yet a basic irony in American history, an irony underscored by the history of American law, is that for all the vaunted individualism of Americans, we are and have always been a nation of joiners.[28]

In fact, we tend, perhaps inescapably, to define individuality in terms of the multitude of groups with which we insistently identify. Even if we put aside wildly varying concepts of family and religious groupings—concepts full of complex psychological and other dimensions that are crucial, not to say integral, to self-conceptualizations—our associations, groups, communities, and causes overlap and have great force in our everyday lives. They are not neatly confined by time or place. By constructing our ideas of communities, we define where we belong and who we are, as well as who we are not.[29] Obviously, it is extremely difficult to sort out how the law should deal with freedom of association claims. But the fact that it will be hard to control this concept should not preclude recognizing and even embracing it. We cannot neatly distinguish between or control weeds and wild flowers, but we still welcome spring.

Associational Rights, Individual Rights, and the First Amendment

Thomas Emerson's famous article, "Toward a General Theory of the First Amendment,"[30] and his elaboration of it in his book, *The System of Freedom of Expression* (1973), solidified his status as the leading First Amendment scholar in the post-World War II period, perhaps for all time. A less well-known article of his, "Freedom of Association and Freedom of Expression,"[31] also proved to be trail-blazing. That article appeared in 1964, when scholarly attention suddenly focused on the "constitutionally protected right of association," as Justice Harlan described what seemed a new right in *NAACP v. Alabama ex rel.*

Patterson.[32] Despite the extensive work of others, Emerson's clarity and careful analysis established his article as the classic treatment of the enormously difficult issue of the appropriate constitutional relationship between associational rights and individual rights.

Emerson celebrated the result of Harlan's opinion for the Supreme Court, which protected the NAACP from southern attempts to dismantle it by going after its membership lists and punishing its members in various ways.[33] Yet Emerson noted that Harlan's opinion for the Court invoked freedom of association first as "derivative from the first amendment rights to freedom of speech and assembly, and as ancillary to them," but then "elevated freedom of association to an independent right, possessing an equal status with the other rights specifically enumerated in the first amendment."[34] Emerson knew that this move was popular with commentators, yet he found it wanting both in terms of consistency and of usefulness in resolving concrete controversies. Indeed, he argued that "as a starting point, an association should be entitled to do whatever an individual can do; conversely, conduct prohibited to an individual by a state can also be prohibited to an association."[35] "Questions of associational rights," according to Emerson, "must be framed and decided in terms of other constitutional theories."[36]

Emerson's article established the modern benchmark for consideration of whether the First Amendment should be interpreted to protect an independent right to form or join an association. The amendment states that "Congress shall make no law . . . abridging the freedom of speech, or of the press, or the right of the people peaceably to assemble, and to petition the Government for a redress of grievances."

I intend here to challenge Tom Emerson's assertion that "it is impossible to construct a meaningful constitutional limitation on government power based upon a generalized notion of the right to form or join an association."[37] I do so not only because Emerson's characteristically meticulous treatment of freedom of association is eminently worthy of attention in its own right. My disagreement does not rest on a quite different notion of the attraction of a generalized theory, nor is it merely an attempt to update Emerson's work in order to take into account many developments in the search for a constitutional theory for groups over the past three decades.[38] It is, rather, based on the belief that Emerson's approach did not adequately reflect the profound psychological and sociological importance and the functional variety of associations, both as amplifiers of different viewpoints and as sources for our individual identities. I suggest that it can and should make a practical difference to recognize an independent right of freedom of association. It would not always trump competing claims: no constitutional right ever does. But the group right I suggest would establish an important rebuttable presumption, to be overcome only upon the demonstration of a conflicting, compelling interest.

Classifying Freedom of Association Claims

In rejecting an independent freedom of association right, Tom Emerson's position would be an accurate description of what had been and generally is still said in Supreme Court precedents. Yet it overlooks important exceptions, exceptions that cry out from the great muddle of recent decisions construing freedom of association. Some groups do merit less constitutional protection than is afforded the sum of their individuals. In other contexts, however, groups should receive more constitutional protection than the sum of the rights of their individual members aggregated.

Thus, for example, racial or gender-based exclusionary practices of certain groups should not be permitted even if their individual members, as individuals, might be protected if they decided to exclude on the same basis. On the other hand, the rights of groups—but not of individuals—to parade, to report the news, and sometimes even to express themselves freely should be protected even under circumstances when group practice would not be permitted for individuals. A group may have a right to march down the middle of the road, for example, when an individual would have no legal claim to do so. Relegating communities and associations to no more, and sometimes less, than the sum of the rights of their members overlooks a crucial, structural element of First Amendment theory.

I do not pretend to be able to meet all of Emerson's powerful doubts about a generalized notion of the right to form or join an association. Instead of "a generalized notion," I seek to suggest a greater emphasis on "operative facts,"[39] a more particularistic focus on the context of varied group functions.

"Abridging the Freedom of Speech . . ., or the Right of the People Peaceably to Assemble, and to Petition the Government for Redress of Grievances"

The text of the First Amendment poses an obvious problem in interpretation. What is the relationship of freedom of expression, peaceable assembly, and petitioning for redress of grievances? The three clauses could be entirely separate, overlapping in several permutations or combinations, or they might constitute a single idea, probably emphasizing political speech, stated in three different ways. Neither original intent nor any clear rule of construction can be invoked to resolve the difficulty.

It is hardly surprising that Tom Emerson suggested a careful classificatory system for thinking about such issues. He was a great systematizer. Emerson's four categories for associational rights included: (1) the general power of the government to regulate the affairs of an organization or its membership; (2) governmental power used to compel an individual to belong to or otherwise to participate in an organization; (3) the rights of an individual or of a minority group vis-à-vis a membership organization; and (4) possible limits on governmental power to punish certain associational relationships, such as those with criminals or with people of different races.

Emerson elaborated his four models after examining the Supreme Court's freedom of association decisions that followed the *NAACP v. Alabama* decision. His development of the problematic cases within his first category, for example, could serve as a model for clear and concise scholarly discussion of judicial decisions. He carefully tracked the Court's treatment of the right of association through its various inconsistencies and mixed metaphors.[40] In conclusion, he explained why he feared that in recognizing an independent right of association, the Court would resort to a weak balancing approach when it sought to apply that right.

To Emerson, the vague and often inconsistent treatment of freedom of association in the cases of the late 1950s and early 1960s illustrated that the right itself was so broad and undifferentiated as to be "essentially obscurantist."[41] Moreover, he claimed that the balancing involved in construing freedom of association was "even less confined and less subject to objective application"[42] than the balancing approach Emerson deplored in cases dealing with specific rights of freedom of speech, press, assembly, or petition.

Emerson traced independent freedom of association analysis through the contexts of forced associations, minority rights, and personal associational freedom. Throughout, he found freedom of association of little or no use. In its place, he suggested ways to reach similar results through alternative doctrinal approaches. He argued that associational expression should be considered simply an extension of individual expression. Therefore, it should enjoy the same protections.[43] It is not surprising that Emerson, having redefined the debate about freedom of expression with his classification system distinguishing "expression" from "action," went on to propose a similar dichotomy for cases involving associational claims.

It must be emphasized that Emerson's system classified a great deal of the conduct of associations as vital to expression. He argued, for example, that public meetings, distribution of literature, solicitation of membership, parades, demonstrations, even the use of sound trucks, and "general organizational activities, including the conduct of schools," must be "as fully safeguarded as the actual utterance of the words themselves."[44]

With some tentativeness, Emerson recognized that associations are not always properly viewed as simply equal to the sum of their individual members. He observed that "the conduct of an association is likely to acquire unique qualities, to have effects which can originate only with an association rather than an individual."[45] This possibility of a qualitative difference between individuals and groups, and the fact that certain conduct (such as collusive price-fixing) requires more than individual involvement, led Emerson to claim that an association must at times be subject to governmental control on a basis different from individual conduct. But "any general right of association must be subordinate to the individual right"[46]; in other words, individual rights always ought to prevail over group rights.

To oversimplify Emerson's elegant argument, he generally regarded associations as entitled to receive the same degree of constitutional protection as an individual should receive for expression, and for conduct surrounding expression. In those respects in which associations are unique, however, he would allow them to be subjected to additional governmental regulation. Though Emerson obviously did not deal with the explosion of doctrine that began in the 1970s—important decisions that protect the freedom of expression of corporations, for example—his theory seems to ally him with Victor Brudney's assertion that "group action . . . is legitimately and traditionally subject to greater regulation by government than is individual action."[47]

Emerson was well aware that freedom of association has been a vital feature of American society for a long time. He also noted the increased importance of associations in recent years. What should we then make of his reluctance to grant associations any constitutional protection beyond what their individual members enjoy? Does Emerson's expression/action classificatory approach—apart from its undoubted significance for consideration of individual activity—adequately handle the range of constitutional ramifications in the wildly diverse litigation involving freedom of association claims today? Consideration of recent Supreme Court decisions will help answer these important questions.

Misery and Politics: Freedom of Association and Political Speech

Recent Supreme Court decisions tend to limit freedom to associate either to intimate associations or to "the freedom of individuals to associate for the purpose of engaging in protected speech or religious activities."[48] In so describing freedom of association, the Court seems, at first glance, to be following Tom Emerson's approach. That is, the justices derive freedom of association from freedom of expression or from the First Amendment's protection for religious freedom. They then render freedom of association nearly or completely otiose.

Occasionally, however, the Court uses freedom of association to accomplish precisely what Emerson feared. Freedom of association is commingled with freedom of speech in a way that makes it easy for judges to balance away both. This whipsaw effect occurs in part precisely because the Court has begun to protect commercial expression. Thus even "a private party"—as the Court described Consolidated Edison—is protected when it speaks through enclosures in its utility bills.[49] Newspapers seek profits, the Court reasoned, so other profit-seeking corporations should be entitled similarly to express themselves on political issues of the day.[50]

In the context of businesses claiming freedom of association and freedom of expression protection, moreover, the justices have begun to stretch judicial notice past any realistic breaking-point. For example, they proclaim themselves unconvinced, absent substantial proof, that requiring the Jaycees organization to admit women and give them full voting rights "will change the content or impact of the organization's speech."[51] Surely the Jaycees then will be a different organization. Surely that difference will be felt throughout an intricate web of relationships and different voices in immeasurable but nonetheless significant ways.

Tocqueville observed: "A false but clear and precise idea always has more power in the world than one which is true but complex."[52] Our difficulty centers around artificial attempts to create a neat, dichotomous view of associations. Despite its appealing result, the decision concerning the Jaycees provides a good illustration of how binary thought helps to create a doctrine that is in danger of becoming an attractive nuisance. It also suggests why groups sometimes should be entitled to less protection than individuals, despite a group's freedom of association claim.

Less Than Meets the Eye: Roberts v. United States Jaycees

In reviewing the Jaycees' discriminatory membership policy, Justice Brennan subdivided freedom of association. He first discerned a substantive due process element, entailing "certain intimate human relationships."[53] The Jaycees could not properly invoke this constitutional basis, however, because their group was "neither small nor selective."[54] But Brennan also spoke of a First Amendment associational element, which protected the Jaycees' expressive activities, albeit not sufficiently to override Minnesota's effort to attack sexual stereotyping in public accommodations.

Brennan considered the first, intimate type of association to be integral and an end in itself. Curiously, he regarded the second expressive type of association as instrumental and therefore subject to greater government intrusion. Though Brennan recognized that the two categories of association are not logically exclusive, he adopted a strongly dichotomous view. Because the Jaycees' association claims were perceived to be only of the second, instrumental variety, Brennan made quick work of finding Minnesota's interest sufficiently compelling to override the freedom not to associate, considered to be inherent in freedom of association. To the Court, this type of associational claim was no more than the sum of its constituent parts.

The most persuasive opinion in the *Jaycees* case—indeed probably the most cogent of all the recent freedom of association opinions—was Justice O'Connor's concurring opinion.[55] Because she viewed the Jaycees as primarily a business and therefore subject to extensive government regulation, O'Connor voted to uphold the regulation. Yet she argued that the same regulation would be invalid if the association were the type of expressive group which enjoys "First Amendment protection of both the content of its message and the choice of its members."[56] Such an association would approach what she termed "the ideal of complete protection for purely expressive association."[57]

O'Connor therefore urged a different approach from that favored by Brennan. She would move along a continuum. Commercial associations, in her view, merit little constitutional protection; expressive associations should receive a great deal. Moreover, O'Connor emphasized the constitutional dimension of governmental intrusion regarding group membership that extended beyond the realm of intimate personal relationships. In this regard, without saying so, O'Connor took up a position much closer to the freedom of association doctrine in the decades prior to the Warren Court.[58] She also was more consistent with the line of NAACP decisions involving freedom of association, dating from Justice Harlan's 1958 Alabama opinion through the Court's strange 1982 opinion in *NAACP v. Claiborne Hardware Co.*[59] *Claiborne Hardware* protected a local NAACP chapter from a huge state court fine imposed for organizing and enforcing a lengthy economic boycott of white merchants in Port Arthur, Mississippi. In *Claiborne Hardware* the Court used a language of dramatic—and puzzling—metaphors. Having begun by describing the concept of group action as "chameleon-like," Justice Stevens's majority opinion in that case concluded with the following memorable statement: "A court must be wary of a claim that the true color of a forest is better revealed by reptiles hidden in the weeds than by the foliage of countless free-standing trees."[60]

Toward a Functional Typology: Federal Election Commission v. Massachusetts Citizens For Life *and* Austin v. Michigan Chamber of Commerce

A little-known Supreme Court decision illustrates the wisdom of an approach that considers both the type of association involved and the type of expression, if any, implicated in the particular litigation. In 1987, the Court decided *Federal Election Commission v. Massachusetts Citizens For Life* (hereafter *MCFL*).[61] Because *MCFL* illuminates several important themes about the freedom of association, it is worth describing what the Court did in some detail.

Read narrowly, *MCFL* invalidated a federal restriction on campaign contributions by a nonprofit organization on the grounds that the federal law infringed upon core political speech.[62] Read more broadly, however, *MCFL* determined that the nonprofit status of the association was what made a constitutional difference to a majority of the justices. This broader reading is more than plausible; it seems the only interpretation to make sense of *MCFL*. Because the vote was so close and the variables so numerous, however, it is not yet time for advocates of robust constitutional protection for nonprofits to begin popping champagne corks. A closer look at *MCFL* underscores its potential and its puzzles.

The case began when a complaint reached the Federal Election Commission alleging that a "Special Election Edition" of the *Massachusetts Citizens for Life Newsletter* in 1978 constituted an expenditure of corporate funds on behalf of certain political candidates. An expenditure for distribution to the general public would violate section 441(b) of the Federal Election Campaign Act.[63] The lower courts disagreed about whether the Federal Campaign Act actually covered the *MCFL* newsletter, but agreed that if it did, the statute would be an unconstitutional restriction on political expression. The Supreme Court agreed that the statute did cover *MCFL*'s newsletter, but the justices vehemently disagreed among themselves as to whether the statute infringed First Amendment rights.

The Court's splintering is not surprising in a case such as *MCFL*. Deep analytic confusion surrounds attempts to reconcile vital but competing public interests in regulation of the political process, freedom of expression, and freedom of association. What does seem clear in *MCFL*, however, is that a majority of the Justices agreed that it made a *constitutional* difference what kind of group was doing the speaking. The *status* of MCFL as a nonprofit was the key factor. In this crucial section of the majority opinion, Justice Brennan wrote for a clear majority when he said, "The concerns underlying the regulation of corporate political activity are simply absent with regard to *MCFL*. . . . Voluntary political associations do not suddenly present the specter of corruption merely by assuming the corporate form."[64] The reason group status makes a constitutional difference is that spending by a business corporation or a union "raises the prospect that resources amassed in the economic marketplace may be used to provide an unfair advantage in the political marketplace."[65]

The fundamental interpretive problem posed by *MCFL* is to determine how much the Court's decision did and should turn on this distinction among corporate forms. Yet there it was: the Massachusetts Citizens For Life group apparently would have lost but for its status as a nonprofit. Yet we must ask: does not the *MCFL* decision really turn on the *type of expression* involved? It was a matter of *political speech*, after all, the kind of speech often defined as most worthy of constitutional solicitude.[66] This is plausible, of course, but the particular type of group involved and its function as a vehicle for group solidarity and amplification surely are two further factors that help explain *MCFL*. In this sense, *MCFL* hints at what role might be played by an independent right of freedom of association.

In *Austin v. Michigan Chamber of Commerce*,[67] the Court further subdivided doctrine and afforded still more constitutional importance to the actual nature of the group. The Michigan State Chamber of Commerce, a nonprofit corporation comprised of over 8,000 members, three-quarters of them for-profit corporations, challenged a state campaign finance act similar to the federal statute in *MCFL*. The Chamber tried to take advantage of the protection afforded nonprofits in *MCFL* as it claimed that Michigan's campaign regulations unconstitutionally burdened its political expression. Writing for the Court, Justice Marshall conceded that Michigan's campaign regulation burdened political expression, and therefore could be justified only by a compelling state interest.

It is usually impossible to meet this stringent standard. But the Chamber's nonprofit status acted as the linchpin for the majority's decision that Michigan had a compelling state interest here. Marshall stressed the unfair advantage corporations could have in the political marketplace through their state-granted ability to amass resources, and the "potential for distortion" that could result. He explained that while the Chamber of Commerce surely was a nonprofit as a formal legal matter, it lacked three essential characteristics of the victorious nonprofit in *MCFL*: first, the Chamber was formed for varied purposes, not all of them inherently political; second, the disincentives to withdraw if members were in political disagreement with the group were much stronger than those for the members of *MCFL*, more akin to those facing shareholders in a business corporation; and finally and most significantly, the Chamber did not seem independent from the influence of business corporations.

Thus *Austin* stands as a modern prototype of a legal realist's opinion. The Court had to stretch doctrine and to pierce legal forms to find a compelling state interest. Yet Marshall did so with an unadorned, almost conclusory focus on *realpolitik*. Corporate structure offers unique state-conferred advantages, Marshall explained. Therefore, "the desire to counterbalance those advantages unique to the corporate form is the State's compelling interest in this case."[68] In *Austin*, realism about groups overrode the impulse—or, said the dissenters, the constitutional necessity—to place all groups that share the same legal form in the same constitutional basket.

The Need for an Independent Right: The Tests Applied in *Citizens Against Rent Control* and *Widmar v. Vincent*

A basic problem associations pose for legal analysis is that lawyers grow accustomed to thinking in binary terms such as government/ individual or group/individual. Perhaps the most appalling character-istic of the spate of recent decisions through which the Court has intervened vigorously to protect political expenditures by associations is the willingness of a majority to use freedom of association in an entirely undifferentiated way. Two decisions within the same week illustrate the phenomenon.

In *Citizens Against Rent Control v. City of Berkeley,* a case about campaign contributions for a vote on rent control, Chief Justice Burger waxed rhapsodic in his majority opinion about the American "tradi-tion of volunteer committees for collective action," a tradition that "manifested itself in myriad community and public activities."[69] This tradition apparently extended to efforts by corporate managers to communicate their dollars-and-cents messages to voters despite con-tribution limitations.[70] The thrust of Burger's opinion was that Berke-ley's limit on election spending offended freedom of association, a right the Court found to overlap and blend with freedom of expression and to require "exacting judicial scrutiny."[71] Ironically, Burger was so taken with the effectiveness of collective efforts in the American past that he found it necessary to state explicitly that not all activities that are legal for individuals are also legal for groups.[72]

Less than a week before the *Berkeley* decision, the Court in *Widmar v. Vincent* explained that religious worship and discussion "are forms of speech and association protected by the First Amendment."[73] Jus-tice Powell's majority opinion therefore applied a rigorous test, a "level of scrutiny appropriate to prior restraint," and struck down an effort by the University of Missouri at Kansas City to deny an evangelical Christian group access to campus facilities for purposes of worship and religious discussion.[74]

The decision in *Widmar* surely was correct. But it seems right largely because frequently "the first amendment's proscription against cen-sorship is itself simply a specialized equal protection guarantee."[75] One of the crucial ways the Court has bogged down in its recent con-sideration of freedom of association claims is that it has lost track of the point Tom Emerson made when he discussed the role of equal protection analysis in the system of freedom of expression. Emerson wrote, "Basically, equal protection requirements demand fairness as between relevant interests in the dispensation of governmental support."[76] It is incoherent simply to assume, as the Court now does quite readily, that the extremely permissive rational relationship test that is standard for equal protection analysis of social and economic classifications is appropriate when freedom of association rights are at stake. Using the equal protection model, any greater judicial protection for the right threatened by such regulations would require proof of a "bad motive." Yet this is entirely misplaced in the sensitive realm of governmental entanglement with the First Amendment. Bad motive may be sufficient to make out a First Amendment violation, but it ought not be a necessary element of proof.

The Court's quest for neutrality is doomed. The protective coloration of purportedly clear, binary choices that are borrowed from the rubric of current equal protection doctrine actually creates unspecified and unaccountable discretion. Neither bureaucrats nor judges need look beyond what groups they feel comfortable in protecting or punishing.

Widmar itself begins to suggest how the crucial role of group identity fades from view when judges simply reason by analogy to equal protection analysis. *Widmar,* and subsequent "public forum" decisions, fail to consider the importance of affiliation itself for group identity and, ultimately, for individual identity. But at least *Widmar* suggests a rigorous constitutional standard, akin to the special scrutiny applied to prior restraints. *Widmar* therefore suggests the extent to which groups such as paraders, journalists, and even evangelicals need their group identities to construct the powerful First Amendment arguments they should have. Unfortunately, *Widmar* has not been followed in this respect. Instead, several wrong-headed approaches to freedom of association in recent decisions illustrate some of the mistakes made when equal protection analysis is imported uncritically into the freedom of association context.

When Freedom of Association Is Less or More than the Sum of Its Parts

The Doomed Search for Governmental Neutrality: A Disastrous Trilogy Concerning NonProfits

Even after the *Jaycees* and *Rotary Club* decisions, a nonprofit association that decides to discriminate in a way that surely would be unconstitutional if perpetrated by a state official might still be able to insulate its action from constitutional scrutiny. Nonetheless, under *Bob Jones University v. United States*,[77] such a victory might prove Pyrrhic. The organization could lose its nonprofit tax status and would have no constitutional recourse. Thus we must consider whether government neutrality is an adequate or even reasonable constitutional standard for administrative decisions about which associations should receive government benefits or burdens.

In *Bob Jones* the Court upheld, on statutory grounds, an Internal Revenue Service (IRS) decision to deny tax-exempt status to private religious schools that practice racial discrimination. Chief Justice Burger's majority opinion did not confront freedom of association explicitly. Moreover, in part because there was some reason to doubt the sincerity of the religious defenses raised by the private schools, the majority slid past the knotty First Amendment issues lurking beneath its construction of congressional intent—and congressional silence.[78] Instead, with more than a nod to Panglossian naive optimism, Burger stressed our nation's unquestioned commitment to the eradication of racial discrimination. By definition, according to Burger, such discrimination is inconsistent with statutory requirements to qualify as a nonprofit organization under the federal tax laws. The majority upheld IRS discretion to determine tax-exempt status with no more particularity than that the nonprofit be consistent with "the public interest," "the common community conscience," and the "declared position of the whole government."[79] Such a standard makes it difficult to determine who, if anyone, is guarding the guardians.

Each April we are too clearly reminded of the pervasive might of the IRS. The Court's way of arriving at the *Bob Jones* decision (while I agree with the result, I deplore the methodology) assigns to the IRS virtually unreviewable discretion to determine what "common law," "common sense," and "history" tell us about whether a nonprofit is comporting with "deeply and widely accepted views of elementary justice."[80] Justice Powell correctly stressed the importance of pluralism, undervalued in the majority's analysis, though he did not find it dispositive in this case.

To make matters worse, in *Allen v. Wright*[81] the Court determined that taxpayers—even when the taxpayers also were parents of minority students within districts under desegregation orders—could not sue to compel the IRS actually to enforce the policy upheld in *Bob Jones*. Even in situations where minority students were stigmatized—a concern at the core of the desegregation cases beginning with *Brown v. Board of Education*[82]—their parents had no standing to sue to compel any remedial administrative response. So much for enforcing "deeply and widely accepted views of elementary justice."

In *Regan v. Taxation with Representation of Washington, Inc. (TRW),*[83] which was handed down the day before *Bob Jones,* the Court unanimously agreed that it was not a denial of either First Amendment or equal protection rights to forbid a nonprofit to lobby Congress if it wished to retain its §501(c)(3) tax exempt status, though other nonprofits such as veterans groups were exempt from the lobbying prohibition. *TRW* deserves more attention than it has received, for two reasons. First, then-Justice Rehnquist's majority opinion viewed tax exemptions as a form of "largess." He stated, "Both tax exemptions and tax-deductions are a form of subsidy that is administered through the tax system . . . [and] has much the same effect as a cash grant."[84] This approach allowed the unanimous Court to emphasize that the Constitution permits great discretion in decisions distributing such largess.

The second significant point about *TRW* is that it illustrates the peculiar application of important principles of neutrality in recent First Amendment decisions. Because the *TRW* Court perceived no invidious discrimination against the particular ideas advanced by the particular nonprofit involved, it was quite willing to find no constitutional violation.[85]

The Court's uncritical approach to hypothetical neutrality in administrative decisions also helps to explain the anomalous holding in *Cornelius v. NAACP Legal Defense and Educational Fund, Inc.*[86] There, in the course of denying a First Amendment and equal protection claim of access to an annual charitable campaign in the federal workplace, Justice O'Connor's majority opinion determined rather mechanistically that the federal campaign constituted a "nonpublic forum." Therefore, the 4–3 *Cornelius* decision held that, absent proof of impermissible motivation in the administrator's decision as to which nonprofits would be included in the combined campaign, administrative discretion would prevail so long as it appeared "reasonable."[87]

The central difficulty with this decision, as with *MCFL* and *TRW,* is that government neutrality is entirely elusive in these cases. The holdings are inconsistent and seem to rest on an unarticulated nexus between the extent to which the justices value the particular expressive act involved and how they perceive the relative worthiness of the particular association seeking constitutional protection. Nonprofit associations that appear to be similarly situated in all relevant respects may be treated very differently. In sharp contrast to *Claiborne Hardware* and *MCFL*, the trilogy of *Bob Jones, TRW,* and *Cornelius* defers to administrators so broadly as to leave them almost unbounded discretion in crucial decisions affecting nonprofit associations. The Court simply applies an extremely deferential "reasonableness" standard of review.

What to Do about Freedom of Association?

Our abhorence of censorship is undeniable. The idea that it could be rooted in a kind of "specialized equal protection guarantee" indicates why much more exacting scrutiny is appropriate than the complete and unquestioning reliance on the presumed neutrality of administrators in the three cases just discussed. It also underscores why the insistence on proof of a "but for" discriminatory motivation in recent equal protection decisions is inappropriate when sensitive First Amendment rights are at stake. Finally, since the status of the association seems determinative, the nascent typology in decisions such as the *Jaycees* and *MCFL* suggests a useful analogy between nonprofits, for example, and the "checking value" we celebrate and expect of a robust free press.

It would be a mistake to belittle the difficulty in deciding the cases analyzed here. Yet the idea that freedom of association is an independent and important right at a minimum suggests that those who seek to regulate nonprofits be required to justify their intrusions with reasons far more significant than those the Court accepted unquestioningly, for example, in *TRW* and *Cornelius*. Because elimination of the ongoing burden of racism and sexism is a compelling, not to say overwhelming, justification in our society, it is easy to applaud the results in *Bob Jones* and *Jaycees* and to pass over the reasons announced by the Court. Even though Tom Emerson suggested that "general organizational activities, including the conduct of schools," should be safeguarded as fully "as the actual utterance of the words themselves,"[88] his analysis might well have led him to join me in approving the outcome, if not the reasoning, in *Bob Jones* and in *Runyon v. McCrary*.[89]

These decisions indicate, however, that group quality makes a profound difference. How can we find a way out of this analytic morass? We probably cannot achieve a general theory, but we may have begun to work toward a few hard-earned generalizations. Surely the status of the association and the type of communicative act emerge as critical factors. Equally clearly, the Court's recent decisions have allowed administrators to treat similar groups differently on no other basis than dubious judicial deference to their presumed neutrality. Finally, while we recognize that there is a need for some government oversight and some means to ascertain that nonprofits actually are what they claim to be, it would be helpful to think about intrusive governmental regulation of nonprofit associations with some of the gingerly concern we are accustomed to affording newspapers. In other words, government intrusions ought to be accepted if and only if the government can demonstrate some very good, even compelling reasons for infringing on the independent freedom of association right.

Whether the press, which is singled out in the First Amendment's text, can claim any exceptional protection has been hotly debated for years.[90] But in numerous ways journalists do, in fact, enjoy special protection. They get access to the best, and sometimes the only seats in courtrooms, legislative galleries, and executive press conferences.[91] Reporters enjoy special formal privileges in a majority of state statutory codes and more privileged status in numerous other ways.[92] Such special protection is sometimes justified on the grounds that reporters serve as surrogates for the public. Yet there can be little doubt that government officials, even judges, treat members of the press with special consideration and that reporters, editors, and publishers surely are not democratically accountable to those they purportedly represent. Members of the fourth estate are members of a special group. Publishers and media executives strive for profit, yet we defer to the press because it helps to check governmental power and seeks to mediate, inform, and entertain. At least in their news and editorial functions, groups denominated "the press" often are thought to merit particular constitutional protection.[93]

It is not a new idea that at least some associations are closely analogous to the press. Tocqueville stressed "a necessary connection between associations and newspapers"[94] and went on to compare and contrast their relative merits and claims for freedom. He underscored the need for associations to function as checks and balances in a democracy and emphasized their educational function, crucial to resisting the alienation he thought was likely to develop in the context of the gentle democratic tyranny of excessive egalitarianism.

Tocqueville optimistically asserted, "An association, be it political, industrial, commercial, or even literary or scientific, is an educated and powerful body of citizens which cannot be twisted to any man's will or quietly trodden down, and by defending its private interests against the encroachments of power, it saves the common liberties."[95] Obviously, much tragic intervening history serves to emphasize the danger to citizens of too much power in the hands of some groups. As Hannah Arendt pointed out, "Power springs up whenever people get together and act in concert."[96] We also have become more aware of the intrusive, often overwhelming power that corporations and other groups can exert. Therefore, it seems particularly appropriate to concentrate our energies and attention on ways to connect constitutional theory to the reality of our identities as members of myriad associations.

Conclusion

This chapter has pointed out why some associations, some of the time, deserve more sensitive, although not absolute, constitutional protection. In particular, those in the voluntary or independent sector may properly be considered a fifth estate, functioning in ways analogous to the fourth estate of the press and to the norm-generating religious associations.[97] For that reason—indeed for the common good—private associations merit constitutional solicitude.

Yet it is a commonplace of American history in general, and American legal history in particular, that we focus on individualism to the virtual exclusion of all else. In turn, the prodigious impact of law schools and judges alike concentrating on the economic profit-maximizing individual exacerbates that trend. That is why this call for the constitutional freedom of association is not a commonplace. Indeed, it seems often out of the picture entirely in a debate posing the choice of individual freedom versus government regulation. The misleading either/or choice between government and individual ignores our nation's extensive tradition of collective responsibility. Unfortunately, this dichotomy tends to ascribe an anachronistic Social Darwinist theory to the minds and motives of the Constitution's founding generation.[98]

The unkickable habit of association in the United States is not the entire story, to be sure, nor is historic description synonymous with normative constitutional proposals.[99] Again, however, Tocqueville's observations and insights are directly pertinent. He stressed the difference between American and European associations. In Europe, associations, like newspapers, tended to represent well-defined classes and sought to influence governmental action directly. Echoing Madison,

Tocqueville argued that "no countries need associations more—to prevent either despotism of parties or the arbitrary rule of a prince—than those with a democratic social state."[100] Tocqueville continued, "In a country like the United States, where differences of view are only matters of nuance, the right of associations can remain, so to say, without limits."[101]

Surely the rights of associations cannot remain "without limits." At the same time, Tocqueville continues to be right in noting how much Americans share beliefs, in contrast to the vigorous clash of ideologies in Europe. There can be no absolute freedom of association right; nor is the right of freedom of association, if given independent status, meant always to carry the same consistent weight. But it is important to note the inconsistency and false rigor in the mechanistic categorical approach to associational rights that is now in vogue in the Supreme Court. With groups, it is not possible to achieve a "philosophically continuous series."[102] Still, an independent right of freedom of association makes better historical, logical, and normative sense.

Gordon Wood sums up a sea-change that began in Philadelphia in the stifling summer of 1787. He writes of "an end of the classical conception of politics and the beginning of what might be called a romantic view of politics."[103] The men who perpetrated this revolution possessed a "more realistic sense of political behavior in the society itself, among the people," according to Wood; they also "embodied a new kinetic sense" and "placed a new emphasis on the piecemeal and the concrete in politics at the expense of order and completeness."[104]

Through the First Amendment, the constitutionalists of two centuries ago—including some who effectively dissented from the Constitution as it stood in unamended form—provided explicit protection for those people concerned enough to assemble together. They linked this right directly to other constitutional protections. Together, these parchment barriers could serve those who would speak, write, petition, or pray against orthodoxy. The First Amendment thereby provided a vital means for people to convince others to join them against injustice. In groups, they could enhance the power of their arguments and the strength of their commitment.

No unified general theory of freedom of association seems possible today, if it ever was. Instead, a kinetic, but grounded constitutional approach could emerge through consideration of some of the dark sides of the intersection of law and associations in the American past, such as the rampant practice of guilt by association discussed in the next chapter. Recently, a great deal of analytic quicksand has encrusted freedom of association. Hence attention to some constitutional roads not taken underscores the importance of clear thinking about the scope of an independent right of freedom of association, often in realms beyond that of the First Amendment.

3 Guilt by Association, Association by Guilt

> In democratic countries knowledge of how to combine is the mother of all other forms of knowledge; on its progress depends that of all others.
>
> *Alexis de Tocqueville*[1]

Mark Twain once said, "The American people enjoy three great blessings—free speech, free press, and the good sense not to use either."[2] A similar point might be made about our clear abhorrence of guilt by association. Guilt must be assessed only on an individual basis, we insist, not because of membership or association with others.[3] Upon closer scrutiny, however, there is a crucial dissonance between this principle and American practice.

Indeed, individualism notwithstanding, guilt by association seems to be a prevalent national tradition endorsed and encouraged by judges. Americans have ascribed to one another guilt by association early and often. Moreover, this phenomenon has not been confined to notorious times of hysteria such as during and after World War I and in the Red Scare of the 1950s. Anyone who recalls President George Bush's effort to link Governor Michael Dukakis with card-carrying members of the ACLU during the 1988 presidential campaign—unfair to ACLU members to smear them by association with Dukakis!—understands the force and commonplace nature of guilt by association attacks.

If assignment of collective guilt is not admirable, it may nevertheless be necessary in modern life. Often we move past or beyond the idea of individual blame and rely on various concepts of social responsibility. This is a crucial element in decisions by some people not to buy German goods, for example, or in refusals to visit or do business with South Africa before apartheid was dismantled. Undoubtedly, some innocents suffer. Yet we continue to assign responsibility in gross for gross national guilt. Innocents also suffer from our complicity, our numerous refusals to become involved despite frequent contacts with anonymous and needy others in everyday life. We constantly make quick judgments about the company we do not want to keep. Generalizations are necessary for utilitarian reasons. We simply do not have the time or energy to make individual judgments.

Paradoxically, the converse also seems true about our most cherished associations. There are human clusters we feel guilty about severing, social constructs we are born into or create through special commitments. They include family and nation, as well as racial, religious, and cultural connections. If both association by guilt and guilt by association are inescapable in the modern world, the quest for full tolerance and for individual justice seems doomed. Even if considerable ambivalence about guilt by association is warranted, such doubts can hardly justify complacency about blatant forms of legalized practice.

The focus in this chapter is not, as it could be, on prosecutorial abuses of the law of criminal conspiracy or the laws against racketeering, for example, but rather on more basic findings of guilt because of membership alone. It centers on what Edmund Wilson termed "the bed-fellow line of argument."[4] Despite pervasive notions of individual accountability, the American legal system has been ready and willing to accept blame based on the company one keeps.

A kind of patchwork guilt enfolds us all. Yet many people today still believe emphatically that the group and status linkages of the past disintegrated long ago. The individual versus the state is perceived as the primary dichotomy. Rights are shields against the state, but the state has no affirmative obligations. *Others* may have duties, but *I* have rights.[5] This individualistic view, a perspective that dominates the American judiciary today, is premised on nostalgia for a golden age that never was. Unfortunately, this skeptical point also can be made about "civic republicanism," the rubric for a critique of the individual/ state dichotomy prevalent in academia today.[6] Consideration of a few moments in American legal history bashes binary choices and shows the illusory aspect of our purported antipathy to guilt by association.

Loyalty and Guilt by Association

Early in 1948 John Lord O'Brian presented the annual address to the New York State Bar Association. This venerable lawyer and public servant chose to discuss "Loyalty Tests and Guilt by Association."[7] His talk is a useful starting point for several paradoxes this chapter explores. By then, O'Brian already had considerable expertise on the subject. Following his graduation from Harvard in 1896 and a very successful legal and political career in Buffalo, O'Brian became head of the Department of Justice War Emergency Board in 1917. He was the lawyer, therefore, who made crucial decisions in 1918 about whether and in what ways Congress ought to broaden the Espionage Act of 1917, and about when and how to prosecute people for espionage, sedition, and interference with the war effort.[8]

It is important to note that O'Brian was a quintessential enlightened liberal, committed to trying to work from within. During World War I, O'Brian and his assistant, Alfred Bettman, carefully reiterated for posterity their view that "freedom of discussion is the very essence of democracy."[9] They believed that the hysteria that was then breaking into violence throughout the country could best be calmed through federal prosecutions overseen by responsible, judicious officials such as themselves. O'Brian and Bettman would not permit prosecutions simply for sedition or disloyalty. They would approve only those prosecutions necessary for "the orderly execution of the laws relating to the raising of armies."[10]

What may be most startling about O'Brian's 1948 speech is its prophetic aspect. O'Brian observed that there is "something peculiarly sinister and insidious in even a charge of disloyalty."[11] He spoke of "our failure to take notice of the growing recognition in our law of the menacing doctrine of guilt by association, for which traditionally we have had distrust amounting to abhorrence."[12] If O'Brian's sanguine claim of longstanding abhorrence to guilt by association was untenable, his warning about President Truman's Loyalty Order and the opening crescendos of the outrages later lumped together as McCarthyism was courageous and prescient.

It is significant that O'Brian's 1948 warning went unheeded, though he was hardly alone in his condemnation of the growing storm. In newspapers, magazines, and law reviews, outstanding law professors such as Erwin Griswold, Zechariah Chafee, Jr., Ernest Gelhorn, and Thomas Emerson—all with very different political beliefs—wrote careful, clear, and convincing critiques of the excesses and dangers of government loyalty programs, congressional witch hunts, and private blacklists.[13]

Unfortunately, the United States Supreme Court had established the crucial precedents in the World War I period, when it upheld far-fetched federal prosecutions for political expression. O'Brian and Bettman had prepared the briefs and argued these cases on the basis of the assertion that the expressions at issue had a forbidden "natural and reasonable effect."[14] Justice Holmes's initial opinions for a unanimous Court revealed the clear and present danger of O'Brian's faith in judicious line-drawing. But there is a more specific reason for considering O'Brian's reflections. Bromides about abhorrence for guilt by association mask pressing and practical legal problems. Law remains our civic religion.

In 1948 O'Brian told the New York Bar Association that until 1920 our law had adhered to the view that "guilt must be personal."[15] This obviously was part of O'Brian's effort to vindicate his own conduct in the World War I period. Both O'Brian and Bettman repeatedly had sounded the theme that "One of the fundamental conceptions of Anglo-American law is that guilt is personal and not by association."[16] With the advantage of hindsight, however, O'Brian also clearly sought to condemn the nefarious activities of the Department of Justice under Attorney General A. Mitchell Palmer, who exploited the nativist and antiradical fever that had gripped the country. Palmer's minions rounded up and deported thousands of aliens without any pretence of due process. The "Palmer raids" effectively torpedoed most notions of freedom of expression and freedom of association that survived the war fought to make the world safe for democracy.

O'Brian's point was to contrast the depredations of the Department of Justice after he left it in 1919 with what happened during his service. Yet his claim that until 1920 legal guilt in the United States was assigned purely on a personal basis hardly withstands scrutiny. One need only consider the declared policies of O'Brian's own Justice Department days, to say nothing of the actual practices of federal and state law enforcement personnel, federal troops, and voluntary patriotic groups. In a largely self-congratulatory 1919 speech reviewing "Civil Liberty in War Time" O'Brian did condemn "spy mania," and he acknowledged serious abuses of civil rights and civil liberties by the state, county, and local councils of defense that proliferated during the war.

Yet in the same speech O'Brian resorted to guilt by association himself, compounded by extremely far-fetched claims about criminal causation, when he discussed the "well-known character" and "menace" of the I.W.W., and defended federal prosecutions on the grounds that "the logical result of the activities of this organization [was] to cripple industries."[17] Moreover, O'Brian's benign recollection of pre-1920 federal law simply ignored the rampant use of guilt by association arguments at the bloody intersection of labor and law in the half century before O'Brian arrived in Washington.

Instead of accumulating evidence about the well-documented legal history in the years after 1948,[18] it may be more useful to consider a few cases of guilt by association in times of relative calm in the United States. Two cases well outside the constitutional law canon prove to be particularly revealing about guilt by association. The affirmative side of association by guilt also merits brief attention.

"The Substitution of Executive Process for Judicial Process": The Colorado Labor War of 1903–04

That most people in the United States lack a sense of history is a cliché that is also a truism. The past has passed—it is in no way thought to be prelude. Thus the judges who now dominate the federal judiciary, appointed by Ronald Reagan and George Bush, seem able to get away with simply announcing that notions of laissez-faire always held sway in American history and were incorporated into the text of the federal Constitution. If we look carefully at the metaphor of a level playing field and its presumption of fair competition for all individuals as individuals, which forms the foundation for the decisions these judges make, we find the field marred by fissures and bumps that reveal a great deal of past aggressive action by government officials that significantly favors some groups and disfavors others.

Even without consideration of the myriad past wrongs perpetrated against African-Americans and Native Americans, for example, there are abundant instances permeating American legal history. In 1890, for instance, the United States Supreme Court upheld the conviction and jail term imposed on a Mormon for registering to vote. He violated an Idaho law that excluded from the franchise anyone who belonged to a church organization that taught bigamy or polygamy.[19]

Both in the century before and the century after that clear example of guilt by association, judges persistently penalized some groups while aiding and abetting others. Often judges declare that, in doing so, they are merely deferring to the wishes of more democratic and accountable legislative or executive officials. In other instances, while proclaiming they are simply neutral referees in a great social race of life, judges tend blatantly to impose their own choices of good and bad groups, purportedly based on the requirements of current social policy or some higher principle. To generalize about judges in this manner, however, itself smacks of guilt by association.

Significant distinctions can be drawn between general collective guilt, legal guilt by association, varying theories of conspiracy, and even the recognition that within contract law—often the paradigm for freely bargaining individuals—longstanding doctrines constrain individual choice and force lawyers and judges to wrestle with the impact that contracts may have on third-party beneficiaries and others in need of protection. Contextual specificity, therefore, is vitally important. *Moyer v. Peabody*,[20] a decision written by the great Oliver Wendell Holmes, Jr., illuminates the pitfalls in facile judicial acceptance of guilt by association. The Court decided *Moyer* in an era of peace and relative national calm, more than a decade before the beginning of legal guilt by association, according to John Lord O'Brian and the generally accepted account.

Colorado Class Conflict and Martial Law: Moyer v. Peabody

In *Moyer* the Court unanimously legitimated a decision by Colorado Governor James H. Peabody a few years earlier. Peabody had declared martial law, suspended habeas corpus, and imprisoned Charles Moyer, president of the Western Federation of Miners. Without filing a criminal complaint, Colorado authorities held Moyer incommunicado for over two months. Governor Peabody took this drastic action even though Colorado's regular courts continued to function throughout the period. Moreover, Peabody simply ignored the fact that a Colorado district judge had ordered Moyer's release.

Holmes's opinion upholding Peabody's action was a far cry from the famous First Amendment dissents Holmes began to write a decade later, in which he expressed sensitivity for the rights of dissenters. By contrast, in *Moyer* Holmes invoked one of his favorite doctrines: the greater power includes all lesser power. Because soldiers might properly fire into a mob during an insurrection, Holmes explained, the exercise of the lesser power of detaining a union president because "trouble was apprehended with the members of that organization" obviously was permissible.[21]

Holmes did sound a skeptical note when he wrote, "it is familiar that what is due process of law depends on the circumstances."[22] Characteristically, however, he then declared it unnecessary to inquire into the facts, although what actually had happened entirely undermined the reasonableness of Peabody's intervention in the decade-long battle between labor and management in the Colorado mines. It was enough that Peabody might have acted in good faith, Holmes wrote.[23] He analogized Peabody's authority to the vast discretion enjoyed by the master of a ship. Holmes was unwilling to consider individual rights at all as he allowed the detention of an individual on the strength of guilt by association with his union, premised on an entirely abstract threat to the government. Holmes's holding was blunt: "When it comes to a decision by the head of the state upon a matter involving its life, the ordinary rights of individuals must yield to what he deems the necessities of the moment."[24] Indeed, Holmes had no qualms about choosing force over law. As he succinctly put the point, "Public danger warrants the substitution of executive process for judicial process."[25]

A Congressional investigation and subsequent careful work by historians such as Vernon Jensen and Melvyn Dubofsky proved how little danger there was and how unfounded was Governor Peabody's declaration of a "qualified state of martial law" for several months in 1903–1904.[26] Moreover, the militia that Peabody sent to break the miners' strike (called in sympathy with a striking smelters' union) was paid directly by the mine owners' association, not by the state. Company managers who commanded this private army repeatedly defied local judicial authority. The militia commander said he had come "to do up this damned anarchistic federation."[27] Long before Holmes made his own Social Darwinist point, antiunion leaders proclaimed that military necessity "recognizes no laws, either civil or social" and announced, "To hell with the constitution, we aren't going by the constitution."[28] Nor did the militia balk at brutal physical violence, tarring and feathering, and extensive use of *agent provocateurs*.

The mine owners and their sympathizers utilized an owners' association and a new Citizens' Alliance network with devastating effectiveness. Their determined effort to squelch the power of unions was part of a well-financed national campaign launched by associations of business leaders and a web of citizens' organizations.[29] The Colorado pattern of the abuse of power by private groups has recurred so often in American history that it should—but generally does not—sober those contemporary scholars who wax almost mystical about the social contributions of groups. The owners and their supporters in Colorado carried out sudden, massive deportations of hundreds of men they believed to be associated with the miners' union. In their close working relationship with Governor Peabody, the mine owners and their allies piggybacked their own power onto the full force of state authority. They thereby triumphed completely in what Dubofsky aptly called "one of the most brutal class conflicts in American history."[30]

The intertwining of private and public power that Holmes ratified quite callously in *Moyer* reflects established practices that became even more blatant in the years that followed. Famous examples include the massacre of at least 45 miners and their families at a tent city in Ludlow, Colorado, in 1914, and the deportation from Bisbee, Arizona, in 1917, where the leading citizens rounded up over 1,200 workers presumed to be associated with the I.W.W. and sent them off at gunpoint, in cattle cars, into the New Mexico desert. (It is worth noting that New York courts subsequently upheld the conviction of Upton Sinclair for leading a peaceful protest against the Ludlow killings outside Standard Oil headquarters in New York City, and that U.S. Army personnel detained many of the Bisbee deportees for several months as possible enemy aliens even after their rescue from the desert.)[31] The army intervened directly and repeatedly in labor disputes against groups perceived to be or depicted as radicals. Not only was guilt by association rampant, but army officers often were explicit about their disregard for legal niceties and their enthusiasm for choosing sides. Military intervention tended to blur or eliminate the traditional public/private distinction. Official enthusiasm for direct participation, or studied indifference in the context of violence aimed at "radicals," prevailed well past the end of World War I.[32]

Normalcy, Threats to Government, and the Great Outdoors: The Rip-Roaring Twenties

In the years after World War I Holmes changed his mind about some forms of guilt by association, after prodding by Justice Brandeis. Yet this doctrine continued to thrive in the streets, the legislatures, and in the courts long after the first Red Scare purportedly faded from view. This casts doubt on accepted historiography that portrays the World War I era and the period of the Palmer Raids as a sort of national fever, a pathological reaction that broke abruptly and then went into remission for several decades.[33]

Brandeis's deservedly famous essay about fear and freedom appeared as a concurrence in the Court's decision as late as 1927 to uphold the conviction of Charlotte Anita Whitney under California's criminal syndicalism act.[34] The majority held that California could impose a jail sentence of one-to-fourteen years because Whitney, already "nearly 60 years old" and a well-known social worker, Wellesley graduate, and niece of a Supreme Court Justice, did not leave a political meeting after the majority had defeated a mild, reformist plank she supported. Because she was present, Whitney was held responsible for the more radical positions the group subsequently adopted.

It might seem hard to find a clearer example of guilt by association, but the Court supplied one in a virtually unknown case decided the same day as *Whitney*. Ms. Whitney's constitutional claims were undercut somewhat by the procedural posture of her case—which helps to explain, if not to excuse, the decision by Brandeis and Holmes to concur in the Court's decision upholding her conviction. The companion case, *Burns v. United States*,[35] presented no such excuse, yet only Brandeis dissented.

The Supreme Court upheld the conviction of William Burns solely on the basis of his organizing for, and being a member of, the I.W.W.[36] In fact, the trial jury acquitted Burns of the charge of having acted "with intent to accomplish a change in industrial ownership and control and effecting a political change."[37] Rousing excerpts from the "I.W.W. Song Book, Joe Hill Memorial Edition," and snippets from various speeches and pamphlets—none by William Burns—put the I.W.W. and not Burns on trial. Yet Burns was "connected with the organization," Justice Butler explained for the Court, and "it cannot be said as a matter of law that the things there mentioned, when taken in connection with facts, may not have been proper for consideration in connection with some element of the criminal syndicalism charged."[38] This remarkable example of cloudy doubletalk about connections suggests the irrelevance of First Amendment values to the *Burns* Court.

Indeed, the lack of constitutional concern is even more startling when one reads the record. For example, the prosecution could not and did not try to connect Burns to any of the testimony against the I.W.W., such as a speech that allegedly advocated sabotage, a speech used as evidence by both the trial judge and the Supreme Court. (Neither court noted that the policeman whose testimony put the speech into the trial said he heard it in Los Angeles, hundreds of miles from the scene and a month *after* Burns's arrest.)[39] The case that landed Burns in prison with a 15-month sentence consisted of a bizarre stew of words and deeds attributed to the I.W.W. anywhere by anyone.

For example, Elbert Coutts was a star witness against Burns. Coutts testified that he was a member of the I.W.W. from 1913 to 1917, during which time he made his living primarily by stealing. Subsequently, his chief source of income was the $250 per case, above expenses, he got from the government for his testimony in more than 40 trials of I.W.W. members.[40] Coutts's testimony was virtually the same throughout the numerous trials, according to the California Supreme Court.[41] And membership in the I.W.W. was the only link connecting Coutts's testimony implicating I.W.W. members in bizarre schemes and boasts, all of which allegedly occurred at least three years before Burns joined the I.W.W. Beneath the Court's mushy language in *Burns* about deference to state criminal processes, its endorsement of guilt by association could hardly have been more stark.

The Court decided a third companion case the same day as *Burns* and *Whitney*. *Fiske v. Kansas*[42] reversed the conviction of an I.W.W. member when the preamble to the I.W.W. constitution was the only significant evidence against the defendant. Although *Fiske* is unusually murky about its constitutional basis, this decision is generally described as the first victory ever for a First Amendment claim in the United States Supreme Court. Yet when *Fiske* is read alongside *Burns*, it is clear that even Thomas Reed Powell's sardonic claim that "Fiske is the one man in the decade whom the free speech clause saved"[43] was something of an exaggeration.

In the United States Supreme Court in the 1920s, free speech decisions saved no one. The contrasting outcome in *Burns* makes clear that Fiske prevailed only by virtue of due process doctrine, given the prosecutor's failure to present adequate evidence against him. By contrast, Burns, improbably an I.W.W. organizer in Yosemite National Park, went to jail because the prosecutor followed the California custom of putting the entire I.W.W. on trial with stale evidence presented by police informers and by notorious professional turncoat witnesses. This evidentiary basis "connected up" general I.W.W. beliefs with Burns's membership in the organization, and satisfied any constitutional scruples of the Supreme Court.

The *Burns* prosecution also illustrates that even after the I.W.W. was thoroughly decimated—the 1925 I.W.W. convention had only 11 delegates representing the pitiful remnant of seven unions—the fervor to impute guilt by association continued with remarkable potency. By a quirk, California's syndicalism act was applicable in a national park, so Burke could be prosecuted and convicted. But it was a display of outright paranoia to uphold Burns's conviction on the premise that an effort to unionize lumbermen in the park (apparently Burns did not try to mobilize the bears) threatened the overthrow of the government.

Finally, *Burns* is most significant for its hint of the bitter labor situation during the 1920s, and of judicial willingness to allow virtually unbridled guilt by association tactics employed to squelch any suspicion of radicalism. John Sayles's movie *Matewan* does a good job of depicting the willingness of management to resort to considerable bloodshed against people organizing in the West Virginia mining towns. What is less well known, however, is that throughout the country union organizers and protesters were constantly denied the opportunity to speak and were forcibly driven out of town after town. Even conservative AFL President Samuel Gompers said in 1924, "The Courts have abolished the Constitution as far as the rights and interests of the working people are concerned."[44] Roger Baldwin, the founder of the ACLU, wrote in 1929 that 90 percent of the protests against infringements of civil liberties involved the assertion of rights by labor in contests with employers or civil authorities.[45] These challenges sometimes led to relatively polite arrests of people such as Baldwin, Norman Thomas, and members of the throng who were denied access to all the nearby meeting halls (and even to the Boston Common, when they wished to protest the execution of Sacco and Vanzetti). But the use of sweeping injunctions and jailings for contempt, syndicalism, or breach of peace, justified by a variety of guilt by association theories, dominated the legal domain in the 1920s and well into the 1930s.

In their zeal to create a venerable pedigree for constitutional protection of freedom of expression and freedom of association, even the most distinguished commentators have ignored or glossed over *Burns*.[46] To see *Burns* for what it was forces us to admit not only that there were no significant First Amendment victories in the Supreme Court until the 1930s, but also that Holmes abandoned Brandeis and left him to dissent alone in *Burns*. The accepted story of a valiant, consistent First Amendment collaboration by these two great justices, beginning with their dissent in *Abrams,* must be reexamined. Finally, as other state and federal decisions make abundantly clear, judges at the end of the 1920s and in the early 1930s had little difficulty in upholding long prison sentences premised entirely on membership in organizations ranging from the Ku Klux Klan to the Communist Party.[47]

Though the Supreme Court had begun to make First Amendment protections applicable to the actions of the states in the 1920s, the Court still found it very easy, for example, to uphold New York's conviction of a Ku Klux Klan officer solely on the basis of his group's failure to disclose its membership list. *New York ex rel. Bryant v. Zimmerman*[48] is a virtually unknown decision that has never been repudiated. The renascent Klan was a menace in the 1920s. Yet the New York Court of Appeals, including Justice Benjamin Cardozo, and the United States Supreme Court, including Holmes and Brandeis, expressed no constitutional qualms about legitimizing a state statute aimed overtly at an unpopular group. These judges thus demonstrated that guilt by association flourished long after the passions of World War I and the Palmer Raids had subsided.[49]

No less a First Amendment giant than Harry Kalven, Jr., found it impossible either to explain or reject the *Bryant* decision. While celebrating the recognition of freedom of association and freedom from disclosure in the NAACP decisions in the late 1950s, Kalven claimed tautologically that it was constitutionally acceptable in *Bryant* to force the Klan chapter to disclose membership because the Klan would thereby be directly deterred from illegal activity. Forced disclosure of NAACP membership lists was categorically different, Kalven proclaimed, despite a flood of allegations by southern state officials that the NAACP either had or was about to engage in activities made illegal by state law.

The crux of the problem, however, is how to explain why direct government intrusions upon freedom of association are permissible when aimed at organizations we do not like, but are clearly unconstitutional when we sympathize with the goals of the organizations under investigation. On First Amendment grounds, the rationale of direct deterrence of illegal activity is hardly a satisfactory way to distinguish the 1928 Klan case from the later NAACP cases or, for that matter, from the troublesome batch of decisions in which the Court upheld, as late as 1961, the requirement that the Communist Party reveal its membership.[50]

The Countertrend

The very first Supreme Court decisions to protect freedom of expression and to condemn guilt by association did not come until the early 1930s, after Charles Evans Hughes had replaced William Howard Taft as Chief Justice. Only after President Franklin D. Roosevelt lost his court-packing battle but won his war against the Court in 1937 did the justices begin to protect peaceful labor picketing, leafletting, use of

public parks, and association. In 1937, for example, the Court voted—
but only by a margin of five to four—to upset Georgia's conviction and
sentencing of a black man to 18–20 years at hard labor for his attempt
to incite insurrection by urging blacks to register and vote for the Communist Party.[51] Other forms of guilt by association, aspects of membership in "involuntary groups" formed by race, ethnicity, or national
origins, soon dominated the news and prevailed in the courts.

Wartime Advances for Civil Liberties and the Internment of the Japanese

It is hardly controversial that wartime is a bad time for civil liberties
and dissent. Yet there were significant advances in constitutional protection from guilt by association during World War II. The high point,
but also the point that marks the start of a precipitous slide, occurred
near the end of the war, when the Court decided *Thomas v. Collins*[52]
in January 1945 (discussed in the next chapter). The anti-Communist
crusade that triggered John Lord O'Brian's 1948 jeremiad surely constitutes the main explanation for the virtual disappearance of *Thomas
v. Collins* overnight. In those years other important precedents bolster,
yet also make more problematic, O'Brian's position that guilt by association was an alien and even sinister concept in the United States.

In 1948 O'Brian had completed recent service as head of the War
Production Board. Being an enlightened lawyer, he could now find
doctrinal support in new Supreme Court decisions for his position that
guilt must be personal. Moreover, the Nuremberg trials cast a long
shadow. These show trials largely operated on the view that even unthinkable guilt had to be personal. Yet they also indicated that standard American conspiracy law was more than puzzling. It was
troublesome in its looseness, even to the prosecutors in friendly
nations. More directly, the Supreme Court during the war had twice
rejected federal government efforts to punish dissent through a typical
combination of guilt by association and federal discretionary authority over citizenship.

In *Schneiderman v. United States*,[53] Justice Murphy's opinion for
the Court noted the deficiencies of proof by imputation in the government's effort to strip a Communist Party leader of the United States
citizenship he had obtained twelve years earlier. Even fifty years ago, it
was clear that "there is, unfortunately, no absolutely accurate test of
what a political party's principles are."[54] As Murphy could not find

precedents to quote, he had to resort to external texts, such as Charles Evans Hughes's famous (unsuccessful) effort to convince the New York Assembly to seat five Socialists who were twice elected but never seated because of their political affiliations.[55]

In another instance, after the federal government repeatedly tried to deport union leader Harry Bridges in retribution for his leftist associations, the Court narrowly voted to halt what Justice Murphy, concurring, called "a concentrated and relentless crusade" by "powerful economic and social forces . . . combined with public and private agencies"[56] to punish someone simply for exercising his freedom. This government attempt to deport Bridges because of his associations, Murphy wrote, "will stand forever as a monument to man's intolerance to man."[57] Less dramatically, Justice Douglas's majority opinion emphasized the need for careful procedures and for sensitivity regarding guilt by "affiliation" prior to any decision to deport the powerful leader of the longshoremen's union. A period of nationwide enthusiasm for a united front with the Soviet Union against the Axis powers, and the threat that Bridges might use his considerable clout to disrupt industry and commerce, helps account for the Court's newfound sensitivity about guilt by association.

The due process niceties the Court observed in *Schneiderman* and *Bridges,* when the justices stressed the need to avoid serious consequences to an individual because of his or her associations in wartime, were conspicuously absent from another category of cases: that of the thousands of Japanese-Americans interned during the war without any legal process whatsoever. How could the Court repeatedly allow that outrage? Sadly, the core of the answer is racism. It now seems irrefutable that by the time of the *Korematsu* decision in 1944 that upheld the internment of Japanese-Americans—and in fact probably considerably earlier—many Americans and the justices specifically knew that there never had been evidence to support the military's initial allegations that the Japanese-Americans on the West Coast posed a massive security threat. *Korematsu*—and much of our history concerning race— illustrates a virulent form of guilt by association that persists and hardly requires the added spice of wartime hysteria.

A 1945 propaganda film, "The House I Live In,"[58] starring young matinee idol Frank Sinatra, displays the common propensity to make collective judgments. In the movie Sinatra comes across a gang of boys chasing a Jewish boy. Frankie says, "You must be a bunch of those Nazi werewolves I've been reading about." "Mister, are you screwy?"

one of the urchins asks. "Not me, I'm an American." Frankie then tells the boys about a mission by a bombing crew made up of Presbyterians and Jews that sank a "Jap battleship." Finally, he advises the boys: "Use your good American heads," because "all races and religions, that's America to me."

In addition to being funny, at least in retrospect, this underestand-able wartime propaganda suggests how readily we find solidarity with some groups because still other groups, variously defined, are desig-nated as outcasts or even the enemy. The perennial hyphenated-American issue is often characterized by efforts to stand firmly on both sides. Adding to the complexity, *Schneiderman* and *Bridges* emphasize autonomous individualism, while *Korematsu*—and *Brown v. Board of Education,* for that matter—are anchored in the power of associa-tions by guilt. In a sense, *Schneiderman* and *Bridges* struggle to define both the limits and the appropriate claims of group solidarity. They echo but are different from the appeal of nonmeltable racial, ethnic, and perhaps religious consciousness. Those groups about which we feel most guilty if we try to reject them, those webs of relationships we cannot enter or leave readily even when we try, are the groups most important to us. Perhaps they are too important to be left to law, as we will explore in later chapters.

Conclusion

Lawyers seem to carry an unusually cumbersome but also notoriously manipulable "stock of old opinions."[59] The brief historical excursion in this chapter suggests that when American judges considered guilt by association, they did little to stop the powerful few and the intolerant many who punished groups perceived to be outside some illusory national consensus. If the assignment of guilt according to one's mates, bedfellows, fellow travelers, or other criteria is inevitable, it neverthe-less is always a matter of degree. That surely is the crux of the matter.

The discussion here is not a critique of joint and several liability, nor of conspiracy law *per se.* Rather, it is a claim that the machinery of legal sanctions must not be employed glibly or complacently to punish associations and relationships. The need to recognize a sensitive con-stitutional right of freedom of association is particularly keen when the passions of the day lead people to fear or to hope via collective pun-ishment. The group right suggested here would establish a presump-tion that could be overcome only for compelling reasons. Although the context differs, this constitutional premise might be thought of as somewhat akin to some existing statutory protections for the environment and for endangered species. The more endangered the group, the more careful constitutional scrutiny ought to be in evaluating actions that intrude upon it.

In a dissent to a decision upholding Minnesota's prosecution of a World War I objector, Brandeis wrote: "Like the course of heavenly bodies, harmony in national life is a resultant of the struggle between contending forces."[60] What our discordant century has taught us about both the heavens and national life undermines even the relatively hardheaded Brandeisian brand of optimism. But our doubts need not silence us. Increasing interdependence and shakier group identities cry out for new, more vigorous legal respect for pluralism. The struggle among contending groups must be a fairer fight, taking past group victimization and pervasive scapegoating into account. Sensitivity to the ways that concepts of guilt by association and strength through association are linked is essential as we grope for that rarest of virtues: toleration.

It is striking that toleration is usually portrayed as mealy-mouthed piety. When it is not wishful thinking, tolerance seems to follow the pattern laid down by Oliver Cromwell. When his forces besieged an Irish village, Cromwell is said to have sent this reply to the villagers' inquiry about what he would tolerate: "As to freedom of conscience, I meddle with no man's conscience; but if you mean by that, liberty to celebrate the mass, I would have you understand that in no place where the power of the parliament of England prevails shall that be permitted."[61]

We badly need a tougher form of toleration. Even a legal optimist such as Zechariah Chafee recognized that "intolerance is the most contagious of all diseases, and no party or creed is immune. . . . Intolerance can always find some crevice in the administration of the law through which to creep and accomplish its purpose."[62] Tolerance, ironically, must be bound to group struggle. It requires recognition of the guilt and fear we all encounter, rooted in uncertainties about our own identities. We strive for independence, yet any meaningful freedom is deeply dependent upon our social networks. To be real, tolerance requires recognition that we all use groups to define ourselves and others, inescapably and differently. Yet to tolerate differences often seems to condescend, to say that *they* do not present real threats to *us*. We put up with others to confirm our power to put them down. It is hardly surprising, therefore, that tolerance has had little legal bite. Tolerance is thought to be the stuff of divinity schools, perhaps of psychologists and social workers and elementary school teachers, but not a topic for hard-headed legal thought.

I argue that the gap between our history and our credo is crucial. Frequent and sometimes zealous practice of guilt by association in a nation that emphasizes individualism is important beyond its value as entertaining iconoclasm. It suggests the necessity and some of the possibilities for needed change.

To be sure, legal declarations will hardly suffice to create tolerance. Nor will tolerance of those who seem intolerant ever be absolute or even easy to weigh on balance. Yet the combination of language and legitimized violence that constitutes law reflects but also shapes social values, perhaps more in the United States than elsewhere. Because in the United States we rely heavily on law to judge others, and to create ourselves, the quest for a firmly based tolerance must involve law.

Legal theorizing about guilt by association has not advanced much since the time when Frederic Maitland denigrated theory and celebrated English law for the "sound instincts" with which it treats associations and "muddles along with semi-personality and demi-semi-personality towards convenient conclusions."[63] Inevitably, however, tolerance is keyed to group ideals, to unfulfilled promise. Philosophers are only beginning to notice that "Our lives are rich because they are complex in the layers and character of the communities we inhabit."[64]

Our glimpse at American legal history is sobering. It undermines confidence in the soundness of the instincts of American judges. It suggests, moreover, that to deny that all of us engage in guilt by association is to appear naive and utopian. Yet to recognize this painful actuality is not to acquiesce in the worst abuses of this practice.

To do something about galloping guilt by association both in and out of law probably requires romantic realism: a leap of hope and charity, even when faith seems more often part of the problem than of the solution. Like going east—or seeking justice—the goal is unattainable. Yet to undertake the journey, and perhaps to reduce the rampant guilt by association that perpetrates injustice through group attribution, is surely a vital constitutional challenge.

4   A Historical Glimpse at Ghostly Personalities

> This little republic . . . in like manner as the River Thames is
> still the same river, though the parts which compose it are
> changing every instant.
>
> *William Blackstone[1]*

> A fiction that we needs must feign is somehow or another
> very like the simple truth.
>
> *Frederic Maitland[2]*

It may be appealing but it would be wrong (as Richard M. Nixon liked
to say) to join today's popular, mystical leap backwards to a golden
age of community. Attention to legal history casts doubt on the notion
that there ever was a time when contented folks knew their places in
some great chain of being. People never did tolerate and appreciate one
another magnanimously in a land where creative craftsworkers practiced civic virtue through robust but respectful dialogic exchange. Our
ancestors, no matter where they lived, never had the time, inclination,
or mutual respect necessary for the many evenings that participatory
democracy seems to require.

The role of groups in both bringing about and resisting the horrors
of recent German and Soviet history, for example, makes American
ambivalence about groups seem something of a curiosity, a singular
parochial tension almost peripheral to the main action of this century's
history. Yet that could be said of most of our constitutional law disputes and all of our constitutional theorizing. Nevertheless, voluntary
associations have played a distinct role in the United States, almost
surely more vital to political and social stability than analogous groups
in other countries. Just as with other matters that end up in litigation
in our culture, legal disputes about group rights are revealing and significant. If it is a common mistake to overemphasize the finality of legal

resolutions, it is also an error to ignore what our lawmakers do and say.

We seem to have a constitutive memory of the functioning of associations. They form elemental aspects of American law both on the books and in action. This chapter seeks to recover some aspects of that memory through intellectual history and case analysis. Then we can begin to reconstruct.

Modernity and the Independent Right of Freedom of Association

It is surely healthy to retain fears about decisions made by unaccountable power elites that gather at exclusive watering-holes. The grip of cults over individuals, the specter of mob violence, and the baleful influence of economic power expressed in lobbying and election spending are all real contemporary dangers. It is impossible and unwise to put all such fears to rest. Nor will my argument for a limited independent right of freedom of association blaze a clear path to an other-directed, altruistic utopia.[3] But we may find glimmerings of clarity in a century-old debate about what Morris R. Cohen called "communal ghosts,"[4] as well as in intriguing, albeit dusty and overlooked, old constitutional decisions.

When we insist on individual rights without inquiring seriously about the internal or external dimensions of the paradigmatic individuals we construct, we ignore much of twentieth century science, psychology, sociology, and anthropology, to say nothing of literary criticism, religion, and history. We have allowed legal fictions about class representation, corporate entities, and formal citizenship to go virtually unchallenged.[5] If we think about the problem of groups carefully, however, we find a number of pragmatic legal examples in which group identity is legally protected even when individuals engaged in the same activity would not be: groups that parade, report the news, engage in certain labor activities and boycotts, find protection from deportation because of persecution in their home countries, and so forth. Perhaps it is a basis for hope rather than despair that we can find no overarching principle to categorize families, people stuck in elevators together, collaborative reproduction units, Native American tribes, religious cults, unions, multinational corporations, and even gaggles of legal academics. No matter what the formal legal form, we have important functioning associations to consider. If Holmes was right that "there is nothing like a paradox to take the scum off the mind,"[6] it is appropriate to pursue the paradoxes of some communal ghosts.

A Brief Historical Excursion

Maitland and the Corporate Personality Debate

In 1900 Frederic W. Maitland published his own translation of German scholar Otto Gierke's *Political Theories of the Middle Age*. In his long introductory essay, this greatest of English legal historians traced the notion of corporate personality in England, Germany, Italy and France back to Roman law roots. In this intriguing and well-told tale, Maitland concentrated on "a middle region where a sociology emulous of the physical sciences discourses of organs and organisms and social tissue, and cannot sever by sharp lines the natural history of the state-group from the natural history of other groups." With characteristic dry wit, Maitland maintained that England was quick to accept a "unicellular state"; this led to a saving of blood and treasure but caused a poverty of ideas regarding "Ireland or of some communities, commonwealths, corporations in America which seemed to have wills—and hardly fictitious wills—of their own."[7]

Maitland's inquiry into the history of corporate forms, and the legal classification of groups as fictional persons, remained his central scholarly concern until his death in 1906.[8] Indeed, Maitland warned that once a person begins to concentrate on the history of groups, it could make other sorts of history seem "superficial" and could lead to the view that "much the most interesting person that you ever knew was *persona ficta*."[9]

Why dust off Maitland's work on groups now—beyond a possible attempt to illustrate the accuracy of his benign curse? Maitland hardly resolved the dilemma of how groups fit into law, or vice versa. He did not even attempt a coherent theory of groups and called "smudgy" the very idea of any group acting collectively. He proclaimed "collectively" to be "the smudgiest word in the English language."[10] Yet it was Maitland who led the brigade of the leading English legal scholars to urge the ubiquitous reality and vital importance of group entities. Moreover, the absence of a sense of history remains one of the most noteworthy and most troubling aspects of recent treatment of groups in legal scholarship as well as at the highest levels of United States and English judge-made law.

Maitland's historical research and his translation and introduction of Otto Von Gierke to an English audience were crucial elements in a great debate about group identity in law. The controversy raged throughout the half-century from the 1870s to the 1930s. English and American legal luminaries, in reaction both to German scholarship's "solemn and high-piled clouds, great and gigantic"[11] and to raging contemporary conflicts about possible legal control of labor unions, businesses, and trusts, argued vehemently—not to say incessantly—about whether there was or should be some corporate or legal personality attributable to unincorporated associations. If such personalities existed, did all such legal entities exist only through concession of authority by a sovereign state? Could some groups exist with rights and duties, and even with attributes of sovereignty, in and of themselves?

Maitland maintained that even to begin to consider group forms in English legal history, we "shall have to think away distinctions which seem to us as clear as the sunshine; we must think ourselves back into twilight."[12] With his usual tenacity and stylistic verve, Maitland then went on to illustrate how unincorporated collective institutions such as trusts had performed crucial roles in English legal development over many centuries. He celebrated the groups known in law as trusts for being experimental and argued that they had characteristically performed significant, innovative work screened off from public regulation or private contractual manipulation.

To ignore the reality of groups as right-and-duty bearing units, Maitland claimed, is to "denature" the facts and to "make a mess and call it law." He had become convinced that "group-personality is no purely legal phenomenon."[13] Such legal devices as the trust provided a hard exterior shell; they protected unincorporated organizations ranging from the Inns of Court, Lloyd's of London, and innumerable clubs to various religious bodies and sensitive cultural and intellectual experiments that take place "in a wicked world" and constantly face "attacks of inadequate and individualistic theories."[14]

Attention to the role of such groups over time allowed Maitland to illustrate that England historically "knew no formal severance of Public from Private Law."[15] Maitland stressed that groups existed and continue to function along a continuum, and he was struck by the intriguing possibility that "morally there is most personality where legally there is none."[16]

Why controversy over group legal identity burgeoned when it did, and why it stopped around the time of the Great Depression and the rise of fascism, are questions that merit further inquiry, but we do not need to answer them here.[17] Instead of extended historiography—a history of the legal history of groups—it is simply important to note both the slipperiness and the still largely uncharted historical significance of the "voluntary groups" that so concerned Maitland and his fellow disputants.[18]

At the end of the last century, Maitland could still assert that "the line of advance is no longer from status to contract but through contract to something that contract cannot explain, and for which our best, if an inadequate, name is the personality of the organized group."[19] In this observation Maitland's identification of "something that contract cannot explain" provides a vital starting place to discuss the role of group rights. It applies not only to the voluntary associations which so concerned Maitland and the virtual hall-of-fame of legal scholars who joined him in the corporate personality debate, but also to the "involuntary groups" we will discuss in a later chapter. We should also note that Maitland's amendment of Sir Henry Maine's famous epigram about movement from status to contract underscores the pervasiveness of teleological faith. Even a skeptical realist such as Maitland still thought in terms of a clear "line of advance" in law. The train of awful events in the years since Maitland's death renders his optimism at the dawn of the twentieth century painfully quaint. Finally, Maitland's quotation is illuminating for the evidence it provides that even an accomplished wordsmith such as Maitland was at a loss for words for what elsewhere, aware of the awkwardness of the locution, he described as "right-and-duty bearing units." We are still at a loss.

Ghostly Footnotes in the Sands of Time

At the turn of the century, judges emphatically recognized the power of associations when they found unions liable for strikes and other activities in famous English and American decisions.[20] This antilabor attitude helps explain why English pluralists such as Harold Laski picked up Maitland's challenge as vigorously as they did. Laski first achieved fame in the United States when he asserted, in the *Harvard Law Review* in 1916, that corporate forms have their own personalities.[21] And, he noted, "Whether we will or no, we are bundles of hyphens."[22] This claim was courageous in view of the virulent nativism that accompanied American intervention in World War I and continued long afterward.[23] Yet in a eulogy for the legal philosopher Morris Raphael Cohen in 1948, Laski credited Cohen for demonstrating the error of Laski's youthful ways, when he had taken "a side which was bound to have reactionary results."[24] Cohen, according to Laski, helped extricate him from a stream muddied by the "torrent of mysticism" of German neo-Hegelians.[25] Without getting our feet wet in such dangerous waters, or delving into why Laski was so insistent on distancing himself from German thinkers in 1948, we might find it worthwhile to consider briefly what curmudgeonly Cohen had to say in his once famous "Communal Ghosts" article in 1919.

Cohen began by noting, "A certain awe for the word *social* is one of the outstanding phenomena of current intellectual life."[26] (The very way he put it is evidence of the cyclical quality of our intellectual fads.[27]) Cohen defined the issue of what is "social" as "the extent to which the principle of unity should be hypostatized or reified"—he expressed a wish to say *"thingified."*[28]

What followed was a trenchant discussion of different kinds of unity—synthetic, chemical, and biologic. Cohen conceded that each actually characterizes diverse human associations in diverse ways. Indeed, the most striking aspect of Cohen's article today is his explicit acknowledgment that no one could deny that "every group has distinctive group marks" and that "there is something uniting the different individuals so that they act differently from what they would if they were not so interdependent."[29] But this concession actually gives away the whole game. Despite himself, Cohen acknowledges the power of ghosts. Old historical battles over corporate personality turn out to produce near-consensus about the reality of groupness.

If a hard-boiled rationalist such as Morris Raphael Cohen—a man whose greatest contribution, according to Laski, was to "push out of the road a good deal of useless, and, not seldom, pretentious lumber that stood in the way of clear understanding"[30]—recognized the relational, kinetic quality of "group marks" and group power to influence individual conduct, the question whether personality is the appropriate terminology for the group ghost seems almost irrelevant. But the debate into which Laski and Cohen and numerous others plunged so vigorously before World War II does illuminate quite starkly the extent to which lawyers and judges still insist on the gnostic power of naming.

As a matter of constitutional law today, with a few narrow exceptions such as heterosexual couples, explicitly political associations, and the NAACP, conglomerations of individuals are treated as if they simply and accurately reflected merely the sums of their individual parts. We no longer even admit that there are "distinctive group marks." What happened?

The Judicial Highwater Mark

The first clearcut Supreme Court victory for a freedom of association claim did not come until 1937. In *DeJonge v. Oregon*,[31] Chief Justice Hughes's opinion for the Court reversed the conviction of an individual for assisting in a meeting sponsored by an organization advocating illegal means to bring about political change. Hughes wrote, "The right of peaceable assembly is a right cognate to those of free speech and free press and is equally fundamental."[32] Hughes made clear that these strong words were no mere slip of the judicial pen when he added that these rights cannot be denied "without violating those fundamental principles of liberty and justice which lie at the base of all civil and political institutions."[33] Still, in retrospect *DeJonge* looks like a relatively easy case; Hughes's language seems tied to the political nature of the association, which might well be protected independently of any freedom of assembly claim.

The crucial point was made in 1945 in *Thomas v. Collins*,[34] a decision that merits close attention though it generally receives little notice today. In contrast to the formal binary categories in recent decisions dealing with freedom of association, Justice Rutledge's majority opinion in *Thomas* was rich in dynamic, relational language. Conversely, in *Roberts v. United States Jaycees*,[35] for example, Justice Brennan found that the Jaycees' exclusionary policy fell right between the "i's": he limited the protected categories to *intimate* or *instrumentally* expressive association.

By contrast, listen to the tone as the *Thomas* opinion protected a union leader from the sentence for contempt imposed when he ignored an *ex parte* judicial order to follow Texas's licensing procedure for paid union solicitors.[36] The Court discerned both an unconstitutional prior restraint on Thomas's speech and an unconstitutional limitation on the right of Thomas and his audience to hold a public meeting.

Rutledge wrote: "It was not by accident or coincidence that the rights to freedom in speech and press were coupled in a single guaranty with the rights of the people peaceably to assemble and to petition for redress of grievances. All these, though not identical, are inseparable.

They are cognate rights . . . and therefore are united in the First Article's assurance."[37] The *Thomas* decision, which recognized "a national right, federally guaranteed . . . (to) some modicum of freedom of thought, speech and assembly which all citizens of the Republic may exercise throughout its length and breadth,"[38] is important for several reasons.

First, Rutledge swept past previous opinions protecting political and religious groups when he noted that the First Amendment "gives freedom of mind the same security as freedom of conscience."[39] The Court in *Thomas* also insisted that the rights of petition and assembly are not limited to religious or political matters, just as the rights of free speech and free press "are not confined to any field of human interest."[40] Moreover, in according "the great, the indispensable democratic freedoms secured by the First Amendment" a "preferred place" in the constitutional scheme,[41] Rutledge directly attacked the old states' rights limitation on the scope of such rights. Finally, Rutledge also emphasized that the rights of speaker and audience, association and members, are "necessarily correlative,"[42] and broad enough to include private as well as public gatherings, economic as well as political subjects, and passionate opinions as well as factual statements.

The vital importance of the *Thomas* decision, however, is in its unified approach to First Amendment rights. Because rights of speech and assembly are "cognate," and rights of speaker and audience are "correlative," *Thomas* adopted a structural approach to First Amendment rights nearly forgotten today. *Thomas* began to suggest the crucial constitutive nature of freedom within the group context. The *Thomas* three c's—cognate First Amendment rights; contextual sensitivity, and, most strikingly today, correlative rights of the union and its members and officials—starkly contrast with the instrumental focus of more recent freedom of association decisions.

An Interlude for Historical Speculation

The virtual disappearance of the idea that groups in themselves at times have their own claims to rights—the opinion by Rutledge in *Thomas v. Collins*—is striking. In the post-World War II period, the Court quickly retreated from this position. The justices began to regard unions and other groups merely as synecdoches for individuals. I will offer a few guesses as to why this happened so abruptly.

First, there was important disaffection, even from within the New Deal, with the corporatist first phase of the federal government's "alphabet agency" approach. Odious comparisons to Mussolini's fascist brand of syndicalism helped to underscore a pervasive American distaste for government recognition of groups. Judicial opinions and lawyers' arguments are full of references to the contrast between good old American individualism and Old World group terms.[43]

Moreover, the internecine warfare within unions over the role of Communists during the height of the Cold War was messy and bitter enough to alert courts to the problematic nature of trying to hang rights on groups themselves. It was like a reprise of the battle more than a century earlier between Congregationalists and Unitarians over which group could rightfully claim church property.[44] Courts believed it the better part of valor to hide as much as possible beneath pious judicial incantations about neutrality, couched in terms that are variations on a theme of benevolent neutrality or benign neglect.[45]

Popular perception of the danger posed by Communist cells and cadres largely explains why lawyers and judges sought refuge in legal process values and found solace in washing the autonomous individual of any traces of his (I use the masculine pronoun advisedly) group marks. Lawyers and even bureaucrats who were not lawyers found it delightfully easy to squeeze the discontented in the passive vices of rules of individual standing, formal representation rules, the need to prove bad motive in one's own particular case claiming discrimination, and so forth. Focusing on the individual also neatly taps into popular nostalgia. It evokes myths about rugged independent cowboys and self-helping entrepreneurs. If groups can be associated with radical threats, individuals can be set up as their dupes or opponents. This technique allows the lawyer to exercise and find support for his role as professional conservative, without actually concerning himself with history.

Much of the legal opposition to *Brown v. Board of Education* sought respectability by claiming that the right of freedom of association necessarily entailed the freedom not to associate with blacks. It followed, according to Herbert Wechsler and numerous lesser legal lights,[46] that though the effect might be undesirable, it was constitutionally inappropriate to invade a decision by a group that defined itself by excluding others on the basis of race. Though many believe that this argument retains some force to this day,[47] considerable guilt by association with segregationists helps to explain the diminished capacity of the independent right of freedom of association as it was developed in *Thomas v. Collins*.

That's all very nice, one may say, but so what? What difference

would an independent right of freedom of association make in what
we jokingly call the real world of litigation? The next chapter suggests
a few of the many categories of cases in which, if the independent right
I propose were taken seriously, the outcomes should be different. (I am
not such a believer in the autonomy of the law, nor such a disbeliever
in the wily wordsmithery of good lawyers and judges, to claim boldly
that it actually will make a difference). But, as Morris Raphael Cohen
put it in his own mystical moment, "words are most potent influences
in determining thought as well as action."[48]

5   Groping for Group Rights: Beyond Politics and Expression

> Let us try to see whether we can frame a theory which will explain the facts without assuming either a fiction or a real group personality.
>
> *W. M. Geldart[1]*

> [T]he conduct of the United States Americans toward the natives was inspired by the most chaste affection for legal formalities. . . . It is impossible to destroy men with more respect to the laws of humanity.
>
> *Alexis de Tocqueville[2]*

The group right I seek to formulate here is not limited to a choice between intimate associations and associations instrumental in the cause of expression. It does not directly implicate either a protected expressive right or an unprotected commercial claim. Like all other rights, this group right will not always be trump. In an important sense, all legal rights are instrumental. To put this somewhat skeptical point another way, in law there are no ends, just means.

Tocqueville early on recognized the great danger of a novel form of "administrative despotism" in the United States.[3] He warned of an "orderly, gentle, peaceful slavery which could be combined, more easily than is generally supposed, with some of the external forms of freedom and . . . [has] a possibility of its getting itself established even under the shadow of the sovereignty of the people."[4] To counter the insidious advance of this "gentle, peaceful slavery," it is essential to amplify the collective free voices of individuals. To build this instrumental case, however, we have to confront a deeply seated popular and legal ambivalence. That ambivalence helps explain why constitutional law generally has overlooked the crucial role of groups.

*   *   *

We all seem to share a paradoxical mass-craving to be loved uniquely: "Not universal love / But to be loved alone."[5] If we cannot find love, each of us at least craves respect. Yet respect, and a range of other social goods that help define us, generally seem meaningful only in group contexts. Declare independence as vigorously as any of us may, we cannot escape interdependence. The individuation of each woman and each man—perhaps an error bred in the bone, perhaps not—originates in others and cannot seem to elude their grasp. It is our numerous associations, our families, politics, ethnicities, religions, and so forth, that offer critical benchmarks for how others evaluate us—and thereby how we evaluate ourselves.

Anglo-American legal thought seems basically to deny and ignore this ambivalence. American law in particular is rooted in the paradigm of relationships between the individual and the state. There is hardly room for the claims of the groups that surround us and serve both as mediators and catalysts. These associations form roots and offer possible routes for escape from the state/individual nexus. Humans develop a sense of self in relation to others, to parents and the complicated social world, in part through the medium of social language. Yet our legal theory sees groups only as sums always divisible into their parts. Constitutional law appears unaware that people live their lives in multiple overlapping groups. Though these associations can sometimes function like little governments, suggesting a kind of private sovereignty, mainstream American constitutionalism has no room for substantive pluralism.

An independent freedom of association right would make a difference in some specific cases and facilitate clarity of thought more generally. The contexts discussed here present situations in which it is more difficult to sustain freedom of association claims than the ones we have seen so far, which focused on relatively clear links between associations and political expression. We turn now to types of associations other than family units, political organizations, civil rights reform, or religious groups, all of which already receive considerable constitutional protection from other categories of rights. Decisions protecting them tend to be about privacy or freedom of speech, and not about the independent constitutional protection and appreciation of a tradition of group identities. For example, I contend that the recent Court decisions involving labor unions and American Indian tribes have been plain wrong; giving substance to a right to freedom of association would have made a difference. Such a right would serve not only the existing groups but it would also provide some constitutional protection to others still in the process of struggling into existence.

It must be emphasized, however, that not every conglomeration of individuals is automatically eligible to invoke the independent constitutional right to the freedom of association I advocate. Rather than adding to the already daunting task of offering a general taxonomy of groups,[6] it is more useful to do some detective work about selected associational claims in specific contexts. For instance, Native American tribal rights constitute an area in which legal protection is distinct from the protection afforded the individuals who constitute the groups.

Native Americans' Claims and the Burden of Historical Irony

For anyone with a sense of ironic—if not tragic—history, the nation's repeated rejection of the legal and moral claims of Native Americans is a familiar story which is generally ignored in mainstream legal discourse.[7] The clash of cultures and the failure of the mainstream Anglo-American thinkers and actors to understand radically different community-based ideas of property, religion, and the meaning of life itself make an oft-told tale.[8] Still, it is astonishing to find that a continuation of the divide-and-conquer tactics used against American Indians for centuries is still vigorously present in the pages of contemporary United States Supreme Court decisions.

Individual versus Tribal Property

There were no dissents, for example, in *Hodel v. Irving,*[9] a virtually unnoticed but starkly illuminating property case. The *Hodel* Court conceded that Congress had made an effort in good faith to respond to a serious, intractable problem: the "extreme fractionation of Indian lands."[10] The federal statute had provided that minutely divided land holdings not disposed of in the lifetime of their owners would return to the tribe. Moreover, the Court agreed that "consolidation of lands in the Tribe benefits Tribe members."[11] But that benefit would have to give way to the vital right of individual holders of property "to pass the property at death."[12]

Justice O'Connor's opinion for the Court drew a sharp contrast between individual claims and tribal claims. Once this binary choice was established, there was no contest. All individuals must be treated alike. The tribal context and the admitted tribal benefit were obliterated by the abstract idea of equality, particularly when that concept was reinforced by the might of individual property rights. The right of the individual had to prevail, almost by definition, over all competing considerations, whether utilitarian or rights-based.

With *Hodel,* the Court could be said to observe a kind of tragic centennial of the Dawes Severalty Act of 1887. The Dawes Act had formalized a federal policy to break up the tribes, on the assumption that tribal units deprived Native Americans of that "selfishness which is at the bottom of civilization."[13] Even after the bitter results (to the Indians) of the ensuing century, the Court held that the Constitution could not permit Congress to try to recognize and enhance the relational aspects of tribal property holding.

Development and Sacred Tribal Lands

As if to demonstrate that insensitivity to tribal interests in *Hodel v. Irving* was no fluke, the Court since has determined in *Lyng v. Northwest Indian Cemetery Association* that, although the road-building and logging operations the government planned "could have devastating effects on traditional Indian religious practices,"[14] this conflict presented no constitutional barrier to development. The Court deferred to the Department of Agriculture, which had decided to ignore the recommendation of a study the Department itself had commissioned. The Court thereby cleared the legal path to begin building six miles of paved highway across a national forest and directly through the ground most sacred to several Northwest Indian tribes.[15]

Justice O'Connor again explained for the majority. She argued that "the crucial word in the constitutional text is 'prohibit.'"[16] Because the Constitution did not say anything explicitly that "prohibited" building a road, no constitutional right was impinged. Moreover, O'Connor insisted, "However much we might wish that it were otherwise, government simply could not operate if it were required to satisfy every citizen's religious needs and desires."[17] This lowest common denominator approach—all citizens have only the rights of every citizen—ignores history and destroys special communal claims that are particularly compelling in the case of Native Americans. Justice O'Connor even added something she apparently took to be the private-property clincher: "Whatever rights the Indians may have to the use of the area . . . do not divest the Government of its right to use what is, after all, *its* land."[18]

Individual Rights and Tribal Zoning Authority

In *Brendale v. Confederated Tribes and Bands of the Yakima Indian Nation*[19] the justices split sharply, but a majority protected the property rights of individual nonmembers of the tribe at considerable cost to tribal sovereignty and to historical accuracy. The crucial factor in Justice Stevens's decisive opinion was his belief that it was unthinkable for individual property holders in fee to be subjected to zoning by a self-governing body—namely, the Yakima Tribe—which they might not be able to join. Analogous situations in which such zoning is permitted, such as huge blocks of real estate owned by foreign nationals, for example, or unaccountable corporate power in a variety of contemporary contexts, did not trouble Stevens and O'Connor.

In this *Brendale* morass, Stevens's opinion underscored the continuing hold of Lockean notions of individual property on American constitutional law. It also echoed the Court's growing fears about minority political power.[20] Had the justices consulted history, they would have had to deal with the uncontested fact of blatant treaty violation by the federal government, as well as Congress's explicit repudiation of the statute upon which the majority relied, the 1887 Dawes Act, in the Indian Reorganization Act of 1934. But judicial myopia about history when Native American rights conflict with the claims of individual fee holders is itself an old story.[21]

What Sort of Sovereign Is a Tribe?

Blatchford v. Native Village of Noatak[22] proves that a story need not be old to be tragic, comic, or both. In this dry technical decision about the sovereign immunity of the states, Native American tribal identity became entangled in one of the most abstract and convoluted categories in American constitutional law. In holding that a Native Village could not sue Alaska, Justice Scalia's majority opinion began by conceding that "Indian tribes are sovereigns."[23] Despite his penchant for claiming strict textualism, Scalia had to admit that the Court could not rely on the text of the Eleventh Amendment, but rather on "the presupposition of our constitutional structure which [the Eleventh Amendment] confirms."[24] Yet our concern is not with a mystical form of Eleventh Amendment doctrine as such. What is significant here about *Noatak* is the Court's glib solution to a basic historical riddle: what is the legal status of Native American tribes?

From the decisions of Chief Justice John Marshall through the Court's most recent precedents, the sovereignty of tribes in North America has been anomalous, inconsistent, and remarkably malleable. Pronouncements on the subject by all the branches of the federal government, and by both federal and state courts, have fluctuated with changing demands made by the majority culture.[25] Today, however, it is allegedly again clear that surviving Native American tribes did retain their sovereignty; tribal self-determination is again repeatedly said to be an overriding value.[26]

The puzzle presented in *Noatak,* therefore, was whether tribal sovereignty is akin to that of foreign states or analogous to that of the fifty states within the federal union. It was crucial to establish this categorization: while Eleventh Amendment doctrine shields states within the United States from suit by foreign sovereigns, any state may sue another state without confronting an Eleventh Amendment barrier.[27] The suit came to the Court from as far away as possible—the Native Village of Noatak lies on the Bering Strait—and the justices got nowhere near either the practical realities of the case or the relevant history. Centuries of development and the Court's own grandaddy decisions about tribal status were simply set aside.

The suit was filed after Alaska reneged on a 1980 statute that granted every Native Village $25,000. On the advice of Alaska's attorney general, however, the legislature later expanded the recipient class to all villages, thereby diluting each Native Village share so that Noatak never received its full initial allotment.[28] The case presented an array of complicated jurisdictional issues, but the Court majority answered them with a simple, sweeping, surprising assertion: Native American tribes are like foreign nations. Such tribes are Native and American; they are under the plenary power and alleged protection of the federal government; and their members are all citizens of the United States, but the tribe as a tribe is more like Monaco than Montana.

The principal appeal of this formulation, of course, was that it immunized states against tribal claims. The Court's holding about tribal identity was anything but the product of enlightened revisionist history. What Scalia offered was a pseudo-formalist choice, purportedly premised on the original intent of the constitutional framers: "Just as in *Monaco* with regard to foreign sovereigns, so also here with regard to Indian tribes, there is no compelling evidence that the Founders thought such a surrender [of immunity] inherent in the constitutional compact." This is remarkably abstract metaphysics. There is no "compelling evidence" about an issue no one imagined at the time.

As Judge John Noonan held in the lower court's opinion in the case, Indian tribes clearly were treated as separate and sovereign long before 1789. They could be found in every original state and relations with them were sensitive and dangerous. But even when a political crisis arose over Georgia's defiance of the Court in the context of the Cherokee Removal during Andrew Jackson's presidency, Chief Justice John Marshall explicitly rejected the idea that tribes were foreign states.[29] It is therefore deeply ironic that the Court in *Noatak* simply waded into the swamp of legal developments over several centuries, in which Indian tribes were deeply, tragically, *sui generis,* and tried to float clear on the flimsy assumption that the relevant inquiry is simply the relative role of the states, foreign nations, and tribes at the time of the Constitutional Convention. According to Scalia, it is plausible to imagine that the states surrendered sovereign immunity on a theory of mutuality in 1789, but "[t]here is no such mutuality with either foreign sovereigns or Indian tribes."[30] Ergo, according to the Court's syllogism, Indian tribes are like foreign nations.

At first glance, the holding of tribal sovereignty analogous to that of foreign nations may seem a great victory for tribal identity. If it were followed in other contexts, it would have important, almost surely unanticipated implications in terms of international law and international human rights guarantees, for example. The analogy to foreign nations also serves to underscore the basic contradictions in the legal status of Native Americans who, for example, within the logic of *Noatak* have had a unique form of dual citizenship thrust upon them. Despite the problems it raises, the Court's approach in *Noatak* is actually but one in a set of extremely statist decisions that have been handed down recently in cases of rights claimed by Native Americans, either as individuals or as members of groups.[31] Hence the Court's belated rediscovery of tribal sovereignty, deemed to be akin to foreign sovereignty in *Noatak,* may lead to further curtailment of the legal claims of Native Americans, whose status is now doubly alienated.[32]

These legal inconsistencies result in constant losses for Native Americans. For example, it is surely a bitter irony that Congress—whose longstanding plenary power over Indian affairs has been the instrument of numerous unilateral treaty violations, uncompensated land seizures, and countless other depredations over the years—should suddenly lack power when it seeks to protect tribal interests in *Hodel.* On the other hand, tribes are said today to be more like foreign nations than they have been deemed to be at any time since the Cherokee cases of the 1830s.[33] Simultaneously, however, the current Court is chipping away at longstanding tribal authority and tribal immunities. Even when it recognizes tribal authority, the Court has reemphasized Congress's plenary power over tribes.[34]

To be sure, it is not easy to classify tribal groups or to categorize the range of their authority. As a legal entity, the tribe has not been respected as "a distinct political society separated from others, capable of managing its own affairs and governing itself"[35] since the days of John Marshall. Even then Marshall's idea of a "dependent domestic nation" marked an unwieldy and ambiguous compromise. But if ever freedom of association ought to have constitutional clout, it surely should be in cases asserting tribal rights brought by remaining Native American tribes.

Just as an excess of formalistic manipulation of categories can be used to defeat tribal legal claims, so can an excess of hard-boiled contemporary policy judgment. The Vermont Supreme Court, for example, recently denied the Abenaki Indians rights to fish in the streams of their ancestral homelands without state licenses. The basis of the unanimous opinion was that the Indian claims had been voided by "the increasing weight of history."[36] It did not matter that the Abenaki never ceded their claims by treaty. The alchemy of the judges' teleological faith transformed old wrongs. The legal status quo trumps clear aboriginal rights.[37]

The Rational Relationship Test for Freedom of Association Claims: *Lyng v. International Union, UAW*

There are less dramatic, more mainstream examples of how sensitivity to an independent right of freedom of association would yield different and better results. These include, for example, the exclusion of the NAACP Legal Defense and Education Fund, Inc. from the general federal charity drive among federal employees on a "mere rationality" basis of review, and several decisions allowing the IRS virtually unchecked discretion in its decisions concerning tax-exempt status.

The mainstream case that most clearly failed to take freedom of association seriously, however, was *Lyng v. International Union,*

UAW.[38] The 1981 Omnibus Budget Reconciliation Act—a statute Justice Stevens once called a "vast piece of hurriedly enacted legislation"[39]—provided that no household could become eligible for food stamps or have an increase in its food stamp allotment while any member of that household was on strike. District Judge Louis Oberdorfer declared the 1981 Act's amendment of the Food Stamp Act unconstitutional on the grounds that it interfered with the strikers' freedom of association with their families, unions, and fellow union members.[40] He also held that Congress had unconstitutionally restricted the First Amendment right of strikers to express themselves free of government coercion and had denied them equal protection by classifying solely on the basis of animus, by treating strikers significantly worse than employees who voluntarily quit jobs, and by placing the onus of the decision to strike directly on the families of the strikers.

The unions and individuals who challenged the food stamp restriction presented uncontested evidence, largely through poignant affidavits that detailed the hardship wrought by the congressional action.[41] Nevertheless, Justice White's majority opinion asserted that on the whole the statute probably had no effect. In any event, the Court noted, the statute did not "order" individuals to stop dining together. In no other way did it "directly and substantially interfere with a family's living arrangements."[42]

This distinction between direct and indirect burdens is reminiscent of the dichotomous judicial approach to interstate commerce and federalism in the years before the constitutional revolution of 1937.[43] But the main thrust of the majority's effort to distinguish direct and indirect harms had a specific aim. Amid rhetorical flourishes such as "[t]he Constitution does not permit" any other result, and "discretion about how best to spend money to improve the general welfare is lodged in Congress rather than the courts," White announced that "[w]e have little trouble in concluding that §109 is rationally related to the legitimate government objective of avoiding undue favoritism to one side or the other in private labor disputes."[44]

White used a footnote to concede, as the precedents obliged him to do, that it is indeed possible for associational rights to be "abridged even by government actions that do not directly restrict individuals' ability to associate freely."[45] But conversely, "[e]xposing the members of an association to physical and economic reprisals or to civil liability merely because of their membership in that group poses a much greater danger to the exercise of associational freedoms than does withdrawal of a government benefit based not on membership in an organization but merely for the duration of one activity that may be undertaken by that organization."[46] This is blatant double-talk. In translation, this circular line of reasoning indicates that the Court will take judicial notice of the level of harm to associational rights when these are threatened by particular governmental action.

Serious, judicially cognizable threats to freedom of association include forced disclosure of membership lists and, in a particular case, a large damage award imposed because of an association's lengthy boycott of all the white merchants in town.[47] These intrusions may be distinguished by judicial fiat, however, from more direct and basic pressure, such as hunger, that is imposed on a worker and a worker's family because of participation in a strike or even because of mere failure to renounce it.[48] Yet this restriction on association is not thought to be punitive or opposed to freedom of association. The Court considered food stamps mere government largess. So long as the governmental decision was couched in terms of neutrality, food stamps could be doled out or cut off for any reason, one reason being, apparently, to penalize an unpopular group.

The Court unquestioningly accepted Congress's claim that it sought to be neutral. "Strikers and their union would be much better off if food stamps were available," the majority acknowledged, "but the strikers' right of association does not require the Government to furnish funds to maximize the exercise of that right."[49] The legislature is entitled "not to subsidize" the exercise of even a fundamental right.[50] This notion of subsidization is a dangerous extension of the purported neutrality the Court accepted in the abortion-funding decisions. Moreover, the Court sought to distinguish precedents invalidating unconstitutional conditions, such as *Sherbert v. Verner*.[51]

The "governmental obligation of neutrality"[52] sometimes does require close scrutiny when fundamental rights originating in the Establishment and Free Exercise clauses of the First Amendment are at stake. Yet freedom of association claims, despite their similar origin in the First Amendment, receive much less, even negligible, attention.

In other words, there is neutrality and then there is *neutrality*. Sometimes, as in the food stamp case, it is claimed that the Constitution obliges the Court to defer to strained, even false, claims of neutrality.[53] But sometimes neutrality obliges the Court to consider carefully whether the government is actually neutral.[54] The Court in the *UAW* case brusquely rejected the relevance of *Department of Agriculture v.*

Moreno, which invalidated a limitation on food stamps aimed at punishing hippies and held that "a bare congressional desire to harm a politically unpopular group cannot constitute a *legitimate* governmental interest."[55] Yet White claimed that *Moreno* merely requires the usual, extremely deferential rational relationship test. When strikers are denied food stamps, this version of neutrality looks bizarre. It defers to legislative action specifically keyed to punishing members of an unpopular group for constitutionally protected action.

For all that, the *UAW* Court would have us sympathize with the plight of Congress. "Congress was in a difficult position when it sought to address the problems it identified," according to the majority.[56] (One hesitates to ask what particular position that was.) It is acceptable for Congress to be "harder on strikers than on 'voluntary quitters,'" according to White, because "the concern about neutrality in labor disputes does not arise with respect to those who, for one reason or another, simply quit their jobs."[57] If you whine, you cannot dine. But winos, dropouts, and those who, like Bartleby the Scrivener, simply prefer not to work are treated much more kindly by a statute "rationally related to the stated objective of maintaining neutrality."[58]

The majority's approach merits attention for what it says and does not say about freedom of association. The way the majority brushed aside the freedom of association right is revealing. White began by conceding that "[w]e have recognized that 'one of the foundations of our society is the right of individuals to combine with other persons in pursuit of a common goal by lawful means.'"[59] Within three paragraphs, however, his discussion ended with reliance on an equal protection decision which held that denial of unemployment benefits to workers thrown out of work in a labor dispute "does not involve any discernible fundamental interest."[60] Etymology to the contrary, freedom of association is thus a foundational right, but somehow not a fundamental one.[61]

In fact, freedom of association so lacked the qualities of a fundamental right that White simply segued into a discussion of traditional, toothless, rational relationship equal protection review. Because the statute had "no substantial impact on any fundamental interest,"[62] the majority only needed to determine that strikers were not a suspect class. The strong doctrinal presumption in favor of legislative line-drawing sufficed. White's discussion of neutrality was a paradigmatic illustration of the point that "one could get out of a premise all that one had put into it."[63] But neither the travesty of neutrality nor the inconsistency with other recent equal protection opinions is the most important flaw.[64] What matters is how glibly, and with what destructive consequences, the Court removed freedom of association from the company it should keep with its First Amendment counterparts. Instead, the right was rendered a makeweight interest. This interest actually thereby carried no weight at all.

If freedom of association truly were "one of the foundations of our society," the union and family claims in the *UAW* case would have required much more careful scrutiny than they received, owing to the majority's extreme deference to government.[65] Comparison to the Native American decisions makes clear that the current Court is not consistent in deciding when to defer to Congress and when to intervene aggressively. If our judges heeded the important—albeit not absolute—freedom of association claims that Justice Rutledge recognized in *Thomas v. Collins,* they might reach different and better results. More significantly, they might begin to hear and tell different, more diverse tales. Ideas are facts, too. The idea of an independent freedom of association right would help groups along the road to better law.

Nascent Groups: Organizing Public Employees

Part of the current legal confusion about groups stems from the standard approach of categorizing and regulating associations. In so doing we sacrifice function to form. It now seems apparent, for example, that workers made something of a Faustian bargain to obtain protections for concerted activity provided by the Wagner Act.[66] That Act's federal labor policy came at considerable cost to spontaneity, older union customs, local control of organizing, political clout, and an array of organizing techniques outside or beyond the formal legal process.[67]

As the Court wrestles with constitutional protection for job security in public employment, one of its difficulties is the idea that custom—beyond formal state or federal law—might be enough to determine a "more than unilateral expectation," which rises to the level of a property right.[68] One explanation for the altered status of public employment lies in recent social and economic changes, ranging from the diminished power of political parties and their patronage to a generally lower threshold of tolerance about how much harshness of life is acceptable.[69] Furthermore, the Court itself has begun to extend limited First Amendment protections into public sector employment.[70] Finally, and most relevant, the very idea of giving weight to custom concedes

that groups, but not isolated individuals, may and do establish understandings, expectations, and reliances that have legal significance. Such
modern customary law stretches beyond the individualistic paradigm
of the employment-at-will labor contract.

The Court, nonetheless, has consistently failed to recognize the crucial role of organizing within the workforce beyond or outside the
formal realm of the National Labor Relations Act or existing political
parties. The Court's denial of the importance of constitutional protection even for nascent groups helps to explain the debacle of *Connick v.
Myers.*[71] The case concerned the effort by Assistant District Attorney
Sheila Myers to solicit the views of her fellow employees about how
the Orleans Parish (New Orleans) District Attorney's office was being
run. The Court held Myers had presented an employee grievance outside normal channels. While the decision to dismiss Ms. Myers for
circulating a questionnaire "may not be fair," the Court ruled the case
was not appropriate for federal judicial review.[72]

Justice White's majority opinion acknowledged that the questionnaire Ms. Myers had sent her co-workers was not "totally beyond the
protection of the First Amendment"; yet "a federal court is not the
appropriate forum in which to review the wisdom of a personnel
decision taken by a public agency allegedly in response to the employee's behavior."[73] (If people are not to go to federal court, one must
wonder where they are to seek legal vindication of First Amendment
rights.)

A perspective that gave freedom of association its due and used a
structural rather than a compartmentalizing approach to First Amendment freedoms would find constitutional protection for this organizing effort. Such an approach would avoid White's unworkable and
illogical test of whether Myers's speech was or was not of "public
concern." More appropriate First Amendment scrutiny would discard
the sharp line White used to divide communications about public concerns, which federal courts apparently will protect, and all other matters. It is curious, incidentally, that Myers's questionnaire about the
often-controversial New Orleans DA's office did not satisfy White's
pigeon-holing test. Employee opinion on how such a public office was
run and whether employees were being unduly pressured to aid political campaigns, White said, "cannot be fairly considered as relating to
any matter of political, social, or other concern to the community."[74]

The majority's narrow view seemed to denigrate the public, even as
it spun out the restrictive consequences of a premise rooted in assump-

tions of individualistic isolation. White's approach required a clear line between communicating and organizing. To deny protection to organizing is to ignore the robust expressive activities that brought about the framing of the federal Constitution.[75] Nor does it make analytic sense. In fact, the Court quickly contradicted its own categorizing approach. On the one hand, Myers could not be protected because "the questionnaire, if released to the public, would convey no information at all other than the fact that a single employee is upset with the status quo."[76] On the other hand, Myers was fired because "[q]uestions, no less than forcefully stated opinion and facts, carry messages."[77] The medium was and was not the message.

In labeling Myers's effort merely "an employee grievance concerning internal office policy," the *Connick* majority protested too much. "Although today the balance is struck for the government," White asserted, "this is no defeat for the First Amendment."[78] It was more likely to prove a disaster. More is needed than labor law statutes to protect efforts such as Sheila Myers's to organize and communicate by considering them within the "preferred position" tradition recognized and advanced in *Thomas v. Collins*. A more sensitive First Amendment approach to group organizing and functioning would better reflect how we work, live, and learn.

Some Limits to Freedom of Association

By now readers may have begun to think that I am always critical of the Court's recent decisions, or that I believe that freedom of association claims should always prevail. To dispel that impression I will mention two recent decisions that upheld the City of Dallas's efforts to regulate morality and clearly reached defensible results, in which freedom of association claims rightly did not prevail. *City of Dallas v. Stanglin*[79] is particularly helpful in clarifying why and where lines must be drawn even in freedom of association cases. Here, while the Court's reasoning was hardly convincing, the decision makes considerable sense.

In *Stanglin*, the owner of the Twilight Skating Rink challenged a city ordinance that had established a class of dance halls open only to persons fourteen to eighteen years old, with limited exceptions for parents, law enforcement personnel, and a few other adults. Patrons at the Twilight Rink whose ages placed them outside the designated age range could skate to the same music, but they could do so only alongside, and separate from, the 1,000 or so patrons of the teenage skating rink/dance hall. The Texas Court of Appeals agreed with the owner's argument that the ordinance deprived his customers of a fundamental right of "social association." Therefore, according to the Texas Court, the ordinance had to be narrowly tailored and to serve a compelling state interest to meet constitutional scrutiny.[80]

In the Supreme Court, "the dispositive question"[81] was the level of judicial scrutiny. Chief Justice Rehnquist's opinion for the Court emphatically disagreed with the Texas judges as to the relevance of any First Amendment rights to the case. Rehnquist summarized, "[W]e do not think the Constitution recognizes a generalized right of 'social association' that includes chance encounters in dance halls."[82] As stated somewhat mockingly, Rehnquist's proposition is narrow and unexceptional. "Chance encounters" in "dance halls" hardly seem the basis for a strong "generalized right." Moreover, ineffective and even silly as the ordinance may be, its effort to protect teenagers does not seem much different from the time, place, and manner of restrictions that are familiar and quite acceptable within our system of freedom of expression. Further, even classic freedom of expression protections may be limited when recipients or participants are still minors. Finally, Rehnquist's words do not preclude, in other freedom of association situations, judicial recognition of some right of "social association." The result in *Stanglin* therefore was at least defensible, and probably correct.

The entire opinion in *Stanglin* made it patently clear, however, that the Court intended a very restrictive view. The Court's approach amounted to a series of on/off applications of the *Roberts v. United States Jaycees* approach. The Court considered it "beyond cavil" that the association involved was "not . . . intimate."[83] Next, the Court determined that the association was not expressive: the participants were "not members of any organized association; they are patrons of the same business establishment."[84] Therefore, the case involved "no constitutionally protected right" and required only "the most relaxed and tolerant form of judicial scrutiny under equal protection."[85]

Stanglin thus exemplifies the application of the rigid categorical approach Brennan introduced in *Jaycees*. As in *Jaycees,* the result is justified. Yet in both cases the analysis is deeply flawed. Though the *Stanglin* Court hinted vaguely that other social associations might warrant constitutional protection, and that it might have made a difference had the would-be dancers been "members of any organized association," the justices obviously showed little sympathy for efforts to form associations—or relationships—not already established.

The unmistakable thrust of the *Stanglin* opinion, including its tightening of the mechanistic *Jaycees* categories, was to confine freedom of association claims as rigidly as possible. The Court simply could not see any constitutional right at stake.[86] If there is "some kernel of expression in nearly every activity a person undertakes,"[87] the very universality of these kernels renders them nugatory nuggets devoid of First Amendment protection.

Jaycees did not go nearly this far. There, Brennan noted that the two categories he discerned in the Court's earlier lines of cases—intimate and expressive associations—often overlapped. Moreover, his categories embraced "a wide variety of political, social, economic, educational, religious and cultural aims." Before *Stanglin*, even lower court judges who tried to distinguish or narrow *Jaycees* still had to concede, for example, that "[d]ating and other social activities are worthy of some protection under the First Amendment even though these activities may lack overt political, religious, or educational purpose."[88] *Stanglin* strangled the very idea of overlap between intimate and expressive association, however, and narrowed to the point of oblivion the Court's earlier recognition that freedom of association extends to relationships that "pertain to the social, legal, and economic benefit of the members."[89]

As if to underscore this categorical approach to freedom of association claims, the Court also upheld a Dallas licensing scheme aimed at "sexually oriented" businesses that prohibited renting motel rooms for less than 10 hours.[90] Justice O'Connor had the support of the entire Court—otherwise sharply divided in the case—when she rejected a freedom of association claim. Again tightening the *Jaycees* criteria, the Court seized the opportunity for some easy moralizing. O'Connor wrote rather snidely, "[W]e do not believe that limiting motel room rentals to 10 hours will have any discernible effect on the sorts of traditional personal bonds to which we referred" in the *Jaycees* case.[91] Further, the type of association taking place in those motel rooms was not the sort that "'played a critical role in the culture and traditions of the Nation by cultivating and transmitting shared ideals and beliefs.'"[92]

The language, if not the holdings, in these two recent Dallas cases provides a virtually unstoppable syllogistic whipsaw. Freedom of association protects only rights already protected by the First Amendment or by substantive due process. To the extent freedom of association claims are broadly based in society, they are easily rejected as commonplaces lacking constitutional clout. Finally, to the extent that an association is small, unusual, or in the process of formation, it can be easily dismissed as untraditional or not part of our shared ideals and beliefs.

It is worth noting how masterfully Judge Posner wielded this new whipsaw against a freedom of association claim. Posner proclaimed that *Jaycees* and *Stanglin* together show that the First Amendment does not protect nonexpressive associations.[93] To Posner, the only expression protected by the First Amendment is expression that seeks to "inform, edify, or entertain." "Casual chit-chat between two persons or otherwise confined to a small group" is therefore "unrelated, or largely so, to that marketplace and is not protected."[94] And if any relational rights are protected beyond the intimate associations shielded by substantive due process, they are properly characterized as "harmless liberties"[95] of no potential constitutional importance. Construed this way, freedom of association begins to devour not only itself but also large chunks of its doctrinal forbears that originally sought to protect freedom of expression and intimate association.

It is difficult to get excited when businessmen lose claims that the Constitution requires that teenagers ought to be able to mix with older people in a dance hall, or that motels ought to be allowed to rent rooms for less than ten hours. Indeed, the outcomes in these two decisions are hardly surprising, even if the Court's efforts to uphold morality seem ineffective at best. But the manner in which the Court rejected freedom of association claims, and instead mechanistically applied and narrowed the *Jaycees* two-part test, surely demonstrates little respect for associational rights that do not involve either direct political expression or intimate association of the sort the Court deems traditional and therefore acceptable. The current Court has a fondness for using dicta to mark rights as if they were trees. They are thereby readied for clear-cutting when some alleged state interest competes for the space they occupy.

The approach to freedom of association in recent cases—a curious blend of mockery and formalistic application of legal categories—hardly bodes well for an earlier tradition, in which "mere public intolerance or animosity cannot be the basis for abridgement" of "the right of the people to gather in public places for social or political purposes."[96] The Court no longer recognizes that freedom of association is an "inseparable aspect" of fundamental speech and liberty values. In addition to dissenters, some centrist justices such as O'Connor and Souter have begun to counter the Court's thrust with the complaint that "[t]here is nothing talismanic about neutral laws of general applicability."[97] In case after case, however, the majority isolates the individual, denies that any fundamental right is at stake, and then easily contrasts her or his puny claim with the extreme deference owed any output of the democratic process under the most permissive equal protection standard.

By no means, however, should group rights claims always trump other constitutional arguments. Two decisions within a week of each other at the end of the Supreme Court's 1993 Term illustrate significant limits to, as well as the necessity for, judicial sensitivity when associational rights are at stake. In *Board of Education of Kiryas Joel Village School District v. Grumet,*[98] the Court rightfully concluded that the New York legislature could not carve out a special new school district exactly coterminous with a Satmar Hasidic village, inhabited exclusively by these separatist Orthodox Jews. Justice Souter's majority opinion invalidated by the 1989 New York law because it "effectively identifies these recipients of governmental authority by reference to doctrinal adherence, even though it does not do so expressly."[99] Despite New York's worthy goal of providing special education for disabled students, the Court held the inextricable link of religious and civil power in the newly minted school district to be too close for constitutional comfort.

The majority's plunge into the complex tensions posed by the coexistence of the Free Exercise and Establishment clauses within the First Amendment is noteworthy in itself. Souter's attention to facts that suggested an unholy alliance between political and religious power made the Court's fear of overweening and unchecked group power convincing in this context. Even if freedom of association is intertwined with, and reinforced by, a strong religious claim, it ought not always prevail. This idea is inherent in the limitation imposed on congruence between government and religious groups by the Establishment clause of the First Amendment.

On the other hand, in *Madsen v. Women's Health Center, Inc.,* the Court clearly erred when it blithely rejected a freedom of association argument made by all those acting "in concert" with protesters who were enjoined from picketing a Florida abortion clinic.[100] In upholding this blatant guilt by association within the sweeping Florida state court injunction, Chief Justice Rehnquist's majority opinion offered only a baldly conclusory explanation. The majority seemed anxious simply to finish a particularly fractious dispute on this final day of its 1993 Term. In its rush to recess, however, the Court's response to a serious associational claim was wholly unsatisfactory and made bad First Amendment law, no matter what one's views of abortion might be.

In *Madsen,* people enjoined simply because of the company they kept complained of the breadth of the injunction against them. Rehnquist answered with a non sequitur that was entirely circular: "The freedom of association protected by the First Amendment does not extend to joining with others for the purpose of depriving third parties of their lawful rights."[101] As stated, Rehnquist's proposition is unremarkable. Yet in presupposing that those enjoined were "joining with others for the purpose of depriving third parties of their lawful rights," this single-sentence response provided a classic example of begging the crucial question. The constitutional argument Rehnquist thereby brushed away was in fact a paradigmatic freedom of association claim. It focused on the Florida judge's injunction against only one side among the groups engaged in an ongoing, bitter dispute outside an abortion clinic. The injunction clearly was viewpoint-based and it clearly imposed a prior restraint upon expression and the associational interests of a particular group of demonstrators.

Justice Scalia's vigorous dissent made it clear that the judge who issued the injunction had explained its reach precisely in terms of which side a person was on. The trial judge repeatedly stated that guilty association was the crucial operative factor.[102] Though it is easy to disagree with Scalia's assertion that the Court's abortion decisions constitute an "ad hoc nullification machine" that now "claims its latest, greatest, and most surprising victim: the First Amendment,"[103] it is hard to ignore Scalia's argument that *Madsen* departs alarmingly from earlier precedent. After *Madsen,* it is no longer clearly established that "mere association with [a] group—absent a specific intent to further an unlawful aim embraced by that group—is an insufficient predicate for liability."[104] The majority's breezy treatment of freedom of association in *Madsen* again illustrates why it is so important to focus upon group claims that, at the least, ought to receive special constitutional concern and respect.

The alternative approach I propose is similar to the approach we are accustomed to using when freedom of the press is at stake. The press certainly does not always win, but the precedents suggest, quite appropriately, that restrictions on or discriminatory treatment of journalists must be handled in a gingerly fashion.[105]

Like the press, many other kinds of associations have a vital "checking value."[106] The form and function of voluntary associations, for example, should not be left to the unbridled authority of government officials. Nor should academic freedom be treated as cavalierly as it often has been in recent decisions.[107] The approach I advocate would help provide a rationale for the Court's conclusion that nonprofits are somehow different for First Amendment purposes.[108]

Like newspapers, which generally do have a profit motive, nonprofit associations ought to enjoy initial constitutional protection. The right that protects them is not absolute, to be sure. It is a rebuttable presumption, creating a constitutional oasis that the government can invade only for a very good reason. At a minimum, this approach would aid courts in paying attention to context. We might thereby avoid the imperatives of the categoricals the Court employs to distinguish political from personal, intimate from social, and individual from relational rights.

Conclusion

It makes sense to think that most judges are inclined to squelch the norms generated by groups other than the state.[109] Judges, after all, legitimize violence on behalf of the state. Unsurprisingly, they want to control or eliminate alternative narratives and competing notions of morality. Yet if deference to the lowest common denominator has appeal as a simple principle for judges, it is not sufficiently sensitive to key constitutional rights that are threatened by statism and by pure majoritarianism. Great judges must be more than bureaucratic followers of the rules—even of the mystical Rule of Law. In their words as in their deeds, the community of judges must stand for alternatives to force. The stories of what judges do—and, equally important, what they do not do—cannot be neatly plotted. Like Bible stories and other great tales, judicial legends are full of tension and complexity. Judges give multidimensional responses to multilayered problems, ranging from the mundane to the profane, from the sensational to the sacred. There is an essential contrariness in legal rules. For example, the clear legal rule in the Bible is that the eldest son should inherit, yet in all the famous Bible stories—Cain and Abel, Ishmael and Isaac, Essau and

Jacob, and Joseph and his brothers—the eldest son loses out to a younger brother.

Various associations create and continue to anchor our deepest instincts. The law is impoverished when it seeks to marginalize the role of groups. To take refuge in the kinds of complacent oversimplifications and binary choices that lawyers delight to call reasonable limits may be temporarily reassuring, but it is a mistake. Gershom Scholem said, "Reason is a great instrument of destruction. For construction, something beyond is required."[110] The fragile materials that make up justice under law include multilayered group stories.

6 Faulkner, Fealty, and Communal Obligations

The confrontation between the prophet Amos and the high priest Amaziah at Beth-el around the year 760 B.C.E. may be the first—and remains the classic—description of a fundamental clash of belief and ritual, righteousness and religion.[1] Amos spoke bravely against established authority, emphasizing his position of solidarity with and for the people. In a message that is approximately contemporaneous with Homer,[2] this herdsman and dresser (or keeper) of sycamore trees explained in stark, passionate words the meaning of "Woe to them that are at ease in Zion" (6:1).

All of Israel and Judah would suffer. Everyone would be punished for thinking themselves special, chosen, immune to the wrath of God because they were different from the Philistines and other nations. Instead of remembering past oppression and sharing the pain of Jacob and Joseph and those who were slaves in Egypt, the children of Israel "swallow the needy, / And destroy the poor of the land" (8:4) as they luxuriate on couches and beds of ivory, devouring the choicest lambs and calves while the wine flows and music plays. Though they perform sacrifices and observe the Sabbath, they are eager to return to business as usual, to cheat and to "buy the poor for silver, / And the needy for a pair of shoes, / And sell the refuse of the corn" (8:6). But ultimately each and every one will suffer destruction and mourning at the end of "a bitter day"(8:10). Amos's riveting words and his cryptic assumption of communal responsibility surely speak to our modern or postmodern dilemmas, obligations, and tragic failings.[3]

The prophet directly challenges the banality and the evil that lie in the mere observance of formal requirements and the attempt to freeze the status quo. He stands alone as he speaks truth to power, knowing he risks madness when he demands that some universalistic justice emerge out of the particulars of Israel's obligation to remember its own oppression.[4] Amos's lonely message requires communal action. Only a deeply historical sense of reciprocal responsibility can give meaning to the pursuit of justice. The failure to remember, to be "grieved for the hurt of Joseph" (6:6), will bring everything to an end, because no strict observance of ritual can replace righteousness.

In the Book of Amos individualism is impossible, responsibility is always shared, and rights appear irrelevant. To discuss the jurisprudence of his awful vision of destruction may at first seem paradoxical. But surely it is noteworthy that Amos's message is anchored in a pervasive theory of obligations. From the top of Carmel to the bottom of the sea, none can hide from communal duty to others. The special qualities of the strong, the swift, and the courageous will give them no advantage; all will be punished in the same way.

Though Amos says "I was no prophet, neither was I a prophet's son" (7:14), he cannot help but prophesy. For himself as for his people there is no refuge: "As if a man did flee from a lion, and a bear met him; / And went into the house and leaned his hand on the wall, / And a serpent bit him" (5:19). There is no individual redemption, and no ceremonies will avert the severe decree. The only hope is for the community to "let justice well up as waters, / And righteousness as a mighty stream" (5:24). It is necessary to act communally to "[h]ate the evil, and love the good, and establish justice in the gate" (5:15).

A more modern and familiar literary work that is relevant to my discussion of rights and collective responsibilities is William Faulkner's "The Bear." It will be illuminating to compare and contrast Faulkner's story with two watershed United States Supreme Court decisions, *Fletcher v. Peck* (1810) and *United States v. Cruikshank* (1876). My quarry is justice more than it is rights. I am intrigued by a sense of communal obligation imposed by past history. Without making any claim that William Faulkner studied or intentionally invoked Amos— though I suspect he did so—I seek for some meaning other than despair, in some place between where "a man did flee from a lion, / And a bear met him" (5:19).

Faulkner, the Court, and Rights: Fictions and Facts

"No man is ever free and probably could not bear it if he were."[5]
"The past cannot be recalled by the most absolute power."[6]

The current Supreme Court seems bent on creating a grand legal fiction, a new natural law premised on formal equality. In case after case, the justices assume an equal start in the race of life. Constitutional law sweeps across a well-kept, level and traditional playing field.

Led by Justice Scalia, this new crusade charges back to a past that never was. The judicial campaign is similar to and as impassioned as the movement to maintain an identifiable core of Western civilization in our college curricula. The Court has embarked on a fruitless Snark hunt for what it idealizes as "tradition."

In this approach, only rights that are explicit in the constitutional text or that can be obviously located within a long, uniform tradition merit judicial protection. Any procedure perceived as traditional, for example, satisfies due process.[7] Rights not textual or traditional cannot be fundamental. No fealty is owed, therefore, to constitutional precedent or principle. Only an extremely rarefied concept, an inconvertible tradition, will suffice as an adequate grounding for constitutional rights.[8]

But facts—such as we can discern them—still do matter. This is so regardless of one's particular point of entry amidst the contemporary maze of trails in search of some Archimedean point.[9] I will show that the facts are found and understood with far more sophistication in Faulkner's fiction than in the sweeping foundational legal fictions that the Supreme Court has long delighted to use. If Faulkner forces us to ponder whether history's hold can ever be escaped or altered, the Court usually proceeds as if a unified past can be frozen and followed blithely or put aside at will both in law and in life.

Uncoupling History and Tradition

Scalia and his colleagues often speak of "history and tradition" as if there were no difference between the two.[10] But the two concepts ought to be uncoupled. In fact, history undermines tradition, at least the single-minded and single-stranded mythical kind of tradition the Court invokes. We are creatures of many habits, accustomed to an extraordinary array of customs that we are quick, even desperate, to dress up as personal or group traditions. People lack the time and energy to innovate constantly. Because it is so scary and lonely even to try, the first and usually the last resort is to rely upon a range of specific traditions grounded in the amazing particularities of overlapping communities. History requires "enlightened skepticism,"[11] as Holmes proclaimed. It also demands close attention to and some attempt at empathy for the past. The proper work of history cannot ignore the constitutive connections anchored in various communities.

Ironically, the law is notorious for repeated, misplaced insistence on disconnection. As Thomas Reed Powell, a flinty constitutional law professor, put it decades ago, "If you think you can think about something which is attached to something else without thinking about what it is attached to, then you have what is called a legal mind."[12] Powell's debunking of commonplace legal reasoning might serve as an accurate description of numerous decisions by the current Supreme Court. But this skeptical legal realist's statement also captures the uses of literary fictions both to comprehend the burden and to keep alive the hope of challenging ideas. The term "fiction" carries many meanings; indeed, elsewhere I have wrestled with the question of whether anything in law can properly be said not to be legal fiction.[13] Fictions of all sorts often explore the tremendous difficulty in any attempt to challenge the established customs and usages of communities in which we all live. At the same time, society pays for the cost of acquiescence in the artificial disconnections produced by customary legal geometry.

Faulkner's Isaac McCaslin, a character in "The Bear," at once understands and demonstrates a key distinction between doing history and owing fealty to tradition. And real Chief Justices, John Marshall and Morrison Waite, illustrate some of the substantial dangers in reasoning from and compounding fiction without recognizing that it is a fiction we are construing.

Faulkner presents a complex, layered account of human identity and of the past. He explores the state of nature as it is played out in the wilderness and in human nature. Often he challenges the weight of the past upon the law of property. His world is further complicated through classical allusions, frequent changes in narrative time frames, and magnificent confusions of past and future, man and beast, and subject and object.

The texture of "The Bear" really can only be communicated through quotation—and finally through careful reading. But even brief quotations illustrate the sharp opposition between Faulkner's vision and the vision that informs formal legal documents that deal with many of the same matters. I do not mean to imply that law ever could do what art does. I do claim, however, that law can do much better than it does, in part by heeding the complexity of overlapping communities and in part by refusing to consider each individual in isolation.

"The Bear": "To Find Such: By Bearings On Trees"[14]

The *Saturday Evening Post* published "The Bear" in 1942. Faulkner included a more complicated version of the same story in his difficult collection *Go Down, Moses,* published later that year. The story has been a kind of rite-of-passage for generations of college students since.

They quest after symbols and sense, resenting or delighting in Faulkner's rhythmic evocation of the "pageant-rite" of the hunt for a totemic bear, Old Ben. The story may have special appeal to those of college age because of its themes of initiation and idealism, particularly because, like so many American heroes, the central character Isaac McCaslin has no living parents to cramp his style.[15] Unlike the sacrifice of Isaac that was demanded in the Bible, however, this Isaac's idealistic decision to relinquish his inheritance because it is tainted by a history of rapacity, slavery, and other sins is a sacrifice of his own choosing.

"The Bear" repeatedly moves back and forth in time. The first crucial event occurs in 1877, when Isaac is ten years old. With marked success from the start, Isaac gradually puts aside the ways of civilization and becomes an accomplished woodsman and hunter. By the time he is sixteen, he knows the ways of the forest better than his elders do, because he was taught by Sam Fathers, "the old man born of a Negro slave and a Chickasaw chief who had been his spirit's father if any had, whom he had revered and harkened to and loved and lost and grieved."[16] In the course of the year when Old Ben the bear, Lion the mongrel dog, and Sam Fathers die, Isaac decodes the plantation ledgers and understands the origins of his inheritance in slavery, exploitation, miscegenation, and incest. His researches are followed by magnificent cascades of argument with his cousin, McCaslin Edmonds, ranging from theology and the meaning of Keats's "Ode on a Grecian Urn" to the history of the western world. At the age of twenty-one Isaac decides to relinquish his inheritance and to live as a carpenter in town.[17]

Old Ben, Sam Fathers, and Isaac are noble, solitary male figures. None has children, yet each is noteworthy for the way he connects across generations with others and with the disappearing wilderness. As admirable as they may be, however, we are left to wonder whether their actions amount to anything more than romantic, tragic gestures in the face of inevitable defeat. Even so, noble gestures are noteworthy parts of communal undertakings.

Within the firm tradition of the annual hunt, the usual social hierarchy is largely upset. Different rules prevail. Skill rather than rank establishes authority.[18] In this respect, too, "The Bear" appeals for its mythic qualities. Here the central American myth of basic equality and of success based on merit is interpreted far differently from the way the Supreme Court puts it. In Faulkner's world, no one ever gets an unhindered or an equal start in life's contests.

"The Bear" follows a logic of parallels, both among characters and in a more direct, physical sense. Its people, animals, and machines travel together on separate, parallel trajectories.[19] Yet "The Bear" complicates and conjoins in a non-Euclidean sense. It is important to note, for example, that the railroad, the planing factory, and even the logic of engineering more generally are not what threatens the hunt and its Edenic world. The greatest threat comes from within the community and each of its linked individuals, even the admirable, mythic, and purportedly free Sam Fathers.

"The Bear" speaks directly to how legal arrangements constitute and are constituted by interlocking groups. It is about fettered freedom, about the overwhelming constraints even on apparently noble efforts to change or relinquish the world. Though they are unusual in that they do exercise some control over timing and manner, even Old Ben and Sam are doomed by their legacies as well as by the shrinking of their natural worlds. Isaac McCaslin's insights about history and the constraints upon him are more complex.

Isaac feels he must explore the direct burden of his own appalling family history and the linkages, black and white, to his grandfather, Carothers McCaslin.[20] Because Isaac's inheritance is rooted in slavery and peonage, he decides to give it up and to try to pay reparations of a sort to black descendants of Carothers. Isaac's wife cannot understand this decision, but nothing, not even her seductive nakedness, will convince Isaac to change his mind. Therefore, she determines that Isaac's sacrifice means he will never have the son he wants. And Isaac is willing to renounce his property without understanding his own action.[21]

Isaac focuses on means, not ends. He is aware that his renunciation is not free: "his life, invincible enough in its needs, if he could have helped himself, not being the Nazarene, he would not have chosen it."[22] Despite Isaac's vaguely grounded idealism and his strong sense of purpose, he too is ensnared. When he works as a poor carpenter, he needs wood from the forest; the wood, ironically, is carried directly to him on train tracks from the planing factory.

Throughout the loosely connected tales of *Go Down, Moses*— dubbed a novel by Faulkner, deemed a challenge by just about everybody else—the people are never free. This is true whether or not any Moses—or Isaac—journeys down to free them. Why not? The short answer is: legal arrangements and the stranglehold of customary law. "The Bear" is only the most explicit one among the doomed assaults on boundaries established by diverse but nonetheless inescapable examples of tradition, custom, usage, and law. The entire jumpy saga of *Go Down, Moses* cuts back and forth to varying forms of the chase after any and all who try to assault or change established boundaries.[23] Section four of "The Bear" is where Faulkner wrestles most directly with the present and past, juxtaposed in overlapping, complex, but inconsistent norms.

Inescapable and Evanescent Legacies

Section four interrupts both the chronology and the main story of Isaac's coming of age. Faulkner added this section after the rest of "The Bear" had appeared in magazine form, and critics have delighted in debating whether this section, which is unusually turgid even for Faulkner, is a net gain or loss. Yet this section is crucial to the rest of the story and the whole of *Go Down, Moses*. Moreover, it should be celebrated for its sense of history and for conveying the complicated but undeniable hold of multiple forms of law.

Section four begins: "Then he was twenty one." Isaac had achieved actual manhood and a sense of freedom years earlier in the woods under the tutelage of old Sam Fathers, but only now is he legally a man. He and McCaslin Edmonds, his closest living relative, had been sitting together in the plantation commissary office, "not the heart perhaps but certainly the solar-plexus of the repudiated and relinquished." It was here Isaac discovered and came to understand the story behind the plantation records. The dusty ledgers recorded slavery, miscegenation, even incest; then "manumission in title at least of Carothers McCaslin's slaves." What followed was "the slow outward trickle of food and supplies and equipment which returned each fall as cotton made and ginned and sold (two threads frail as truth and impalpable as equators yet cable-strong to bind for life them who made the cotton to the land their sweat fell on)."[24]

Later Faulkner reiterates his bleak vision of contractual freedom and peonage: "the whole edifice intricate and complex and founded upon injustice and erected by ruthless rapacity and carried on even yet with at times downright savagery not only to human beings but the valuable animals too."[25] Moreover, this system remains "solvent and efficient and, more than that: not only still intact but enlarged, increased."

As Isaac seeks to challenge the status quo with his renunciation of his inheritance, he wants to capture "the whole plantation in its mazed and intricate entirety." His public gesture and his private understanding operate together "like a stereopticon." Isaac links past and present, the inseparably mixed lineage of black and white, the dubious origins of all property claims, and the important but empty fact of inheritances. He "condenses into one instantaneous field the myriad minutia of its scope."[26] Isaac has become a skilled historian, and it is noteworthy that his stance is hardly neutral. Through Isaac, Faulkner conveys the tragic and factual basis of foundational traditions.

In effect, Isaac's gesture did little to counter the continuing presence of the past. In a like manner, a local folk tale about a form of antislavery rebellion by Isaac's father and uncle, Uncle Buck and Uncle Buddy, exemplifies the constraining force of communal limits. Before the Civil War, Buck and Buddy refused to live in a house built by slave labor. As soon as their father was buried, the twin brothers moved out of his magnificent, unfinished plantation house. They turned it over to their slaves, and the two white owners lived in a simple log-cabin they built themselves. Each sundown, one of the brothers herded all the slaves they owned into the "tremendous abortive edifice" and nailed shut the front door. But the plantation house lacked glass in half its windows and the back door had not been installed. Thus there was an "unspoken gentleman's agreement between the two white men and the two dozen black ones":[27] once the front door was nailed shut, the slaves were free to go where they pleased so long as they returned by the time the brother who drove in the nail withdrew it at daybreak. If this private customary arrangement is a relatively benign mummery, it undeniably remains a crucial link in "the general and condoned injustice and its slow amortization."[28] It is inescapably part of the legacy Isaac attempts to reject.

Section four brims over with the problematic nature of legacies.[29] Isaac declares that all the legacies he has uncovered are cursed. He claims that the curse is traceable to the moment when a Chickasaw chief realized that he could sell land for money. Man was intended "not to hold for himself and his descendants inviolable title forever, generation after generation, to the oblongs and squares of the earth, but to hold the earth mutual and intact in the communal anonymity of brotherhood, and all the fee He asked was pity and humility and sufferance and endurance and the sweat of his face for bread."[30]

There are many ways to read Isaac's effort to realize his utopian vision. Isaac relinquishes his powers as Prospero gave up his magic in *The Tempest*, yet remains part of his community. Indeed, he may be hopelessly naive, admirable, or so self-righteous as to be at least par-

tially to blame for the grief and the recurrence of old patterns he witnesses when he is "past seventy and nearer eighty than he ever
corroborated any more, a widower now and uncle to half a county and
father to no one."[31] In "Delta Autumn," set on the eve of World War
II, Isaac finally realizes why "the ruined woods I used to know dont cry
for retribution!"[32] His bitter epiphany is that the very people he knows
so well have destroyed the woods and much more. They are accom-
plishing nature's revenge themselves. At best, it will take thousands of
years of suffering and love to change things.

The last time readers encounter Isaac, he gives the hunting horn
General Compson had willed to him, and the last of the blood money
owed Carothers McCaslin's black descendants, to the "almost white"
mistress of his cousin. She is an unnamed Beauchamp directly
descended from Old Carothers's incestuous union. Although this
young woman is pregnant by Roth McCaslin, Isaac's wealthy cousin
to whom the land passed when Isaac renounced his inheritance, neither she nor Isaac tells Roth about the family connection. Moreover,
Roth's mistress forcefully rejects Isaac's advice to forget and to start
anew in the North. "Old man," she said, "have you lived so long and
forgotten so much that you dont remember anything you ever knew or
felt or even heard about love?"[33] The romantic hope she raises about
love and self-sufficiency is overridden by the sadness of Isaac's urging
to forget the past. In retrospect, his singular renunciation, his youthful
effort to redeem history, seems to have been a futile gesture.

Faulkner places his dark view of confounded free will in sharp relief
against a backdrop of confining customary and legal power. His complex, ultimately harsh view of inexorable communal pressures undermines the crisp polarities often invoked today to schematize the recent
turn to law and literature. Faulkner does give some voice to the voiceless.[34] Yet he continuously punctures idealist claims that attention to
literature might help humanize lawyers through empathy, set us free to
do better interpretations of texts, or provide pragmatic grounding for
ideas somewhere between the real and the ideal. Today, there is great
discomfort as well as a strong sense of the past in the particular version
of fidelity Faulkner celebrates in his dedication of *Go Down, Moses*:
"To Mammy/ Caroline Barr/ Mississippi/ [1840–1940]/ Who was
born in slavery and who gave to my family a fidelity without stint or
calculation of recompense and to my childhood an immeasurable
devotion and love."

History's complicated webs became Faulkner's obsession. By the
time the writer could delight in his role as Nobel laureate, he had

begun to sound like Justice Holmes: "[N]o man is himself, he is the sum of his past. There is no such thing really as 'was' because the past 'is'."[35] Yoknapatawpha County overflows with the most basic evils of domination, but normative jurisdiction is always fluid and authority both inescapable and always doubtful. It is a land flooded with violence and with words. Standard legal process is far away, but legal authority is inescapably present.

Faulkner's world abounds with complicated characters indissolubly linked with each other. Each one judges and must in turn be judged. All, even slaves, play roles in the diversified community whose unspoken rules govern them all. In various ways everyone is implicated in communal law-making. Intuition and custom are crucial but not sufficient for understanding and justice. There is no such thing as a free hunch. Faulkner's persistent attack on binary choices aspires to the multileveled determinism of myth. It emphasizes the grasp and force of the past.

Isaac McCaslin is particularly tethered to history, in a most unusual way. As soon as he comes of age in the wilderness, still only sixteen years old, he begins an aggressive pursuit of the facts of his communal past, to make amends and to escape. Nonetheless, Isaac's empathy and sense of community tie him inextricably. The self-sufficient hero able to comprehend and live in harmony with the wilderness without gun or compass is also able, through research and a sense of interlocking connections, to achieve an unusual understanding of history. Neither he nor anyone else, Isaac learns, can float free of the burden of communal constraints.

At the end of his life, to honor his dead wife, Isaac McCaslin pretends to accept property she willed to him. But he insists that the property "was not his, will or not, chancery dying wishes mortmain possession or whatever."[36] By contrast, in a series of steps purportedly based upon fundamental legal principles, the Supreme Court set about inventing grand fictions about the foundations of property, contract, and federalism. The justices thereby created an unpeopled past that nevertheless could grasp and control the future with its ghostly hands.

Fletcher v. Peck (1810)

The great case of *Fletcher v. Peck* parallels Faulkner's world in significant ways beyond sharing the physical location of Faulkner's Yoknapatawpha in the Yazoo River delta of northern Mississippi. Chief Justice John Marshall's opinion for the Court illuminates the legal understandings that helped make that land the way it was in 1877, when Sam Fathers began to teach ten-year-old Isaac McCaslin the ways of his vanishing natural world. It explains how crucial and inexorable ownership had become, even for the hunt, even for the place where Old Ben, Lion, and Sam Fathers were buried. Indeed, direct echoes from the context of *Fletcher,* full of adventurers who used slaves to gouge out claims to land seized, swapped, or purchased from the Indians, pervade Faulkner's work. At the end of "The Bear," four concrete markers, "lifeless and shockingly alien,"[37] set off fresh legal claims of property, contract, and suzerainty. *Fletcher v. Peck* also marked the beginning of that end.

In January 1795 Georgia sold 35 million acres of western land claimed by the state to four companies of land speculators for $500,000 in specie currency. The Georgia legislature, in what has been called and might well have been "the greatest real estate deal in history," turned over virtually all of what is currently Alabama and Mississippi, then known as the Yazoo lands after the river that traversed much of the territory.[38] The sale took place after politically prominent speculators and their partners bribed most if not all of the Georgia legislature. But the deed did not go unchallenged: for once, the theory of accountable democratic government actually seemed to function. James Jackson, the most powerful figure in Georgia politics, known as the "Prince of Savannah Duelists," resigned his U.S. Senate seat to fight "the rapacious grasping of a few sharks."[39] The voters of Georgia promptly tossed the corrupt legislators out of office.

Jackson and his allies in the new Georgia legislature quickly enacted a law that nullified the 1795 sale as a blatant violation of "equal rights." Accompanying this February 1796 act was another law to obliterate the 1795 sale from the public record entirely. Georgians conducted a ritualistic public burning of "the usurped act." After prolonged, remarkably byzantine machinations, one of the directors of the New England Mississippi Land Company, Robert Fletcher of New Hampshire, bought 15,000 acres of Yazoo land from another land speculator, John Peck of Massachusetts, who had purchased part of the Yazoo grant. Fletcher contrived to invoke diversity jurisdiction to maneuver into federal court a test case for breach of covenant against Peck, based on the alleged invalidity of the 1795 sale. The Company paid all the expenses for both sides. They hired some of the brightest lights of the bar, including John Quincy Adams, Robert Goodloe

Harper, and Joseph Story, to represent Peck. They retained Luther Martin for what purported to be the other side, though the Court reportedly had to adjourn until Martin sobered up enough to continue his argument.[40] It may be useful to reduce the legal complexity of *Fletcher* to terms as simple as: A (absolute rights); B (balancing); and C (community).

Absolute Vested Rights

Behind all the entertaining playacting in *Fletcher* stands Marshall's famous opinion for the Court. The opinion is well known because it marked the first time the Supreme Court invalidated state legislation on constitutional grounds. As in many of his other famous decisions, Marshall had to stretch quite far. He had to determine initially that the 1795 land sale actually was a contract, the necessary premise for his argument. This he managed with assertions about the nature of things, questionable analogies from private law, and implications he drew as needed. But Marshall went further. Georgia's attempt to repeal its grant-as-contract was invalid, he argued, "either by general principles which are common to our free institutions, or by the particular provisions of the constitution of the United States."[41]

After protesting too much, as he often did, about his awareness of the particular delicacy of the task the Court was performing, Marshall advanced to the claim that it ought to be relevant that the 1795 Georgia legislature undoubtedly was corrupt. After considerable handwringing about the very possibility of contamination and impure motives in the governments of our infant republics, Marshall raised a series of practical questions. What if legislators have mixed motives? How much corruption is enough to invalidate legislation? What if public sentiment still favors the law in question? But he finally used a pleading technicality to duck the corruption issue.

"It would be indecent, in the extreme," Marshall said, to address such public questions in a private contract dispute between two individuals.[42] Thus the case was really only between A and B, two individual abstractions. Marshall reduced nearly two decades of controversy and intrigue over 35 million acres to plaintiff and defendant as single integers. In fact, he insisted on it. The Court was obliged only to choose between, or balance, two individual rights. The lands in controversy had "vested absolutely" in the original purchasers in 1795.[43] To interfere with absolutely vested rights would be "a mere act of power," and could only be vindicated "in a train of reasoning not often heard in courts of justice."[44]

Marshall then hammered together a chain of binary, seemingly logical links to get to the crux of his argument. Either a legislature or a court had to decide the legitimacy of what Georgia had done. Any court of justice knows that if a title to property has been perfected through the requisite legal forms, any subsequent buyer is "innocent."[45] Even if the original transaction had been tainted, "those who purchased parts of it were not stained by that guilt which infected the original transaction."[46] In the dichotomous world Marshall manipulated, "great principles of justice, whose authority is universally acknowledged" are overriding.[47] When he went on to add that these great universal principles "ought not to be entirely disregarded,"[48] Marshall's studied understatement, couched in a clever lawyerly double negative, provided the logical coup de grace.

Balancing and the Judicial Refusal to Balance

On the off chance that anyone might still consider expropriating the innocent subsequent purchaser in defiance of universal principles of justice, Marshall offered a practical sketch of how steep such a slippery slope would be. If the legislature could be "itself absolved" from "those rules of property which are common to all the citizens of the United States, and from those principles of equity which are acknowledged in all our courts,"[49] no property would be secure and all commerce would be very seriously obstructed.

Marshall's point distilled common law rules and universal principles of equity common to all American citizens into a single sweeping principle: the absolute vested right of an innocent property buyer. Only the Court could forestall the legislature's attempted "annihilation"[50] of the property right it had transferred. Georgia might try such a maneuver, but the United States Supreme Court ultimately would evaluate whether Georgia law was inconsistent with the federal constitution. Georgia "is part of a large empire," Marshall argued, and "the American union" has a Constitution that imposes limits on the legislatures of the several states.[51] In characteristic fashion, Marshall invoked an abstract version of the framers' original intent. "[I]t is not to be disguised," he claimed, that the framers of the Constitution viewed, "with some apprehension," the sorts of "violent acts" that "grow out of the feelings of the moment," and that the people of the United States in adopting the Constitution thereby determined "to shield themselves and their property from the effects of those sudden and strong passions to which men are exposed."[52]

These words are anything but an invitation "to constitute and reconstitute our community and culture anew" and "to build on what I have made."[53] While "The Bear" begins with "voices quiet and weighty and deliberate for retrospection and recollection and exactitude among concrete trophies,"[54] Marshall insists on preempting discussion with his authoritative, magisterial pronouncement. For Marshall, the past is fully occupied by absolute, abstract rights; Faulkner's past is dominated by relative, specific wrongs. Faulkner constantly considers those who try to escape or challenge what has gone before, while Marshall has eyes only for the glorious status quo that he creates with his grand fictions.

The *Grundnorm*—today we might call it ground zero—is Marshall's stark assertion: "The past cannot be recalled by the most absolute power."[55] (In thus foreclosing "recall," Marshall surely does not mean to speak to the dilemma every historian faces in trying to reconstruct the past accurately. In context, he is actually doing quite the opposite.) Basically, Marshall's idea was that a property right had become irrevocable—a thing or a fact. When he considered "vested legal estates," Marshall argued "that they originally vested is a fact, and cannot cease to be a fact."[56] This reification was so powerful that Marshall declared it irreversible even if some sovereign authority were to try to seize what he termed absolute individual rights.

Community: Who Decides?

The rights of citizenship, the fundamental principles of law and equity, and the relevant community all merge in *Fletcher v. Peck*. Marshall described an indefeasible national common denominator where the only relevant community was the national community of citizens. Each individual citizen in this "empire" could expect the same protection against any and all attempts by any majority or any other power to annihilate his absolute, vested rights. The battlefield having been leveled, American law now was ready for fair, equal, and traditional legal contests. The transmogrification of a small democratic republic into a broad capitalistic nation could proceed smoothly. What else need be said?

There was one questionable item that caused Marshall's entire approach to change drastically. Dropping the sure-footed protection of absolute individual rights, Marshall suddenly became a blatant trimmer and compromiser when he addressed the problem of "the extinguishment of part of the Indian title"[57] to the lands in question. After a notably sparse recitation of official British colonial actions pertaining to the land, including the explicit reservation of the lands for the Indians in 1763 in conjunction with a prohibition against settlement or purchase by anyone else, Marshall alleged only that the 1763 reservation "appears to be a temporary arrangement."[58] Subsequent commissions to Georgia's colonial governors were enough, he claimed, to remove any doubt. Moreover, because the question of whether "vacant lands"[59] belonged to the national government or to the states had threatened the new American confederacy after the Revolution and had produced difficult compromises, that status quo must stand.

Marshall concluded, as he had begun, by protesting too much. In this first Supreme Court opinion to discuss the claims of American Indians, a blatant double standard marked his interpretation. Marshall ended his opinion with the argument that "the nature of the Indian title, which is certainly to be respected by all courts, until it be legitimately extinguished, is not such as to be absolutely repugnant to seisin in fee on the part of the state."[60] In other words, the nature of the Indian title was so different from the nature of the white man's title that the Indian title carried no absolute or vested right. Therefore, Marshall maintained, respect for the Indian title did not preclude government power to buy and sell or grant away the land in fee if that is what the government wished to do.

While recent commentators on Native American law have commented insightfully on this double-talk and its implications, Marshall's rhetorical ploy in referring to the land as "vacant" may be even more significant, though it has not been noticed.[61] To call the land "vacant" allowed logic to push Indian claims off the legal map entirely. By so declaring, the law made it so. This became a form of conquest by legal fiction. Deep-seated assumptions about property could and did undergird such a move. Those settlers and lawmakers who followed Marshall delighted in their freedom to acquire land by such legal manipulation.

The ability to take land that is not occupied or used by its owner by "prescription" has long been and remains a crucial building block in Anglo-American property law. Yet this doctrine rests on a concept of change and active use that competes with and undermines the basic role of settled expectations in property. The ability of a newcomer to take property by prescription has its foundation, according to Holmes, in "the position of the person who gains [rights], not in that of the loser." Holmes linked this newcomer's ability to trump older but inactive ownership to something "further back than the first recorded history." Its basis can be traced to "the deepest instincts of man." Holmes asserted that law could ask for no better justification. When something—property or an opinion—is held and used for a long time, Holmes continued, it "takes root in your being and cannot be torn away without your resenting the act and trying to defend yourself, however you came by it." If you fail to demonstrate such active identification with something you own and do not warn away or stop others who wish to use your property, "in justice" you lose it.[62] Holmes thus emphasized the importance of active connection between land and man. But the nexus in Holmes's exploitative world contrasts sharply with the complex connections between community and nature that Faulkner celebrated in "The Bear." Holmes applauded the process of development that Faulkner vehemently decried.

The legal doctrine of prescription, allegedly so instinctual as to stretch back further than recorded history, is simply a conclusory way of saying that use and development ought to prevail. The doctrine creates an even stronger legal case when the property to be seized can be deemed "vacant." To hold property in fee merges with the need to use it actively. This kind of protected expectation in property is intertwined with the dominant American myth of progress that Faulkner directly challenged in "The Bear."

There is a basic historical and etymological link between holding land in fee and owing fealty (in the sense of homage and service) to the sovereign. Land held in fee was held in theory under a royal grant, because the monarch owned all property within the royal jurisdiction. In return, a vertical hierarchical system demanded identification with one's lord to the extent of swearing "to love what he loves and to hate what he hates."[63] In using, abusing, and creatively destroying English land law and history, Marshall performed a crucial juggling act.

Marshall embraced a great national commercial republic, and this meant constitutionalizing the claims of huge land speculators, himself included. In his quest for free speculative individualism, he tried to forswear the authority of any power to recall the past. Marshall's craftiness was so great that his linked series of breathtakingly bold fictions managed to revoke the factual past and put in its place an autonomous and absolute individual property right. The steps he took helped channel American law and legend in crucial ways. Marshall's *Fletcher* opinion added to the prevalent denial of history against which Faulkner and Isaac McCaslin struggled.

Coda: Disagreement from within

Marshall's reversal of his natural law/absolute right of property premise when it came to applying it to Indian claims was too much for Justice William Johnson. Johnson, who had not yet begun to earn his title as the Court's first dissenter, wrote separately, though he concurred in the result. Johnson destroyed the logic-chopping in Marshall's constitutional argument and his treatment of the status of Indian tribes and land by attacking him on both broad and narrow flanks.

Johnson first argued for a more sweeping vision of natural law principles. He agreed that Georgia could not revoke its own grants, but he went even further, putting his trust "on a general principle, on the reason and nature of things."[64] He thus entirely rejected Marshall's far-fetched reliance on the text of the Constitution. The unwritten principle Johnson invoked was so broad, he insisted it "will impose laws even on the deity."[65]

Johnson also proclaimed that once an individual has a vested property right, that right is so important that it "becomes intimately blended with his existence, as essentially so as the blood that circulates through his system."[66] That is a potent natural right principle indeed. But Johnson also suggested a series of important distinctions that Marshall's opinion elided. They included the differences between power and interest and between the right of jurisdiction and the right of soil.

Johnson said he could imagine no solid objection to Marshall's adoption of Blackstone's technical definition of "contract," even after contemplating strikingly modern-sounding concerns about "[t]he etymology, the classical signification, and the civil law idea of the word." What he did object to, however, was the absolutism with which Marshall approached contract claims and the notion that the state might not impair contracts. Johnson here attacked from the narrow flank. He could have been a modern legal realist when he pointed out the "extreme difficulty" in determining "where to draw the line, or how to define or limit the words, 'obligation of contracts'." He objected to stretching constitutional language to restrict state powers in favor of private rights and—in a style remarkably similar to the language of *West Coast Hotel* and the post-1937 Supreme Court[67]—complained of judicial restriction of "that right which every community must exercise, of possessing itself of the property of the individual, when necessary for public uses."[68] The states remained relevant communities within the American Union, and Marshall's avid nationalism threatened to make local authorities unable to deal with local problems at the local level.

United States v. Cruikshank (1876): The Colfax Riot

The *Cruikshank* case affords a tragic example of how hard it is to achieve significant change. The pinched legal response to the Colfax, Louisiana, race riot on Easter Sunday of 1873 tells us a great deal about irrepressible racial violence in the Reconstruction period. Moreover, the setting and the story of the Colfax riot are Faulknerian in several senses. The violent events in this remote Louisiana county resonate directly with the period of Isaac McCaslin's youth and with his vanishing rural Southern world. The racial tensions that exploded into open warfare in 1873 were hardly unique. The bloody events along the Red River underscore the intertwining of race, face-to-face relationships, and violence. This aspect of communal life forms a vital undercurrent throughout *Go Down, Moses* and most of Faulkner's work. Finally, the Colfax riot together with the Court's parsimonious response illuminate the malign and ineluctable aspect of community solidarity. As in Faulkner, terrible facts and the prevalent lack of concern or acquiescence in them demonstrate that the absence of accountability can have horrific consequences. Lawlessness occurs in many guises; sometimes it is even enfolded in judicial robes.

The Supreme Court's narrow, formalistic holding in the wake of the riot provides evidence of the dangers of legal abstractions. Contemporary accounts and an extended congressional investigation capture a sense of the unsettled and violently contested basic political and legal norms in Reconstruction Louisiana. In this context the opinion in *United States v. Cruikshank* did a great deal to legitimate vigilante justice and to hasten the rise of Jim Crow. *Cruikshank* simply ignored the kind of intense violence Faulkner describes that can occur between people who know each other all too well. Instead of dealing with that reality, the Court found false security in syllogisms about federalism. The justices thereby ignored civics and civilians alike.

Accounts of events in the rough world of Grant Parish, Louisiana, in the early 1870s include stories by white survivors who still gloried in their actions half a century later. They might serve as a useful corrective for those among us who are excessively deferential to local community values.

In 1873 the rich plantation land along the Red River, 350 miles northwest of New Orleans, had achieved parish status so recently that it was named after President Grant, and its tiny parish seat bore the name of Vice President Schuyler Colfax.[69] The peculiarity of honoring Republican politicians in the middle of Reconstruction Louisiana only begins to suggest the level of discord within state and community politics. Louisiana was so bitterly divided, in fact, that after the 1872 state election two governments claimed legitimacy and neither would back down. The immediate excuse for the riot in Colfax was the attempt by Republican Governor William Pitt Kellogg to install a few of his followers, including several blacks, in local offices.

Whites in Grant and surrounding parishes organized into the White League and other paramilitary groups and proclaimed their mission to rid this "white man's country" of "Black Devils."[70] When they sought to oust the new Republican office holders, armed blacks occupied the courthouse, formerly a stable and the only brick building in Colfax at the time. They set about digging trenches and establishing a defensive perimeter.

Early on Easter morning, armed whites from nearby parishes joined local whites in surrounding the defenders of the courthouse. In the early afternoon, the whites launched an all-out, two-front attack on "the unsuspecting darkies," even using cannon fire from a boat on the river. They quickly defeated the black defenders. After the blacks surrendered, the courthouse was surrounded and burned, immolating dozens of blacks trapped inside. Many of those who tried to escape were shot as they ran from the building and others "were ridden down in the fields and shot without mercy."[71] Other blacks were shot or bayoneted long after their capture. Estimates of the number of blacks killed range from sixty-nine to over one hundred, with some accounts numbering the dead at nearly four hundred. Apparently only two white men died in the riot.[72]

Some whites murdered blacks at random while others used the opportunity to carry out personal vendettas. As one of the whites recalled, for example, in an account Faulkner might have used: "Captain Dave Paul and Mr. Yawn came walking by me and says, 'We got most of them, but the man which we want. We don't see him among the dead.' I says, 'Examine them carefully, maybe you can find him in there [the garden].' We walked down the line and there was a negro with his hat pulled down over his eyes. Jim Yawn was laying for the man who killed Jeff [in 1871]. Yawn lifted his hat up and grabbed him by the coat and says, 'I got you,' and took him about twenty steps away and shot him.'"[73]

Remarkably, federal troops captured some of the white perpetrators, and a few courageous federal officials sought criminal indictments in the wake of the riot. They even managed to convince a jury to convict William Cruikshank and two others, out of nearly one hundred defendants tried on numerous counts of interfering with the civil rights of citizens of the United States of African descent, for violations of the Enforcement Act of May 31, 1870. The jury would not convict Cruikshank and his two co-defendants of murder, but they did convict them on sixteen counts of conspiracy to "injure, oppress, threaten, or intimidate" several named "persons of African descent" in their exercise of a number of rights of citizenship.

In the lower court opinion, Judge Woods and Justice Bradley (sitting on circuit) disagreed about the appropriate scope of the 1870 Enforcement Act. Bradley argued for a relatively broad interpretation, claiming that "whenever a right is guarantied by the constitution of the United States," the government has "the correlative duty . . . to protect." This duty either arises when the right is conferred or when Congress invokes its general power under the Necessary and Proper Clause of Article I. Bradley's argument created confusion. He first described rights that exist as part of a citizen's birthright, to be protected and affirmatively enforced by the state in which he is a citizen, and only guaranteed by the federal government. The Thirteenth Amendment, however, "had an affirmative operation the moment it was adopted." Indeed, the amendment abolishing slavery and involuntary servitude "enfranchised four millions of slaves." Bradley added that because "disability to be a citizen and enjoy equal rights was deemed one form or badge of servitude," the Thirteenth Amendment gave Congress the power to "place the other races on the same plane of privilege as that occupied by the white race."[74]

For Bradley, Congress' power to eliminate all forms and badges of servitude meant that federal civil rights statutes had to contain a racial *mens rea* requirement. The crucial test of federal jurisdiction thus became whether a deprivation of rights occurred because of "a design to injure a person or deprive him of his equal right of enjoying the protection of the laws, by reason of his race, color, or previous condition of servitude." The central problem with Bradley's approach is the difficulty of producing evidence that isolates race as the motivating factor. A basic failing of contemporary Thirteenth Amendment and equal protection doctrine, for example, is that the Court today requires proof of discriminatory motive to make out a constitutional claim.[75]

When *Cruikshank* reached the Supreme Court, however, Bradley joined a majority of the Court in invalidating the indictments on sweeping, and more destructive, grounds. Two years earlier the Court, in its first construction of the Fourteenth Amendment, used an extremely strained distinction between national and state citizenship to limit severely what constitutional claims could be premised on the Fourteenth Amendment.[76] Yet it was *Cruikshank* that ended any hope that Reconstruction law enforcement might protect blacks from the depredations, legal and illegal, directed against them across the South.[77] Chief Justice Waite's theory was breathtakingly simple. He offered a syllogism about separate spheres of sovereignty. This theory had devastating consequences for race relations over the next century.

Absolute Rights

Waite agreed that all citizens have fundamental rights. In fact, "The very highest duty of the States, when they entered into the Union under the Constitution, was to protect all persons within their boundaries in the enjoyment of these 'unalienable rights with which they were endowed by their Creator.'"[78] Moreover, the right of the people peaceably to assemble for lawful purposes "existed long before the adoption of the Constitution of the United States."[79] The trick was that all such fundamental rights, so basic as to be preconstitutional, could be vindicated only by some preconstitutional authority. Sovereignty for such purposes, Waite alleged, "rests alone with the States."[80] Thus the very fact that any right "is and always has been, one of the attributes of citizenship under a free government" precluded the federal government from doing anything to protect such a right.[81]

Balancing

Like Marshall in *Fletcher v. Peck,* Waite saw no need to strike a balance. His was also an either/or world. The federal and state governments are distinct, with citizens owing allegiance separately to each.

"The powers which one possess, the other does not. . . . The citizen . . . owes allegiance to the two departments, so to speak, and within their respective spheres must pay the penalties which each exacts for disobedience to its laws. In return, he can demand protection from each within its jurisdiction." No variegated, overlapping pluralism here. Neither the Civil War nor the amendments and statutes that followed it altered this geometry, this essential fact of American legal life. Occasionally there might be some apparent overlap, but government was made up of decisively separate spheres. The duty of the courts was to keep them carefully apart.

Community

In *Cruikshank,* the state is the essential community, and the federal government possesses only limited powers. The bloody proof that there was no law and no lawful government with enforcement powers in Louisiana in 1873 was not relevant to the Court. Even the blatant racial motivation for the crimes committed, including mass murder despite the white flag of surrender, had no relevance unless and until the only significant community, the sovereign state of Louisiana, chose to make it so. If that community could not or would not act, the Court would allow a Hobbesian world to prevail. Deep-seated custom and the untrammeled use of fear and violence to sustain it demonstrated the danger in leaving matters to local control and in acquiescing in whatever communal norms and practices might dominate in a raw struggle for power. Rights would be defined by the passions of the crowd, and law would be established by the victors.

Conclusion

In the above cases the judges manipulated abstract fictions with devastating results for the Chickasaw and the other tribes in the Southeast and for other American Indians and blacks throughout the nation.[82] There was and is iron beneath the hermeneutic trappings. The importance of the conjunction of a government of laws and a government of people can hardly be overstated. Yet only the literary intuition of someone of the caliber of Faulkner can help us comprehend some of the ways that concepts of contract and property, and other community norms, complicate and confine no matter what courts say or do.

Although the Supreme Court eviscerated most of the Reconstruc-

tion era's federal civil rights statutory package in *Cruikshank* and
many cases that followed, the remnant that survived and that is most
frequently invoked today is codified as 42 U.S.C. Sec. 1983. Literally
thousands of federal cases each year are anchored in Section 1983,
derived from the Ku Klux Klan Act of 1871, but it is striking that this
section still contains forgotten language. Section 1983 provides a civil
rights remedy for all citizens against anyone "who, under color of any
statute, ordinance, regulation, *custom or usage*" (emphasis added)
subjects any United States citizen "to the deprivation of any rights,
privileges, or immunities secured by the Constitution and laws."
Astonishingly, this clear textual reference to "custom and usage" has
no legal bite whatsoever.[83] Any customary denials and prevalent usages that deprive citizens of their rights are still not legally relevant
today. It is a measure of the success of the world of laws, but not
people, which Marshall and Waite set about to construct, that the
customs and usages of our diverse and sometimes oppressive communities have no role whatsoever in contemporary federal law concepts
of civil rights and liberties.

Faulkner documented deprivations and depredations perpetrated at
the ground level of community. He explored the threads of action and
omission that are "frail as truth and impalpable as equators yet cable-
strong to bind for life." Faulkner's awareness of overlapping community practices, in which interdependent people driven by passions and
the burdens of varying histories cooperate and clash, is beyond the
purview of "tradition" that dominates contemporary American law.
Yet these constraints—devastating, frequently oppressive but also necessary to our individual identities—are of our own making. Notwithstanding the current Supreme Court, we ought not to be able any
longer to think seriously of impermeable separate governmental
spheres, nor of the separateness of the public realm from private
existence.

Sam Fathers taught Isaac McCaslin that to get one's bearings, you
must know where you have been and where you want to go. While "no
man is ever free,"[84] even to attempt to cross the lines that confine us,
as Isaac tried to do, requires both historical awareness and the ability
to dream. Any idealist's dream needs to be steered by history. Inescapably, we are all heirs, no matter how much we struggle to be free of the
past. A sense of inheritance is necessary alongside awareness that the
past contains unfulfilled promises. In his famous "I Have a Dream"
speech in 1963, for example, Martin Luther King, Jr. proclaimed "the

fierce urgency of now" and announced that he had come to Washington with hundreds of thousands of other people "to cash a check"[85] of unredeemed past promises. As King put it, "When the architects of our Republic wrote the magnificent words of the Constitution and the Declaration of Independence, they were signing a promissory note to which every American was to fall heir. This note was a promise that all men—yes, black men as well as white men—would be guaranteed the unalienable rights of life, liberty and the pursuit of happiness."

King thus merged the demands of past and future and of religious vision and commercial paper. Yet he did so without Faulkner's underlying bleakness. And he still echoed Faulkner's sense of interdependent freedom even as he tried to move beyond anything Faulkner dreamed possible. King praised whites who "have come to realize that their freedom is inextricably bound to our freedom. We cannot walk alone." Costly and even futile as it no doubt was, Isaac McCaslin's effort to relinquish his inheritance proclaimed a similar sense of interdependent obligation across time. What remains most deeply appealing about Isaac is probably his methodology, rather than his eccentric, perhaps utopian effort to reform or escape communal guilt. Isaac's careful attention to the impact of the past and his empathetic understanding of history led him to resist the flow of his community's present ways. He acted despite awareness that "no man is ever free," even though he knew freedom probably would be unbearable.

In contrast, the Supreme Court has tended to rely both historically and in its recent output on abstract undifferentiated tradition, as it did in *Fletcher* and *Cruikshank*. The justices perpetrate grandiose legal fictions, apparently unconcerned about historical facts and willing to ignore the way communities actually interlock. Abstractions transcend real conflicts. An invented, unified tradition trumps ingrained customs and usages, in a world populated with theoretical individuals who stand freely, firmly, and voluntarily upon absolute rights that must be protected in either/or judicial decisions. The justices repeatedly insist, ironically, that they are bound by the past. Moreover, they delight to announce that they lack discretion to consider the present and future impact of their decisions in terms of doing justice.[86]

In literature, as in law, we cannot escape communal inheritances. As Robert Cover said, "History corrects for the scale of heroics that we would otherwise project upon the past. Only myth tells us who we would become; only history can tell us how hard it will really be to become that."[87] Both law and literature are forms of art. Both ought to combine history and myth. Keen awareness of what has come before is necessary, but passion and vision also are needed to improve upon the past.

This helps explain a striking thing: despite Amos's terrifying message, he was not killed and is not forgotten. His demand for justice in relational terms has endured. It remains integral to the variegated, misshapen, multifarious communities that fetter and link us all as we struggle to move forward.

7 Involuntary Groups and the Role of History in American Law

All Nature's difference keeps all Nature's peace.

Alexander Pope[1]

This history goes forward and goes backward, as occasion calls. Nimble center, circumference elastic you must have.

Herman Melville[2]

History is crucial in identifying the groups that warrant particular legal protection.[3] Yet it is common to try to cut off the past so as to approach the future with wholehearted optimism. In the United States we are notorious for assuming that the past has emphatically passed. Still, it is worthy of notice when even the justices of the United States Supreme Court are willfully blind to the burdens of the past. Judges today evince a profoundly ahistorical approach to groups that most obviously warrant special judicial concern on the basis of past wrongs.

During the civil rights struggles of the 1870s and the 1960s minority groups attempted to force the United States and its courts to deliver on glittering historical promises. At such times various judges chose the patina of neutrality over the demands of equality. Today, many leading judges also opt for a static, abstract ideal over what is complex, contextual, and historically real. The pleasant judicial assumption that all citizens of the United States have reached parity now extends even to racial matters. A majority of the justices go so far as to suggest that a combination of the federal Constitution and their judicial oaths compels them to reject solicitude for dispossessed and victimized groups.

My criticism of judicial ahistoricism differs from the more commonplace critique of "law office history," though surely there is validity to that criticism as well.[4] I do not claim that what has come before should automatically continue,[5] nor that the past reveals a line of clear, inescapable development. In discussing legal claims rooted in the special histories and perspectives of members of discrete and insular minorities, I will not argue that such claims should always prevail. But memory does reveal past burdens, as well as the richness of resources available to deal with our troublesome heritage. The diverse backgrounds of the groups with which we define ourselves and are defined by others help constitute the context a judge ought to consider even when—perhaps particularly when—legal arguments challenge complacent faith in the sweeping generalities of the legal status quo.

Legal claims may involve the definition of families, tribes, and racial, ethnic, national and religious groups. In combination or in opposition, these relationships inescapably define who we are. Such groups sometimes are bunched together under the rubric of "involuntary associations."[6] This appellation lacks definitional precision, however. It also tends to deprecate the vital, albeit almost infinitely varied, importance of such collectivities in constituting individual identities. Still, it is important to distinguish generally "innate" or virtually "immutable" group characteristics from the "voluntary associations" we have already discussed. In the hands of American judges committed to seeing only how individuals play life's game, these fundamental social groupings are wild cards. Sometimes "natural associations" trump everything else. Recently, however, judges have taken to sweeping them off the table as superfluous, worthless, or worse.

Only eighteen years after the formal abolition of slavery, as Jim Crow began to dominate the South, the United States Supreme Court declared it high time that the former slave "take[] the rank of mere citizen, and cease[] to be the special favorite of the law."[7] Today, again for the sake of presumed equality, the Court cuts off consideration of past racial wrongs. The Court's own complicity in legitimating segregation has been expunged.[8] Now everyone is presumed formally equal, unencumbered by the past. All groups—voluntary and involuntary, white and black, corporations and Indian tribes—compete fairly in the political marketplace. Indeed, it would violate judicial neutrality to show special concern even for a group with a long history of being victimized. Special concern, in fact, may be unacceptable. It denies equality in the great race of life. In their enthusiasm for a world of free individuals without any past, judges have begun to resemble those "most unlearned of most learned men" whom Maitland described as "rigorous logicians, afraid of no conclusion that was implicit in their premisses."[9] The recent, extremely parsimonious approach of the United States Supreme Court to "natural" groupings such as family, tribe, and racial, ethnic, and national identities demonstrates that these categories are neither natural nor neutral. Judges themselves play active roles in establishing and legitimating criteria that define involuntary groups.

Discrete and Insular Minorities

Equal Protection: "The Usual Last Resort of Constitutional Arguments"

In his infamous opinion for a United States Supreme Court majority in *Buck v. Bell,*[10] Justice Oliver Wendell Holmes, Jr., seized the opportunity to indulge his eugenic beliefs by upholding the sterilization of a young woman who, it was alleged, was feeble minded.[11] That holding, and the accompanying *apercu* that "three generations of imbeciles are enough,"[12] are sufficiently appalling to merit notice. But it is Holmes's reference to equal protection as "the usual last resort of constitutional arguments"[13] that requires brief consideration here. What did he mean by that?

Of course, this phrase may simply reflect Holmes's inability to resist a well-turned phrase, his love of judicial *machismo* that includes a frequent embrace of arbitrariness, his customary desire to provoke, and his interest in denigrating what appeared to be a sympathetic claim made by Carrie Buck's lawyer. But another reason may be more significant: the forgotten, aggressive use of equal protection by the activist Supreme Court of Holmes's time.

It is quite well known that during the 1920s the Court vigorously invoked the Due Process Clause of the Fourteenth Amendment to invalidate numerous state laws. Justices Holmes and Brandeis generally dissented from what they considered antidemocratic judicial intrusions against the will of popularly elected, often progressive, legislatures.[14] What has not been much noticed, however, is that for many decades, and most emphatically still in the 1920s when William Howard Taft was Chief Justice, the Supreme Court delighted to use Equal Protection as a weapon against progressive legislation.

Truax v. Corrigan[15] exemplifies the phenomenon. In 1913 the Arizona legislature passed a statute to protect labor unions. Arizona law would no longer consider peaceful picketing and the circulation of leaflets unlawful, *per se,* although federal courts and many state courts elsewhere still readily enjoined such union activity. No Arizona court would issue an injunction against peaceful union activity, unless it was deemed necessary to prevent irreparable injury. The Arizona Supreme Court upheld this new law, claiming it was a mere change in the rules of evidence. The legislature simply had eliminated a "conclusive presumption"; they did not deprive employers of vested property rights.[16]

Chief Justice Taft vehemently disagreed. His Court's majority opinion held that Arizona's attempt to protect unions violated the Equal Protection Clause of the federal Constitution.[17] The Fourteenth Amendment "was intended to secure equality of protection," Taft wrote with a Hobbesian echo, "not only for all but against all similarly situated."[18] The government had an affirmative obligation to provide protection to all against all. "Indeed," Taft proclaimed, "protection is not protection" unless the state meets this equal obligation to everyone.[19] In considering all participants in the marketplace to be "similarly situated," Taft followed mainstream equal protection doctrine. Judges had used the equality argument for decades to invalidate social and economic legislation they perceived to be "class legislation."[20] It was precisely this aggressive use of equal protection that made the concept of judicial enforcement of equality a target of ridicule for Holmes. And Holmes's facile dismissal of equality claims in 1927 generally carried the day, and most of the next decade.

Another Footnote in the Sands of Time: April 25, 1938

The spring of 1938 rescued equality claims from Holmes's dustbin of constitutional history. The Supreme Court began to suggest a new approach to prejudice and discrimination against groups. Because of two judicial pronouncements, April 25, 1938, probably was as significant to American law as May 17, 1954, when the Supreme Court unanimously invalidated official segregation in public schools in *Brown v. Board of Education*.[21] Unlike *Brown*, however, the judicial handiwork that April day attracted virtually no public attention.[22] The two key decisions involved obscure plaintiffs and seemed to decide only issues of "lawyers' law." Yet these two cases marked a watershed. That cloudy spring day, a new majority of the Court struggled to reduce general activism by federal judges on the one hand, while encouraging judicial intervention in a select category of cases on the other. That approach has dominated constitutional discourse in the United States ever since.

The first decision, *Erie Railroad v. Tompkins*,[23] need not detain us long. (Because Brandeis's decision was a watershed in federalism and

civil procedure, it remains part of virtually every American law student's troubled introduction to the perplexity of trying to "think like a
lawyer" in our peculiar federal judicial system.)[24] The day's other crucial judicial pronouncement suggested that the federal Constitution
might compel judges to play an activist role when they review discrimination against "discrete and insular minorities." Ironically, this influential idea appeared only in footnote four to an obscure opinion
written by Justice Harlan Fiske Stone, *United States v. Carolene Products.*[25] Its three paragraphs suggested a new approach that was to
prove crucial in the treatment of minorities in American law.[26] The
brief description of the footnote that follows will also illuminate the
pervasive retrenchment from this perspective in recent Supreme Court
decisions.

Carolene Products

The *Carolene Products* holding was part of a trend toward a new,
limited role for federal courts. In contrast to the rash of decisions that
had invalidated important elements of the New Deal and triggered
Franklin Delano Roosevelt's court-packing scheme in 1937, the new
judicial outlook proclaimed extreme judicial deference to the social
and economic policies of the popularly elected branches. Justice
Stone's majority opinion sought to consolidate the developing
restraints on judicial intervention in economic matters.[27] The opinion
suggested an almost ironclad presumption in favor of the constitutionality of all social and economic legislation, including Congress' power
to regulate the quality as well as the price of milk shipped in interstate
commerce.[28] In footnote four, however, Stone suggested several categories of constitutional claims that might deprive government action
of the extreme deference it otherwise should enjoy.

The first paragraph, added at the urging of Chief Justice Hughes,
voiced special judicial concern for rights explicit in the text of the
Constitution. This individualistic, interpretivist position involved less
of a judicial leap than the possibility, mentioned in the rest of the
footnote, of additional grounds for judicial refusal to defer to judgments of other governmental branches.

The second paragraph urged special judicial skepticism regarding
challenges to any state action that might interfere with "those political
processes which can ordinarily be expected to bring about repeal of
undesirable legislation." This paragraph appears to rest on the premise
of a regulated social life gradually purifying itself of undesirable leg-

islation through well-working political mechanisms. To illustrate the ways in which clogged political channels might be grounds for unusually exacting judicial review, Stone cited earlier decisions invalidating restrictions on the right to vote, the dissemination of information, freedom of political association, and peaceable assembly.[29]

The footnote's third and final paragraph is the most important for our purposes. Government action directed at particular religious, national, or racial minorities, Stone said, might merit special judicial scrutiny. Hence "prejudice against discrete and insular minorities," Stone asserted, in a language that was notably cautious and abstract, "may be a special condition, which tends seriously to curtail the operation of those political processes ordinarily to be relied upon to protect minorities, and which may call for a correspondingly more searching judicial inquiry."[30]

Judicial and scholarly disagreement has continued and intensified about when and what sort of activist role is appropriate for judges confronting claims by "discrete and insular" groups.[31] The main arguments centering on footnote four can be put in terms of two questions: first, if we assume that the category "discrete and insular minorities" includes African-Americans, what, if any, other groups ought to be included? Second, does paragraph three of the footnote essentially overlap with the footnote's other paragraphs, or does it supplement them by suggesting additional judicial solicitude for certain groups?[32]

The minorities Stone had in mind were longstanding outgroups, groups in which membership itself often became a cause for mistrust or hostility. These unmeltable groups experienced "special vulnerability" to "predictable perversions of majoritarian government."[33] In other words, they repeatedly have been made scapegoats. Majoritarian politics has been—and still is—manipulated through explicit or encoded racism. African-Americans seemed the paradigmatic "footnote four" minority. Past discrimination and present membership yield current injury.

Moreover, this is a special injury, to which attention must be paid. The injury is uniquely prone to being exacerbated, either by invidious legislation or by the absence of legislation. This makes apparent judicial neutrality not neutral but complicit in perpetuating past wrongs.

Footnote four appeared the month after Hitler took over Austria, in the year that Stalin's show trials disposed of the last of the old Bolsheviks, and just as Italian and German aid decisively turned the tide for Franco in the Spanish Civil War.[34] Even within the largely isolationist United States, labor battles and ethnic and racial tension added to what seemed a particularly explosive spring.[35] As Robert Cover put it, "[M]inorities . . . in the sense we use the term today—religious, ethnic, national, and racial minorities—became a special object of judicial protection only with footnote four, which was written at almost the exact moment when majoritarianism became the dominant constitutional perspective."[36] The paragraph suggested the need for imposing judicial limits on permissible democratic action, and even inaction, that perpetuates the burdens of past victimization of special groups.

As new groups, such as mentally retarded, physically handicapped, and lesbian and gay citizens began to allege discriminatory treatment, the meaning of "discrete and insular minorities" became increasingly problematic.[37] Moreover, determining what groups are "similarly situated"—the *Grundnorm* for assuring them legal equality—depends on where you are when you happen to look. The Court vividly illustrated this when it rejected an equal protection challenge to the denial of state disability benefits to pregnant women on the grounds that the distinction drawn by California was between "pregnant women and non-pregnant persons," rather than between women and men.[38] Despite a flood of equal protection decisions, the legal argument still focuses on whether it is appropriate to relegate those who claim discrimination at the hands of the majority to the economic or political marketplace.

Most of the justices today apparently share in the pervasive national nostalgia for a simpler, freer, and happier time-that-never-was. Now only a smoking gun—that is, incontrovertible proof of a specific racially discriminatory motive that an individual plaintiff can tie directly to his or her own plight—will move the Court to acknowledge discrimination adequate to make out a constitutional case.[39] Judges thus simplify their work by deferring to the outcome of any social struggle, and each citizen has only himself to blame if he loses. The sobering history of different groups has been canceled. The dream of equality for all individuals already has arrived.

The Fifty-Year Gap: Freedom from Association with Guilt

Patterson v. McLean Credit Union I: "External Criteria"

To love history is to love coincidence. Fifty years to the day after *Carolene Products,* the United States Supreme Court announced, by a 5–4 vote, that a case involving alleged racial harassment in the workplace, *Patterson v. McLean Credit Union,*[40] would be set down for reargument. The Court on its own initiative asked the lawyers to address a question not previously raised: should the Court overrule a 1976 decision, *Runyon v. McCrary,* that held that the 1866 Civil Rights Act prohibited private schools from excluding qualified children solely because of their race?[41] This question touched off a passionate public debate unusual even in a nation obsessed with the Supreme Court. The language used by the five justices who voted to pose that question for reargument merits close attention. The brief *per curiam* opinion captures the recrudescence of an extreme, abstract individualistic ethos in American courts today.

To begin at the conclusion: the *per curiam* opinion ended by responding to an argument, made in both dissenting opinions,[42] that the Court should be particularly loath to upset an important statutory precedent that favors civil rights plaintiffs. The majority answered:

> We do not believe that the Court may recognize any such exception to the abiding rule that it treat all litigants equally: that is, that the claim of any litigant for the application of a rule to its case should not be influenced by the Court's view of the worthiness of the litigant in terms of extralegal criteria. We think this is what Congress meant when it required each Justice or judge of the United States to swear to 'administer justice without respect to persons, and do equal right to the poor and to the rich . . .'[43]

Three distinct though interrelated reasons make the majority's rhetoric in *Patterson* both illuminating and troubling. First, the *per curiam* opinion expressed the notion that race—the very criterion which constitutes the basis for civil rights claims—is fungible with other "extralegal criteria." A higher judicial duty requires judges to treat all litigants abstractly and, thereby, to treat them formally as equal.

Second, the majority apparently believed the specific judicial obligation to do "equal right to the poor and to the rich" to be synonymous with the idea that all litigants should be treated as if they are exactly the same. The majority justices insisted that the judicial obligation to do "equal right" requires judges to be blind to what they know as women and men. They would have to ignore different starting places, significant encumbrances, and the weight of the past. This view rejects a basic point made by John Winthrop in the early days of the Massachusetts Bay Colony: "If the same penalty hits a rich man, it pains him not, it is not affliction to him, but if it lights upon a poor man, it breaks his back."[44] Litigants are not interchangeable ciphers.

They are defined by their histories and their group associations. Thus an earlier Court noted, as it struck down state court enforcement of restrictive covenants in 1948, "Equal protection of the laws is not achieved by indiscriminate imposition of inequalities."[45]

Finally, the *per curiam* opinion went further than allowing the "indiscriminate imposition of inequalities." It suggested that indiscriminate treatment is obligatory. Upon close reading, however, the judicial oath the majority invoked does not define "equal right" as lack of awareness of group differences. Nor does it hint of distinguishing intrinsic from extrinsic characteristics. The meaning of "respect to persons" is considerably more complex in terms of both etymology and history than the *per curiam* opinion allows.[46] Yet the Court aggressively presumed that no approach to justice would allow judges to protect the downtrodden. This willed obliviousness toward history coexists awkwardly with recent judicial activism in constructing the very categories the judges elsewhere consider immutable, natural groupings such as race, tribes, and families.

Patterson v. McClean Credit Union II

In *Patterson II* the Court unanimously agreed not to overrule *Runyon v. McCrary*.[47] The justices reaffirmed that section 1981 prohibits racial discrimination in the making and enforcement of private contracts. But they disagreed vehemently about the extent of that prohibition. Justice Kennedy's majority opinion held that "the right to make contracts does not extend, as a matter of either logic or semantics, to conduct by the employer after the contract relation has been established, including breach of the terms of the contract or imposition of discriminatory working conditions."[48] On this formalistic view of contract law, the Court ignored both the substance and the historical context of the 1866 Civil Rights Act, passed primarily to protect newly freed slaves. That was strange, given the historic backdrop. Congress had premised the 1866 Act on its new power under the Thirteenth Amendment, declared to be ratified only the previous December.[49] The newly freed slaves hardly had the time to take advantage of their initial opportunities to make and enforce contracts with equal bargaining power. Lengthy congressional hearings and debates concerned ways to guarantee equality, particularly because of extensive evidence of virulent, racially based harassment of free contractual relationships in the South.

Justice Kennedy not only failed to heed this historic context but belittled it. Kennedy proclaimed, at the conclusion of his majority opinion, that the Court was not "signaling one inch of retreat from Congress' policy to forbid discrimination in the private, as well as the public, sphere." "Nevertheless," he added, "in the areas of private discrimination, to which the ordinance of the Constitution does not directly extend," the Court must play a role "limited to interpreting what Congress may do and has done." By diminishing the amendment that abolished *private* slavery and involuntary servitude throughout the nation, and by declaring that it was not a direct part of the Constitution's "ordinance" (whatever that means), the majority led not a retreat but a rout.

The Inversion of Footnote Four

My bleak view of *Patterson* is underscored by several other recent civil rights decisions by the Supreme Court. *City of Richmond v. J. A. Croson Co.*[50] is most revealing. In invalidating a Richmond, Virginia, city council plan that set aside 30 percent of city contracts for minority businesses, the majority noted: "The dream of a Nation of equal citizens in a society where race is irrelevant to personal opportunity and achievement would be lost in a mosaic of shifting preferences based on inherently unmeasurable claims of past wrongs."[51] To avoid mosaic law, therefore, the majority found it necessary to restrict remedial efforts by state and local entities to situations in which the effects of identified discrimination within the relevant jurisdiction could be specifically demonstrated. Otherwise, "racial politics" would prevail.[52] The history of Richmond, the capital of the Confederacy and a leading site in resistance to school integration, was thus put aside.

As Justice Marshall pointed out in passionate dissent, when the majority adopted strict scrutiny for the first time in the context of an equal protection challenge to race-conscious remedial measures, it had done something radical. The Court had now ignored the profound difference between "governmental actions that themselves are racist, and governmental actions that seek to remedy the effects of prior racism or to prevent neutral governmental activity from perpetuating the effects of such racism."[53] Because the battle against racism has hardly been won, Marshall argued, race remains germane in constitutional law "precisely because race remains dismayingly relevant in American life."[54]

This is not to say that issues of affirmative action are easy—they are gut-wrenchingly difficult. In this case, though, the economic interest of a white-owned contractor, curiously the only bidder for the relevant city contract, seemed a bizarre occasion for aggressive protection of the equal dignity and respect of the individual plaintiff. But the central failure of the Court's decision lay in its willingness to operate in a vacuum, to wrench Richmond and its attempt to remedy past wrongs entirely out of the specific historical setting of those wrongs. To Justice Scalia, who concurred in the judgment, "The relevant proposition is not that it was blacks, or Jews, or Irish who were discriminated against, but that it was individual men and women, 'created equal,' who were discriminated against."[55]

In emphasizing the need for specific proof and individualism, in denigrating group identity as a relevant factor, and in rushing to jettison racial history as relevant to current reality, *Patterson* and *Croson* illustrate the complete rejection of the footnote four approach. Indeed, *Croson* comes perilously close to resuscitating *Truax v. Corrigan*. The majority aggressively employed what it claimed were neutral equal protection principles to invalidate reform measures not to their liking. Concern for "discrete and insular minorities" is gone.[56] In its place, a white-owned business now may trigger strict judicial scrutiny of a remedial government contracting scheme.

Involuntary Groups as Judicial Constructs

Tales of Origins: Families and Tribes

Much law is devoted to macadamizing and pulverizing.[57] Our essential perception involves individuals on one side of the scales of justice and agencies of the state on the other. The role of courts is to balance between the two. To introduce even a third component seems unacceptable: it cannot be handled neatly in the either/or world of legal winners and losers. We picture Justice blindfolded.[58] But if she could see, she would need powerful bifocals.

The current Supreme Court has emphasized the need to demonstrate particular individual harm in decisions ranging from who may enter a courtroom to who leaves with a death sentence.[59] Almost despite itself, however, the Court frequently must deal with groups that anchor individual identities. In several decisions in the 1988 Term, for example, the justices wrestled with the active role of law in the construction of family units. The Court also confronted several cases involving Native American tribes, social groupings so anomalous that their stories generally are omitted from American constitutional law accounts.[60] The deeply paradoxical approaches the Court took in its decisions about families and tribes illustrate the importance of thinking more clearly about involuntary groups. Surprisingly, so-called conservative judges do not accept what they believe to be natural. Categories such as parent-child relationships at birth, genetics, and ethnicity are decidedly problematic in themselves. Yet these judges use such categories as essentialist decisive factors.

In a decision handed down the same day as *Patterson* II, Justice Scalia's plurality opinion celebrated "the historic respect—indeed, sanctity would not be too strong a term—traditionally accorded to the relationships that develop within the unitary family."[61] But the Court's proclaimed devotion to "historic respect" did not respect history. It actually honored only abstract legal categories. In *Michael H. v. Gerald D.* the Court upheld California's conclusive presumption that precluded a biological father from introducing as evidence blood tests that provided clear evidence of his paternity—paternity that he and the mother had acknowledged but that he now wished to establish legally. California's legislative presumption, grounded in the common law, was that in a marital relationship the husband must be presumed the father of any child born to the mother during the marriage.[62] This legal construct prevailed over undisputed contrary facts. It did not matter to the Court that the child in question—she was eight years old at the time of the decision—joined her biological father in his constitutional challenge to California's irrebuttable presumption. California thus precluded the "real" father and daughter from continuing their relationship unless the other parties permitted them to do so outside the framework of the law.

Scalia was undoubtedly snide when he said, "The facts of the case are, we must hope, extraordinary."[63] But his sneering turned out to be essential to the plurality's approach. "California law, like nature itself, makes no provisions for dual fatherhood," Scalia added.[64] In the face of a law-and-nature dichotomy, he chose California law over nature without further ado.[65]

The due process claim by the natural father and his daughter could not be upheld, Scalia claimed, because the liberty they invoked lacked roots "in history and tradition."[66] Indeed, to avoid the breakdown of the rule of law he believed to be threatened by the dissenters' pluralistic approach, Scalia asserted that there must be a rule to determine the appropriate level of historical generality to identify constitutional tradition.[67] The tradition behind the conclusive presumption was fundamental because its ancient common law roots could be traced. By contrast, the biological parent-child relationship lacked tradition.

Even if Scalia's bizarre notion of tradition as determinative were to be accepted, his narrow view of what counts as tradition in general is inadequate. Minority groups are simply left out, as are racial and ethnic mixtures, combinations and recombinations of white masters and black slaves, for example, and the diverse family structures of Native Americans, Hawaiians, and Spanish-speaking peoples. But attention to the family histories of such subgroups would demolish Scalia's happy homogenization. Perhaps because the history of families in the United States has such inconvenient jagged edges and recalcitrant chunks, Scalia chose to replace the complex past with a fairy tale tradition. His recipe produced a nondescript concoction: an imaginary master blender combined all distinct ingredients into one great, frothy, tasteless legal soup.[68]

In sharp contrast, Brennan's vehement dissent argued for an ongoing, open-ended assessment of fundamental values. Rather than view the Constitution as "a stagnant, archaic, hidebound document steeped in the prejudices and superstitions of a time long past," the Court should recognize that "[w]e are not an assimilative, homogenous society, but a facilitative, pluralistic one, in which we must be willing to abide someone else's unfamiliar or even repellent practice because the same tolerant impulse protects our idiosyncrasies."[69] Brennan condemned Scalia for "exclusively historical analysis" and for seeking the "tradition" Scalia considered determinative by "poring through dusty volumes of American history."[70] At the same time, he too readily conceded the relevant history to Scalia.

The dissenters failed to make an affirmative alternative historical case. They attacked Scalia's reliance on Mandarin texts, but they did not suggest that the past, viewed from other than the formal vantage point of law books and treatises, would disclose a different history of families. Real life histories would complement the arguments the dissenters made about the advent of reliable blood tests and changes in societal values. They explode Scalia's parochial definition of tradition.

Ironically, Brennan and Scalia were on the same side in *Mississippi Band of Choctaw v. Holyfield*[71] when the Court again rejected the claims of natural parents. Justice Brennan's majority opinion in this case had to stretch considerably to give exclusive jurisdiction to the Choctaw tribal court. Twin babies, whose formal state court adoption three years earlier was challenged by the tribe, had been adopted by nontribal parents through regular state court procedures. The children were born 200 miles away from the Choctaw reservation and had never lived on it or visited it. Their biological parents, both of them members of the tribe, voluntarily surrendered the twins for adoption a few weeks after the babies' birth and continued to appear alongside the adoptive parents to urge that the initial state court adoption not be upset. Despite all this, Brennan's latitudinarian statutory interpretation held that the domicile of the twins remained on the reservation they had never seen. Their biological parents' consistent efforts to avoid such a connection did not matter. The Court also found that Congress had intended the tribal court to have exclusive jurisdiction over the adoption of American Indian children, even when this meant reopening an adoption that had endured without problems for over three years.[72]

From the perspective of biological parents, these two decisions are surprising in themselves. As legal rulings, they are difficult to reconcile with one another and impossible to reconcile with other recent decisions that deal with the overlapping realities of family, tribe, and racial groupings. At first glance, the Court in both *Michael H.* and *Mississippi Choctaw* simply decided to defer to the judgments of the relevant legislatures, California and Congress respectively. Upon scrutiny of what the Court said as well as what it did, however, the two decisions acquire more significance. The Court majority advanced particular legal constructs of the family while ignoring the biological reality and the wishes of biological parents.[73] Elsewhere, ironically, biology and the wishes of biological parents loom large in Supreme Court decisions that deal with family and tribal units.[74]

Less than two months before *Mississippi Choctaw,* for example, the Court held that Joshua DeShaney had no constitutional basis upon which to claim protection from the state. Joshua was four years old when beatings by his father culminated in head injuries so severe that Joshua is now destined to spend the rest of his life in an institution for the severely retarded. The Court conceded that the record showed that state authorities knew of Joshua's plight. But the Court held, in an opinion by Chief Justice Rehnquist, that "While the State may have been aware of the dangers Joshua faced *in the free world,* it played no part in their creation, nor did it do anything to render him any more vulnerable to them."[75]

Rehnquist divided children in two—not at all like Solomon. Some children are in state custody; all others are in "the free world." All these free-world children are relegated to the protection of their own families and state law, or perhaps the kindness of strangers. Because Joshua DeShaney was not actually in state custody at the time he was battered, Wisconsin had no constitutional duty to protect him. As Joshua sustained beating after beating from the time he was two years old, he could rely only on the father who was beating him, because a state court had given that father custody of Joshua after his parents' divorce.[76] Though the record disclosed numerous contacts between government doctors, social workers, police, and young Joshua, Rehnquist reasoned that to hold that these interventions obliged Wisconsin to protect Joshua would weaken the rights of families and would transform the state into "the permanent guarantor of an individual's safety by having once offered him shelter."[77] According to the *DeShaney* decision, a family with custody of a child is the only source of protection for that child as a matter of constitutional law, unless and until the state formally takes or reassigns custody.

Destruction of the Tribe

It should be obvious that the extension of tribal jurisdiction in *Mississippi Choctaw* took place in a thought system ruled less by binary choices than was the free world/custody reasoning in *DeShaney*. Lest anyone think that the Court suddenly grew soft when a case involved Native American tribal rights, however, it is necessary to consider a few contrasting decisions. For example, *Hodel v. Irving*[78] can hardly be distinguished from *Mississippi Choctaw*. Both cases involved recent congressional legislation passed to protect Indian tribes. Both also arguably aided individuals by emphasizing benefits Native Americans derive from their tribal contexts. The dramatically contrasting results in the two cases suggest an unpleasant truth about the relative priority of property and children in the Court's view. In addition to *Hodel,* we have seen that other recent decisions likewise fail to concede constitutional weight to tribal entities. Respect for freedom of association is absent from these rulings.

Another decision that involved a constitutional claim by an individual Native American underscores the analytic emptiness, not to say cynicism, of the current Court's approach to minority claims. The background and litigation history of *Employment Division v. Smith,*[79] in which two members of the Native American Church were fired from their jobs and denied employment benefits because of their ritual use of peyote, is a tangled and important story in itself, but it need not detain us. What was particularly significant about the decision, beyond its reversal of over forty years of precedent and common understanding about free exercise of religion doctrine,[80] was the double divide-and-conquer approach Justice Scalia took for the majority.

First, Scalia argued that because the Oregon law making peyote use unlawful was not motivated by a desire to harm religion, any otherwise valid law of general application could not violate free exercise rights. Scalia set about to distinguish whole batches of free exercise of religion precedents on the grounds that they all involved this right in conjunction with other constitutional rights, such as freedom of expression or freedom of the press. Free exercise claims alone had become superfluous, and all the leading free exercise precedents now were reinterpreted to cover only a "hybrid situation" of free exercise plus another fundamental right. The *Smith* case, Scalia went on to say, presented only "a free exercise claim unconnected with any communicative activity or parental right."

At first glance, Scalia appeared here to underscore the importance of freedom of association claims. He noted that "it is easy to envision a case in which a challenge on freedom of association grounds would likewise be reinforced by Free Exercise concerns."[81] But this was simply a throw-away line. Instead of attending to the history of the Native American Church, and the essential role of the group in the peyote ceremony and other rituals of the religion—which were amply described in the case—Scalia isolated the individual claimants by judicial fiat and then mechanistically used that isolation to deny that there was any group religious element in the case. The rest of his opinion in *Smith,* as well as in a number of other recent decisions, makes it quite clear that the formal addition of a freedom of association claim under the approach newly minted in *Smith* would make no difference.

In *Smith,* for example, Scalia inexplicably put aside the line of unemployment benefits precedents most on point, in which the Court protected those with religious claims. Instead, he emphasized Oregon's criminal law interest, which was simply not involved in this unemployment benefits case. Moreover, the majority now rejected the established requirement that the state demonstrate a compelling state interest when it burdens religious practice in such a context, calling this a "constitutional anomaly."[82]

Any minimally rational state claim will suffice to override competing religious claims. It is, according to the Court, a matter of basic political science. "Values that are protected against government interference through enshrinement in the Bill of Rights," Scalia explained, "are not thereby banished from the political process."[83] Although Scalia conceded that "leaving accommodation to the political process will place at a relative disadvantage those religious practices that are not widely engaged in," this was simply the "unavoidable consequence of democratic government." The Free Exercise Clause had become redundant. Appeal to majoritarian processes was the sole avenue available for the religious practices of minorities. Absent proof of a discriminatory motive, or a boost from some other First Amendment right, those claiming that their religious practices had been invaded would have to prevail at the polls, because the courts would not listen to their claims.

According to the majority, any other holding would be "courting anarchy" and would "open the prospect" of broad religious exemptions.[84] If the Court did not defer to the laws the majority imposed, the result would be one of two awful alternatives: "a system in which each conscience is a law unto itself or in which judges weigh the social importance of all laws against the centrality of religious beliefs."[85] Yet the prospect of anarchy did not disturb the Court when a single individual made a parallel claim to unemployment benefits. Illinois violated an individual's free exercise right when it denied him benefits for his unwillingness to work on his sabbath. This was so regardless of whether the individual's refusal to work on Sunday was in response to the command of a particular religious sect.[86] Sincere religious belief by an individual was the only touchstone, the unanimous Court insisted.

The rejection of free exercise claims rooted in the longstanding beliefs and practices of religious groups contrasts with respect for an entirely individualistic religious claim in *Frazee*. Together, these decisions provide yet another illustration of the way in which the contemporary American legal climate is losing sympathy with group identification.

In the modern welfare state in which government programs serve as invaluable sources of both wealth and status, purportedly neutral policies that actually impinge on the group identifications of distinct and insular minority groups should be the paradigmatic cases for special judicial scrutiny. Instead, as Justice O'Connor charged, the Court has begun to relegate "a serious First Amendment value to the barest level of minimal scrutiny that the Equal Protection Clause already provides."[87]

The Court may still accept the claims of individuals, but the majority is vigorously unsympathetic to any constitutional claims that conditions imposed on government benefits may be in conflict with the religious beliefs of members of discrete and insular groups.[88] It is true that *Smith* introduces the notion that a hybrid of such claims blended with freedom of association claims might produce a different result. The results in the Court's recent cases tell a different story. The contrast between the parallel *Smith* and *Frazee* unemployment benefits cases, and the Court's obvious lack of sympathy for group religious claims in decisions such as *Northwest Cemetery Protective Association*, suggest that the more religion is grounded in a highly structured, longstanding minority group tradition, the more likely is the Court to fear anarchy and to jettison precedents protective of minority religious practices.

In *Smith* Scalia relied on the *Gobitis*[89] decision in 1940 that upheld a mandatory school flag salute over the religious objections of Jehovah's Witnesses. He thus pointedly ignored *Barnette*,[90] the 1943 decision that explicitly overruled *Gobitis* and invalidated a mandatory salute on free exercise grounds. Just as each individual now purportedly participates freely and fairly in the economic marketplace and in the political arena, so a nation of individuals may follow any religious beliefs so long as they do so in splendid isolation. Minority religions must use the majoritarian political process to convince their fellows to grant them exemptions or to provide subsidies for their beliefs. The Court indicates that if citizens gather together and produce alternative normative sources through their groups, anarchy is threatened. To interpret the Constitution to protect the rituals and sacraments of such groups would be to slide down a slippery slope into judicial imperialism.

Construction of Racial, Ethnic, and National Groups

The basic question of who is a member of a family or a tribe is never trouble free. Likewise, judicial deference to tribal or family norms may defeat principles as important as the elimination of gender discrimination.[91] Judicial struggles to define membership in racial, ethnic, and national groups further illuminate the dangers of purported neutrality when there are important legal consequences of group identity at stake.

In contrast to the two *Patterson* opinions discussed above, the United States Supreme Court decided in 1987 that the 1866 Civil

Rights Act at issue in *Patterson* may be invoked by both Arabs and Jews to attack alleged discrimination against them. An antic sense of humor may have informed the Court's decision to consider *Saint Francis College v. Al-Khazraji*[92] and *Shaare Tefila Congregation v. Cobb*[93] together. Prior decisions had determined clearly that discrimination against whites was actionable under sections 1981 and 1982, but now the Court had to wrestle with alleged discrimination based on the plaintiffs' Arab and Jewish identities, respectively.

In *Saint Francis College,* an Arab professor alleged discrimination when a Catholic college denied him tenure. The issue, as the Court framed it, was, "whether a person of Arabian ancestry was protected from racial discrimination under Sec. 1981."[94] Justice White's answer for the unanimous Court was that it was unnecessary to determine the current racial characterization of Arabs.[95] "The understanding of 'race' in the 19th century"[96] should be decisive.

The Court sought that understanding primarily through a brief survey of nineteenth-century dictionaries and encyclopedias, supplemented by a smattering of the legislative history of Sec. 1981. Because these sources defined "race" in terms of "stock," "lineage," and "ancestry," and because encyclopedias and Congressmen alike seemed to distinguish "Arabs, Englishmen, Germans and certain other ethnic groups" from one another as separate races, the Court claimed "little trouble" in concluding "that Congress intended to protect from discrimination identifiable classes of persons who are subjected to intentional discrimination solely because of their ancestry or ethnic characteristics."[97] While White noted that distinctive physiognomy is not essential to qualify under section 1981, he added that if Al-Khazraji had claimed discrimination based "solely on the place or nation of his origin, or his religion," the statute would not have protected him.[98]

After anti-Semitic slogans were sprayed on the walls of a suburban synagogue, Jewish plaintiffs tried to claim that although "Jews are not a racially distinct group," they ought to be protected as Jews under Section 1982 because the perpetrators of the spray-painting "viewed Jews as racially distinct and were motivated by racial prejudice."[99] The Court refused to thread so fine a needle. Nevertheless, the unanimous Court, mostly by reference to its treatment of Al-Khazraji's case, held that when Section 1982 was adopted, "Jews and Arabs were among the peoples then considered to be distinct races and hence within the protection of the statute."[100]

The result, if perhaps not the reasoning, seems right in both these cases. The 1866 Civil Rights Act did seek to reach "at a minimum," as the Court of Appeals put it, "discrimination directed against an individual because he or she is genetically part of an ethnically and physiognomically distinctive sub-grouping of *homo sapiens*."[101] Yet the Court's reliance on selections from a few dictionaries and encyclopedias is glib, an example of the methodology of law-office history. Moreover, even the few snippets from the congressional debates illustrate the implausibility of the distinction White tried to draw between discrimination based on racial or ethnic characteristics and discrimination based on place or nation of origin.[102] The malleability of these categories is further underscored by their subsequent history. Nevertheless, there is obviously still resonance in calling Jews a race, for example, and it has variable weight that depends on the perspective of the identifier perhaps more than on those identified.[103] To ignore the baggage of that history is both myopic and woefully unrealistic.

"To Know . . . What We See"

During the early days of the Gilded Age, Justice Stephen Field had to decide whether it was constitutional for the San Francisco sheriff to cut the hair of all prisoners to within an inch of their scalps. This equal haircut rule was not challenged by hippie prototypes but by Chinese prisoners. Field generally embraced formal judicial principles and free competition with an enthusiasm (and inconsistency) similar to that of current justices. But he viewed this case differently and invalidated the rule: "When we take our seats on the bench we are not struck with blindness, and forbidden to know as judges what we see as men."[104]

Consideration of "a fact in its history"[105] convinced Field that San Francisco had targeted Chinese prisoners. Sheriff Nunan cut off the queues the Chinese considered sacred. Field held this "altogether disproportionate" suffering unconstitutional.[106] Justice Field thus was a pioneer in recognizing prisoners' rights, but his opinion is important beyond the anti-Chinese attitudes he perceived behind the neutral mask of equality.[107] His decision illustrates why there must be judicial willingness to grasp "a fact in its history" in dealing with minority groups. That sensitivity includes cognizance of discrimination in the guise of evenhandedness, as well as more overt bigotry.

In contrast, the modern tales we considered are full of self-satisfied legal abstractions. They lack specifics about diverse people and traditions that give rise to group exceptionalism. Our contemporary judicial narratives reflect and produce Whiggish law and set aside any complexity, and certainly any bleakness. To consider that past wrongs may be visited upon current group members would sap teleological faith in the neutral, evenhanded principles of the current legal system. Therefore, contemporary judges must squelch particularized historical arguments. Yet, as William Wiecek put it, "oppressed peoples have an acute sense of their past . . . they must: it is the crucible of their identity and their cohesion. Without it their present oppression becomes either meaningless or natural."[108]

Conclusion

Tragic history cannot be decisive in every legal contest. But putting everyone on one level sacrifices the diverse history of groups for abstractions about deracinated individuals who float equally above reality. Yet we have not reached once upon a time. Judicial declarations alone cannot purge the past.

The traditions and historical sense of different groups are part of "the factual surround of legal arrangements."[109] Footnote four's suggestion of special scrutiny for claims of discrete and insular minorities never flourished fully. At the same time, it is vital not to lose sight of the clashing norms anchored in groups. Sentimental haze obscures history. Judges pave over the shards of the past. As they do so, these judges proclaim that they are merely doing a bit of groundskeeping on a lovely, smooth, and level playing field open to all.

Despite a few sometimes paradoxical success stories, group differences still count.[110] Yet in *Patterson, Croson,* and *Hodel v. Irving,* for example, the Court intervened to invalidate efforts by popularly elected bodies to remedy past wrongs perpetrated against paradigmatic discrete and insular minorities. Moreover, judicial struggles to define membership in families and tribes, and in racial or ethnic groups, underscore how aggressive judges have become in constructing the problematic group categories they prefer to consider natural, almost Platonic, essences.

The decisions we considered are particularly dismaying because judges were in a position to help legitimate ideals not otherwise widely accepted.[111] But the trend of the judicial treatment of involuntary groups still veers toward the conception of a unified, homogenized past.[112] Neutral rules crisscross with presumed equality. There is no iron, only velvet, as pleasant abstractions beyond history stretch back to a golden time immemorial.

It is important, in dealing with human rights, "to climb down to earth."[113] Yet if particularism is to be the foundation for Jacob's Ladder, an entirely *ad hoc* approach would end in a lawless morass. Legal actors must consider similarities and differences between group experiences to produce thoughtful decisions in cases that arise from particular contexts. Therefore, a few normative suggestions for judicial treatment of minority rights seem in order:

(1) Judges scrupulously must scrutinize both public and private actions and omissions that harm or stigmatize members of traditionally victimized groups. Legitimacy ought not to be presumed in actions—or even failures to act—directed at members of those involuntary groups scapegoated repeatedly in the past.

(2) Proof of biased motivation for acts against members of such groups must be sufficient, but not necessary, to allege discrimination. For example, Section 1 of the 1866 Civil Rights Act[114] includes a group *mens rea* concept. It does not require explicit proof of a discriminatory motive in a denial of equality, but it allows judges or juries to infer discriminatory motive in the way that American law generally allows such inferences to be drawn. This approach is consistent with the statute's history; it also parallels a trend toward group liability in other areas.[115]

(3) At times, judges may have to seek evidence on "subjective" ideas about the identity of a particular involuntary group. Discerning group wishes is always difficult. Yet to ignore a collectivity's perceptions—and the question of whether an individual is, or perceives herself to be, part of the collectivity—is to hide behind the false universalism of conclusive presumptions.[116] Group history plays a crucial role in such questions.

Diverse minority groups undoubtedly will survive and even thrive no matter what judges say. Group identities free and fetter what we are and what we can become. Perceptions of diverse histories will help sustain these groups as they struggle to overcome inertia, legal precedents, ignorance, or ill will. Consideration of history and context is also vital for judges.

Carl Becker, famous for his relativism, once stated, "Let us then admit that there are two histories: the actual series of events that once occurred; and the ideal series that we affirm and hold in memory."[117]

It is important to try to make these two histories correspond as nearly as possible. "One of the first duties of man is not to be duped," Becker asserted, "to be aware of his world."[118]

Awareness of history is bound to make the job of judges more complex. They will find no single objective historical account.[119] But heeding history is different from invoking a single tradition. Neither history nor tradition correlates with the invention of an appealing, simple, reusable, but fundamentally ahistorical past.[120] Historical facts also do not speak for themselves. It thus becomes important for Everyperson—and vital for those who combine force with their opinions—to heed a full array of social memory.

The nitty-gritty quest to "do equal right" requires that all those involved with law heed the complex, dark, even harrowing histories of discrete groups. Repeatedly, these factual stories remind us that "The key to redemption is remembrance."[121]

8 Judges and Identity Problems

> You cannot become thorough Americans if you think of your-
> selves in groups. America does not consist of groups. A man
> who thinks of himself as belonging to a particular national
> group in America has not yet become an American.
>
> *Woodrow Wilson*[1]

Ought judges to judge people differently because of who those persons are? In cases involving society's stigmatized and downtrodden, for example, should a judge pay special attention, listen with more sympathy, at times perhaps even grant what Federal Judge David Bazelon jokingly called a writ of *rahmonis* (mercy)? Fine recent work by John Leubsdorf, John Noonan, and Judith Resnik among others illustrates how seductively, but elusively, neutrality beckons to judges.[2]

Neutrality appeared to be the goal of Justice Felix Frankfurter. His opinions display his well-known, overly insistent antipathy toward taking ancestry into account. His emphasis is on the irrelevance of "race or religion or the accidents of antecedents."[3] The question then is: when, if ever, should a judge refuse to check her (the biblical Deborah serves as an example of a tough, early female judge) antecedents at the door? When should precedents trump antecedents?

An instructive aspect of Jewish jurisprudence may merit general attention. As Robert Cover summarized, "In a jurisprudence of *mitzvoth* [obligations] the loaded, evocative edge is at the assignment of responsibility."[4] To combine obligations we all incurred in the past with the responsibility to assure at least the minimal threshold of rights, any decent social contract would require close attention to the rights of others.

Felix and Fealty: The Accidents of Antecedents

Barnette and the Parvenu Thesis

Felix Frankfurter, the paradigmatic parvenu in Robert Burt's *Two Jewish Justices* (1988), has been criticized cogently by many others, notably by Jerold Auerbach, Richard Danzig, and Sanford Levinson.

They all point to Frankfurter's painfully overanxious quest to melt in the American melting pot, to become a new, *parve* (neither milk nor meat) American. Surely there is much to attack in Frankfurter's opinions and more still in what was often a remarkably convoluted self-definition of his role. And Frankfurter was astonishingly blind to his inability to separate his judicial from his personal machinations. On the day *West Virginia Board of Education v. Barnette* came down in 1943, this self-deluding judge insisted in his diary, "But I do not see what is 'personal' about referring to the fact that although a Jew, and therefore naturally eager for the protection of minorities, on the Court it is not my business to yield to such considerations, etc."[5]

If we needed a proof text for the assimilationist stance of the neutral judge, it is surely Frankfurter's opening paragraph in his *Barnette* dissent. There it is clear that being a Jewish judge obliges him to bend over backwards to eschew values rooted in his antecedents. The judicial world of detached judgment is a world of obligatory confinement, a realm of boundaries and being bound. Legal precedents banish antecedents.

Frankfurter begins his dissent, ironically, by asserting that he is "[o]ne who belongs." The group he belongs to is "the most vilified and persecuted minority in history." In a classic lawyerly double negative, Frankfurter claims that this makes him "not likely to be insensible to the freedoms guaranteed by our Constitution."[6] His words fold back on themselves. He declares that if his "purely personal attitude" were relevant, "I should wholeheartedly associate myself with the general libertarian views" contained in Justice Jackson's opinion for the Court. But Frankfurter cannot be wholehearted, or even half-hearted; he must use only his head, even if that means rejecting his own views "representing the thought and action of a lifetime."

Next comes the crux (as it were): "But as judges we are neither Jew nor Gentile, neither Catholic nor agnostic." Judges are confined equally. "We owe equal attachment to the Constitution and are equally bound by our judicial obligations." The origin and length of citizenship cannot matter, nor can any other background fact, not even the thought and action of a lifetime. Frankfurter dissents because he can do nothing else. This is precisely the moral/formal dilemma Robert Cover explored in *Justice Accused: Antislavery and the Judicial Process* (1975). Frankfurter's "Judicial Can't" eerily echoes the antislavery judges Cover studied who personally were opposed to slavery, but who, like Herman Melville's Captain Vere, obeyed law's "fearful symmetries" because their judicial role required that they do so.

For Frankfurter to respond to the sense of identification he insists he feels with the Jehovah's Witnesses would be to allow his own antecedents to link with the special characteristics of the persons before the Court. In Frankfurter's definition of what judging "without respect for persons" requires, however, a judge should be proud to be equally obligated with his fellow judges to transcend his background and personal values in order to do his duty. Frankfurter's dissent in *Barnette* revealed his inability or unwillingness to reclassify the Jehovah's Witnesses' legal claim (they sued against being forced to salute the flag in the public schools) as a freedom of expression or freedom of conscience claim rather than simply a freedom of religion argument. It was this dissent, according to some observers, that marked the point at which Frankfurter distanced himself irretrievably from his judicial colleagues.

But we should ask further what made Frankfurter, in his enthusiasm to demonstrate patriotic support of national security even at the local school board level, assert that Jews were "the most vilified and persecuted minority in history." Wasn't this reliance on extraneous and antecedent evidence far beyond the record in the case? It appears that Frankfurter could not even imagine possible competing claims on behalf of African-Americans, for example. This Jew, who so delighted in his role as constant adviser to President Roosevelt, apparently never tried to use his influence to urge action against the Nazi concentration camps. The judge compartmentalized so desperately, and with such apparent success, that he was oblivious to his own numerous violations of his role boundaries. To Frankfurter, a good, properly trained lawyer was "an expert in relevance . . . a person who has intellectual disinterestedness, who penetrates a problem as far as the human mind dealing with affairs is capable of penetrating, and who is free, who is not entangled in exercising a fair judgment and is not thwarted by personal, partial or parochial interest."[7]

A chilling vignette tells much about this master of relevance. A few months after *Barnette,* Jan Karski, a member of the Polish underground who had been smuggled into the United States, told Frankfurter in a secret meeting about Nazi death camps. Karski reports that Frankfurter responded that he did not believe him. When the exiled ambassador of the Polish government who had set up the meeting with Karski pressed Frankfurter as to how he possibly could not credit this awful report, Frankfurter emphasized the importance of distinguishing between the belief that Karski was lying, which he did not assert, and his disbelief. "My mind, my heart," Frankfurter said, "they are made in such a way that I cannot conceive it."[8]

It is deeply ironic that Frankfurter could not credit Karski's information. Now Frankfurter had horrific support for his earlier assertion in *Barnette* that Jews undoubtedly were "the most vilified and persecuted minority in history."[9] The judge surely was extreme in his denial and his apparent cognitive dissonance as he sought to ignore the costs of suppressing the personal, untethering the law from its communities, and ignoring the background and context of those he judged.

Frankfurter refused to yield to the urging of some of his friends that he delete the opening, personal paragraphs of his *Barnette* opinion. He wrote in his diary that though "any kind of manifestations are temperamentally disturbing to me," at times "one has to forego one's personal dislikes."[10] *Barnette* was one such time because "to keep all reference to anti-Semitism or anti-Catholicism hidden is the best kind of cover under which evil can operate."[11]

Frankfurter's rather convoluted image of detached judgment might be thought to be typical of his times. The same could be said of his desire to prove his success in assimilating fully into a prestigious professional role. He assumed his success was representative. Frankfurter insisted on meritocracy. He was a courageous and outspoken opponent of restrictive quotas at Harvard. Yet he sometimes took pride in not ignoring personal backgrounds. When he was "a Harvard Law School professor who happened to be a Jew," Frankfurter recalled, "I know I exacted higher standards from Jews than from other people, and perhaps that was on the whole a good thing for Jews who have any capacity."[12] Frankfurter celebrated this particular toughening process within Harvard's battle of all against all immediately before he described himself as "a great believer in reason," someone with "a romantic view about reason" because "You've got nothing else except that poor reed of reason to lean on in order to get away as far as possible from the jungle and the earth from whence we all come and a good deal of which we have in us."[13] Frankfurter often spoke of his "quasi-religious feeling about the Harvard Law School"—an institution he termed "the most democratic institution I know anything about."[14] Yet he saw no inconsistency as he bragged that he put a thumb on the scale against his Jewish students.

Lest it be said that Frankfurter's statements were mere reflections of the times in which he lived, a Second Circuit opinion by Judge Jerome Frank handed down in 1943, a few months after *Barnette* and Frankfurter's meeting with Karski, supplies a vigorous contrast. In deciding whether a Special Master in a contested corporate bankruptcy proceeding should have been removed for bias, Frank commented that "Much harm is done by the myth that, merely by putting on a black robe and taking the oath of office as a judge, a man ceases to be human."[15] Frank warned that to conceal the human element in the judicial process "allows that element to operate in an exaggerated manner."[16] This prominent legal realist, probably most famous (and notorious) for his flair in introducing psychoanalysis into legal analysis, described the judge as himself a witness who "must cannily penetrate through the surface of [lawyers'] remarks to their real purposes and motives."[17] Indeed, Frank asserted that the judge "has an official obligation to become prejudiced in that sense. Impartiality is not gullibility. Disinterestedness does not mean child-like innocence."[18] As if commenting on Frankfurter directly—the two had a well-known public falling out—Frank then announced that "a judge who purports to be superhuman is likely to be dominated by improper prejudices."[19]

Willie Francis and Role Utilitarianism

If Frankfurter's lack of self-awareness is striking in itself, it is also instructive. At times he practiced a crude form of role rather than rule utilitarianism. This is clear in the case of Willie Francis, a barely literate black teenager convicted of committing a murder when he was fifteen. Louisiana executed Willie Francis twice. The first execution failed when the portable electric chair failed to deliver enough current to Francis's writhing body, probably because the jailers who set up the chair were drunk at the time. When J. Skelly Wright took the *Francis* case to the Supreme Court to try to stop a second execution, Frankfurter fought to get and sustain a majority to allow Louisiana to proceed; in the end he cast the deciding vote. In his separate concurrence, Frankfurter emphasized that he had to guard against allowing his personal disapproval to influence his vote. Though "[s]trongly drawn" to sentiments of the dissenters, "I cannot rid myself of the conviction" that to vote against the second execution "would be enforcing my private view rather than that consensus of society's opinion which, for purposes of due process, is the standard enjoined by the Constitution."[20]

Yet Frankfurter soon began to pursue his private view in a private manner. He set to work to try to have Willie Francis's execution stopped through executive clemency by Louisiana's governor or some other political means. He wrote secretly to his old friend and Harvard roommate, Monte Lemann, at the time an influential Louisiana lawyer, and began to orchestrate a campaign to attempt to save Francis. Several commentators, including Frankfurter himself, celebrated his vote in the *Francis* case as "a classic proof of the judicial process at its best."[21]

Frankfurter's attempt to separate his roles so completely is strange and frightening. If his passion for the institutional constraints of a judge was unrestrained, his behind-the-scenes maneuvering went too far in the other direction. In trying to maintain the dichotomy of judicial versus personal so mechanistically, Frankfurter became a paradigm of too much respect for persons: he revered the impartial robe, but thought he could successfully manipulate backdoor influence. Yet Frankfurter's belated attempt at humane flexibility was not merely too little, too late. His handling of the Willie Francis case also lacked any sense of acceptance of paradox, of the possibility of humane wisdom *within* the role of legal interpreter.

Frankfurter had a penchant for protesting his own disinterestedness too much. Thus, for example, he argued that a judge "must think dispassionately and submerge private feeling on every aspect of a case."[22] Unlike his posturing about his ability to put aside his personal feelings in *Barnette,* for example, in a lawsuit challenging the practice of playing the radio on District of Columbia buses, Frankfurter found it necessary to recuse himself. He explained that his feelings were "so strongly engaged as a victim of the practice in controversy that I had better not participate in judicial judgment upon it."[23] Despite "a good deal of shallow talk,"[24] the judicial robe does indeed change the person within. Judges learn to put aside their private views "through training, professional habits, self-discipline and that fortunate alchemy by which men are loyal to the obligation with which they are entrusted."[25] Yet in this case Frankfurter felt he ought not sit in judgment, though he presumably was not satisfied when the Court refused to invalidate the intrusion of the broadcasts on a "captive audience."

"History Also Has Its Claims"

As artful a dodger as Frankfurter surely was even to himself, he could not consistently keep up the mask. Brief mention of a few of his opinions from the early 1950s will make this clear—though the early 1950s were not the best of times for either Frankfurter or the country.[26] Frequently self-deluded, arrogant, and inconsistent, Frankfurter had moments of success, perhaps even courage. The most important example occurred out of the public view. Frankfurter now is credited both with building the unanimous coalition in *Brown v. Board of Education* and with uttering the wittiest line.[27]

Other moments bolster Frankfurter's diminished reputation and add weight on the side of the scales where we place impartial procedures and judicial efforts to be disinterested. The most striking instance occurred in a famous case in which Frankfurter's role is often forgotten. The story of Julius and Ethel Rosenberg is by now deeply embedded in American iconography.[28] The story of the execution, the gripping pictures of Ethel and Julius and of their sons wearing their Brooklyn Dodger baseball caps, make it a case in which "the story is more important than the events."[29] For many Jews, apparently including Judge Irving Kaufman, the Rosenberg case called for extraordinary procedures precisely because all the crucial players were Jewish at a time when suspicion of Jews as subversives was abroad in the land.

It was particularly striking, therefore, for Frankfurter to file a dissent after the Rosenbergs' execution, objecting to the Court's hasty decision to convene in special session to reverse the stay Justice Douglas had granted on the basis of new legal issues. "To be writing an opinion in a case affecting two lives after the curtain has been rung down upon them has the appearance of pathetic futility," Frankfurter acknowledged, yet his opinion was necessary because "history also has its claims."[30]

With characteristic self-preoccupation and typical concern for legal process, Frankfurter explained the need to consider history for the sake of progress in the "long and unending" struggle to "develop and enforce justice according to law." Specifically, "necessary habits for detached and wise judgment" could only be accomplished through "sturdy self-examination and self-criticism." Frankfurter closed by noting, "Perfection may not be demanded of law, but the capacity to counteract inevitable, though rare, frailties is the mark of a civilized legal mechanism."

If it is accurate to consider Frankfurter "the most conspicuous example of the phenomenon [of court Jew] in American history,"[31] it should be added that even court Jews have on occasion been unpredictable and outspoken against the powerful. In a sense, Frankfurter's argument in his *Rosenberg* dissent is consistent with his ongoing, doomed attempt to achieve pure due process liberalism. The Rosenbergs should get a stay because the Court has not taken adequate time, has not followed settled procedures. This miscarriage of justice is a blip in the nation's course of progress. And it was fitting that the only Jewish Justice, famous for his outspoken activity on behalf of fair procedures for Sacco and Vanzetti and often vilified as a Red, a radical, and an alien, now cried out against the profound procedural injustice perpetrated against the Rosenbergs in the frenzied atmosphere of the early summer of 1953.[32]

Nor was this the first time Frankfurter stood up for fair procedures. In *Sacher v. United States*,[33] for example, Frankfurter dissented forcefully as the Court upheld criminal penalties against the lawyers who defended Communist Party leaders in the *Dennis* case. The lawyers were cited for contempt by Judge Harold Medina on extremely dubious grounds only after the trial had concluded. Frankfurter's concern for procedural justice again led him not only to buck the trend of the times, but to be willing to do so in a much publicized case involving a named Jewish defendant. Frankfurter detailed all the exchanges between Medina and Sacher and the other lawyers in a lengthy appendix, and argued that every contemptuous act by the lawyer "had its reflex" in inappropriate behavior by the judge, whose judicial conduct seemed to Frankfurter to "manifest[] a failure of moral mastery."[34]

It would be a mistake to overstate Frankfurter's courage or to theorize that he grew in the judicial role or gained confidence about his own stature. All his life he likely wrestled with his apparent embarrassment about his "father" and his "face." Certainly even he was aware that he had determined to exchange his upbringing and the religious rituals of his youth for extreme patriotism for his new country and faith in the rituals of the law. But his words in the *Rosenberg* and *Sacher* cases and his emphasis on history's claims suggest a more tangled outcome. As Jerold Auerbach put it, "no other Jew in American public life engaged in such a prolonged, tormenting, and conspicuous struggle over Jewish identity."[35]

Writing for the Court in the key early "hate speech" precedent, *Beauharnais v. Illinois,* Frankfurter recognized the importance of "groups with whose position and esteem in society the affiliated individual may be inextricably involved."[36] Based on a pattern of repeated historical incidents of racial violence in Illinois, from the murder of abolitionist Owen Lovejoy in 1837 through several vicious race riots in the World War I era and in Cicero in 1951, Frankfurter wrote that "we would deny experience to say that the Illinois legislature was without reason in seeking ways to curb false or malicious defamation of racial or religious groups."[37] Thus, for a 5–4 majority, Frankfurter determined that Illinois could constitutionally criminalize group libel.

Justice Hugo Black led the dissenters in charging that the majority had given libel "a more expansive scope and more respectable status than it was ever accorded even in the Star Chamber" by allowing a group libel statute to withstand First Amendment scrutiny.[38] This dissent marked an important way-station in the development of the absolutist approach to the First Amendment for which Black is famous. He argued that the First Amendment "absolutely forbids" punishing free expression.[39] Black also asserted that, far from being a victory for minority groups, the decision should make minority group members realize that "Another such victory and I am undone."[40]

Frankfurter's defense against these and other rather bitter charges by the dissenters was two-pronged. First, Frankfurter simply equated the Illinois statute with laws that had been upheld which allowed individual libels and "fighting words" to be punished. With these analogies, Frankfurter somewhat cursorily placed Beauharnais's pro-segregation, anti-Negro leaflets within the "well-defined and narrowly limited classes of speech" beyond the realm of First Amendment protection.[41]

Frankfurter's second line of defense was to emphasize the importance of group identity. He cited union labor cases from the 1920s and law review articles published during World War II by David Reisman to support the reasonableness of Illinois's legislative belief that "a man's job and his educational opportunities and the dignity accorded him may depend as much on the reputation of the racial and religious group to which he willy-nilly belongs, as to his own merits."[42] Frankfurter found it convenient to ascribe awareness of the weightiness of group identity to the Illinois legislators who had passed the challenged group libel statute in 1917, but both the tone and the substance of the point were very much his own.

Even Frankfurter recognized that no matter how hard one seeks for impartial justice, one cannot escape one's history and the group affiliations that help constitute every self. This may be near the core of Justice Cardozo's point that "We may try to see things as objectively as we please. Nonetheless, we can never see them with any eyes except our own."[43] Moreover, our forbears helped determine the shape and color of those eyes. They also shaped the theories that in turn shape what we can see. It is self-deluding to think we can put aside our origins. It is naive to believe it is ever possible to be impervious to the intersecting group realities that influence how we judge others in everyday life. But we also need reflection; reflection not in the sense of mirroring groups that have passed before us, but in the much more difficult sense of striving—despite the remarkably complex embeddedness that constitutes each of us—to do better, to reconstitute, to be more just.

Old Lines in New Battles: Hate Speech

The prickly issue of "hate speech" has returned to legal and national consciousness with a vengeance. If Frankfurter's somewhat cavalier dismissal of categories of expression is no longer supported by leading precedents as it was in 1952, the *Beauharnais* Court's struggle to resolve a clash between competing, basic values is very much still with us. The legal literature on the subject of whether it is valid to regulate hate speech is already vast.[44] A new burst has followed Justice Scalia's majority opinion that invalidated a St. Paul, Minnesota ordinance that made it a misdemeanor to place "a symbol, object, appellation, characterization or graffiti, including, but not limited to, a burning cross or Nazi swastika" on either public or private property "which one knows or has reasonable grounds to know arouses anger, alarm or resentment in others on the basis of race, color, creed, religion or gender."[45]

For sharply different reasons, the justices all agreed that it was unconstitutional to convict a juvenile under the ordinance for burning a cross on the lawn outside the home of an African-American family. If nothing else, the bitterness of the disagreement among the justices provides further evidence that judges do care about legal approaches as well as results. The various opinions as to why the conviction could not withstand constitutional scrutiny will keep legal scholars writing for years.[46] Without becoming entangled in the fascinating doctrinal underbrush in *R.A.V.*, it is worth simply noting that much of the disagreement among the justices revolved around whether "fighting words" are, "despite their verbal character, essentially a 'nonspeech' element of communication."[47]

Scalia analogized fighting words to a noisy sound truck. He insisted that neither could be regulated because of hostility or sympathy toward a given message. In a characteristic *aperçu* he summed up: "St. Paul has no such authority to license one side of a debate to fight

freestyle, while requiring the other to follow the Marquis of Queens-
bury [sic] Rules."[48] The majority expressed no doubt that St. Paul had
a "compelling" interest in trying to ensure "the basic human rights of
members of groups that have historically been subjected to discrimination, including the right of such group members to live in peace
where they wish."[49] But St. Paul had acted unconstitutionally because
it did not use content-neutral alternatives. It protected either too little
or too large a group. The majority's equal protection approach to the
First Amendment question is both innovative and confusing. But what
is most significant here is the degree to which this all-or-nothing
approach forces law makers to ignore the salience of particular groups.

It has never made sense to seek an entirely subjective or an entirely
objective standard to determine what expression constitutes "fighting
words." Neither an individual's subjective feelings about an insult nor
some theoretical common denominator can capture adequately what
is at stake. The difficulty ought to have been clear from the inception
of the "fighting words" exception to First Amendment protection in
1942 in *Chaplinsky v. New Hampshire.*[50] It should have made a constitutional difference that Chaplinsky had been arrested for distributing Jehovah's Witnesses literature, and that the object of his insulting
words was the city marshal. Surely the official status of a city marshal,
even in the small New Hampshire town of Rochester in the early
1940s, ought to carry weight in determining whether the words at
issue were in fact fighting words. Context is vital. No city marshal
should respond with violence even if called "a God-damned racketeer"
and "a damned Fascist," part of "the whole government of Rochester
[who] are Fascists or agents of Fascists."[51]

Unfortunately, the prevalence of "hate speech" seems to be on the
rise around the nation and the world. The constitutional problems
raised by attempts to penalize such expression, either with civil or
criminal sanctions, are still largely unresolved. But an all-or-nothing
approach such as the Court's in the *R.A.V.* decision makes the crucial
error of ignoring the different meanings and different impacts words
may have in different communities. This case is more a clash of two
alien cultures than it is a traditional legal paradigm of individual versus the state. Obviously, it is not possible or desirable for both sides to
win, though some of the best proposals for dealing with hate speech
would couple a legal victory for the hateful speech with a vigorous
communal demonstration of support and reinforcement for the victims. It may be unfortunate that we are what we are, but this state of

affairs cannot be merely washed away by some formal faith that we have already reached the dispassionate legal universe where all are protected equally and neutrally by our laws.

Juries might seem the best institutions to fight over and resolve the overlapping norms of a multitude of pluralistic communities. This jury function has been enhanced significantly by several recent Supreme Court decisions that limit the use of peremptory challenges on the basis of race in the jury selection process.[52] In other decisions, however, the Court has exacerbated the false objectivity of formal law by, for example, limiting such challenges to instances of clear-cut racially motivated jury selection practices that are remarkably difficult to prove.

In *Hernandez v. New York,*[53] for example, the Court allowed a prosecutor to challenge and remove potential jurors who were Spanish-speaking. The prosecutor did so on the "neutral grounds" that these Spanish-speaking citizens could not swear that they would be able to ignore their understanding of the testimony given in Spanish. In a bizarre epistemological twist, the Court accepted the prosecutor's assertion of the need to insure that all the jurors would be confined to the official translator's version of the Spanish-language testimony. With particular zaniness in *Hernandez,* inadequate judicial attention to communal values, practices, and understandings makes the concept of a unified, objective law look silly and allows it to operate in perverse ways. Judges must deal with the recognition that they and those they judge are "thick with particular traits"[54] when they arrive in court.

Conclusion

In E. L. Doctorow's *The Book of Daniel,* the lawyer Jacob Ascher defends a fictional couple based directly on the Rosenbergs. Attorney Ascher "was said to have worked for years on a still unfinished book demonstrating the contributions of the Old Testament to American law."[55] There is at least a whiff of mockery in that description of Ascher; one might criticize him for thinking he "could wear a homburg and a *tallis* at the same time" and "perceive[] in the law a codification of the religious sense of life."[56] But Ascher's decisions might also make his a life worth living, for all its complexities and lack of neatly bounded true belief.[57]

If Jacob Ascher ever finished his book, he might have focused on the controversial role of judges and judicial oaths in Massachusetts Bay Colony, a community self-consciously attempting to use the Bible as the source for its laws. These people were not about to adopt the custom of consensus judgment Native Americans seemed to practice, but they found themselves adrift and largely free to create their own rules.

In Massachusetts Bay, a central source of the ongoing contention between the two "houses" of the Massachusetts General Court concerned the judicial function. The bicameral General Court combined legislative and judicial rules. The larger of the two institutions, the Deputies, represented the towns and elected the Assistants or Magistrates, a kind of executive committee that was supposed to make sure that Massachusetts Bay would not be "a meere democratie" but rather "A forme mixt of an Aristocracy and Democracy."[58]

At least from the time of the celebrated case of Goody Sherman's sow in 1643, however, the two parts of the General Court fought for decades over their respective roles in adjudication. A major source of disagreement focused on the different oaths their members took before performing as judges. Each magistrate took an oath to carry himself and behave "according to the Lawes of God, and of this land." On the other hand, each deputy, when acting as a judge in the General Court, swore "to deale uprightly and justly, according to my judgement and conscience."[59] These competing oaths disclose radically different premises about the judicial role. We need hardly be surprised that the magistrates spent most of the century trying to get the more democratic deputies out of the judging business altogether. But even these bickering leaders were remarkably unified within their little face-to-face community concerning the need and the justice of expelling and even executing nonconformists on occasion.

As yet we have made little progress toward reconciling the two Massachusetts approaches or, more realistically, finding the appropriate position among a number of other competing practical choices along a broad continuum. Perhaps that is because we want judges who feel both obligations. Certainly we desire impartial justice, though we know it is impossible to obtain. Just as certainly, we seek judges rooted in and encumbered by their communities, so long as they can leave them behind when it is appropriate to do so. We want formal impartiality along with focused perception of underlying realities.

Judging ought not be viewed as static or binary but as kinetic and paradoxical. It is a tightrope act: in John Noonan's words, "Abandonment of the rules produces monsters; so does neglect of persons."[60]

Work by Judith Resnik, Lynne Henderson, and Martha Minow has greatly advanced our understanding of how problematic it is to proclaim disengagement, impartiality, and independence as central judicial virtues. Yet the dangers of abandoning these ideals are painfully obvious. There can be too much empathy, too much willingness to understand and then to embrace one party and to punish another.[61] Judges fail when they are inadequately committed to detached judgment. They also fail when they are so detached that they think they can fly high above the communities that encumber them as well as the rest of us.[62]

9   Oaths and the Communities of Judges

> Judges and other public officers habitually appeal to the pre-
> tended obligation of their oaths, when about to perform some
> act of iniquity, for which they can find no other apology, and
> for which they feel obliged to offer some apology.
>
> *Lysander Spooner*[1]

Before his confirmation hearings exploded into high drama, Clarence
Thomas's mantra was that he had no agenda. He even offered a
description of the judicial ideal: "You want to be stripped down like a
runner."[2] Thomas was hardly alone among judicial nominees to
emphasize repeatedly that he carried no baggage to his judicial appointment.[3] Yet he also stressed that because he was an African-
American who had come far from Pinpoint, Georgia, and had
overcome poverty and racial discrimination, his life experience would
bring a different and valuable perspective to the Court.

To some, coming up with the image of a judge as a stripped-down
runner might already suggest lack of qualification.[4] As William Rehnquist stated a few months after his own appointment as Associate Justice in 1971, "Proof that a Justice's mind at the time he joined the Court
was a complete *tabula rasa* in the area of constitutional adjudication
would be evidence of lack of qualification, not lack of bias."[5] At the
very least, Thomas's image of the unencumbered judge—and the Sen-
ate's willingness to accept it as an appropriate judicial ideal—underscores the problematic nature of the judicial role.

The core of Justice Rehnquist's explanation about why he did not
recuse himself in a case involving matters on which he had worked and
testified prior to his appointment was: "Every litigant is entitled to
have his case heard by a judge mindful of this [federal judicial] oath."
Rehnquist went on to say that neither that oath nor anything else
"guarantee a litigant that each judge will start off from dead center."[6]

Why does the image of Thomas's nearly unclothed judge seem so
unsatisfactory? On the other hand, why does the conflicting excuse by

Rehnquist seem facile and unconvincing? In part the explanation is that "to have character is to know I move in a history I neither summon nor command, which carries consequences none the less for my choices and conduct."[7] But no judge can or should constantly pierce some personal robe of authority. At the same time, most of us reject a judicial model that could be programmed by a computer or run by rule-bound bureaucratization. There is good reason that "mechanistic" judging is decried in our culture. We also fear the chill at dead center. There ought to be a complex relationship between a judge's struggle to come to terms with her own background, and her effort to ignore at least some characteristics of the litigants before her. Additionally, the judge swears fealty to an oath that requires the pursuit of justice, even if all judges know that justice can never be fully achieved.

In this chapter the text of the federal judicial oath will be used to explore the relationship of personal associations and legal rules. Although a close analysis of the language of the federal judicial oath shows it to be wonderfully illuminating, my argument does not depend on that text. The point here is to confront the very act of judging, with or without specific formal obligation. My claim is that a sense of history and precedent is crucial; this sense of the past ought to liberate rather than bind judges. If the judge is aware of the groups that she and the parties before her come from, she can pursue justice better, and may escape the pitfalls of deracinated expertise that seem to accompany sitting in judgment of one's fellows.

A careful assessment of the oaths that judges take can tell us much about the tensions with which they ought to live. These oaths underscore the problematic nature of the central concept of neutrality in regard to persons before any court. One question is whether and how much ought a judge to take into account the associations from which the judge herself has emerged, as well as the group identities of persons to be judged. In exploring the oath's apparent commitment to neutrality, we will discover various nettlesome dilemmas about what we want judges to leave behind.

Opposing Views of the Judicial Oath: Recent Invocations within the Supreme Court

Justice Thomas's statements during his confirmation hearings about his lack of agenda and baggage were simply ritualistic: others had responded in just this way to questions that probed their notions of what might bind them as judges. In what Sanford Levinson has termed a "most subtle degradation ceremony,"[8] judicial nominees are now expected to provide assurances that they will subordinate any and all private moral or religious beliefs to what the Constitution commands. But a good deal may be learned from those rare occasions when sitting justices invoke the oaths they have already taken as directly relevant to their decisions. Moreover, in making an unusual move of taking the federal judicial oath seriously, we can examine the role of the judge itself as a remarkable social construct, simultaneously a vehicle for the imposition and legitimation of force and, at its best, also a constraint even upon popularly endorsed force.

Means, Money, and a Great Tradition

Recall that in *Patterson v. McClean Credit Union*, discussed in Chapter 7, the majority's *per curiam* opinion relied on what it called the essential command of the federal judicial oath: the requirement that "the claim of any litigant for the application of a rule to its case should not be influenced by the Court's view of the worthiness of the litigant in terms of extralegal criteria."[9] The key question, of course, is what criteria are properly considered to be extralegal. In *Patterson,* the Court's view of the oath obliged judges to ignore race and the civil rights context of the case.

The oath was to figure again in a vehement disagreement among the justices in a far less dramatic setting. The Court decided to amend its own Rule 39. As of July 1, 1991, the Court could deny a motion to proceed *in forma pauperis*—a waiver of the usual fees for those without adequate financial resources—if the justices are satisfied that the petition or jurisdictional statement is frivolous or malicious. In other words, the petitions and writs of poor people now could be turned away for a reason that does not apply to those who can afford filing fees: even frivolous or malicious claims of people wealthy enough to pay are considered differently and more fully than those of poor claimants.[10]

Justice Marshall, dissenting from this revision of the Rule, argued with considerable sarcasm that the Court "once had a great tradition: 'All men and women are entitled to their day in Court.'"[11] Now, Marshall said, "All men and women are entitled to their day in Court only if they have the *means* and the *money*."[12] This time it was Marshall who invoked the text of the federal judicial oath to illustrate a basic

prior commitment, unfortunately now to be "conditioned on mone-
tary worth." He highlighted the oath's obligation to "do equal right to
the poor and to the rich."[13] Thus, the oath's paradoxical quality is
underscored by different, even diametrically opposed recent judicial
views of what it commands.

To be sure, the oath hardly provides a clear tie-breaker between the
formal notion of equal treatment expressed in *Patterson* and the gist of
Marshall's dissent, which points to a lack of equal treatment if some
claims are excluded entirely from the process. Perhaps history and
earlier texts will help illuminate the problem. Is the quest for justice
furthered if judges specially heed the claims of members of groups with
particular disabilities, or of people who suffer the ongoing ramifications of massive past victimization?

The Federal Judicial Oath: A Little History

The text of the judicial oath suggests how complicated the judicial role
ought to be. Ever since the first job posting in the Judiciary Act of
1789, for example, all federal judges have sworn or affirmed that they
will "administer justice without respect to persons, and do equal right
to the poor and to the rich."[14] But to judge "without respect to persons" seems curious. Can that obligation be consistent with the duty to
"do equal right to the poor and to the rich?" Both phrases address, but
only seem to deepen, the conundrum of how a judge's awareness or
lack of awareness of her or his own rootedness affects administering
justice.

If federal judges think about the solemn obligation they undertake
as they begin their new jobs, they surely simply presume that they have
agreed to be impartial.[15] Yet to "administer justice without respect to
persons" seems difficult to reconcile with the idea that respect for persons is a good thing, even an admirable goal.[16] Moreover, to "do equal
right to the poor and to the rich" emphasizes the dilemma of formal
equality—as in Anatole France's famous example of forbidding the
rich and the poor alike to sleep under bridges—and may hint that a
judge ought not be entirely blind as to who is rich and who is poor in
aspiring to "administer justice without respect to persons."

Even if most judges pretend to be unaware of the problem, every
judge ought to know that to judge in a self-aware manner is to be
unable to jump free and to float above the battle. Every judge is necessarily pressed from behind by the past and blocked and driven back

by the future.[17] The argument here is that judges cannot and should not entirely ignore the group identities that shaped them, nor the communities and statuses of persons who are to be judged.

That there seems to be a basic antinomy within the oath itself has something to do with its origins. Most of the oath's wording reached the American colonies as an old English royal judges' oath from the General Court in Chancery. But George Wythe did some important tinkering when he composed an oath for Virginia judges.[18] He was a charter member of Virginia's High Court of Chancery and taught law to John Marshall, Thomas Jefferson, James Madison, Henry Clay, and many other famous Americans. Wythe also became the first law professor in the United States when Virginia Governor Thomas Jefferson abolished a Chair of Divinity at William and Mary during the Revolutionary War so he could put his old teacher Wythe into a new Chair of Law and Police. Wythe resorted to biblical sources for the oath he created: the phrase "without respect to persons" is from the King James translation of the Bible.

The Quest for Neutrality

Images of neutrality seem to revolve around not seeing things, making ourselves blind to what we usually take into account. Yet as Martha Minow put it, "Veiling the standpoint of the observer conceals its impact on our perception of the world . . . [and] leads to the next assumption: that all other perspectives are either presumptively identical to the observer's own or do not matter."[19] Nonetheless, we cling to the need for impartial procedures and unbiased judges.

Judith Shklar emphasized our society's customary blindness to the faces of injustice, but she nevertheless suggested the importance of impartial judicial procedures.[20] There seems to be widespread agreement that "the keenest of human torments is to be judged without a law."[21] But the torment might be almost as bad, or perhaps even worse, when an apparently fair procedure is actually a mask for mob domination or some predetermined result.[22]

Reason and logic, principles and precedents, offer security if not certainty. They raise issues to an elevated plane and heighten the appeal of formalism in the judicial role. They help compensate judges for the discomfort they feel at the tug of their original communities when they are no longer quite in them. And judges must decide. In judging, they must disappoint and hurt. There always seems to be another side. Some claimants are patterned and predictable; a few may even be unworthy of empathy.[23] Judges must decide; they do not merely engage in dialogue. Yet they cannot entirely escape their own inner dialects. As judges struggle with the task of judging, it matters how much of law is logic, how much experience. And the obligations that judges undertake ought to matter, too, both as instructive ideals and as practical obligations. This would be so even if there were not a long tradition that claims judging is the work of the Lord.[24]

Knowing and Judging Your Neighbor and Yourself

At the beginning of Deuteronomy, Moses specifically charges the judges he has organized in a decentralized network as follows:

> Hear the causes between your brethren, and judge righteously between a man and his brother, and the stranger that is with him.
> Ye shall not respect persons in judgment; ye shall hear the small and the great alike; ye shall not be afraid of the face of any man; for the judgment is God's; and the cause that is too hard for you ye shall bring unto me, and I will hear it.   (Deut. I, 16–17)

What is the meaning of the command to "not respect persons in judgment"?[25] How is this prescription linked to the obligation to hear the small and great alike, and not to be "afraid of the face of any man; for the judgment is God's"? There is extensive commentary on these elliptical sentences, of course, but this is not the place to review it, or to discuss the role of judges as administrators and officers as well as adjudicators in biblical times. Nonetheless, we should note some important paradoxes directly rooted in the biblical text.

Moses tells these judges to hear the causes first, not to prejudge them. Also, they are to consider the litigants as "your brethren," not as anonymous, even arms-length plaintiff A and defendant B. In fact, even the stranger is explicitly included as if among the judge's brothers. So the judge clearly knows who the parties are, and is expected to strive to be neither fearful of the powerful nor to discriminate against the stranger. Ultimately, after all, "the judgment is God's." Although the directive does not seem to envision a virtuously passive judiciary, Moses does emphasize the benefits of modesty (at least for others) and specifies, "and the cause that is too hard for you ye shall bring unto me, and I will hear it" (Deut. I, 17).

If legal realists were to consider this text, their initial concern—beyond what manna the judge had for breakfast—would be how these judges were selected. Moses has just asked the children of Israel, "How can I myself alone bear your cumbrance, and your burden, and your strife?" (Deut. I, 12). Obviously, he will have to encumber others. "Get you from each one of your tribes wise men, and understanding, and full of knowledge, and I will make them heads over you" (Deut. I, 13). We quickly learn that Moses has to settle for wise men, full of knowledge. Apparently, it is impossible to find those who might also be "understanding."[26] And the judges are to be local, rooted in their tribes.

The point is made repeatedly in the Bible that judges are not to be respecters of persons. This is said in different contexts, however, and in language that seems to vary slightly but significantly. In *Kedoshim* (Holy Things), the portion of Leviticus that is said to contain the essentials of the entire Torah, for example, "And the Lord spoke unto Moses: Speak unto all the congregation of the children of Israel, and say unto them, ye shall be holy, for I the LORD your God am holy" (Levit. XIX, 1, 2). Much is made of the universalism of this passage. It seems to connect the entire people to a God who is merciful, who demands that every child obey his father and mother, who requires that gleanings be left for the poor and for the stranger, and who forbids oppression and requires the payment of prompt wages for the hired servant. This chapter contains the single concept said by Rabbi Hillel to be the essence of the entire Torah: "thou shalt love thy neighbor as thyself" (Levit. XIX, 18). But what if thou must judge thy neighbor?

A problematic juxtaposition addresses precisely the issue of impartiality and evenhandedness. First, the text commands that "Thou shalt not curse the deaf, nor put a stumbling-block before the blind, but thou shalt fear thy God: I am the Lord." Immediately next is "Ye shall do no unrighteousness in judgment; thou shalt not respect the person of the poor, nor favour the person of the mighty; but in righteousness shalt thou judge thy neighbor" (Levit. XIX, 14–15).

We may be struck first by the apparent difference between judging brothers and the strangers included among the brothers, and judging neighbors whom we are to love as ourselves. It is hard to anticipate which formulation is most likely to yield impartial judgment. Moreover, awareness of difference seems essential in the case of the command not to curse the deaf or put hurdles before the blind. Surely we ought not curse anyone nor set up stumbling-blocks as a general matter. Yet the text specifically enjoins us to pay special respect to certain categories of people, notwithstanding the inherent dangers of special treatment and paternalism.[27]

The inconsistency is compounded by the parallelism in the command to "not respect the person of the poor," "nor favour the person of the mighty." As with the Supreme Court, perhaps it seemed too difficult or too unjust for biblical judges to think of wealth as a suspect classification akin to the disadvantages people are born with that seem immutable and often lead to stigma and discriminatory treatment. In Exodus there is an explicit warning against favoring the poor in a legal setting: "neither shalt thou favour a poor man in his cause" (Exod. XXIII, 2). This is placed directly after the warning against following a multitude to do evil or to pervert justice. A few verses later, however, we are reminded of another familiar danger: "Thou shalt not wrest the judgment of thy poor in his cause" (Exod. XXIII, 6). If there is often a humane tendency to lean in sympathy toward the poor, there may be a still stronger impulse for the rich to coerce the poor or for others to think it natural somehow for the rich to prevail.

The Pursuit of Justice

It is striking that judges and judging are important enough to merit a whole portion of Deuteronomy, called *Shofetim* (Judges), and they precede kings, priests, and prophets. Again we learn that judges are to be sought at the communal level, "tribe by tribe," and they are to be established in every town (Deut. XVI, 18). These judges receive the standard command to "not wrest judgment" and "not respect persons." They also are told, "neither shalt thou take a gift; for a gift doth blind the eyes of the wise, and pervert the words of the righteous" (Deut. XVI, 19). It is necessary to "judge the people with righteous judgment." The key word here is *tzedek*. Next, in fact, is the classic command, *"tzedek, tzedek tyrdoof,"* generally translated as "Justice, justice shalt thou follow [or pursue]," so that "thou mayest live, and inherit the land which the LORD your God giveth thee" (Deut. XVI, 20).

This communal *quid pro quo*—the oft-stated duty to pursue justice in return for getting the Promised Land—may seem ironic to modern eyes. The irony is underscored because some rabbis take this precise phrase about pursuing justice to warn against unjust means used even in pursuit of just ends.[28] A skeptic might note further that within *Shofetim* the famous demand for justice is followed by the clear command that, if a city refuses to make peace with the Israelites and is delivered into their hands by the Lord, all the men of that city are to be slain and all the women and children taken captive; all, that is, except for six specific cities that are to be extirpated entirely (Deut. XX, 10–18).

The pursuit of justice is complicated elsewhere by stories of a vengeful God who, for example, punishes Saul for being insufficiently genocidal against the Amalekites (I Samuel XV, 1–34). Likewise, David demands on his deathbed that Solomon, in judging, must wreak vengeance for reasons of state against David's enemies (1 Kings II, 5–9).

The apparent paradox deepens when we consider an earlier Deuteronomic passage describing God in the process of judging. "For the LORD your God, He is God of gods, and Lord of lords, the great God, the mighty, and the awful, who regardeth not persons, nor taketh reward. He doth execute justice for the fatherless and widow, and loveth the stranger, in giving him food and raiment. Love ye therefore the stranger; for ye were strangers in the land of Egypt" (Deut. X, 17–19). As judge, at least, God is said to be able not to regard persons and yet to be particularly aware of the character and plight of the fatherless, the widow, and the stranger.[29]

Righteousness for the Poor; Equity for the Meek

Isaiah offers what is probably the most famous example of what it means to judge without respect for persons. This passage is read in synagogues on the final day of Passover, prior to the reading of Isaiah's vision of animals which are natural enemies lying down together. It seems to usher in utopia: "And he shall not judge after the sight of his eyes, neither decide after the hearing of his ears; but with righteousness shall he judge the poor, and decide with equity for the meek of the land" (Isaiah XI, 3–4). Thus in Isaiah's messianic version of the judicial role, a judge must not judge by what he sees or hears but must strive to get to the essence. This struggle requires attention to judging the poor with righteousness and particularized concern to judge the meek with equity. Not to respect persons, then, begins to look less like a directive to be formally neutral, and more like a prescription to try to dig beneath surface appearances, because that is what is necessary in order to do justice.

A biblical judge performed many functions, of course, and they were markedly different from the duties of an Article III judge. And in several places the biblical text admonishes against the tendency to have pity or exercise favoritism toward the poor. But there is also a countertrend. The thrust of the aspiration for perplexed judges seems to be:

"think of the strangers before the court as if they were persons you know well." In other words, neighbors are to be treated and judged as one would judge oneself, and strangers are to be judged as brothers. Judges must not detach themselves from the familiar world but try to connect others to it, and to take into account who the persons to be judged really are beneath their appearances. Only in seeking this essence through empathy can the judge overcome giving excessive respect but inadequate dignity to those who are to be judged.

Like the judges appointed by Moses, a modern judge lacks understanding when she takes the judicial oath. She must constantly grow into it. Thus "no respect for persons" becomes the duty to look through the disguises, costumes, and masks donned by others, and by oneself.[30] As Maimonides ponders what is meant by the biblical command "in righteousness shalt thou judge thy neighbor" (Levit. XIX, 15), he explains that a righteous judgment is "a judgment marked by perfect impartiality to both litigants." The judge must not "show courtesy to one, speaking softly to him, and frown upon the other, addressing him harshly." Moreover, "[i]f one of the parties to a suit is well clad and the other ill clad, the judge should say to the former, 'Either dress him like yourself before the trial is held, or dress like him, then the trial will take place.'"[31]

The impartiality of a righteous judgment, then, implies a relationship between the parties as well as an involvement on the part of the judge to insure that the litigants at least approach an equal footing. The judge is hardly a passive or neutral bystander. Judicial activism is triggered by inequality. The judge perceives differences and then demands that any differences between the parties be set aside. Only in this way can a righteous judgment can be rendered.

The Rabbi, the Chicken, and the Law

My friend Allan Feld is knowledgeable about some of the biblical mysteries I thought I perceived concerning the judicial role. Feld, like many other practicing Orthodox Jews, insisted that both the Bible and the body of Jewish law generally require neutrality in judging between man and man. But then Allan told me a story his favorite rabbi had told him when he was a boy.

That rabbi said that when a question arises about the *kashrut* of a chicken (was it a healthy, intact fowl, ritually slaughtered in the correct way?), the rabbi ought to take into account whether the person asking is rich or poor. If the poor man has spent a great part of his meager resources on the chicken, the rabbi stretches the law as much as possible to find the chicken kosher. If a rich questioner asks about the same chicken, the result may be different.

This story is fairly typical, at least of the kinds of rabbis and judges we want and are commanded to seek out for ourselves. (A person has discretion in choosing who will be his or her rabbi.) The story, also typically, provides a striking paradox. Why should judging the law between man and man demand strict neutrality, while judging the law of God seems to incorporate a little leeway, a bit of equity at the margin? Some rabbinic texts suggest that because it is essential for everyone, even judges, to "do that which is right and good in the sight of the LORD, that it may be well with thee" (Deut. VI, 18), it is not enough to follow the strict letter of the law; judgment must follow a higher justice, which is equity. Moreover, the erstwhile neutral judge is required to be grounded in the community. Finally, Jewish law is directed more at members of the community than at the judge. The role of rabbi or judge is less that of an umpire than that of an interpreter of obligations to those who agree that they are obliged.[32]

Maimonides stated that a judge should be wise and sensible, learned in law and full of knowledge, and acquainted with subjects such as medicine, arithmetic, astronomy, and astrology, as well as the ways of sorcerers, idolaters, and the like. Also, a judge must not be too old, a eunuch, or childless. He must be pure in body as well as mind, imposing in stature, and conversant in many languages so that he will not need an interpreter. Maimonides's seven fundamental qualities of a judge include love of people, love of truth, wisdom, humility, fear of God, disdain of money, and a good reputation.[33]

It could be that affective ties to people are essential for a man to avoid being "a scoundrel within the four corners of the Torah," as Nachmanides described the danger of excessive formalism. Yet anti-formalism hardly meant limiting judicial power. Nachmanides insisted that the command "Thou shalt not depart from the word which they shall tell thee, to the right nor the left" meant obeying a judge of the Great Sanhedrin no matter what. Rashi enjoined obedience, "Even if he tells you of the right that it is the left or about the left that it is the right."[34]

Why was one of Maimonides' criteria that a judge not be childless? This further hints at the benefits of rootedness. Perhaps Maimonides meant to invoke the humility many of us have to learn in trying to deal with family disputes and disagreements that are much too deep to be resolved by determining who did what or whether procedures were formally equal. Equality in a family is always relational. Protection at its best must be keenly aware of dependence, yet active in quest of independence. To be a good judge may be akin to being a good parent. Both require questioning and adjusting. Neither should involve playing favorites, and both require constant attention to the changing character of messages and messengers. Both parent and judge follow rules and try to know when old rules ought to be broken. The past matters much, but the future ought to matter more.

The First Jewish Federal Judge and a Question of Social Justice

When Jacob Trieber died after twenty-seven years as a federal judge, the *Arkansas Gazette* provided a typical, almost generic obituary that included a characteristic, apparent inconsistency. Trieber "was perhaps best known on the bench for his *impartiality*. In criminal cases he was as severe, *if not more severe*, with law violators who had wealth and influence under ordinary circumstances, as with those lacking friends or funds to fight for them in court."[35] No mention was made of the religion of this "staunch Republican," though his role as a Mason was described in detail, and the newspaper reported that several bishops were among the honorary pallbearers.[36]

In 1900, the *Gazette*'s report that President William McKinley was about to appoint Trieber a federal judge mentioned that Trieber's maternal grandfather and great-grandfather were rabbis. The *Gazette* also noted, "By his conscientious loyalty to his convictions and clients, and by the charm of his address, he has succeeded in overcoming various adversities and prejudices that threatened to impede his early progress."[37]

With this appointment, the first federal judge in the United States known to be Jewish ascended to the bench. (Judah P. Benjamin had turned down President Millard Fillmore's offer in 1853 of a Supreme Court appointment—perhaps Fillmore's finest hour, but then the competition was not fierce.)[38] Actually, Jacob Trieber was a most improbable pathfinder. His career was a classic, mainstream American success story in many ways. He was born in Prussia in 1853 and educated in a German gymnasium. His parents decided to immigrate to the United States in 1866, when they joined an elder son in St. Louis. The family then followed the river down to Helena, Arkansas, where Jacob worked as a clerk in a dry-goods store and began to study law with a former Arkansas Supreme Court Justice, M. L. Stephenson, who later became Trieber's law partner in representing "an extensive and wealthy clientage."

Trieber quickly became active in Republican Party politics once he passed the bar in 1880, and he held many party posts and repeatedly ran unsuccessfully for major federal and state posts. After being elected treasurer of Phillips County in 1892, Trieber was appointed U.S. Attorney by McKinley in 1897 and District Judge three years later, with strong support expressed by black citizens, who wrote of their need for federal protection from the poisonous local atmosphere.[39]

For the most part, Trieber's judicial career was smoothly unexceptional. He wrote a number of law review articles and frequently sat by designation on the Eighth Circuit Court of Appeals and in the Southern District of New York, where he could be near his daughter who had settled in Scarsdale. Interestingly, William Howard Taft, Jr., known for his virulent opposition to Louis Brandeis's appointment in 1916 and often described as antisemitic, apparently was a friend and admirer of Trieber. The *New York Times* also celebrated Trieber, editorializing about his skill in moving cases and his keen understanding and quick recall of all pivotal federal decisions. The *Times* called Trieber "the most perfect out-of-town judge who ever presided in the big town."[40]

Trieber thus provides a predictable story of an influential Republican politician who became a steady, dependable judge. But that portrait is complicated by his opinions dealing with race discrimination. The story of his involvement, despite his initial partial recusal from proceedings growing out of the bloody race riot in Phillips County in 1919, is fascinating in itself. Trieber, in fact, played a crucial part in the dramatic events preceding the Court's pathbreaking decision in *Moore v. Dempsey*,[41] which held that mob-dominated proceedings violated due process and could be attacked through a writ of federal habeas corpus. *Moore* thereby vindicated Justice Holmes's earlier dissent from the Court's refusal to upset the conviction of Leo Frank. (Despite his general position of deference to the popular will, Holmes had objected strenuously when the Court refused to allow federal habeas corpus to cut through the tissue to the bone, thereby allowing Frank's conviction to stand despite blatant mob domination of the courtroom in the infamous case that led to the lynching of Leo Frank.[42])

Still more significant was Trieber's decision early in his judicial career in *United States v. Morris*.[43] A local group of "whitecappers"—

white citizens who specialized in intimidating blacks and Jews—tried to drive blacks from their agricultural and factory jobs.[44] These white-cappers were precursors of the renascent Ku Klux Klan of the World War I period. In *Morris,* Trieber rejected a demurrer to a federal indictment against several whitecappers. To do so, he had to distinguish away a long series of Supreme Court precedents stretching back at least to *United States v. Cruikshank* in 1876.[45] Moreover, as it was clear that Trieber's sympathies lay not with the defendants but with their victims, he ran the risk of appearing biased, particularly because black citizens had been among his most ardent supporters for his federal judgeship.

Trieber read the 1866 Civil Rights Act—the very statute at stake in *Patterson*—as no other judge ever approached reading it, from the 1870s when the Supreme Court eviscerated the statute until it was resuscitated in 1968 in *Jones v. Alfred H. Mayer Co.*[46] In fact, Trieber's reading may still be the broadest ever, and, for reasons many have discussed at great length elsewhere, also the most accurate.[47] Reflecting the dominant mood of the 39th Congress, the judge stated initially that "Every citizen and freeman is endowed with certain rights and privileges, to enjoy which no written law or statute is required."[48] He then went on to quote an amalgam of the Declaration of Independence, the Arkansas Constitution, and several concurring opinions and circuit court opinions by Supreme Court Justices. But Trieber's basic approach was to note the prevalence of "unjust discriminations against the negroes" and to assert that "Congress enacted this civil rights act, intending thereby to protect them in the enjoyment of those rights which are generally conceded to be fundamental and inherent in every freeman."[49]

Indeed, Trieber had the wonderful temerity—we might even term it *chutzpah*—to cut to the core. He asked, "Shall the courts be less liberal in construing constitutional provisions in favor of freedom than those in favor of slavery?"[50] Even to ask that question rhetorically, Trieber had to be willing to reject both popular will and precedent; it is fair to speculate that his own background helped him empathize unusually closely with another class of victims. As he probably anticipated, good lawyer that he was, the appeal of an unreported companion case also handed down by Trieber gave the Supreme Court the opportunity again to make clear that it would have none of Trieber's broad definition of freedom and of what constituted a form of involuntary servitude.

In contrast with Trieber's decisions, Justice Brewer's opinion in

Hodges v. United States[51] insisted that it could not be a federal offense for a mob to drive eight blacks from their jobs at a lumber mill. The Thirteenth Amendment, Brewer argued, was "not an attempt to commit [blacks] to the care of the nation."[52] They would have to seek redress exclusively in the Arkansas courts. Otherwise, blacks would be treated as "wards of the government."[53] No special treatment should be meted out to anyone, because all citizens must be treated alike. In the long run, the best interests of all, including blacks, would be served, if everyone simply competed equally and corrected any problems at the state level.[54] In opposition to this view, Trieber had discerned more clearly than any other federal judge of his era that it simply did not answer the problem to direct Negro victims of violence and intimidation away from the special protection of the federal courts to "tak[e] their chances with other citizens in the states where they shall make their homes."[55]

The Supreme Court thus clutched for the blindfold of justice, at a terrible cost to justice itself.[56] Both past and present realities were ignored in pursuit of detachment and impartiality. Trieber had recognized that the Thirteenth Amendment authorized Congress to legislate "against acts of individuals, as well as of the states, in all matters necessary for the protection of the rights granted by that Amendment."[57] To Trieber, impartiality entailed awareness of who was before the court and how they were situated in life. The Supreme Court, however, made the comfortable assumption that adequate equality had already been achieved, and that to leave people to take their chances in life's struggle constituted the entire judicial obligation.

Conclusion

What, if anything, can we learn from the apparent contrast between the judicial roles played by Trieber and Frankfurter? These two assimilated Jewish judges reacted differently to the fundamental issue of whether and when to consider group identities. But for them, as for all of us, there inevitably came the crunch, a time to test their values. The wisdom of Solomon's famous judgment depended on his ability to transcend the usual rules and precedents in order to do justice in a particular case. And the story of Solomon and his threat to cut the baby in two emphasizes context and history. Its crucial subtext undercuts the stubborn theory of evenhandedness in favor of pre-existing and ongoing relationships. This story captures elements of the horror, power, and angst that should go with the job of judging, as well as some of what it takes to be a good or great judge attuned to the role's constructive possibilities.[58]

A number of our leading judges today appear to relish the Solomonic judicial power to go it alone, yet they proclaim that their actions are actually compelled by judicial restraint. Such judges claim to be bound by the past. They regard their unique personal understandings of the national will, discerned in a constitutional text that is luminous to them, as the only source to which they owe loyalty. When the language of the Constitution beckons, the views of past and contemporary colleagues must be ignored. In a dissent from a decision not to overrule a two-year-old precedent that he regarded as overly tender toward criminal defendants, for example, Justice Scalia accused his colleagues of following the rule of binding precedent simply to preserve the Court's legitimacy. Scalia proclaimed, "I would think it a violation of my oath to adhere to what I consider a plainly unjustified intrusion on the democratic process in order that the Court might save face."[59]

The zest of this lone gun-slinger approach, currently exemplified best by Scalia but practiced by many other appellate judges in the federal system, helps explain the passionate disagreement within the Court's conservative bloc in the recent Pennsylvania abortion decision, discussed above. In the 1990s macabre judicial machinations in death penalty cases also illustrate the phenomenon. For example, in a death penalty case from Texas in the spring of 1992, four justices voted to grant *certiorari,* thus garnering the requisite number for the Court to take a case under its longstanding "Rule of Four." Collegial respect on the Court is apparently at such a low ebb, however, that the five other justices had no compunction about voting immediately to dissolve the stay of execution in the case.[60] The prisoner could therefore be electrocuted quickly, and the case thereby mooted and never heard.

The Supreme Court itself is an association—a collegial body that is terribly important to a large number of people, and it both generates and maintains its own customs and mores. The old ways of the Court now seem under obvious stress and there is a danger that the Court could become simply an amalgam of separate legal shops. Purportedly for the sake of democratic processes, several current justices repeatedly insist on the need to go it alone. This tends to result in parallel statist decisions by these same justices, an outcome that leaves individual litigants in isolation as they face the full force of some vague, general democratic will.

The judicial desire to view the world in increasingly dichotomous terms is especially troubling. Judges currently are eager to declare that their decisions turn on crisp opposing categories, such as public/private, state/individual, and neutrality/bias. Thereby they seek to insulate themselves and their decisions from the need to wrestle with morality. The pursuit of justice simply vanishes. From atop their lofty neutral benches, these judges delight to use the easy option of deference to either the individualistic instrumentalism of the marketplace or the presumed majoritarianism of the state—or to both.

It is uncomfortable to recognize that our culturally rich communities are brimming with varying definitions of the good life. Both their conflicts and their shared emphasis on transcending individual self-interest demand intellectual engagement and tough tolerance. Instead, our legal system divides and conquers. Insisting on the autonomy and absolute sovereignty of the individual, our law bleaches away the real normative alternatives that surround us.

Too often, the individual—and what he or she alone values—is portrayed in law as the essential building-block of our secular public world, the only source of rights. Yet what would happen if we did not think it necessary to follow the "method of avoidance" that John Rawls recommends because of "the fact of pluralism?"[61] What a challenge it would be if the legal world rejected Rawls's prescription for politics, that "we try, so far as we can, neither to assert nor to deny any religious, philosophical or moral views, or their associated philosophical accounts of truth and the status of values."[62]

Our law is inevitably and inextricably bound together with our nation's civic, public, and political life. Law would be both more realistic and more just if we did not strain so hard to ignore our varied group cultures and contexts. The communities in which we live define and enrich our lives, even as their boundaries confine and complicate us. Our communities help establish who we are alone and together.

In these last chapters I have tried to soften some traditional harsh judgments, to make more complex what is often taken to be simple and dichotomous, and to propose a vision of the judicial role in which judges are comfortable with paradox, not debilitated by it. Their oaths and roles as judges for the state—and our oaths and roles as jurors, lawyers, litigants, and citizens—connect us in commonalities. But the encumbrances of our particular groups produce inevitable tensions for each and all of us.

No particular homburg, tallis, or robe can be a determining factor in the quest for just rights and responsibilities. No single role will suffice.

No one, not even within the interpretive community of judges, can escape the impossibility and frustration inherent in seeking justice. We also cannot elude a multitude of harsh communal realities. Painfully, moreover, each of us needs to be judged by others to gain and maintain the respect we crave. It is both tragic and hopeful, therefore, that all people are encumbered in many ways before the law.

Conclusion

Justice Holmes was almost ninety when he told an admiring correspondent: "I have said to my brethren many times that I hate justice, which means that I know if a man begins to talk about that, for one reason or another he is shirking thinking in legal terms."[1] This illustrates Holmes's penchant for provocative statements; it also underscores a commonplace among lawyers who seem to delight in their insistence that there is a necessary bifurcation between the concept of justice and legal thinking. Our dominant legal paradigm makes it seem natural to ignore what *ought* to be in order to honor past precedent and to defer to what *is*.

Pluralism *is* a central reality, and we *ought* to attend better to the substance of pluralism in American law. Because groups are so pervasive and powerful in "real life," anyone who wishes to reach others directly must focus on these groups. In addition, legal doctrine and the outcomes reached will be more coherent if we acknowledge that groups *qua* groups have significant legal impact. We will be in a better position to connect "reality" with the patterned, changeable conglomeration we delight to call "law." The final reason for paying attention to pluralism is tied to obligations that are generated by the complicated company we keep. The building blocks of any quest for justice include the groups—social, professional, political, civil, interpretive, religious and so forth—from which we derive and apply our ethical standards in search of a better life.

For Holmes, and for most legal thinkers today, the legal system rests upon the presumed equality of all individuals before the law. Individuals are autonomous. We are all fundamentally fungible for legal purposes. Within the arena of deracinated legal equality, one person primarily deals with another on a one-to-one basis. Economic, political, and social competitions reflect individual choices made in pursuit of varying definitions of the good life. To the extent that anyone is concerned about the pursuit of justice, that concern is but one of many equally vague and unrealizable goals. It is akin to, and more or less interchangeable with, other hortatory concepts.

Within today's individualistic legal ethos, justice has principally become an issue of whether, as a formal matter, political, economic, and legal markets are open to all individuals. At best, the sovereignty exercised by legislators, bureaucrats, and judges is merely bound to follow pre-existing rules and procedures and to reflect the wishes and interests of aggregated constituencies. Among legal thinkers, talk of justice occurs somewhere above or beneath—but surely outside—normal law.

I have argued for a different model. Under this approach, for pragmatic and other important reasons, attention must be paid to group context. For this approach it is necessary to accept that while justice is unattainable in this life, we still must always pursue justice. In other words, justice is not one of many goals. It is the ultimate obligation of our legal system. To seek justice, moreover, requires constant reflection as well as attention to particularistic nuances. Sensitivity to a complex, changing network of mutual relationships inextricably grounded in history provides the only plausible hope for a more just future.

My primary focus has been the law judges make. They have the advantage of force behind their words, but they often have made quite bad law. Nevertheless, from Prospero and Plymouth through Yazoo and Yoknapatawpha to Amos and Jacob Trieber, we have seen that all of us do and must judge. The ability to step outside a doctrinal box composed only of individuals and government will help not only legal thinkers but every thinker to reason toward a juster justice.

I emphasized that "The past gives us our vocabulary and fixes the limits of our imagination; we cannot get away from it."[2] Sadly, an individualistic ethic only makes sense in a society that has lived up to its individualistic ethic in the past.[3] This has never happened. But we have learned from the past that, precisely because justice ought to be the indispensable element of all law, legal thinking must inevitably and inexhaustibly confront group conflict and competition. The burdens of history create a floor, but history provides no ceiling. Our best, perhaps our only hope is that the prism of our groups may "cool the fierce glow of moral passion by making it pass through reflection."[4]

This book in no way denies the importance of individual autonomy. Such autonomy, however, always entails dependence on others. It is both unrealistic and distorting—and ultimately unjust—to pretend otherwise. Our multitude of groups, both voluntary and involuntary, establish the preconditions for the dignity we all need for any individual action to make sense. When we really do treat an individual as an individual, in fact, we must take into account that person's history and aspirations, defined largely by group identities.

The view of legal justice I suggest is, to be sure, deeply paradoxical. It posits an overarching obligation that remains within the free choice of individuals. At the same time, these individuals must depend on identification with others to be themselves. It is sensible to return to Tocqueville once more. He observed: "Providence did not make mankind entirely free or completely enslaved. Providence has, in truth, drawn a predestined circle around each man beyond which he cannot pass; but within those vast limits man is strong and free, and so are peoples."[5]

Tocqueville defined the limits that encircle man's freedom as mores, products of any individual's social state. The social state of Americans, Tocqueville observed, may be considered "the prime cause of most of the laws, customs, and ideas which control the nation's behavior." Moreover, the social state "modifies even those things which it does not cause" and it is "commonly the result of circumstances, sometimes of laws, but most often of a combination of the two."[6]

I make no argument that individual rights ought to be jettisoned entirely, nor that any group right should be absolute. Indeed, groups often are unjust to their own members as well as to each other. The claims of dissenters and persons excluded, the rights of those who seek escape and of those who are forced to leave, cannot be ignored. Yet if we heed the complexity introduced by group claims, we return to an essential conundrum about individuals, groups, and time.

The wonderful Humphrey Bogart character, "Rick," in the movie "Casablanca" (1942), offers a more familiar referent for the same crucial points. Surely nearly everyone recalls that Rick, the proprietor of the Cafe Americain in occupied Casablanca, insists that he has no past, that he is neutral and above the fray. He proclaims he is in it for himself and will not get involved for love, money, or anything else. The happy ending—when Rick finally gets off his barroom stool and puts himself at risk, only to give up both the woman he loves (Ingrid Bergman) and his own chance to escape the social Darwinism of Casablanca—moves us. Rick's gruffly unstated attention to his better self, his sacrifice to aid the Resistance, is anchored directly in his group obligations. The ending may be shrouded in fog, but it is clearly just.[7]

The essence of any effort to do justice in this life is captured in three questions by the great Rabbi Hillel: "If I am not for myself, then who is for me? And if I am not for others, then who am I? And if not now, when?"[8] Hillel's third question focuses on a pressingly present sense of obligation that contrasts with the more familiar, complacent acceptance of the legal status quo. His first and second questions seem to describe an inescapable Möbius strip that links and loops individual and social identity.

Throughout this book, I have suggested that we construct, and are constituted by, the overlapping groups within which we live. Inevitably, we are the creatures and the creators of these groups. We also make our law. To reconstruct law realistically and with justice, we must become more protective of group identities and increasingly aware that we constantly judge and are judged. It is necessary to push beyond the assumption that if we do get down to cases, hard questions can be answered with facile dichotomies such as individual and state, autonomy and coercion, mine and yours. Groups confine us. Yet groups may set us free to pursue justice through, rather than under, law.

Notes

Preface

1. Tim O'Brien, *The Things They Carried* (Boston: Houghton Mifflin, 1990), 40.
2. The New York Court of Appeals noted drily the "differences" between the Satmar Hasidim and the surrounding communities, and the Satmarer insistence on the separation of the sexes which "have led to a series of court cases." Grumet v. Board of Education of Kiryas Joel School District, 1993 N.Y. LEXIS 1866*2 (NY Ct. App. July 6, 1993), *cert. granted*, 114 S.Ct. 10 (1993). The United States Supreme Court's consideration of the case has attracted a great deal of attention. It involves an Establishment Clause challenge to a 1989 New York statute that created a public school district coterminous with the Satmar religious enclave to provide handicapped children with public educational services. New York's highest court struck down the statute, terming the separate Satmar (or Satmarer) school district "de jure segregation for the benefit [of] one school religious group" and holding that "[a] forbidden denominational preference can result from a grant of benefits to one religious groups as readily as discrimination against sects." id. at *31.

   Having obtained approximately $6 million for 200 special needs children, the Satmar Hasidim now are willing to educate handicapped boys and girls together and to have them taught by outsiders. In earlier legal contests, the Satmar had insisted on strict separation. This change seems to echo compromises in religious positions that figured in the Bob Jones University case, discussed in Chapter 5. The challengers of the Satmar school district invoked Satmar suppression of internal dissent, but at oral argument in the Supreme Court this argument was rebuffed as irrelevant. For a brief summary quoting state police reports of "hundreds of calls from people who've been stoned, their house and car windows broken, their sidewalks stenciled with Hebrew profanities" because they disagreed with the Satmar Grand Rabbi, see Michael Winerip, "Pious Village Is No Stranger to the Police," *New York Times*, Sept. 20, 1992. For the 1994 Supreme Court decision see Chapter 5.

Introduction

1. The example of the impact of the butterfly's wings on the weather in New York is drawn from James Gleick, *Chaos: Making a New Science* (New York: Viking Penguin, 1987), 8–31, 23 (discussing the Butterfly Effect as only a half-joking example of "sensitive dependence on initial conditions"). There have been numerous forceful attacks on both the coherence and the objectivity of accepted classificatory schemes across many disciplines. Some of the most accessible include: Martha Minow, *Making All the Difference: Inclusion, Exclusion, and American Law* (Ithaca: Cornell University Press, 1990) (law); Peter Novick, *That Noble Dream: The 'Objectivity Question' and the American Historical Profession* (Cambridge: Cambridge University Press, 1988) (American history); George Lakoff, *Women, Fire, and Dangerous Things: What Categories Reveal about the Mind* (Chicago: University of Chicago Press, 1987) (linguistics); Stephen J. Gould, *The Flamingo's Smile: Reflections in Natural History* (New York: W. W. Norton, 1985) (history of science).

2. Abraham Lincoln faced a similar difficulty with "liberty"—"the apple of gold" established by the Declaration of Independence, then "pictured" and "framed" by the Union and the Constitution. Abraham Lincoln, *The Collected Works of Abraham Lincoln* Roy P. Basler, ed. (New Brunswick: Rutgers University Press, 1953) IV, 169.

    By 1864, however, Lincoln ruefully noted: "The world has never had a good definition of the word liberty, and the American people, just now, are much in need of one. We all declare for liberty; but in using the same *word* we do not all mean the same *thing*." Id., VII, 301. In contrast to the constitutional positivism dominant today, Lincoln stressed that "The *picture* was made for the apple—*not* the apple for the picture." Id., IV, 169. Lincoln was not alone to comment upon the charged, associational basis for language. See Maurice Olender, *The Language of Paradise: Race, Religion, and Philology in the Nineteenth Century*, Arthur Goldhammer, trans. (Cambridge, Mass.: Harvard University Press, 1992).

3. Michael S. Dukakis, "Acceptance Speech," July 21, 1988, #54 *Vital Speeches of the Day* (1988), 642. President Ronald Reagan loved to quote—actually to misquote slightly—another passage from Governor Winthrop's speech about creating "a city upon a hill," as a paean to American exceptionalism. John Winthrop's complete speech aboard the Arbella, "A Model of Christian Charity," is reprinted in *Puritan Political Ideas*, Edmund S. Morgan, ed. (Indianapolis: Bobbs-Merrill, 1965), 75.

    That the settlers of Massachusetts Bay neither celebrated diversity nor always practiced tolerance is well known. Similar limitations may still dominate small-town U.S.A. See David Potter, "Social Cohesion and the Crisis of Law," in *American Law and the Constitutional Order*, Lawrence M. Friedman and Harry N. Scheiber, eds. (Cambridge, Mass.: Harvard University Press, 1978), 420.

4. George Bush, "Acceptance Speech," August 18, 1988, #55, *Vital Speeches of the Day* (1988), 2.

5. CNN Specials, Transcript #86–11, Nov. 4, 1992, p.6. Vice President-Elect Al Gore similarly talked about "the values of community," and specified that "among them is our obligation to protect the environment in which we live." CNN Specials, Transcript #86–12, Nov. 4, 1992, p. 9.

6. Peter Hamilton, "Editor's Foreword" to Anthony Cohen, *The Symbolic Construction of Community* (New York: Tavistock Publications, 1985), 7.

7. Mary Ann Glendon, "Individualism and Communitarianism in Contemporary Legal Systems: Tensions and Accommodations" (1992) (draft on file with author).

8. Jack H. Hexter, *Reappraisals in History* (Chicago: University of Chicago Press, 1963), 39. In discussing the common misuse of Ferdinand Tonnies's famous competing sociological types, *gemeinschaft* versus *gesellschaft*, Hexter described this fallacy as the belief that "any flow of social energy in the direction of one such pole can only take place by way of substraction from the flow of energy to the opposite pole" (40). For an application of Hexter's point to historical studies of American communities, see Thomas Bender, *Community and Social Change in America* (New Brunswick: Rutgers University Press, 1978).

9. Thomas Grey, *The Wallace Stevens Case: Law and the Practice of Poetry* (Cambridge, Mass.: Harvard University Press, 1991), 7, quoting John Keats on Shakespeare's ability to live "in uncertainties, mysteries, doubts, without any irritable reaching after fact and reason" and to "remain with half-knowledge." John Keats, Letter to George and Thomas Keats, December 21, 1817, in *The Selected Letters of John Keats*, Lionel Trilling, ed. (New York: Farrar, Straus and Young, 1951), 92.

10. J. Willard Hurst, *Justice Holmes on Legal History* (New York: Macmillan, 1964), 39. A classic discussion of this American propensity is Arthur Schlesinger, "Biography of a Nation of Joiners," 50 *Am. Hist. Rev.* 1 (1944).

11. This point about the tendency of legal thought is hardly new, of course. Perhaps it is put best in "The Mystery of Jurisprudence," in Thurman Arnold, *The Symbols of Government* (New Haven: Yale University Press, 1935), 59–71. Another leading legal realist, Jerome Frank, put it this way: "Once trapped by the belief that the announced rules are the paramount thing in the law, and that uniformity and certainty are of major importance, and are to be procured by uniformity and certainty in phrasing the rules, a judge . . . refuses to do justice in the case on trial. . . . Such injustice is particularly tragic because it is based on a hope doomed to

futility, a hope of controlling the future." Jerome Frank, *Law and the Modern Mind* (1930; rpt. New York: Brentano's, 1963), 165–66.

12. Arthur Bentley, *The Process of Government,* Peter Odegard, ed., (1908, rpt. Cambridge, Mass.: Harvard University Press, 1967), 277. Karl Llewellyn thought so highly of Bentley that he described his own work in the early 1930s as simply "a rediscovery of Bentley"; Karl Llewellyn, "The Constitution as Institution," 34 *Col. L. Rev.* 1, 1 n.1 (1934). An earlier European version of Bentley's point about pluralism may be found in Georg Simmel's essay, "Conflict," in his *Conflict and the Web of Group Affiliations,* K. Wolff, trans. (1964), quoted in Carol Weisbrod, *The Boundaries of Utopia* (New York: Pantheon Books, 1980), 113. For an elaboration of Llewellyn's concern about differences among groups of merchants, see Zipporah Batshaw Wiseman, "The Limits of Vision: Karl Llewellyn and the Merchant Rules," 100 *Harv. L. Rev.* 465 (1987).

13. Karl Llewellyn, "What Price Contract?—An Essay in Perspective," 40 *Yale L. J.* 704, 734 n.63 (1931).

14. Bob Cover often advanced a seemingly bleak vision, particularly concerning the role of judges. See Robert Cover, *Justice Accused* (New Haven: Yale University Press, 1975); Robert Cover, "Violence and the Word," 95 *Yale L. J.* 1601 (1986). But he also expressed great hope in law as "a challenging enrichment of social life"; see Robert Cover, "Nomos and Narrative," 97 *Harv. L. Rev.* 4, 68 (1983), that might provide "the bridge—the committed social behavior which constitutes the way a group of people will attempt to get from here to there." Robert Cover, "The Folktales of Justice: Tales of Jurisdiction," 14 *Cap. U. L. Rev.* 179, 181 (1985).

If we embrace communal ghosts even while we recognize their dangerous tendencies, we may create more and better room for ourselves and our posterity. A room entirely of one's own, Virginia Woolf notwithstanding, is a tough place in which to live. We need privacy, but we also need others to make sense of our efforts at communication. As Willard Hurst stated, "Individuals realize their humanity only in society, but they realize their individuality only in self-awareness, which consists in some sense of separateness." J. Willard Hurst, *Justice Holmes on Legal History* (New York: Macmillan, 1964), 15. Yet Milner Ball recently asked, "Isn't the primary reality and real mystery the community? Is it I or is it the neighbor and our binding that is wonderful?" Milner Ball, "Humanizing Law," Book Review of Joseph Vining, *The Authoritative and the Authoritarian* 35 *U.C.L.A. L. Rev.* 547, 554 (1988). For an important exploration of what "belonging" ought to mean in the context of national citizenship, see Kenneth L. Karst, *Belonging to America: Equal Citizenship and the Constitution* (New Haven: Yale University Press, 1989).

15. Even Tocqueville, whose observations on the importance of groups in the

United States are extraordinary, pointed out that in Europe by the 1830s "within associations, there often prevails a tyranny more intolerant than that exercised over society in the name of the government they attack." Alexis de Tocqueville, *Democracy in America,* J. P. Mayer, ed. (Garden City: Doubleday Paperback, 1969), 195. Tocqueville contrasted this situation with America, where associations generally featured "civil government," "a place for individual independence," and "no sacrifice of will or of reason." Id.

1. Authority and Freedom

1. Richard Helgerson, *Forms of Nationhood: The Elizabethan Writing of England* (Chicago: University of Chicago Press, 1992), 3.
2. Martha Minow, "Speaking and Writing Against Hate," 11 *Cardozo L. Rev.* 1393, 1397–98 (1990)(quoting Catharine MacKinnon).
3. John Locke, *Second Treatise of Government,* Peter Laslett, ed. (Cambridge: Cambridge University Press, 1988), sect. 49, 301 (emphasis in original).
4. J. G. A. Pocock, "The Common-Law Mind: Custom and the Immemorial" in his *The Ancient Constitution and the Feudal Law* (Cambridge: Cambridge University Press, 1987), 35. See also the famous "I'm sorry . . . it's turtles all the way down" story (misattributed to William James) about the conflict between science and faith, discussed in Roger Cramton, "Demystifying Legal Scholarship," 75 *Geo. L. J.* 1, 2 (1986).
5. Sir Edward Coke, Seventh Reports, *Calvin's Case,* reprinted in John Henry Thomas and John Farquhar Fraser, *The Reports of Sir Edward Coke* (London: J. Butterworth and Son, 1826), IV, 6. As Joseph Henry Smith put it, "The report of *Calvin's Case* remained for many a day the point of departure of subsequent judicial discourse respecting dominions not parcel of the realm." Joseph H. Smith, *Appeals to the Privy Council from the American Plantations* (New York: Columbia University Press, 1950), 469.
6. There is considerable internal evidence that Shakespeare took some specific details, ranging from St. Elmo's Fire in the rigging to the reactions of men of all ranks to their imminent death, from William Strachey's report of the wreck of the *Sea Venture* as a source for *The Tempest.* This theme, and much of the general history of the *Sea Venture* on which I rely, is summarized in sprightly fashion (as it were) in Avery Kolb's posthumous article, *"The Tempest,"* 34 *American Heritage* 26 (April/May, 1983). See generally Samuel Purchas, *Hakluytus Posthumous or Purchas His Pilgrimes, Contayning a History of the World in Sea Voyages and Lande Travells by Englishmen and others* (Glasgow: J. MacLehose and Sons, 1906), which reprints William Strachey's *True Reportory of the Wrack,*

dated July 15, 1610, but first published in 1625, and Sylvester Jourdain's *A Discovery of the Bermudas* (1610, facsimile ed. 1940). The Virginia Company also published an apologetic version in 1610, entitled *True Declaration of the state of the Colonie in Virginia, with a confutation of such scandalous reports as have tended to the disgrace of so worthy an enterprise,* which is available in Peter Force, *Tracts and Other Papers* (1844, rept. New York: Peter Smith, 1947), vol. III.

7. Edmund S. Morgan, *American Slavery-American Freedom: The Ordeal of Colonial Virginia* (New York: Norton, 1975), 72–108. Morgan succinctly and powerfully makes the case that the English actions suggest a bizarre, "suicidal impulse" (75). The English settlers committed numerous atrocities against the Indians upon whom they depended. While starving and engaging in cannibalism, the colonists remained unwilling to sow their own crops or even to hunt or fish, reserving their energy for bowling in the streets. We know these things largely from the written record kept by the settlers; the unwritten reality may have been even more brutal.

8. All citations in the text are from William Shakespeare's *The Tempest,* Frank Kermode, ed. (Cambridge, Mass.: Harvard University Press, 1958).

9. Edmund S. Morgan, *Inventing the People: The Rise of Popular Sovereignty in England and America* (New York: Norton, 1988), 100.

10. Id. 21.

11. Wayne Booth points out that the term "character" comes from the Greek word for "stamp" or "mark," but also can be translated as "ethos." Wayne Booth, *The Company We Keep* (Berkeley: University of California Press, 1988), 232 n.5. Much of the discussion about the character of Caliban through the centuries is centered on the nature/nurture controversy.

12. G. F. Parker, *Johnson's Shakespeare* (New York: Oxford University Press, 1989), 119, quoting S. Johnson, *Notes on The Tempest.*

13. Mark Van Doren, *Shakespeare* (New York: H. Holt, 1939), 282–83, reissued as a Doubleday Anchor book in 1953. Similar views were expressed in the year of *Brown v. Board of Education,* 347 U.S. 483 (1954), by Derek Traversi, in his *Shakespeare: The Last Phase* (New York: Harcourt, 1954) and even in part by Frank Kermode in his famous edition of *The Tempest* (1954). For a stinging critique of the views propounded by Traversi and, to a lesser extent, by Kermode about Caliban and Prospero, see William Empson's 1964 essay, "Hunt the Symbol," reprinted in William Empson, *Essays on Shakespeare,* David B. Pirie, ed., (Cambridge: Cambridge University Press, 1986), 238–43 (accusing Traversi of "expressing . . . the pure milk of master-race doctrine . . . with the usual glum sanctimoniousness" and finding "something very shambling and sub-human about the whole [Moral Critic] movement").

14. For significantly more upbeat views of Prospero than my own, see John Denvir, "William Shakespeare and the Jurisprudence of Comedy," 39 *Stan. L. Rev.* 825, 835–37 (1987) (viewing Prospero as a fair, even benevolent, judge); Winfried Schleiner, "Prospero as a Renaissance Therapist," 6 *Literature and Medicine* 54 (1987) (arguing that Prospero may be seen as a crafty therapist with a moral and curative large design); but see Jan Kott's much darker portrait of Prospero in "Prospero's Staff," reprinted in *Shakespeare: The Tempest: A Casebook* D. J. Palmer, ed. (London: Macmillan, 1968), 244. Compare W. H. Auden's "Prospero to Ariel" in "The Sea and the Mirror," W. H. Auden, *Collected Longer Poems* (New York: Random House, 1969), 204. ("When I woke into my life, a sobbing dwarf / Whom giants served only as they pleased, / I was not what I seemed. . . . Now, Ariel, I am that I am, your late and lonely master, / Who knows now what magic is:—the power to enchant / That comes from disillusion.")

15. Palmer, "Introduction," *Shakespeare,* 16.

16. Leo Marx, *The Machine in the Garden: Technology and the Pastoral Ideal in America* (New York: Oxford University Press, 1964), 34–72. For a survey of the scholarly debate on the relevant narratives, and the view that "nobody who impartially surveys the evidence . . . will deny that Shakespeare was interested in the Gates expedition, and in the New World generally," see Kermode's Introduction to *"The Tempest,"* xvi–xvii n.3. Despite the reference to the "still-vex'd Bermoothes," however, if the play is anywhere on earth, it is set in the Mediterranean, somewhere off the coast of Africa.

17. Stephen Greenblatt, *Shakespearean Negotiations: The Circulation of Social Energy in Renaissance England* (Berkeley: University of California Press, 1988), 40.

18. Id. 4.

19. Stanley Cavell, *Disowning Knowledge in Six Plays of Shakespeare* (Cambridge, Cambridge University Press, 1987), 3. Cavell argues that skepticism, which he describes as "privatization of the world, . . . repudiation of assured significance, repudiation of the capacity to improvise common significance" (19), is central to Shakespearean tragedy. But he suggests that the second half of *The Winter's Tale,* for example, shows that such profound skepticism is inherently unstable, seeking recovery through reconceiving—"in finding skepticism's source (its origin, say, if you can say it without supposing its origin is past)" (198). While my reading of *The Tempest* is also concerned with skepticism and with questions of "participation and parturition" (200), my sense of the burden of history, both intergenerational and "public" history, may be even darker than is Cavell's. It is also obvious, however, that we share an interest (perhaps a grasping for hope would be a more apt de-

scription) in reading Shakespeare to suggest a quest to transcend skepticism.

20. III.iii.28–49. For a fine brief description of this phenomenon in Plato, see Mary Ann Glendon, *Abortion and Divorce in Western Law: American Failures, European Challenges* (Cambridge, Mass.: Harvard University Press, 1987).

21. This theme seems to cut across academic fields. Consider, for example, the work of Richard Rorty, Michael Sandel, and Charles Taylor in philosophy and political theory; Wayne Booth, among many others, in literary criticism; David Hall, David Konig, and Bruce Mann among historians of colonial New England; and Milner Ball and Martha Minow among law professors. This current trend also helps to explain the renewed interest in Charles Peirce and his claim a century ago that even science depends upon membership in an infinite "community of inquiry," quoted in R. Jackson Wilson, *In Quest of Community: Social Philosophy in the United States, 1860–1920* (New York: Wiley, 1968), 41, an excellent general discussion of an earlier search for community by intellectuals in the United States.

22. William Bradford, *Of Plymouth Plantation,* Samuel E. Morison, ed. (New York: Knopf, 1952), 75. On the occasion of the return of the original Bradford manuscript from England to Massachusetts, Senator Hoar proclaimed it to be nothing less than "the only authentic history of what we have a right to consider the most important political transaction that has ever taken place on the face of the earth." Address of Senator Hoar in William Bradford, *Bradford's History 'Of Plimoth Plantation'* (Boston: Wright and Potter, 1898), xxxix.

23. I am not so determined to draw the connection between Shakespeare and the New World as to claim that he had this specific incident in mind fully a decade before it happened, when Stephano says, upon meeting Caliban, "Where the devil should he learn our language?" (I.ii.66–67). Since we have been told that Caliban learned his language from Prospero, however, this passage may be more suggestive than it first seems.

24. *The Story of the Pilgrim Fathers, 1620–1623 A.D., as told by Themselves, their Friends, and their Enemies,* Edward Arber, ed. (Boston: Houghton Mifflin, 1897), 470–72.

25. John Abbot Goodwin, *The Pilgrim Republic: An Historical Review of the Colony of New Plymouth* (Boston: Houghton Mifflin, 1920), 406–08.

26. Id.

27. Id. The Head Master of the Roxbury Latin School notes that Stephen Hopkins was "a man of more than ordinary force and character" who "bulked large in the early life of the Plymouth colony." Daniel Ozro Smith Lowell, *A Munsey-Hopkins Genealogy* (Boston: priv. print, 1920), 28–29. It is left to another, however, to claim that Stephen Hopkins was

the great-grandfather of the Stephen Hopkins who signed the Declaration of Independence "with a weak hand but a stout heart," and of Ezekiel Hopkins, "the first admiral of our national navy, the co-equal with Washington himself." Goodwin, *The Pilgrim Republic,* 435 n.2.

28. David D. Hall, *World of Wonder, Days of Judgment* (New York: Knopf, 1989), 19. Hall's account focuses generally on conflict within the many belief systems of seventeenth-century New Englanders; he cogently probes how these settlers chose and mediated among meanings and how ambivalent they were in doing so.

29. Bruce H. Mann, *Neighbors and Strangers: Law and Community in Early Connecticut* (Chapel Hill: University of North Carolina Press, 1987), 5.

30. *The Tempest* is hardly unique in Shakespeare's attention to this issue, of course. In *The Winter's Tale,* for example, Polixenes's famous paradox is: "This is an art / Which does mend nature—change it rather—but/ The art itself is nature" (IV.iv.95–97). For a provocative discussion of this theme in the context of the contemporary abortion debate, no less, see John Denvir, "Comic Relief," 63 *Tulane L. Rev.* (1989), 401.

31. Ralph Waldo Emerson, "English Traits," quoted in Marx, *The Machine,* 42.

32. George D. Langdon, *Pilgrim Colony: A History of New Plymouth, 1620–1691* (New Haven: Yale University Press, 1966), 21–22, 29, 59, 79.

33. Pocock, supra n.4, 37, 41, 42, 51; Morgan, supra n.9, 290. In his response to Hobbes in the 1650s, George Lawson had the Whigs in mind. In the Convention of 1688, the Whigs distinguished between the Community that came into existence prior to government by a "popular contract," and a commonwealth or government established by that Community through a "rectoral contract." Id. 87, 109.

34. George Orwell, "Lear, Tolstoy and the Fool," in his *Collected Essays* (London: Heinemann, 1961), 414.

35. John Winthrop,"A Model of Christian Charity," reprinted in *Puritan Political Ideas,* Edmund S. Morgan, ed. (Indianapolis: Bobbs-Merrill, 1965), 75. I am grateful to Saul Touster for reminding me of this passage. The reference to Micah is, of course, "to doe Justly, to love mercy, to walke humbly with our God." Winthrop goes on to say "wee must uphold a familiar Commerce together in all meekenes, gentlenes, patience and liberallity, wee must delight in eache other, makes others Condicions our owne rejoyce together, mourne together, labour, and suffer together, allwayes haveing before our eyes our Commission and Community in the worke, our Community as members of the same body" (92).

36. Henry Wolcott's notebook excerpt on Thomas Hooker's Sermon delivered to the General Court on May 31, 1638, quoted in M. J. A. Jones, *The Fundamental Orders of Connecticut* (Bicentennial ed., 1988), 17.

37. Emma Lazarus, "The New Colossus," written in aid of the Bartholdi

Pedestal Fund in 1883 and now inscribed on a plaque on the Statue of Liberty, reprinted in Emma Lazarus, *Emma Lazarus: Selections from Her Poetry and Prose,* Morris U. Schappes, ed. (New York: Emma Lazarus Federation of Jewish Women's Clubs, 1967), 48. Perhaps Lazarus was inspired by earlier American dreamers. For example, George Washington advised his countrymen "humbly and fervently to beseech the kind Author of these blessings . . . to render this country more and more a safe and propitious asylum for the unfortunates of other countries," and Thomas Jefferson asked, "Shall we refuse the unhappy fugitives from distress that hospitality which the savages of the wilderness extended to our forefathers arriving in this land? Shall oppressed humanity find no asylum on this globe?" Quoted in Arthur D. Morse, *While Six Million Died: A Chronicle of American Apathy* (New York: Random House, 1968), 135.

2. The Right to Form and Join Associations

1. Alexis de Tocqueville, *Democracy in America,* J. P. Mayer, ed. (Garden City: Doubleday, 1969), 513.
2. Academics like to dress up the rediscovery of groups in the garb of fashionable notions about interpretive communities, neo-republican virtues, the politics of meaning, and "a living tradition [that] is an historically extended, socially embodied argument." Alasdaire MacIntyre, *After Virtue: A Study in a Moral Theory* (Notre Dame: University of Notre Dame Press, 1981), 206–07. See also Anthony Cohen, *The Symbolic Construction of Community* (New York: Tavistock Publications, 1985), 11–21; Owen Fiss, "Objectivity and Interpretation," 34 *Stan. L. Rev.* 739 (1982); Stanley Fish, "Fish v. Fiss," 36 *Stan. L. Rev.* 1325 (1984).

    For a critique of such approaches see Paul Kahn, "Community in Constitutional Theory," 99 *Yale L. J.* 1 (1989). Comprehensive discussions of republicanism are available in Symposium, "The Republican Civic Tradition," and, in particular, comment by Kathryn Abrams, 97 *Yale L. J.* 1591 (1988); Symposium, "Roads Not Taken: Undercurrents of Republican Thinking in Modern Constitutional Theory," 84 *Nw. U. L. Rev.* 1 (1989). For a detailed critical response to republicanism from an historical standpoint, see Joyce Appleby, *Liberalism and Republicanism in the Historical Imagination* (Cambridge, Mass.: Harvard University Press, 1992); and for a concise historiographic treatment of the recent republicanism phenomenon see Daniel T. Rodgers, "Republicanism: The Career of a Concept," 79 *J. Am. Hist.* 11 (1992).
3. This binary world seems to attract people on the political right and left alike. For the conservative side, see Robert Bork, *The Tempting of America: The Political Seduction of the Law* (New York: The Free Press, 1990),

and many of the Rehnquist and Scalia opinions discussed in later chapters. Conversely, many of those who glorify the role of the people-out-of-doors and others who have rediscovered civic republicanism in American history are strange bedfellows with these conservative judges on issues of majoritarianism, local control, and the role of judges. See, for instance, James Gray Pope, "Republican Moments: The Role of Direct Popular Power in the American Constitutional Order," 139 *U. Penn. L. Rev.* 287 (1990) and the writers discussed supra n.2.

4. See generally Mary Ann Glendon, *Rights Talk: The Impoverishment of Political Discourse* (New York: Free Press, 1991). For snappy, but nearly forgotten, earlier explorations of related themes by other eminent legal scholars, see Wesley Sturges, "Unincorporated Associations as Parties to Actions," 33 *Yale L. J.* 383 (1924) (arguing that unincorporated entities ought to be considered parties to legal actions); Zechariah Chafee, Jr., "The Internal Affairs of Associations Not for Profit," 43 *Harv. L. Rev.* 993 (1930) (arguing that "the central idea of our law is relation" and analyzing four policies concerning judicial interference with different types of associations: "the Strangle-hold Policy, the Dismal Swamp Policy, the Hot Potato Policy, and the Living Tree Policy").

5. See McKleskey v. Kemp, 481 U.S. 279, 290–92 (1987) (defendant challenging imposition of capital punishment failed to prove that "the decision makers in *his* case acted with discriminatory purpose") (emphasis in original); Valley Forge Christian College v. Americans United for Separation of Church and State, 454 U.S. 464, 471 (1982) (litigant must show, among other factors constituting "an irreducible minimum" for Art. III purposes, "that he personally has suffered some actual or threatened injury as a result of the putatively illegal conduct of the defendant"). The best-known recent example probably is still Justice Powell's deciding opinion in Regents of the University of California v. Bakke, 438 U.S. 265, 295 (1978). See John Noonan, *Persons and Masks in the Law* (New York: Farrar, Straus and Giroux, 1976).

6. See Stephen Yeazell, *From Medieval Group Litigation to the Modern Class Action* (New Haven: Yale University Press, 1987) (tracing groups in litigation, from the medieval assumption of the natural, inevitable role of groups through ambivalence about representation by attribution to current confusion regarding consent and interest of individual members of the class); Morton Horwitz, "*Santa Clara* Revisited: The Development of Corporate Theory," in Warren Samuels and Arthur S. Miller, *Corporations and Society: Power and Responsibility* (New York: Greenwood Press, 1987) (tracing the development of various theories of the corporation prior to the triumph of the entity theory around 1900). For a wonderful illustration that there may be no such thing as an original idea, see Frederic Maitland's introduction to his translation of Otto Gierke, *Polit-*

ical Theories of the Middle Age (Boston: Beacon Press Paperback, 1958), discussed below in Chapter 6.

7. Tocqueville, supra n.1, 189.

8. Recent scholarship tends to use Tocqueville simply as a launching-pad for discussion of the lack of, and need for, communal orientation today. See Robert N. Bellah et al., *Habits of the Heart: Individualism and Commitment in American Life* (Berkeley: University of California Press, 1985); *The Responsive Community* (a publication launched in 1990 to oppose the idea of a society run like a marketplace and to counter "Me-ism"). For a discussion of the communitarian political movement following a "communitarian teach-in" in Washington, D.C., see Michael D'Antonio, "Tough Medicine for a Sick America," *Los Angeles Times,* March 22, 1992, Sunday Magazine, 32; Peter Steinfels, "Communitarianism Takes From Left and Right," *New York Times,* May 24, 1992, sect. 4, 6.

9. Tocqueville, supra n.1, 189–90.

10. Id. 193.

11. The Assembly's Declaration of August 18, 1792, eliminated the corporate form. It did not thereby solve the problem of who would inherit the property of the Church and villages, for example, and it thus ironically helped to make the nineteenth century in France "the century of associations." Frederic Maitland, "Moral Personality and Legal Personality," Sidgwick Lecture at Newnham College (1903), reprinted in Frederic Maitland, *Selected Essays,* H. D. Hazeltine et al., eds. (Cambridge: Cambridge University Press, 1936), 230. Moreover, it would be a mistake to focus exclusively on the attack on associations in the context of the Revolution. As Maitland described the developments leading up to 1789, "In France, we may see the pulverizing, macadamizing tendency in all its glory, working from century to century, reducing to impotence, and then to nullity, all that intervenes between Man and State" (229). Maitland makes the further point that groups are remarkably resilient, however, and that they tend to persist no matter what the dominant theory or political reality.

12. Tocqueville, supra n.1, 515. Tocqueville treated the crucial educational role of associations in greatest detail in his chapter "On the Use Which the Americans Make of Associations in Civil Life." On the propensity to form civil associations, which he defined as those associations that do not have a political object, he wrote: "Americans of all ages, all stations in life, and all types of disposition are forever forming associations. . . . If the inhabitants of democratic countries had neither the right nor the taste for uniting for political objects, their independence would run great risks, but they could keep both their wealth and their knowledge for a long time. But if they did not learn some habits of acting together in the affairs of daily life, civilization itself would be in peril" (513–14).

13. Id. 517.
14. Id.
15. Arthur Schlesinger, "Biography of a Nation of Joiners," 50 *Am. Hist. Rev.* 1, 3 (1944), reprinted in Arthur Schlesinger, *Paths to the Present* (New York: Macmillan, 1949), 25. For a similar point, see Wilson Carey McWilliams, *The Idea of Fraternity* (Berkeley: University of California Press, 1973), 224–31.
16. Schlesinger, supra n. 15, 9 n.16. The spirit of association was neither limited to joining forces in order to accomplish specific ends, nor to a specific period in American life. Sometimes, of course, Americans sought what Julius Goebel called the "creative magic of mere association" in order to confirm their own identities at the expense of others (quoted id. 24). But the outburst of collective activity in the 1820s, for example, produced a plethora of new associative ventures, including Owenite utopian experiments, penological and social welfare reforms, workingmen's associations, pro- and anti-Masonic activity, and various forms of Christian communalism. See Anthony Wallace, *Rockdale: The Growth of the American Village in the Early Industrial Revolution* (New York: Knopf, 1978), 275–92, and Carol Weisbrod, *The Boundaries of Utopia* (New York: Pantheon Books, 1980). For a famous early example of protection of association in the labor context, see Commonwealth v. Hunt, 45 Mass. (4 Met.) 111 (1842) (Shaw, C. J.). For the political implications of Masons and anti-Masonic movements, see Dorothy Lipson, *Freemasonry in Federalist Connecticut, 1789–1835* (Princeton: Princeton University Press, 1977). For the social context of the growth of asylums, see David Rothman, *The Discovery of the Asylum: Social Order and Disorder in the New Republic* (Boston: Little, Brown, 1971). This flourishing of the collective impulse attempted to revive the spirit of the Revolution and to keep threatening forces of industrialization, materialism, and urbanization at bay.
17. Journal entry dated October 17, 1840, in Ralph Waldo Emerson, *The Journals and Miscellaneous Notebooks of Ralph Waldo Emerson, 1838– 1842*, A. W. Plumstead and Harrison Hayford, eds. (Cambridge, Mass.: Harvard University Press, 1969), VII, 408. See Joel Porte, *Representative Man: Ralph Waldo Emerson in His Time* (New York: Oxford University Press, 1979).
18. Journal entry dated April, 1841, in Emerson, *Journals*, VII, 437–38. For a fine recent discussion of the "curious paradox" of Transcendentalists who celebrated individualism yet joined together to start the utopian experiment of Brook Farm, see Carl Guarneri, *The Utopian Alternative: Fourierism in Nineteenth-Century America* (Ithaca: Cornell University Press, 1991), 44–51. Guarneri believes that Emerson's views about individualism hardened as he reached the tough decision not to join his fellows in their communitarian venture. Emerson wrote "Self-Reliance" the

month he attended Brook Farm planning sessions; in it he resolved that society is necessarily in tension with the individualism he celebrated: "Society is a joint-stock company, in which the members agree, for the better securing of his bread to each shareholder, to surrender the liberty and culture of the eater." Ralph Waldo Emerson, "Self-Reliance" in Ralph Waldo Emerson, *The Complete Works of Ralph Waldo Emerson* (Boston: Houghton Mifflin, 1903–04), II, 30, 33.

It is surely not a coincidence that the nineteenth century's most famous decision recognizing the rights of workers to organize in unions, Chief Justice Lemuel Shaw's Commonwealth v. Hunt, 45 Mass (4 Met.) 111 (1842), was handed down at a time of remarkable ferment over group activity. During this era judges also wrestled with the issue of which religious group could rightfully claim church property in the context of the bitter split between Unitarians and Congregationalists; the prolonged litigation about whether Pennsylvania was bound to honor the will of Steven Girard, which sought to endow a nonsectarian school entirely for white males; and some of the most famous disputes about the rights of, and appropriate constitutional restraints upon, business corporations. See sources in Stephen Presser and Jamil Zainaldin, *Law and American History: Cases and Materials* (St. Paul: West Publishing, 1980); Leonard Levy, *The Law of the Commonwealth and Chief Justice Shaw* (Cambridge, Mass.: Harvard University Press, 1957); Robert Ferguson, *Law and Letters in American Culture*, (Cambridge, Mass.: Harvard University Press, 1984); and Stanley Kutler, *Privilege And Creative Destruction: The Charles River Bridge Case* (New York: J. B. Lippincott, 1971).

19. Raymond Jackson Wilson, *In Quest of Community: Social Philosophy in the United States, 1860–1920* (New York: Oxford University Press, 1970), 5. Wilson's important book traces how, to Charles Sanders Peirce, G. Stanley Hall, and other intellectuals of the post-Civil War period, "the idea of community seemed the best response to the disintegrating effects of evolution and industrial capitalism that threatened both their minds and their society" (31).

20. A good, concise discussion of these factors is provided by Guarneri, supra n.18, 60–90.

21. A collection of sources that deal with these themes in detail, as well as my interpretation of their impact on selected aspects of legal history, may be found in Aviam Soifer, "The Paradox of Paternalism and Laissez-Faire Constitutionalism: United States Supreme Court 1888–1921," 5 *Law and Hist. Rev.* 249 (1987) and Aviam Soifer, "Status, Contract, and Promises Unkept," 96 *Yale L. J.* 1916 (1987).

22. Morton Keller, *Affairs of State* (Cambridge: Harvard University Press, 1977), 7, 517. The U.S. Sanitary Commission, Union League Clubs, the first national trade associations, and a variety of organizations formed to

aid the freedmen were among the most influential examples. According to Keller, however, voluntary associations gained even greater importance toward the end of the century.

23. James Bryce, *The American Commonwealth* (London: Macmillan, 1888), III, 44.

24. Quoted in Schlesinger, supra n.15, 1.

25. Pierre Proudhon is quoted in Robert A. Nisbet, *Community and Power* (New York: Oxford University Press, 1962), xiii, originally published as *The Quest for Community* (New York: Oxford University Press, 1953). The Bohemian Club filed an *amicus* brief along with the Century Club and numerous other private associations urging the Supreme Court to strike down an effort by New York City to force most private clubs in the city either to admit women as full, voting members or to lose their liquor licenses and other benefits. See New York State Club Ass'n v. City of New York, 487 U.S. 1 (1988).

It is both sobering and a bit encouraging to discover that enthusiasm for community is a particularly hardy perennial in American intellectual, utopian, and legal history. See generally Wilson, supra n.19; McWilliams, supra n.15; Rosabeth Kanter, *Commitment and Community: Communes and Utopias in Sociological Perspective* (Cambridge, Mass.: Harvard University Press, 1972); Weisbrod, supra n.16.

26. See Kai Erikson, *The Wayward Puritans: A Study in the Sociology of Deviance* (New York: Wiley, 1966) (discussing and applying Emile Durkheim's theory of we/they group identification in the context of New England Puritans and penology); Bellah et al., *Habits of the Heart* (contemporary examination of nostalgia for and diminishing commitment to community identification); Philip Selznick, "The Idea of a Communitarian Morality," 75 *Cal. L. Rev.* 445 (1987) (advocating "morality of the implicated self" and "anchored rationality" within "community of reason").

27. Shakespeare, *The Tempest,* II.ii.

28. Schlesinger, supra n.15, 1.

29. For a good survey of and commentary on social anthropology supporting this point, see Cohen, supra n.2.

30. 72 *Yale L. J.* 877 (1963).

31. 74 *Yale L. J.* 1 (1964).

32. 357 U.S. 449, 463 (1958). See M. Glenn Abernathy, *The Right of Assembly and Association* (Columbia: University of South Carolina Press, 1961); Charles Rice, *Freedom of Association* (New York: New York University Press, 1962); David Fellman, *The Constitutional Right of Association* (Chicago: University of Chicago Press, 1963); Drucilla Cornell, "The Problem of Normative Authority in Legal Interpretation," 54 *Tenn. L. Rev.* 327 (1987); Robert Cover, "Foreword: *Nomos* and Narrative,"

97 *Harv. L. Rev.* 4 (1983); and Ronald R. Garet, "Communality and Existence: The Rights of Groups," *56 S. Cal. L. Rev.* 1001 (1983).

33. Unsurprisingly, the most important cases that raised and decided issues of freedom of association in the late 1950s and 1960s grew out of the civil rights movement. In *The Negro and the First Amendment* (Columbus: Ohio State University Press, 1965), Harry Kalven, Jr. illuminated this connection with panache.

34. Emerson, supra n.31, 2.

35. Id. 4.

36. Id. 35.

37. Id. 6.

38. My disagreement with Tom Emerson, my former teacher and an admirable role model, is not a thinly veiled psychological or generational assault on authority. I tried to express my appreciation for Emerson in Aviam Soifer, "'Toward a Generalized Notion of the Right to Form or Join an Association': An Essay for Tom Emerson," 38 *Case W. Res. L. Rev.* 641 (1988).

For some of the best recent legal work on community, see Paul Kahn, "Community in Contemporary Constitutional Theory," 99 *Yale L. J.* 1 (1989); Martha Minow, "Foreword: Justice Engendered," 101 *Harv. L. Rev.* 10 (1987); Frank Michelman, "Foreword: Traces of Self-Government," 100 *Harv. L. Rev.* 4 (1986); "Symposium on Law and Community," 84 *Mich. L. Rev.* 1373–1541 (1986); William Marshall, "Discrimination and the Right of Association," 81 *Nw. U. L. Rev.* 68 (1987); Deborah Rhode, "Association and Assimilation," 81 *Nw. U. L. Rev.* 106 (1987); Ronald Garet, "Communality and Existence: The Rights of Groups," 56 *S. Cal. L. Rev.* 1001 (1983); Robert Cover, "Foreword: *Nomos* and Narrative," 97 *Harv. L. Rev.* 4 (1983).

39. Arthur Corbin, whom Karl Llewellyn identified as his "father in the law," was known for his attention to an incredible array of what Corbin termed "operative facts" in the contract cases he collected for his treatise. Grant Gilmore, *The Ages of American Law* (New Haven: Yale University Press, 1977), 79–80.

40. In Louisiana ex rel. Gremillion v. NAACP, 366 U.S. 293, 296 (1961), for example, the Court placed freedom of association within "the bundle of First Amendment rights" (Justice Douglas for the majority, striking down Louisiana statute requiring principal officer of "benevolent" associations to file list of names and addresses of all officers and members). In Gibson v. Florida Legislative Investigation Commission, 372 U.S. 539, 568–69 (1963), Justice Douglas, concurring, combined this bundle image with locating the right at "the periphery of the First Amendment" within a single sentence.

41. Emerson, supra n.30, 14. Emerson pointed out that, except for silent

acquiescence in the Alabama NAACP decisions, Justice Black refused to adopt the doctrine of an independent right of freedom of association. Justice Douglas took what Emerson kindly dubbed "an intermediate position" (15).

42. Id. 15.

43. To the extent that the cases treated associational and individual rights differently, Emerson argued, those differences merely involved standing issues (23).

44. Id. 25.

45. Id. 4.

46. Id. 5.

47. Victor Brudney, "Business Corporations and Stockholders' Rights under the First Amendment," 91 *Yale L. J.* 235, 259 (1981). Given Emerson's emphasis on individual freedom of expression, however, he probably would not agree with Brudney's extension of the argument to any group action, "whether in the form of speech or otherwise."

48. Board of Directors of Rotary International v. Rotary Club of Duarte, 481 U.S. 537 (1987). See also Roberts v. United States Jaycees, 468 U.S. 609 (1984), discussed below; New York State Club Association v. City of New York, 487 U.S. 1 (1988).

49. Consolidated Edison Co. v. Public Serv. Comm'n, 447 U.S. 530, 535, 540 (1980). Justice Powell's majority opinion also described ConEd as "one group of persons" and explained that regulation of their bill enclosures "strikes at the heart of the freedom to speak." This odd variation on the marketplace-of-ideas theme added another element to the confusion the Court began to create when it protected commercial speech in Virginia State Bd. of Pharmacy v. Virginia Citizens Consumer Council, 425 U.S. 748 (1976). For a demonstration of the Court's lack of harmony—almost of self-parody—in its four-part tests and the like, see Posadas de Puerto Rico Associates v. Tourism Co. of Puerto Rico, 478 U.S. 328 (1986) (greater power includes the lesser power, so Puerto Rico may forbid advertisements about gambling in newspapers aimed at the local population).

For devastating critiques of the recent expansion of commercial speech protections, see Brudney, supra n.47; C. Edwin Baker, "Commercial Speech: A Problem in the Theory of Freedom," 62 *Iowa L. Rev.* 1 (1976); Daniel Farber, "Commercial Speech and First Amendment Theory," 74 *Nw. U.L. Rev.* 372 (1979); William Patton and Randall Bartlett, "Corporate 'Persons' and Freedom of Speech: The Political Impact of Legal Mythology," 1981 *Wis. L. Rev.* 494 (1981).

50. First National Bank of Boston v. Bellotti, 435 U.S. 765 (1978).

51. Roberts v. United States Jaycees, 468 U.S. 609, 628 (1984). Justice Brennan's majority opinion suggested that it would be indulging in sexual

stereotypes to think differently. But see Minow, supra n.38. The Court's facile distinction is reminiscent of one of the ways it ducked the freedom of association claim in Runyon v. McCrary, 427 U.S. 160 (1976). In that decision, in dismissing the freedom of association argument made by a segregated academy, Justice Stewart failed to distinguish the Court's defense of discrimination by a private club in Moose Lodge No. 107 v. Irvis, 407 U.S. 163 (1972). Moreover, *Runyon* appears to turn on the nature of the school's commercial solicitation, but the distinction Stewart drew between regulating whom the school would admit, but not what the school could teach, is hardly convincing.

52. Tocqueville, supra n.1, 164. Presumably Tocqueville did not anticipate American legal education when he wrote: "Generally speaking, it is only the simple conceptions which take hold of a people's mind."

53. 468 U.S. 617. Brennan's reference here was to the line of modern decisions, beginning with a successful challenge to Connecticut's proscription of birth control in Griswold v. Connecticut, 381 U.S. 479 (1965), which have relied upon a variety of theories of personal privacy—thought to include elements of individual autonomy and secrecy—but have been extended to other family relationships as well. See Kenneth Karst, "The Freedom of Intimate Association," 89 *Yale L. J.* 624 (1980); Mary Ann Glendon, *State, Law, and Family: Family Law in Transition in the United States and Western Europe,* 2nd ed. (New York: North-Holland, 1988).

54. 468 U.S. 621.

55. O'Connor concurred in part of Brennan's opinion and in the judgment. Rehnquist concurred only in the judgment, without opinion. There were no dissents, but Burger and Blackmun took no part in the decision.

56. Roberts v. Jaycees, 468 U.S. 633.

57. Id. 635.

58. See Thomas v. Collins, 323 U.S. 516 (1945); De Jonge v. Oregon, 299 U.S. 353 (1937); Hague v. CIO, 307 U.S. 496 (1939); United States v. Cruikshank, 92 U.S. 542 (1875), discussed in Chapter 6.

59. NAACP v. Claiborne Hardware Co., 458 U.S. 886 (1982). The decision was unanimous, but Justice Rehnquist concurred only in the judgment without opinion. Justice Stevens's opinion for the Court went so far as to state that "The claim that the expressions were intended to exercise a coercive impact . . . does not remove them from the reach of the First Amendment" (911). The opinion is surely to be understood at least in part as a response to the Court's perception that "the white establishment of Claiborne County" had denied blacks "the basic rights of dignity and equality that this country fought a civil war to secure" (918). For a similar emphasis on the underlying facts in the NAACP decisions by the Supreme Court in the late 1950s and early 1960s, see Kalven, supra n.33.

60. 458 U.S. 934.

61. 479 U.S. 238 (1986). In this decision the Court was as sharply divided as it could be. Justice Brennan wrote for only three other justices in one crucial section of his majority opinion, and Justice O'Connor concurred separately and discussed her concerns over the disclosure requirements of the Federal Election Campaign Act. Chief Justice Rehnquist's dissent for four members of the Court argued that business corporations should not be treated differently from nonprofits. Justice White joined the dissent, but noted separately that he continues to disagree with the string of recent decisions extending First Amendment protections to corporations.

62. This interpretation is reinforced by the Court's decision less than a week before in Tashjian v. Republican Party of Connecticut, 479 U.S. 208 (1986), holding it unconstitutional for Connecticut to make voting in the Republican Party primary conditional on a registration requirement not desired by the Republicans. Justice Marshall's majority opinion rests on freedom of association for political purposes.

63. 2 U.S.C. sect. 441(b).

64. 479 U.S. 263. Brennan was anything but formalistic when he noted that "Some corporations have features more akin to voluntary political associations than business firms, and therefore should not have to bear burdens on independent spending solely because of their incorporated status."

65. Id. 257. At this point, Brennan emphasized the dangers of corruption arising from the determination that resources in a corporate treasury are no indicator of public support. Elsewhere in the opinion, however, he conflated for-profit corporations and unions for purposes of his First Amendment analysis (264). While relevant, an extended discussion of labor law matters is beyond the scope of this chapter. For a provocative introduction to the tangles of labor law, see NLRB v. City Disposal Systems, 465 U.S. 822 (1984) (individual can engage alone in "concerted activity" protected under Sec. 7); Staughton Lynd, "Communal Rights," 62 *Tex. L. Rev.* 1417 (1984).

66. The most famous statement of this approach is in Alexander Meiklejohn, *Political Freedom: The Constitutional Powers of the People* (New York: Harper Row, 1960). A more recent indication of how limiting this approach might prove to be is available in Robert Bork, "Neutral Principles and Some First Amendment Problems," 47 *Ind. L. J.* 1 (1971). The Court often has emphasized the "indispensable" and "core" quality of political speech.

67. 494 U.S. 652 (1990). Marshall wrote for the majority and Brennan and Stevens concurred separately, while Scalia and Kennedy, joined by O'Connor, wrote dissents.

68. Id. 665. Marshall was less convincing as to why Michigan could exempt unions from the statutory regulation, though his point that dissenting

union members are not faced with an all-or-nothing situation has some merit. A line of recent decisions assures dissenters that they may decline to contribute to any union political activities they do not support. The majority also accepted the partisan leaning of Michigan's lesser restrictions on media corporations, holding that the unique role played by the press supplies a compelling state interest.

69. 454 U.S. 290, 294 (1982).

70. See also First National Bank of Boston v. Bellotti, 435 U.S. 765 (1978); California Medical Association v. Federal Election Commission, 453 U.S. 182 (1981).

71. 454 U.S. 298.

72. Burger wrote, "There are, of course, some activities, legal if engaged in by one, yet illegal if performed in concert with others, but political expression is not one of them." Id. 296. In this, therefore, Burger implicitly accepted Tom Emerson's general approach to freedom of associations claims, though in the context of the case, the two men seem strange allies indeed.

    Burger also implicitly rejected even the limited claim for an independent freedom of association right that was made, for example, in Reena Raggi, "An Independent Right to Freedom of Association," 12 *Harv. C.R.-C.L. L. Rev.* 1 (1977). Raggi sought recognition of "the basic principle . . . that whatever action a person can pursue as an individual, freedom of association must ensure he can pursue with others." Id. 15. Relying primarily on NAACP v. Alabama ex rel. Patterson, Raggi used the dictum that an association and its members "are in every practical sense identical," id. (quoting 357 U.S. 449, 459 (1958)), to claim that an association is no more than the sum of its individual members and to assert that this notion "seems essential in a society in which it is the 'individual who is the ultimate concern of the social order.'" Id. (quoting Tom Emerson, supra n.30, 4). She thereby undercut the idea of an independent freedom of association right that her article's title advanced.

73. 454 U.S. 263, 269 (1981). Justice Stevens concurred in the judgment and Justice White dissented. One might have thought the free exercise clause of the First Amendment directly relevant, and sufficient to provide a basis for the decision in Widmar v. Vincent. Therefore, it is noteworthy that while the majority repeatedly invoked freedom of association, the justices also employed the extremely protective analogy of a prior restraint test to that right, at least when freedom of association was discerned to be in combination with freedom of expression.

74. 454 U.S. 268 n.5 (1981) (quoting Healy v. James, 408 U.S. 169, 181, 184 (1972), which held it unconstitutional for a university to exclude an S.D.S. chapter on grounds of freedom of expression and freedom of association). The Court has since cut back considerably on such vigorous

protection of group religious rights, particularly in the context of Native American religious claims.

75. Perry Local Educators' Ass'n v. Hohlt, 652 F.2d 1286, 1296 (7th Cir. 1981) (Wisdom, J.), *rev'd* 460 U.S. 37 (1983).

76. Thomas Emerson, "The Affirmative Side of the First Amendment," 15 *Ga. L. Rev.* 795, 802 (1981). Emerson noted that when the government participates in the system directly, however, new difficulties arise that might usefully be approached by distinguishing between macro and micro levels of the government's affirmative First Amendment involvement.

77. 461 U.S. 574 (1983) (upholding the authority of Internal Revenue Service to deny sect. 501(c)(3) tax exempt status to schools that discriminated on the basis of race in admissions or school policies, despite claims of a religious basis for such discrimination).

78. For example, Chief Justice Burger's majority opinion spoke cryptically of an "unusually strong case of legislative acquiescence" implicitly ratifying IRS rulings, thus ignoring years of litigation. Burger argued that "Non-action by Congress is not often a useful guide, but the non-action here is significant." Id. at 599, 600. See also Moose Lodge No. l07 v. Irvis, 407 U.S. 163 (1972) (holding state insufficiently implicated to find state action in racial exclusion, except in one minor particular).

79. 461 U.S. 592, 599.

80. Id. 592.

81. 468 U.S. 737 (l984) (denying standing to parents of black school children who claimed that the IRS was not enforcing the *Bob Jones* decision and was failing in its statutory duty to deny sect. 50l(c)(3) tax exempt status to private academies that discriminated on the basis of race).

82. 347 U.S. 483 (1954).

83. 461 U.S. 540 (1983). Rehnquist wrote the majority opinion and Blackmun, joined by Brennan and Marshall, concurred.

84. Id. 544, 549.

85. Justice Blackmun's concurring opinion for three justices stressed that, as actually administered by the IRS, TWR had a readily available opportunity to create a lobbying affiliate under sect. 501(c)(4). This was crucial to their rejection of TWR's challenge to the sect. 501(c)(3) restriction. But the majority's approach was quite different. Applying a standard that "[i]t is . . . not irrational" for Congress to subsidize lobbying by veterans groups, Rehnquist's opinion invoked the abortion funding decisions, Harris v. McRae, 448 U.S. 297 (1980) and Maher v. Roe, 432 U.S. 464 (1977) to support the proposition that so long as government regulations are not affirmatively aimed at suppression, the government is entitled to encourage action it favors. 461 U.S. 550.

86. 473 U.S. 788 (1985). O'Connor wrote for four justices. Blackmun, joined by Brennan, dissented, as did Stevens. Marshall and Powell did not take

part in the decision. The case reached the Supreme Court after extensive and somewhat complicated maneuvering in the lower courts and within the executive branch, and the Court remanded for consideration of whether it could be proved that the administrator acted with a bad motive.

87. Id. 811–12.
88. Emerson, supra n.31, 25.
89. 427 U.S. 160 (1976) (42 U.S.C. § 1981 held to reach and prohibit racial discrimination by "private, commercially operated, nonsectarian schools").
90. See Anthony Lewis, "A Preferred Position for Journalism?" 7 *Hofstra L. Rev.* 595 (1979) and other articles in the same symposium, as well as the symposium articles in 34 *U. Miami L. Rev.* 785 (1980). The debate was touched off by Justice Stewart's theoretical discussion in Potter Stewart, "Or of the Press," 26 *Hastings L. J.* 631 (1975).
91. See the cases collected and discussed in Aviam Soifer, "Freedom of the Press in the United States," in *Press Law in Modern Democracies: A Comparative Study,* Pnina Lahav, ed. (New York: Longman, 1986), 79, 108–17.
92. By 1974 over half the states had enacted laws to shield reporters who confronted demands for information by government officials or grand juries. Joel Gora, *The Rights of Reporters: The Basic ACLU Guide to a Reporter's Rights* (New York: E. P. Dutton, 1974), 243–48 (summarizing state shield laws). See also Jon Sylvester, "How the States Govern the News Media: A Survey of Selected Jurisdictions," 16 *Sw. U. L. Rev.* 723 (1986), and Willard Eckhardt and Arthur McKey, "Reporter's Privilege: An Update," 12 *Conn. L. Rev.* 435 (1980). In response to Zurcher v. Stanford Daily, 436 U.S. 547 (1978), which rejected a constitutional claim that a newspaper should enjoy special protection from a newsroom search, Congress enacted the Privacy Protection Act of 1980, 42 U.S.C. sect.2000aa et seq., 94 Stat. 1879 (1980), providing special protection from searches for those engaged in "public communication."
93. This is not to say that newspapers always, or even generally, enjoy clearcut special constitutional protection. In Cohen v. Cowles Media Co., 501 U.S. 663 (1991), for example, Justice White's majority opinion found no First Amendment barrier to a breach of contract suit brought by a news source when a newspaper failed to protect that person's anonymity. The Court split 5 to 4 in *Cohen,* however, and four justices joined in Justice Souter's strong dissent proclaiming a constitutional basis for a shield that would protect newspapers from such suits. Ironically, the Court decided against shielding the newspaper in *Cohen* the same day as it established an Eleventh Amendment barrier to shield Alaska against a suit by a Native American tribe in Blatchford v. Native Village of Noatak,

501 U.S. 775 (1991), criticized in Chapter 4. In both cases the Court rejected claims of significant associations, acting in a manner protective of states but not of groups.

94. Tocqueville, supra n.1, 518.

95. Id. 697.

96. Hannah Arendt, *On Violence* (New York: Harcourt, Brace, 1970), 52. Arendt is quoted and discussed with insight in C. Edwin Baker, "Scope of the First Amendment Freedom of Speech," 25 *U.C.L.A. L. Rev.* 964, 1031–35 (1978).

97. For development of definitions for and a defense of activism by the independent sector, see John Simon's "Foundations and Public Controversy: An Affirmative View." For a spirited contrary view, see Jeffrey Hart's "Foundations and Social Activism: A Critical View," in *The Future of Foundations,* Fritz Heimann, ed., (Englewood Cliffs: Prentice Hall, 1973). The *locus classicus* for current discussions about norm-generating communities in legal circles is the work of the late Robert Cover.

98. For some of the convincing historical studies demonstrating the intimate involvement of government with the private sector in our early history, see Carter Goodrich, *Government Promotion of American Canals and Railroads,1800–1890* (New York: Columbia University Press, 1960); Oscar Handlin and Mary Flug Handlin, *Commonwealth: A Study of the Role of government in the American Economy: Massachusetts, 1774–1861* (New York: New York University Press, 1947); Louis Hartz, *Economic Policy and Democratic Thought: Pennsylvania, 1776–1860* (Cambridge, Mass.: Harvard University Press, 1948); Morton Horwitz, *The Transformation of American Law, 1780–1860* (Cambridge, Mass.: Harvard University Press, 1977); J. Willard Hurst, *Law and the Conditions of Freedom in the Nineteenth Century United States* (Madison: University of Wisconsin Press, 1956); and Harry Scheiber, *Ohio Canal Era: A Case Study of Government and the Economy, 1820–1861* (Athens: Ohio University Press, 1969).

99. For a famous negative reaction, see George Washington's Farewell Address, in which he expressed his concern about "combinations and associations . . . with the real design to direct, control, counteract, or awe the regular deliberation and action of the constitutional authorities." *A Compilation of the Messages and Papers of the Presidents, 1789–1897,* James D. Richardson, ed. (Washington, D.C.: Government Printing Office, 1896–1899), I, 217–19. Washington's warning and his famous rejection of overtures by the Society of Cincinnatus indicate an early ambivalence in the response to the proliferation of associations in America.

As Gordon Wood makes abundantly clear in his *The Creation of the American Republic, 1776–1787* (Chapel Hill: University of North Caro-

lina Press, 1969), the men who wrote the Constitution feared both factions and the power of the governors over the governed. Rather than
attempt to eliminate factions, however, or to diminish necessary national governmental power, Madison and his supporters attempted to
employ factions and private associations to counterbalance each other
and to check government power.

100. Tocqueville, supra n.1, 192.
101. Id. 194. For support of the idea that a tendency toward the middle, and
     toward the claims of the middle class, is a master fact in American his-
     tory, see Lawrence Friedman, *A History of American Law,* 2nd ed. (New
     York: Simon and Schuster, 1985).
102. Grant Gilmore discusses how even Holmes fooled himself about his
     ability to accomplish the task he set himself as a judge, to create a "philo-
     sophically continuous series" through his decisions. Gilmore, supra
     n.39, 53 (quoting Holmes).
103. Wood, supra n.99, 606.
104. Id.

3. Guilt by Association, Association by Guilt

1. Alexis De Tocqueville, *Democracy in America,* J. P. Mayer, ed. (Garden
   City: Doubleday, 1969), 517.
2. Quoted by Roger N. Baldwin in "The Myth of Law and Order," in
   Behold America, Samuel D. Schmalhausen, ed. (New York: Farrar and
   Rinehart, 1931), 659.
3. A recent United States Supreme Court decision may exemplify this
   point. Chief Justice Rehnquist, known to allow considerable leeway in
   capital cases, nevertheless wrote for the majority in Dawson v.
   Delaware, 112 S. Ct. 1093 (1992). The Court refused to allow a stipulation as to the defendant's membership in a white racist prison gang,
   the Aryan Brotherhood, to be used by the prosecution at a death penalty sentencing hearing without a firm evidentiary basis. Admission of
   the stipulation was held to violate the defendant's First Amendment
   associational rights. Justice Blackmun concurred separately, and Justice Thomas dissented vigorously. It should be noted, however, that
   Rehnquist suggested that the constitutional error might have been
   harmless, thus leaving open the possibility that Dawson still might be
   executed.
4. Edmund Wilson, *Europe without Baedeker* (New York: Noonday Press,
   1966), 154.
5. See Mary Ann Glendon, *Rights Talk: The Impoverishment of Political
   Discourse* (New York: Free Press, 1991); J. Willard Hurst, *The Growth
   of American Law: The Law Makers* (Boston: Little, Brown, 1950), 3.

6. Joyce Appleby, *Capitalism and a New Social Order: The Republican Vision of the 1790s* (New York: New York University Press, 1984); Linda Kerber, "Making Republicanism Useful," 97 *Yale L. J.* 1663 (1988).

7. John Lord O'Brian, "Loyalty Tests and Guilt by Association," Annual Address, 71st Meeting, New York State Bar Association, Jan. 23, 1948, reprinted in 61 *Harv. L. Rev.* 592 (1948).

8. The role of O'Brian and his close associate, Alfred Bettman, in crucial decisions about legislation and about prosecutions and legal arguments during World War I is discussed briefly in Richard Polenberg, *Fighting Faiths: The Abrams Case, The Supreme Court, and Free Speech* (New York: Viking, 1987) and in Arnon Gutfeld, *Montana's Agony: Years of War and Hysteria, 1917–1921* (Gainesville: University Press of Florida, 1979).

9. Polenberg, supra n.8, 30 (quoting Alfred Bettman, "Regulation of Free Speech," April 25, 1919, O'Brian MSS, Box 18).

10. Bettman to O'Brian, Sept. 1, 1918, Box 17, quoted in Polenberg, id., and Gutfeld, supra n.8, 45, who explains O'Brian's dominant role in amending the Espionage Act, in response to widespread outrage at the courageous decisions by Federal District Judge George M. Bourquin in Montana.

11. O'Brian, supra n.7, 608.

12. Id. 602. O'Brian pointed to "the sinister developments which have been taking place in broadening the scope of our criminal conspiracy statutes and in the increasing acceptance of this doctrine of guilt imputed by association" (599).

13. Thomas Emerson and David Helfeld, "Loyalty Among Government Employees," 58 *Yale L. J.* 1 (1948), a characteristically careful discussion of the articles by other scholars. Undoubtedly, a later article by Bill Donovan and Mary Gardner Jones, "Program for a Democratic Counter Attack to Communist Penetration of Government Service," 58 *Yale L. J.* 1211 (1949), had greater impact than the scrupulous elaboration of constitutional doubts by courageous legal scholars—if law review articles ever have any impact—at least in part because of "Wild Bill" Donovan's fame as head of the Office of Special Services during World War II.

14. John Lord O'Brian, "Civil Liberty in War Time," 1919 N.Y. Bar Ass'n Rep. 275, 307. O'Brian and Bettman briefed and argued the three famous *Schenck-Frohwerk-Debs* Espionage Act cases, and played vital roles in other First Amendment cases as well, such as Abrams v. United States, 250 U.S. 616 (1919). See generally Zechariah Chafee, Jr., *Free Speech in the United States* (Cambridge, Mass.: Harvard University Press, 1941). For an example of an inflammatory approach that was far more typical of the period see the address by Attorney General Thomas W. Gregory, reprinted in 4 *A.B.A.J.* 305, 316 (1918), applauding lawyers who proclaimed it unpatriotic and unprofessional to represent anyone seeking to

escape the draft. Gregory argued that "[t]he greatest menace is the so-called 'respectable pacifist,'" and he labeled such a person "a physical or moral degenerate."

15. O'Brian, supra n.7, 602.

16. Alfred Bettman, *Hearings on H.R. 438 Before the Comm. on Rules,* 66th Cong., 2d Sess. 125–28 (1920), quoted in Chafee, supra n.14, 471.

17. O'Brian, supra n.14, 298, 299. In fact, the Department of Justice put prosecutions of I.W.W. members on a separate administrative track during and after World War I. O'Brian subsequently criticized this procedure as a deliberate plan to preclude internal review. William Preston, Jr., *Aliens and Dissenters: Federal Suppression of Radicals, 1903–1933* (Cambridge, Mass.: Harvard University Press, 1963), 258–59. Often, as Stanley Kutler put it, "The State . . . is some obscure clerk, hidden in the recesses of a Government bureau, into whose power the chance has fallen for the moment to pull one of the stops which control the Government function." Stanley Kutler, *The American Inquisition: Justice and Injustice in the Cold War* (New York: Hill and Wang, 1982), xiii.

18. The Supreme Court allowed guilt by association to dominate from the *Dennis* decision in 1951, which upheld the conviction of the Communist Party leadership, through various decisions after the fever subsided in the early 1960s. Dennis v. United States, 341 U.S. 494 (1951). In upholding New York State's loyalty oath for public school teachers in 1952, for example, the Court found it clearly acceptable that "One's associates, past and present, as well as one's conduct, may properly be considered in determining fitness and loyalty. From time immemorial, one's reputation has been determined in part by the company he keeps." Adler v. Board of Education, 342 U.S. 485, 493 (1952).

See also David Caute, *The Great Fear: The Anti-Communist Purge Under Truman and Eisenhower* (New York: Simon and Schuster, 1978); Kutler, *supra,* n.17. Harold Medina, the judge who presided over the rancorous trial in *Dennis,* died at age 102 in March 1990. *New York Times,* March 16, 1990, B7. Medina's remarkable longevity, along with that of John Lord O'Brian—O'Brian died at age 99 in 1973—might lead one to speculate about some correlation between which side you are on and your longevity. But Roger Baldwin, the founder of the ACLU, died in 1981 at age 97 and undermines such a theory. And the theory is exploded if you credit the great I.W.W. ballad about Joe Hill. Despite the accuracy of a Utah firing squad in 1915 when Hill was only 36 years old, Joe Hill says he never died—and goes on to organize.

19. Davis v. Beason, 133 U.S. 333 (1890). There was no allegation that Davis himself practiced or even advocated bigamy or polygamy. The Idaho law made mere membership in the church the decisive factor, and the Court went along when it upheld his conviction for violating a criminal law that

excluded all Mormons from the franchise and from holding office on grounds of membership alone.

20. 212 U.S. 78 (1909). For lower court treatment of the case, see 148 F. 870 (1906), 91 P. 738 (1905), 85 P. 190 (1905). Particularly noteworthy was the vigorous dissent by Justice Steele of the Colorado Supreme Court, invoking the principles of Ex parte Milligan, 71 U.S. (4 Wall.) 2 (1866) (holding that the President, the Congress, and the Judiciary cannot disturb the civil liberties incorporated in the Constitution, and that therefore military commissions cannot try, convict, or sentence citizens unconnected with the military).

21. 212 U.S. at 84.

22. Id.

23. The procedural posture of the case is only a partial explanation, and Holmes played cat-and-mouse with the formal procedural rules in any event. He claimed that though the record of the habeas corpus proceeding in the Colorado Supreme Court was made part of the complaint by agreement, "that did not make the averments of the petition for the writ averments of the complaint." Id. That left Holmes free simply to assume that a state of insurrection existed and that the governor acted without sufficient reason but in good faith. He then proceeded to mention the guilt by association point about Moyer, not as a material fact, "but simply to put in more definite form the nature of the occasion on which the governor felt compelled to act." Id.

24. Id. 85.

25. Id.

26. Melvyn Dubofsky, *We Shall Be All: A History of the Industrial Workers of the World* (Urbana: University of Illinois Press, 1969); Vernon Jensen, *Heritage of Conflict: Labor Relations in the Nonferrous Metals Industry up to 1930* (Ithaca: Cornell University Press, 1950). Governor Peabody's action, while extreme, nevertheless merely served to cap a period in Colorado history (1880–1904) when governors called out the state militia to deal with labor matters ten times. Paul Murphy, *The Meaning of Freedom of Speech: First Amendment Freedoms from Wilson to FDR* (Westport: Greenwood, 1972), 51.

27. Jensen, *Heritage*, 130.

28. Id. 131.

29. See George G. Suggs, *Colorado's War on Militant Unionism: James H. Peabody and the Western Federation of Miners* (Detroit: Wayne State University Press, 1972).

30. Dubofsky, supra n.26, 49.

31. People v. Sinclair, 149 N.Y.S. 54 (Gen. Sess. 1914); William Preston, Jr., supra n.17, 93.

32. Arnon Gutfeld, supra n.8; H. Hyman, *Soldiers and Spruce: Origins of the*

Loyal Legion of Loggers and Lumbermen (Los Angeles: Institute of Industrial Relations, University of California, 1963); Preston, supra n.17. A wave of bloody race riots swept the country in 1919. The Elaine, Arkansas, riot was the culmination, and once again the army was called in after between 50 and 100 blacks were killed by rampaging whites, who were often formally deputized or otherwise sanctioned by a committee consisting of both public and private powers in Phillips County. See Arthur Waskow, *From Race Riot to Sit-In, 1919 and the 1960s: A Study in the Connections Between Conflict and Violence* (Garden City: Anchor Books, 1967). F. Scott Fitzgerald conveys something of the group tensions, violence, and poignant personal difficulties encountered by returning World War I veterans in his short story, "May Day," in *The Short Stories of F. Scott Fitzgerald: A New Collection*, Matthew J. Bruccoli, ed. (New York: Charles Scribner's Sons, 1989), 97.

33. See Murphy, supra n.26. But see also Frederick L. Allen, *Only Yesterday: An Informal History of the 1920s* (New York: Perennial Library, 1931, rpt. 1964), 49–52, 63 (hysteria did not subside quickly and the Red Scare died very slowly, often replaced by nativism).

34. Whitney v. California, 274 U.S. 357 (1927).

35. 274 U.S. 328 (1927).

36. Id. 331. He was guilty of associating with an "organization, society, group and assemblage of persons organized and assembled to advocate, teach, aid and abet criminal syndicalism, to wit, the Industrial Workers of the World, commonly known as I.W.W." The trial judge instructed the jury that advocacy of sabotage would suffice. The jury acquitted Burns on one count, but convicted on the second. Justice Butler wrote the majority opinion; Justice Brandeis dissented alone, but argued that because the federal trial judge had committed reversible error, it was not appropriate to discuss possible constitutional violations as well.

37. Bill of Indictment, Print Transcript at 2.

38. 274 U.S. 328, 332.

39. Testimony of Charles Wykoff, speech by Leo Stark, May 23, 1923, Tr. at 53. Burns was arrested on April 10, and the grand jury handed up the indictment against him on May 22, 1923, the day Wykoff alleged he heard Stark urge men to load telephone poles in the ship's hold in a way that would make it list and require the ship to return to port. This was a key example of the alleged sabotage the I.W.W. was said to advocate in violation of the California Syndicalism Act.

40. Id. 25–26.

41. See People v. Wright, 226 P. 952 (1924); People v. LaRue, 226 P. 627 (1923). For a general discussion of the California custom in I.W.W. cases, see Chafee, supra n.14, 326–42.

42. 274 U.S. 380 (1927). May 16, 1927, was described by the *New York Times* as a "colorless" day for news. It reported that Charles Lindbergh

again had to delay his attempt to fly across the Atlantic because of bad weather—and that French General Duval condemned his plan and others like his as "immoral" and "shameful"; Mrs. Whitney told the press that "I have done nothing to be pardoned for . . . [but] I have nothing to complain of in comparison to Sacco and Vanzetti"; and Ty Cobb, Lou Gehrig, and Babe Ruth homered, while the Boston Red Sox lost a game.

43. Quoted in Paul Murphy, supra n.26, 367 n.34. Zechariah Chafee, whose work on the background and analysis of the Supreme Court's First Amendment decisions during this decade is still unmatched, viewed *Fiske* similarly, albeit with considerable caution.

44. Samuel Gompers, "The Courts vs. Natural Rights and Freedom," 31 *Am. Federationist* 865 (1924). See also Murphy, supra n.26, 258.

45. Quoted in Murphy, 132.

46. Fine articles such as Robert Cover, "The Origins of Judicial Activism in the Protection of Minorities," 91 *Yale L.J.* 1287 (1982) and David Rabban, "The Emergence of Modern First Amendment Doctrine," 50 *U. Chi. L. Rev.* 1205 (1983) ignored the decision, while Chafee and Murphy, supra nn. 14 and 26, mentioned it only in passing.

47. See State v. Boloff, 4 P.2d 326 (1931), *aff'd*, 7 P.2d 775 (1932) (upholding conviction and ten-year sentence imposed on an unemployed, illiterate sewer digger for violation of the Oregon Syndicalism Act, based solely on his membership in the Communist Party); New York ex rel. Bryant v. Zimmerman, 278 U.S. 63 (1928), discussed below.

48. 278 U.S. 63 (1928). The Court upheld New York's "Walker Law" of 1923, compelling every "membership corporation" or "unincorporated association having a membership of twenty or more persons" that required an oath for membership to file a sworn copy of its oath, constitution, by-laws, rules, regulations and "a roster of its membership and a list of its officers." The law specifically exempted labor unions and benevolent orders mentioned in New York's Benevolent Orders Law. Justice Van Devanter's majority opinion sustained the law against attack based on privileges and immunities, due process, and equal protection claims by a Kleagle of the Ku Klux Klan in Buffalo, who had been convicted and jailed for his knowing membership in a group that did not comply with the law. The prosecution of Bryant followed a fatal revolver duel between a police undercover agent and a visiting southern Klansman. *New York Times*, Nov. 20, 1928, p.20. Only Justice McReynolds dissented, saying he did so on jurisdictional grounds.

49. Bryant v. Zimmerman, 150 N.E. 497, 500 (1926). The highest New York Court unanimously upheld the statute "as not 'actually and palpably unreasonable and arbitrary' on the authority of precedents which have gone far to uphold legislative power in matters of classification." The statute rested "on an opinion reasonably permissible for its validity," because "the Legislature may take notice of the potentialities of evil in

secret societies" (500, 498). For a compelling retelling of the story of the growing strength of the Klan in the 1920s, when "intolerance became an American virtue," see Frederick Lewis Allen, supra n.33, 39–63, 49.

50. Harry Kalven, *The Negro and the First Amendment* (Chicago: University of Chicago Press, 1965), 91–94. In Communist Party of the United States v. Subversive Activities Control Board, 367 U.S. 1 (1961), Justice Frankfurter's majority opinion upheld forced disclosure because the SACB had a reasonable basis to inquire about the danger of "a world-wide integrated movement which employs every combination of possible means, peaceful and violent, domestic and foreign, overt and clandestine, to destroy the government itself" (96).

   Justice Black's dissent in this 1961 case, along with similarly vigorous dissents in related decisions such as Barenblatt v. United States, 360 U. S. 109 (1959), mark some of the best innings ever for a justice who is in nearly everyone's judicial Hall of Fame. Black asserted that to ban an association, whether political or not, is "a fateful moment in the history of a free country," and he castigated the idea of "[g]overnment . . . as . . . paternal guardian." 367 U.S. 137, 139. Black drew parallels to the Sedition Act of 1798—"one of the greatest blots" in American history (155). He warned against beliefs such as that held by arch-Federalist Harrison Gray Otis that "The spirit of association is a dangerous thing in a free government, and ought carefully to be watched" (quoted, 161). Instead, Black asserted, "The creation of public opinion by groups, organizations, societies, clubs, and parties has been and is a necessary part of our democratic society" (167).

51. Herndon v. Lowry, 301 U.S. 242 (1937). See Kendall Thomas, "*Rouge et Noir* Reread: A Popular Constitutional History of the Angelo Herndon Case," 65 *S. Cal. L. Rev.* 2599 (1992).

52. 323 U.S. 516 (1945). A notable precursor was Hague v. C.I.O., 307 U.S. 496 (1939) (Jersey City officials were forbidden to interfere with speeches and assemblies publicizing the National Labor Relations Act). Justices Black and Roberts viewed the rights involved as privileges of national citizenship; Justices Stone and Reed anchored the rights in the First Amendment, applied to the states through the Fourteenth Amendment. For a fine account, see Benjamin Kaplan, "The Great Civil Rights Case of *Hague v. CIO*: Notes of a Survivor," 25 *Suffolk U. L. Rev.* 913 (1991).

53. 320 U.S. 118 (1943).

54. Id. 154.

55. Id. 154 n.41. Ironically, *Schneiderman* was handed down the same day as Hirabayashi v. United States, 320 U.S. 81 (1943), the decision in which the Court unanimously upheld the West Coast curfew imposed on all persons of Japanese ancestry, pursuant to President Roosevelt's Execu-

tive Order No. 9066, promulgated on February 19, 1942. See Peter Irons, *Justice at War* (New York: Oxford University Press, 1982).

56. Bridges v. Wixon, 326 U.S. 135, 157 (1945). For a lucid account of the protracted efforts to "get" Harry Bridges, and the involvement of numerous legal and political leading lights of the times, see Kutler, supra n.17, 118–51.

57. 326 U.S. 157.

58. Steve Wizner told me about this film and Mary Dudziak introduced the reference to the world of law reviews; Mary Dudziak, "Desegregation as a Cold War Imperative," 41 *Stan. L. Rev.* 61, 68–69 (1988).

59. William James, *Pragmatism: A New Name for Some Old Ways of Thinking* (New York: Longmans, Green, 1907), 59, lucidly discussed with reference to law and precedent in Thomas Grey, "Holmes and Legal Pragmatism," 41 *Stan. L. Rev.* 787 (1989).

60. Gilbert v. Minnesota, 254 U.S. 325, 338 (1920).

61. Quoted in Zechariah Chafee, Jr., *The Inquiring Mind* (New York: Harcourt, Brace, 1928), 147–48. On several significant recent efforts to ground practical legal ethics in tolerant religious frameworks, see Thomas Shaffer with Mary Shaffer, *American Lawyers and Their Communities: Ethics in the Legal Profession* (South Bend: University of Notre Dame Press, 1991); William Park, "Spiritual Energy and Secular Power," in *The Influence of Religion on the Development of International Law*, Mark Janis, ed. (The Netherlands: Kluwer Academic Press, 1991), 171.

62. Chafee, supra n.61, 146–47. Therefore, "The only remedy is to build up every day and every hour the opposite spirit, a firm faith that all varieties and shades of opinion must be given a chance to be heard, that the decision between truth and error cannot be made by human beings, but only by time and the test of open argument and counter-argument, so that each citizen may judge for himself." For a little-known, intriguing attempt to answer both New Left and right-wing critics of tolerance, while also critiquing the traditional justifications of the concept that rely on the individualism, rationalism, and historical optimism of Locke and Mill, see Glenn Tinder, *Tolerance: Toward a New Civility* (Amherst: University of Massachusetts Press, 1976). Recently, Joseph Raz has developed a jurisprudential argument for toleration based on a related theory of value pluralism, stressing the fallibility of ordinary knowledge; see his "Liberalism, Skepticism, and Democracy," 74 *Iowa L. Rev.* 761 (1989), and *The Morality of Freedom* (New York: Oxford University Press, 1986), 401. ("Toleration is a distinctive moral virtue only if it curbs desires, inclinations and convictions which are thought by the tolerant person to be in themselves desirable.")

63. Frederic W. Maitland, "Moral Personality and Legal Personality," Sidgwick Lecture at Newnham College (1903), in *Maitland: Selected Essays,*

H. D. Hazeltine et al., eds. (Cambridge: Cambridge University Press, 1936), 237. Maitland insisted on "the morality of common sense," in which "the group is a person, is right-and-duty-bearing unit" (233). Tragically, the wars, genocide, and ethnic strife of the twentieth century have destroyed both his era's general teleological faith, and Maitland's particular, appealing form of sanguine functionalism. See, for example, "The Body Politic" (1899), id. 240. If guilt by association is potent in the relatively benign context of political and economic associations within the United States, it is emphatically more powerful when we move to the types of blame, guilt, and stereotyping connected to racial, ethnic, religious, and national groupings discussed in Chapter 7. See generally Harold Isaacs, *Idols of the Tribe: Group Identity and Political Change* (Cambridge, Mass.: Harvard University Press, 1989).

64. Ronald Dworkin, *Law's Empire* (Cambridge, Mass.: Harvard University Press, 1986), 215. Dworkin notes that associative obligations are "complex, and much less studied by philosophers than the kinds of personal obligations we incur through discrete promises and other deliberate acts," although, for most people, associative obligations are "the most consequential obligations of all" (196).

4. A Historical Glimpse at Ghostly Personalities

1. William Blackstone, *Commentaries* (1765), I, ch. 18, describing incorporated groups, is quoted in Frederick Pollock, "Has the Common Law Received the Fiction Theory of Corporations?" 27 *Law Q. Rev.* 219, 224 (1911). After cautionary notes against mistaking the "borrowing of exotic phrases" for "serious reception," Pollock argued that "the artificial identity of a corporation is, within its own sphere and for its own purposes, just as real as any other identity." Id. 219, 220, quoting his own *Principles of Contract* (1876), 81. It was possible to go back to Bracton for a similar image of ongoing, organic group identity. Bracton had observed that "in colleges and chapters the same body endures for ever, although all may die one after the other, and others may be placed in their stead; just as with flocks of sheep, the flock remains the same though the sheep die," quoted in H. Ke Chin Wang, "Corporate Entity Concept (or Fiction Theory) in the Year Book Period," 58 *Law Q. Rev.* 498, 499 n.12 (1942). Wang argued that there was no fiction theory in early English legal history, but that churches, chapters, and boroughs were treated as groups not distinct from their members.

2. Frederic Maitland, "Moral Personality and Legal Personality," Sidgwick Lecture for 1903, Newnham College, in *Maitland: Selected Essays*, H. D. Hazeltine et al., eds. (Cambridge: Cambridge University Press, 1936), 235.

3. In thinking seriously about our myriad communities, we ought to beware of usages such as the one exemplified by President Reagan's Exec. Order No. 12,333, 3 C.F.R. 200 (1981), reprinted in 50 U.S.C. § 401 (1988), in which: "Maximum emphasis should be given to fostering analytical competition among appropriate elements of the Intelligence Community" (201). The executive order reconstituted National Security Council procedures to enhance government secrecy (and thereby facilitated the Iran-Contra tangle). A month after his first inauguration, President Reagan stressed the common concern of "the Intelligence Community." This oxymoronic statement reveals how easily sponge-like words such as "community" and "intelligence" can be devalued or manipulated.

4. Morris Raphael Cohen, "Communal Ghosts and Other Perils in Social Philosophy," 16 *J. Phil.* 673 (1919), republished in generally the same form as "Communal Ghosts in Political Theory" in Morris Raphael Cohen, *Reason and Nature* (New York: Harcourt, Brace, 1931), 386.

5. But see Stephen Yeazell, *From Medieval Group Litigation to the Modern Class Action* (New Haven: Yale University Press, 1987); Meir Dan-Cohen, *Rights, Persons and Organizations: A Legal Theory for Bureaucratic Society* (Berkeley: University of California Press, 1986); Joseph Vining, *Legal Identity: The Coming of Age of Public Law* (New Haven: Yale University Press, 1978); Kathryn Abrams, "Raising Politics Up: Minority Political Participation and Section 2 of the Voting Rights Act," 63 N.Y.U. L. Rev. 449 (1988).

6. *Holmes-Laski Letters: The Correspondence of Mr. Justice Holmes and Harold J. Laski, 1916–1935,* Mark Howe, ed. (Cambridge, Mass.: Harvard University Press, 1953), 389.

7. Frederick William Maitland's introduction to Otto Gierke, *Political Theories of the Middle Ages,* F. W. Maitland, trans. (Cambridge: Cambridge University Press, 1900), x–xi.

8. Maitland began to focus in earnest on the problems of "juristic persons" in 1890, when he began work on the second edition of the *History of English Law.* He later joked that his own epitaph might be: "Hic jacet persona ficta" (Here lies a fictional person). Henry Esmond Bell, *Maitland: A Critical Examination and Reassessment* (Cambridge, Mass.: Harvard University Press, 1965), 9, 42.

9. Maitland, supra n.2, 227.

10. Id. 237. He added with characteristic acerbic wit: "[t]he largest 'collection' of zeros is only zero." Id.

11. E. Barker, Introduction to his translation of Otto Gierke, *Natural Law and the Theory of Society, 1500 to 1800* (1934; rpt. Cambridge: Cambridge University Press, 1958), xvi–xvii. Barker believed that dense German constructs such as Gierke's theory of society "become (at any rate to the realist) a matter of billowy cloud and rolling nebulosities" which

ultimately "are not our natural sky." It is particularly sobering to note Barker's warnings, in a book published in 1934, that German group theory "may end, in practice, in little more than the brute and instinctive automatism of the hive," providing "an idealisation whose effect may be to brutalise romance, and to romanticise cynicism." If Gierke's effect on Maitland is "the most famous example of German influence on British [legal] writing," in the words of Detlev Vagts, Foreword, in Ingo Müller, *Hitler's Justice: The Courts of the Third Reich* (Cambridge, Mass.: Harvard University Press, 1991), then Maitland and his followers apparently accepted that influence with considerable skepticism.

12. "Township and Borough," reprinted in *Selected Historical Essays of F. W. Maitland,* Helen M. Cam, ed. (Cambridge: Cambridge University Press, 1957), 3, 10.

13. Maitland, supra n.2, 232–33. He added that in "the morality of common sense" the group is a person, is a "right-and-duty-bearing unit." Moreover, though the moral philosopher may call such a thing an illusion, it is an illusion "persistently and progressively triumphing over certain philosophical and theological prejudices." In his wonderful introductory essay to his Gierke translation Maitland went so far as to say that such a unit "Itself can will, itself can act." Maitland, supra n.7, xxvi.

It is worth noting that Maitland repeatedly celebrated the English fear of what he called "the petrifying action of juristic theory"; see his "Trust and Corporation" in *Maitland: Selected Essays,* 189. As history illustrates, "Men often act first and think afterwards" (164). In this, as well as in other significant ways, Maitland may be viewed as a precursor of legal realism. An intriguing mystery in the intellectual history of Anglo-American legal thought is why Maitland was not more influential in this regard, and why English law seemingly never experienced anything like the outpouring of legal realist thought in the United States in the 1920s and 1930s.

14. Id. 186–88. Maitland suggested that the development of the trust idea over the centuries was "the greatest and most distinctive achievement performed by Englishmen in the field of jurisprudence"; see his "The Unincorporate Body," in *Maitland: Selected Essays,* 129.

15. Id. 216. Maitland warned that "public law" and "private law" remain "not technical terms" but only "potential rubrics" (144).

16. Id. 201. "A man thinks of his club as a living being, honourable as well as honest, while the joint-stock company is only a sort of machine into which he puts money and out of which he draws dividends." W. M. Geldart sounded a similar theme in his inaugural lecture as successor to Dicey in the Vinerian chair at Oxford, discussing "those bodies which seem to stand lowest in the scale of apparent group-personality, those whose aim is the acquisition of individual gain." W. M. Geldart, "Legal Personality," 27 *Law Q. Rev.* 90, 97 (1911).

17. Controversy about corporate personality raged (politely) for 50 years in Anglo-American legal discourse. By translating Gierke and by adding much of his own historical work to the concerns of Gierke, Ihering, and other continental thinkers, Maitland clearly was the premier thinker about such matters. But within the English legal elite, leading lights such as A. V. Dicey and W. M. Geldart, along with Frederick Pollock, Harold Laski and numerous others on both sides of the Atlantic, continuously debated the origins and significance of the fiction of corporate personality throughout the early part of this century. In a sense, John Dewey punctured the entire balloon with his functionalist critique in "The Historic Background of Corporate Legal Personality," 35 *Yale L. J.* 655 (1926). Clearly, however, the nexus between corporatism and fascism also helped to quiet the debate. See Edward A. Purcell, Jr., *The Crisis of Democratic Theory: Scientific Naturalism and the Problem of Value* (Lexington: University Press of Kentucky, 1973); James Q. Whitman, "Of Corporatism, Fascism, and the First New Deal," 39 *Am. J. Comp. L.* 747 (1991).

18. Kathleen Sullivan, "Rainbow Republicanism," 97 *Yale L. J.* 1713 (1988), offers a lucid introduction to several basic problems posed by "intermediate groups"—those affiliations that exist somewhere between individuals and the comprehensive state—for constitutional law generally and for the currently fashionable strand of "republicanism" in particular. She also mentions the tendency to overstate the voluntary/involuntary dichotomy (1714).

19. Maitland, supra n.2, 233. Maitland referred, of course, to Sir Henry Maine's famous assertion that "the movement of the progressive societies has hitherto been a movement from status to contract." Henry Sumner Maine, *Ancient Law: Its Connection with the Early History of Society and Its Relation to Modern Ideas* (1861; rpt. New York: Dorset Press, 1986), 182. Maine's specific examples were the movement from slave status to free contract, and from family hierarchy to individual independence. For a discussion of how the history of judicial reactions to Reconstruction in the United States suggests that Maine's observation is problematic, see Aviam Soifer, "Status, Contract, and Promises Unkept," 96 *Yale L. J.* 1916 (1987).

20. Taff Vale Railway Co. v. Amalgamated Society of Railway Servants, AC 426 (1901), cited in the opinion by Chief Justice Taft in United Mine Workers of America v. Coronado Coal Co., 259 U.S. 344 (1922). It may be worth noting that not everyone who agreed with Maitland about the reality of group identity did so for sympathetic or "liberal" reasons. For example, in the course of his customary decrying of the end of individualism, if not of civilization, Dicey agreed that "When a body of twenty, or two thousand, or two hundred thousand men bind themselves together to act in a particular way for some common purpose, they create a body,

which by no fiction of law, but the very nature of things, differs from the individuals of whom it is constituted." A. V. Dicey, "The Combination Laws as Illustrating the Relation Between Law and Opinion in England During the Nineteenth Century," 17 *Harv. L. Rev.* 511, 513 (1904). Similarly, Holdsworth commented on the excessive power of groups in labor matters in the course of his history and scolded that the failure to employ the crime of conspiracy in this context "has in effect set up a new feudalism, which is every whit as retrogressive in its ideas, and as mischievous, as the feudalism of the Middle Ages." Sir William Searle Holdsworth, *A History of English Law,* 3rd ed. (London: Methuen, 1944), IX, 46.

21. Harold Laski, "The Personality of Associations," 29 *Harv. L. Rev.* 404 (1916).

22. Id. 425.

23. See Arthur Mann, *The One and the Many* (Chicago: University of Chicago Press, 1979); John Higham, *Strangers in the Land: Patterns of American Nativism, 1860–1925* (New Brunswick: Rutgers University Press, 1955).

24. Harold Laski, "Morris Cohen's Approach to Legal Philosophy," 15 *U. Chi. L. Rev.* 575, 578 (1948).

25. Id.

26. Cohen, supra n.4, at 386 (emphasis in original). An insightful summary of the importance of community in the thought of Progressives is available in David Price, "Community and Control: Critical Democratic Theory in the Progressive Period," 68 *Am. Pol. Science Rev.* 1663 (1974).

27. For detailed historical treatments of this cyclical phenomenon, see Robert Nisbet, *Community and Power* (New York: Oxford University Press, 1962), originally published as *The Quest for Community* (New York: Oxford University Press, 1953); Raymond J. Wilson, *In Quest of Community: Social Philosophy in the United States, 1860–1920* (New York: Wiley, 1970).

28. Cohen, supra n.4, 390 (emphasis in original).

29. Id. 388.

30. Laski, supra n.24, 576.

31. 299 U.S. 353 (1937).

32. Id. 364.

33. Id.

34. 323 U.S. 516 (1945). A notable precursor was Hague v. C.I.O., 307 U.S. 496 (1939).

35. 468 U.S. 609 (1984).

36. R. J. Thomas was president of the International U.A.W., a vice president of the C.I.O., and one of the country's most influential labor leaders. In 1943, when Thomas came to Texas to solicit for union members, Presi-

dent Roosevelt put him on a special five-person labor commission created to deal with labor disruptions (and perhaps to co-opt the political
thrust of the left) during World War II. Thomas traveled to Bay Town,
Texas, to address the oil workers there and specifically to challenge a
1943 Texas statute that required licensing of paid union solicitors. (The
statute is set out, and accepted as intended to protect the laboring class,
in Ex parte Thomas, 174 S.W.2d 958 (1943).) Thomas made it a point
to address "one Pat O'Sullivan, a nonunion man in the audience," and
to urge him by name to join the Oil Workers Union. 323 U.S. at
522–23.
37. Id. 530.
38. Id. 543.
39. Id. 531.
40. Id.
41. Id. 530.
42. Id. 534.
43. This story is still to be fully told, but parts of it may be found in Peter
Irons, *The New Deal Lawyers* (Princeton: Princeton University Press,
1982), and Edward Purcell, Jr. and James Q. Whitman, supra n.17.
44. For a vivid description of these church schisms in antebellum Massachusetts, see Leonard Levy, *The Law of the Commonwealth and Chief Justice
Shaw* (Cambridge, Mass.: Harvard University Press, 1957), 29–42; for
an overview of various attempts to settle disputes outside of law in America, see Jerold Auerbach, *Justice Without Law?* (New York: Oxford University Press, 1983).
45. As Robert Cover put it, "Prudential deference . . . is the great temptation,
and the final sin of judging." Robert Cover, "The Folktales of Justice:
Tales of Jurisdiction," 14 *Cap. U. L. Rev.* 179, 190 (1985). To be sure,
the enactment of the National Labor Relations Act in 1934 created a new
framework for labor litigation. Nonetheless, it should be noted that
Thomas came a decade after the NLRA, and that the Court has never
been bound to defer to the administrative expertise of the National Labor
Relations Board or to ignore constitutional problems when they are discerned beneath the NLRA scaffolding. Justice Thomas's first opinion for
the Court, for example, Lechmere Inc. v. N.L.R.B., 112 S.Ct. 841 (1992),
disregarded the views of even a conservative NLRB and went further in
denying any statutory right of access for union organizers to a workplace
so long as they might conceivably reach potential union members by "other alternative means" (849). For a fine historical overview, see Christopher Tomlins, *The State and the Unions: Labor Relations, Law and the
Organized Labor Movement in America: 1880–1960* (Cambridge: Cambridge University Press, 1985).
46. Herbert Wechsler, "Toward Neutral Principles of Constitutional Law,"

73 *Harv. L. Rev.* 1, 34 (1959). But see Charles Black, "The Lawfulness of the Segregation Decisions," 69 *Yale L. J.* 421 (1960); Louis Henkin, "Shelley v. Kraemer: Notes for a Revised Opinion," 110 *U. Pa. L. Rev.* 473 (1962). For more on John W. Davis and his argument for South Carolina in *Brown,* see Richard Kluger, *Simple Justice* (New York: Knopf, 1976).

47. See Moose Lodge No. 167 v. Irvis, 407 U.S. 163 (1972) (Douglas, J., dissenting).
48. Cohen, supra n.4, 389.

5. Groping for Group Rights

1. W. M. Geldart, "Legal Personality," Inaugural Lecture for Vinerian Chair, Oxford, published in 27 *Law Q. Rev.* 90, 97 (1911).
2. Alexis de Tocqueville, *Democracy in America,* J. P. Mayer, ed., George Lawrence, trans. (Garden City: Anchor Books, 1969), 339.
3. Id. 693. Devotion to equality, according to Tocqueville, might produce elected leaders who would not be tyrants but rather schoolmasters, and a populace in "perpetual childhood" who ultimately became "no more than a flock of timid and hardworking animals with the government as its shepherd" (692).
4. Id. 692–93.
5. See "September 1, 1939" in W. H. Auden, *The Collected Poetry* (New York: Random House, 1945), 58–59.
6. See Anthony P. Cohen, *The Symbolic Construction of Community* (London: Tavistock Publications, 1985); Constance Smith and Anne Freedman, *Voluntary Associations: Perspectives on the Literature* (Cambridge, Mass.: Harvard University Press, 1972).
7. See the discussion of Indian tribes in Milner Ball, "Constitution, Court, Indian Tribes," 1987 *Am. B. Found. Res. J.* 3; Robert Williams, Jr., "The Algebra of Federal Indian Law: The Hard Trail of Decolonizing and Americanizing the White Man's Indian Jurisprudence," 1986 *Wis. L. Rev.* 219; Ronald Garet, "Communality and Existence: The Rights of Groups," 56 *S. Cal. L. Rev.* 1001, 1035–43 (1983).
8. See Petra Shattuck and Jill Norgren, *Partial Justice: Federal Indian Law in a Liberal Constitutional System* (New York: Berg, 1991); Vine Deloria, Jr., and Clifford Lytle, *American Indians, American Justice* (Austin: University of Texas Press, 1983); William Cronon, *Changes in the Land: Indians, Colonists, and the Ecology of New England* (New York: Hill and Wang, 1983).
9. 481 U.S. 704 (1987). Justice O'Connor wrote the Court's lead opinion and there were no dissents. Justice Brennan, joined by Justices Marshall and Blackmun, concurred separately; so did Justice Scalia, joined by Chief

Justice Rehnquist and Justice Powell; and Justice Stevens, joined by Justice White.

The primary cause for these *seriatim* opinions among Justices who concurred in the result was their disagreement about whether the decision in *Hodel* to invalidate a congressional statute on the basis of minimal property claims undercut other recent precedents, particularly Andrus v. Allard, 444 U.S. 51 (1979) (upholding ban on sale of all artifacts containing eagle feathers, on the theory that the value of the artifacts nevertheless was not entirely destroyed).

10. 481 U.S. 704. The decision invalidated the original version of the Indian Land Consolidation Act of 1983, Pub. L. No. 97–459, 96 Stat. 2519.

11. Id. 705. Indeed, Justice O'Connor described the policy of allotment as "disastrous for Indians" and noted that the problem of fractionation would continue to compound over time. Nevertheless, none of the justices expressed any qualms about the Court's activist intervention to protect admittedly attenuated individual property against clear, nearly contemporaneous congressional action.

12. Id. 711. The statutory section at issue affected only fractional interests that represented 2 percent or less of the total acreage of a tract and that had earned the owner less than $100 the previous year. The Court also acknowledged the headaches and expense in administering tracts subdivided into hundreds of interests, many of which generate only pennies a year in rent. Yet O'Connor extolled the significance of inheritance as "part of the Anglo-American legal system since feudal times" (716). The rights of tribes, and their members, simply were no match for longstanding—one might almost say "inherited"—individual rights.

13. Senator Dawes is quoted in A. Debo, *And Still the Waters Run* (Princeton: Princeton University Press, 1940), 21–22.

14. 485 U.S. 439, 451 (1988).

15. The Ninth Circuit had predicted that the road would "virtually destroy the Indians' ability to practice their religion," Northwest Cemetery Protective Ass'n. v. Peterson, 795 F.2d 688, 693 (9th Cir. 1986), but Justice O'Connor's majority opinion argued that, even if this prediction materialized, "The First Amendment must apply to all citizens alike, and it can give to none of them a veto over public programs that do not prohibit the free exercise of religion." 485 U.S. at 452. This time, Justice Brennan, joined by Justices Marshall and Blackmun, dissented; Justice Kennedy did not take part.

16. 485 U.S. at 451.

17. Id. 452.

18. Id. 453 (emphasis in original). This is reminiscent of President Reagan's memorable remark during the 1980 New Hampshire primary: "I paid for this microphone." It merely amounts, however, to a restatement of the

idea that the greater power necessarily includes the lesser power. For further discussion of the renascence of this argument, see the discussion of Moyer v. Peabody in Chapter 3 and Employment Division v. Smith in Chapter 7.

19. 492 U.S. 408 (1989). In this decision, and two consolidated cases, the Supreme Court split into three camps on the question of whether the Yakima Tribe had exclusive zoning jurisdiction over property within its reservation in the state of Washington. The decisive duo—Stevens joined by O'Connor—used their swing votes to determine that the tribe could continue to exercise control over a site in what had been the closed area of the reservation, at least when the owner sought to develop the land in a way that might harm the environment. But, they determined, the tribe had to cede authority to the local county zoning process in the case of a parcel held in fee on the more open part of the reservation. The second group of justices—White, joined by Chief Justice Rehnquist and Scalia and Kennedy—would have deprived the tribe of zoning authority entirely. The third group—Blackmun, Brennan, and Marshall—would have given the tribe exclusive authority over all the land at issue. For a powerful, detailed critique of *Brendale* and its broad implications, see Joseph William Singer, "Sovereignty and Property," 86 *Nw. U. L. Rev.* 1 (1991).

20. See the discussion of City of Richmond v. J. A. Croson Co. in Chapter 7.

21. See Milner Ball, supra, n.7; Robert A. Williams, Jr., *The American Indian in Western Legal Thought: The Discourses of Conquest* (New York: Oxford University Press, 1990); Rennard Strickland, "Dances with Lawyers: Wolves, Judges, and Other Medicine Men," 69 *Tex. L. Rev.* 995 (1991).

22. 501 U.S. 775 (1991). Justice Scalia wrote for the majority and Justice Blackmun dissented, joined by Justices Marshall and Stevens.

23. Id. 780.

24. The Eleventh Amendment states: "The Judicial power of the United States shall not be construed to extend to any suit in law and equity, commenced or prosecuted against one of the United States by Citizens of another State, or by Citizens or Subjects of any Foreign State." For the remarkably convoluted history of the amendment, see John Orth, *The Judicial Power of the United States: The Eleventh Amendment in American History* (New York: Oxford University Press, 1987); for a critique of the particular notions of a deep structure of federalism invoked by conservative justices in recent decisions, see sources cited in Aviam Soifer, "Truisms That Never Will Be True: The Tenth Amendment and The Spending Power," 57 *U. Col. L. Rev.* 793 (1986). That Scalia and his fellow textualists practice a peculiar and inconsistent brand of originalism is obvious to any reader of the Court's opinions, but the point is captured

succinctly in George Kannar, "The Constitutional Catechism of Antonin Scalia," 99 *Yale L. J.* 1297 (1990); Glenn Reynolds, "Penumbral Reasoning on the Right," 140 *U. Pa. L. Rev.* 1333 (1992).

25. Milner Ball, supra n.7, provides a wonderfully clear and convincing demonstration of inconsistencies and obtuseness within the "shabby tales composed by the Supreme Court" as the justices repeatedly have manipulated legal doctrine to reassert the apparent paradox that "the law is that might is the basis of federal power over Indian nations." 1987 *Am. B. Found. Res. J.* 139, 137.

26. See Nell Jessup Newton, "Federal Power Over Indians: Its Sources, Scope and Limitations," 132 *U. Pa. L. Rev.* 195 (1984). The Court celebrated self-determination in Oklahoma Tax Commission v. Citizen Band Potawatomi Indian Tribe of Oklahoma, 498 U.S. 505, 510 (1991), for example, quoting California v. Cabazon Band of Mission Indians, 480 U.S. 202, 216 (1987): "These Acts reflect Congress' desire to promote 'the goal of Indian self-government,' including its 'overriding goal' of encouraging tribal self-sufficiency and economic development."

27. Compare Monaco v. Mississippi, 292 U.S. 313 (1934) with South Dakota v. North Carolina, 192 U.S. 286 (1904). For the current doctrine and background of the legal tangle surrounding the "anachronistic fiction" of sovereign immunity, see Oklahoma Tax Commission, 498 U.S. 514 (Justice Stevens, concurring); Vicki Jackson, "The Supreme Court, the Eleventh Amendment, and State Sovereign Immunity," 98 *Yale L. J.* 1 (1988); J. Orth, supra n.24.

28. Noatak was joined by two other tribal entities in its suit. The state attorney general had advised that the 1980 statute, in specifying Native Villages for beneficial treatment, violated equal protection. Though Alaska has run into equal protection difficulties in attempts to distribute some of the bounty from the oil pipeline to state citizens, on the basis of their relative longevity within the state, Zobel v. Williams, 457 U.S. 55 (1982), the attorney general's opinion here seems very dubious. It would not have been difficult, for example, to prove through the totality of circumstances the kind of past discrimination needed to defend the statutory plan if any plaintiff actually had been able to overcome jurisdictional difficulties and wished to launch an equal protection attack.

At the most basic level, the treatment of Alaska's Native Peoples, who welcomed white settlers, as directly analogous to "conquered" tribes in the "lower 48" states, flies in the face of history, despite the lumping together of all Native Americans for purposes of federal government control upheld in Tee-Hit-Ton Indians v. United States, 348 U.S. 272 (1955). Moreover, recently the Court has upheld differential treatment of Native Americans quite readily, arguing that such classifications are political, not racial, and therefore need only be rationally related to some acceptable governmental purpose. See Morton v. Mancari, 417 U.S. 535 (1974); Washington v. Yakima Indian Nation, 439 U.S. 463 (1979).

29. Cherokee Nation v. Georgia, 30 U.S. (5 Pet.)1, 17–18 (1831). Marshall specifically held that an Indian tribe might be a nation, but that a tribe "is not a foreign state, in the sense of the constitution" (18). In this decision, and again in Worcester v. Georgia, 31 U.S. (6 Pet.) 515 (1832), Marshall emphasized the relationship between the federal government and the Indian tribes against claims of state sovereignty that Georgia had vigorously pursued, to the point of creating a national crisis. Marshall's approach as well as his language cannot be reconciled with that of the *Noatak* Court's embrace of Alaska's state sovereign immunity claims. Instead, Marshall constructed the "dependent domestic nations" categorization of the tribal relationship to the federal government that has dominated, and haunted, Indian law ever since. For a careful study of the background of the Georgia cases, see Joseph Burke, "The Cherokee Cases: A Study in Law, Politics, and Morality," 21 *Stan. L. Rev.* 500 (1969).

30. 501 U.S. 782. The state sovereign immunity issue had been discussed earlier only in scattered dicta, largely because the prevalent theory was that the federal government had plenary power over the tribes, including the right and the duty to sue states on their behalf, thus overcoming any Eleventh Amendment barrier. A 1966 statutory change explicitly altered federal court jurisdiction to give tribes the ability to sue by themselves, but the Court in *Noatak* held that Congress had not been explicit enough to lift the states' Eleventh Amendment barrier.

31. When Native American religious claims were at stake, for example, Scalia again wrote for the Court and purported to recognize the "relative disadvantage" of such minority religious practices. Yet he relegated such religious claims exclusively to protection through the political process, proclaiming this the "unavoidable consequence of democratic government." Employment Division, Department of Human Resources v. Smith, 494 U.S. 872, 890 (1990), discussed in Chapter 7.

32. See U.S. v. Alvarez-Nachain, 112 S.Ct. 2188 (1992)(foreign citizens not entitled to protection from kidnapping by agents of U.S. government); Vine Deloria, Jr., "Laws Founded in Justice and Humanity: Reflections on the Content and Character of Federal Indian Law," 31 Ariz. L. Rev. 202 (1989); Vine Deloria, Jr., and Clifford Lytle, *The Nations Within: The Past And Future of American Indian Sovereignty* (New York: Pantheon Books, 1984).

33. For a snappy overview, with particular attention to the Cherokee cases, see Shattuck and Norgren, supra n.8.

34. In addition to the *Hodel, Northwest Cemetery, Yakima,* and *Noatak* decisions discussed in the text, see also Oklahoma Tax Commission v.

Citizen Band Potawatami Indian Tribe of Oklahoma, 498 U.S. 505 (1991) (unanimous decision holding that state may not tax tribal members but, despite longstanding practice, may prospectively tax sales by tribal members to nonmembers); Santa Clara Pueblo v. Martinez, 436 U.S. 49 (1978) (rejecting individual sex discrimination claim against tribe on jurisdictional ground, holding that Indian Civil Rights Act of 1968 protects tribal sovereignty but emphasizing Congress's plenary power to override tribal authority if it sees fit).

35. Cherokee Nation v. Georgia, supra n.29, 17–18.

36. State of Vermont v. Elliott, 616 A.2d 210 (1992), cert. denied, 113 S.Ct. 1258 (1993). The local state attorney defended the decision: "We think this affirms our position all along . . . that all Vermonters are equal before the law." "Vermont Court Says History Voids Land Claims of Abenaki Indians," *New York Times,* June 18, 1992, D23.

37. For an anthropologist's critical perspective on a similar recent legal clash of cultures, see "Identity in Mashpee," in James Clifford, *The Predicament of Culture: Twentieth-Century Ethnography, Literature, and Art* (Cambridge, Mass.: Harvard University Press, 1988), 277.

38. 485 U.S. 360 (1988).

39. Sorenson v. Secretary of Treasury, 475 U.S. 851, 867 (1986)(Stevens, J., dissenting).

40. International Union, U.A.W. v. Lyng, 648 F. Supp. 1234 (D.D.C. 1986) and International Union, U.A.W. v. Block, 648 F. Supp. 1241 (D.D.C. 1985).

41. Some of the affidavits are summarized in Judge Oberdorfer's opinion granting summary judgment for the plaintiffs. The government agreed that the strikers' choices were "leaving their households, abandoning a strike by returning to work, quitting their jobs, or attempting to persuade their unions to call off the strike." U.A.W. v. Lyng, 648 F.Supp. 1236. Some strikers remained disqualified even though their employers had replaced them and therefore foreclosed any chance to return. Judge Oberdorfer indicated that the 1981 House Agriculture Committee report explained that the amendment was rejected previously because it was "the non-neutral act of pressuring the worker to abandon the strike," id., quoting H.R. Rep. No. 106, 97th Cong., 1st Sess. 142 (1981).

42. 485 U.S. at 364–5, quoting Lyng v. Castillo, 477 U.S. 635, 638 (1986) (holding that statutory definition of "household" for food stamp purposes satisfied rational relationship test). Justice White asserted that *Castillo* "foreclosed" the claims of associational rights asserted in the striker-food stamp case.

43. See Peter Irons, *The New Deal Lawyers* (Princeton: Princeton University Press, 1982); Carter v. Carter Coal Co., 298 U.S. 238 (1936) (Congress lacked power over coal-mining); United States v. Butler, 297 U.S. 1

(1936) (Congress lacked power over agriculture); Hammer v. Dagenhart, 247 U.S. 251 (1918) (Congress lacked power to regulate indirect effect on interstate commerce of child labor). The direct/indirect approach was vigorously attacked and rejected in several lonely opinions by Justice Cardozo and subsequently by a majority of the Court. It has nearly disappeared—at least for the moment—from explicit Supreme Court decisions about federalism and the constitutional reach of the Commerce Clause. Garcia v. San Antonio Metropolitan Transit Authority, 469 U.S. 528 (1985). Nevertheless, the approach is dear to lawyers and still echoes mightily within the doctrinal morass in current labor law concerning such matters as boycotts and handbilling. See Michael Harper, "The Consumer's Emerging Right to Boycott: *NAACP v. Claiborne Hardware* and Its Implications for American Labor Law," 93 *Yale L. J.* 409 (1984); James Gray Pope, "The Three-Systems Ladder of First Amendment Values: Two Rungs and a Black Hole," 11 *Hastings Const. L.Q.* 189 (1984).

44. 485 U.S. at 373, 371.

45. Id. 367 n.5,(citing Bates v. Little Rock, 361 U.S. 516, 523 (1960) and Healy v. James, 408 U.S. 169, 183 (1972)).

46. Id.

47. The Court referred here to NAACP v. Claiborne Hardware Co., 458 U.S. 886, 919–20 (1982) and to NAACP v. Alabama ex rel. Patterson, 357 U. S. 449, 462 (1958). Both decisions involved the NAACP, of course, and neither was a model of clarity about the extent of the freedom of association right embraced by the Court or about why traditional limitations such as standing and state action requirements were relaxed in these cases. These decisions share some similarity with New York Times Co. v. Sullivan, 376 U.S. 254 (1964), though they have lacked *Sullivan*'s capacity to grow beyond its initial, very sympathetic fact pattern.

48. See Thomas Emerson, "Freedom of Association and Freedom of Expression," 74 *Yale L. J.* 1 (1964); Michael Harper, *supra* n.43; but see International Longshoremen's Association, AFL-CIO v. Allied International, 456 U.S. 212 (1982) (secondary political picketing) and compare DeBartolo Corp. v. Florida Gulf Coast Bldg. and Const. Trades Council, 485 U.S. 568 (1988) (sect. 8(b)(4)(B) construed in light of constitutional problems raised by secondary handbilling).

49. 485 U.S. at 368. The majority also conceded: "It would be difficult to deny that this statute works at least some discrimination against strikers and their households" (371), but considered that discrimination not to be of constitutional significance. Instead, the Court adopted the idea that the greater power automatically includes the exercise of any degree of lesser power. This idea seems to be increasingly popular with the Court; see Posadas de Puerto Rico Associates v. Tourism Co. of Puerto Rico, 478 U.S. 328 (1986) (government power to ban gambling necessarily includes

government power to exercise the lesser power of banning advertising of gambling in newspapers targeted at local population); Harris v. McRae, 448 U.S. 297 (1980) (government may influence an indigent pregnant woman's constitutionally protected, fundamental right to choose abortion by subsidizing childbirth, but not abortion, because government need not provide any comprehensive medial care). Cf. McAuliffe v. Mayor of New Bedford, 155 Mass. 216, 220, 29 N.E. 517 (1892) (Holmes, J.) ("The petitioner may have a constitutional right to talk politics, but he has no constitutional right to be a policeman.")

An older, even less appealing greater power/lesser power argument was used as the leading rationale for slavery in the 1600–1700s, based on the claim traceable to Roman roots that slaves were captives in war and could therefore be killed. Merely enslaving people was said to be actually favorable treatment, clearly included within the greater power to kill them. See David B. Davis, *The Problem of Slavery in Western Culture* (Ithaca: Cornell University Press, 1966), 83–121; Winthrop Jordan, *White Over Black: American Attitudes Toward the Negro, 1550–1812* (Chapel Hill: University of North Carolina Press, 1968); Edmund S. Morgan, *American Slavery, American Freedom: The Ordeal of Colonia Virginia* (New York: W. W. Norton, 1975). For a demurrer concerning the reality of the justification in Graeco-Roman culture, see Moses I. Finley, *Ancient Slavery and Modern Ideology* (New York: Viking, 1980), 82–92.

50. 485 U.S. 368, quoting Regan v. Taxation with Representation of Washington, 461 U.S. 540, 549 (1983).

51. 374 U.S. 398 (1963) (Free Exercise Clause violated when woman denied unemployment benefits because her religious beliefs did not permit her to work on Saturday).

52. *UAW*, 485 U.S. 369 n.7, quoting Maher v. Roe, 432 U.S. 464, 475 n.8 (1977).

53. Justice Marshall's dissent, joined by Justices Brennan and Blackmun, convincingly demonstrated the absence of neutrality in several ways. Marshall used legislative history, excerpts from the affidavits of strikers, and responses by the government in the course of the litigation to show that the statutory intent, and its sometimes devastating actual effect, was to punish strikers and to force them into hard choices such as between living with their families and being loyal to their unions. Moreover, Marshall made the important point that "[o]n a deeper level," the neutrality argument actually "reflects a profoundly inaccurate view of the relationship of the modern federal government to the various parties to a labor dispute" (382). He pointed to tax subsidies, Small Business Administration loans, bankruptcy law protections, and similar advantages afforded management in strike situations.

54. See Personnel Adm'r v. Feeney, 442 U.S. 256, 274–79 (1979) (absolute

preference for veterans for civil service jobs valid since not "inherently non-neutral"); Young v. American Mini Theatres, Inc., 427 U.S. 50, 67 (1976) ("absolute neutrality" the essence of the First Amendment rule prohibiting content regulation); Lemon v. Kurtzman, 403 U.S. 602 (1971) (three-pronged test developed to measure crucial government neutrality regarding religion).

55. 413 U.S. 528, 534 (1973) (emphasis in original) (invalidating restrictive definition of household for food stamp purposes, clearly aimed at "hippies").

56. 485 U.S. 371.

57. Id. 372. Nevertheless, White was certain that "[i]t was no part of the purposes of the Food Stamp Act to establish a program that would serve as a weapon in labor disputes" (371).

58. Id. 373. Having decided this, the majority mentioned but did not rely on the money-saving or aid-to-the-neediest rationales suggested by the government. The first would explicitly end review of restrictions in government programs, and the second could not be supported, given the eligibility criteria for the Food Stamp program.

59. Id. 366, quoting NAACP v. Claiborne Hardware Co., 458 U.S. 886, 933 (1982).

60. Id. 368, quoting Ohio Bureau of Employment Services v. Hodory, 431 U.S. 471, 489 (1977).

61. The words "foundation" and "fundamental" share the same derivation and at one time shared the same meaning, pertaining to the base or bottom of a building. *Oxford English Dictionary,* 2nd ed. (Oxford: Clarendon Press, 1989). My friend Hugh Macgill reminded me that Dr. Johnson once caused great laughter when he remarked that "the woman had a bottom of good sense," which he amended to proclaim, "I say the *woman* was *fundamentally* sensible." *Boswell's Life of Johnson,* G. Hill, ed. (New York: Harper and Brothers, 1891), 114–15.

In Village of Belle Terre v. Boraas, 416 U.S. 1, 7 (1974), Justice Douglas's majority opinion insisted that the village ban on groups of three or more unrelated by blood or marriage sharing a household was constitutional because "it involves no 'fundamental' right guaranteed by the Constitution, such as . . . the right of association." The other fundamental rights Douglas sought to distinguish were voting, the right of access to the courts, and rights of privacy. Justice Marshall's dissent argued that "deference does not mean abdication" when, as in the case of the Belle Terre zoning ordinance, government action "infringe[s] upon fundamental constitutional rights" (14). Justice Brennan also dissented, primarily on jurisdictional grounds.

62. 485 U.S. 369.

63. Thomas Reed Powell is quoted, in turn quoting this aphorism by William

Graham Sumner, in John Braeman, "Thomas Reed Powell on the Roosevelt Court," 5 Const. Comm. 143, 145 (1988).

64. White did not mention his own majority opinion in City of Cleburne v. Cleburne Living Center, Inc., 473 U.S. 432, 439, 450 (1985), which indicated that even without strict or intermediate scrutiny there should be some bite in judicial consideration of whether similarly situated persons are treated alike. Differential treatment of specific groups may still indicate that the true goal of government action is illegitimate. See also Plyler v. Doe, 457 U.S. 202 (1982).

65. The majority relied on the minimal scrutiny proclaimed in decisions such as Massachusetts Bd. of Retirement v. Murgia, 427 U.S. 307 (1976) and Dandridge v. Williams, 397 U.S. 471 (1970).

66. See Christopher Tomlins, *The State and the Unions: Labor Relations, Law, and the Organized Labor Movement in America, 1880–1960* (Cambridge: Cambridge University Press, 1985); James Atleson, *Values and Assumptions in American Labor Law* (Amherst: University of Massachusetts Press, 1983); Staughton Lynd, "Communal Rights," 62 *Tex. L. Rev.* 1417 (1984); Karl Klare, "Labor Law as Ideology: Toward a New Historiography of Collective Bargaining Law," 4 *Indus. Rel. L. J.* 450 (1981).

67. See Tomlins, supra n.66, 99–243; Peter Irons, supra n.43, 203–71; *Working Class America: Essays on Labor, Community and American Society,* Michael Frisch and Daniel Walkowitz, eds. (Urbana: University of Illinois Press, 1983); David Montgomery, *Workers' Control in America: Studies in the History of Work, Technology and Labor Struggles* (New York: Cambridge University Press, 1979); Karl Klare, "Judicial Deradicalization of the Wagner Act and the Origins of Modern Legal Consciousness, 1937–1941" 62 *Minn. L. Rev.* 265 (1978).

68. Board of Regents v. Roth, 408 U.S. 564, 577 (1972). See Cleveland Bd. of Education v. Loudermill, 470 U.S. 532, 541 (1985) (holding that "the 'bitter with the sweet' approach misconceives the constitutional guarantee"); Wygant v. Jackson Bd. of Education, 476 U.S. 267 (1986) (Powell's plurality opinion, joined only by Rehnquist and Burger in Section IV, stressed the impact of even a temporary layoff on an employee, arguing that "the rights and expectations surrounding seniority make up what is probably the most valuable capital asset that the worker 'owns,' worth even more than the current equity in his home," 476 U.S. 283, quoting James Fallon and Paul Weiler, "Conflicting Models of Racial Justice," 1984 *Sup. Ct. Rev.* 1, 58; compare with Arnett v. Kennedy, 416 U.S. 134 (1974); Perry v. Sindermann, 408 U.S. 593 (1972).

69. See Mary Ann Glendon, *Rights Talk: The Impoverishment of Political Discourse* (New York: Free Press, 1991); Lawrence Friedman, *Total Justice* (New York: Russell Sage Foundation, 1985).

70. See Branti v. Finkel, 445 U.S. 507 (1980)(assistant public defender could not be discharged solely because of political beliefs); Elrod v. Burns, 427 U.S. 347 (1976) (public employment could not be conditioned on membership in or loyalty to political party in power). But see Brown v. Glines, 444 U.S. 348 (1980) (upholding Air Force regulations requiring prior approval of commanding officers before circulating petitions to Congress on a military base); United States Civil Service Commission v. National Association of Letter Carriers, 413 U.S. 548 (1973) (reaffirming limitation on active participation by civil servants in political parties).

71. 461 U.S. 138 (1983).

72. Id. 146. Sheila Myers chose to circulate the questionnaire after she objected to a transfer, was transferred anyway, and was told that her concerns about how the office was being run "were not shared by others in the office" (141).

73. Id. 147. The concession of a First Amendment element in the case, combined with the majority's denial that federal courts ought to be open to such concerns, must give one pause. The majority's position grows curiouser and curiouser, however, when we learn that one of Ms. Myers's questions—the one her employer was particularly upset about because it would be damaging if discovered by the press (167)—concerned pressure to work in political campaigns. If substantiated, this would clearly violate the Constitution. The Court segregated this question from all the other issues it considered to be not of public concern. Then the majority used only a balancing test and determined that Ms. Myers had raised only an unprotected employee grievance. Cf. Mt. Healthy City Bd. of Education v. Doyle, 429 U.S. 274 (1977) (school teacher could be fired for no reason whatever, but not for exercise of First Amendment right).

74. 461 U.S. 146. Not only did this statement of what can be fairly said gratuitously insult the four dissenters—Justice Brennan, joined by Justices Marshall, Blackmun, and Stevens—but it required the majority to reverse the fact-finding of the District Court, upheld by the Fifth Circuit, on the grounds that, "The inquiry into the protected status of speech is one of law, not fact. Thus, we are not bound to the views of the District Court unless clearly erroneous" (148 n.7).

75. See Leonard Levy, *Emergence of a Free Press* (New York: Oxford University Press, 1985); David Rabban, "The Ahistorical Historian: Leonard Levy on Freedom of Expression in Early American History," 37 *Stan. L. Rev* 795 (1985). But see John Reid, *Constitutional History of the American Revolution: The Authority of Rights* (Madison: University of Wisconsin Press, 1986).

76. 461 U.S. 148.

77. Id. 152.

78. Id. 154.

79. 490 U.S. 19 (1989).
80. 744 S.W.2d 165, 168 (Tex. App. 1987).
81. 490 U.S. 23. Chief Justice Rehnquist wrote for the majority; Justice Stevens, joined by Justice Blackmun, concurred in the result.
82. Id. 25.
83. Id. 24.
84. Id.
85. Id. 28.
86. "[W]e do not think the Constitution recognizes a generalized right of 'social association' that includes chance encounters in dance halls" (25).
87. Id. At the end of the following Term, the Court went further in distinguishing the dancer from the dance and decided that nude dancing was not expression protected by the First Amendment.
88. IDK, Inc. v. Clark County, 836 F.2d 1185, 1194 (9th Cir. 1988) (denying summary judgment in facial challenge to Las Vegas licensing scheme for sexually oriented escort services). See also Wilson v. Taylor, 733 F.2d 1539 (11th Cir. 1984) (invalidating dismissal of policeman for dating daughter of convicted felon who was a reputed mobster); Aristotle P. v. Johnson, 721 F. Supp. 1002 (D. Ill. 1989) (denying motion to dismiss claim by children in foster care of freedom of association right to remain in contact with siblings).
89. 490 U.S. 25, quoting and rejecting conclusion of Griswold v. Connecticut, 381 U.S. 479, 483 (1965).
90. FW/PBS, Inc. v. City of Dallas, 493 U.S. 215 (1990). The justices disagreed on questions of standing and whether the licensing scheme provided constitutionally adequate procedural safeguards, with a majority holding that for the most part it did not.
91. Id. 237.
92. Id., quoting *Roberts,* 618–19.
93. Swank v. Smart, 898 F.2d 1247, 1252 (7th Cir.), *cert. denied,* 498 U.S. 853 (1990). Posner had a good time—perhaps too good a time—rejecting the substantive claims but remanding for further consideration the procedural claims brought by policeman Gary Swank, who lost his job after he took Tina Millin, a 17-year-old college student, for a motorcycle ride one early morning while off duty. Posner's analysis of *"l'affaire* Tina" is entertaining, but it also affords a classic example of how to divide and conquer overlapping constitutional claims. In deprecating "Tina"— whom he repeatedly calls by her first name in contrast to "Mr. Swank"— Posner seemed insensitive to the gendered quality of language. Cf. Deborah Tannen, *You Just Don't Understand: Women and Men in Conversation* (New York: Morrow, 1990). Posner's sardonic factual description paved the way for him to denigrate the freedom of association claim. When he segregated serious expression from idle chit-chat, he missed a

point made by Justice Holmes, whom Posner generally admires: "The difference between gossip and philosophy lies only in one's way of taking a fact." Oliver Wendell Holmes, Jr., *Collected Legal Papers* (New York: Harcourt, Brace, 1920), 159.

94. Swank v. Smart, at 1251.
95. Id. 1252, using Ellwest Stereo Theatres v. Wenno, 681 F.2d 1243, 1247 (9th Cir. 1982) as an illustration. That decision rejected a constitutional attack—including the allegation of a constitutional right of customers to fondle themselves—on a Phoenix ordinance requiring that booths in which sexually explicit films were shown remain open to view from the outside.
96. Coates v. Cincinnati, 402 U.S. 611, 615 (1971). Justice Stewart's majority opinion invalidated an anti-loitering law but was limited to associating in public places. Stewart cited an Ohio Municipal Court decision that pointed out how arrests and prosecutions for loitering and congregating would have been effective weapons against patriots outside the Raleigh Tavern in Williamsburg, Virginia in 1774. But see Boos v. Barry, 485 U.S. 312, 328–29 (1988) (invalidating District of Columbia ban on displaying signs, but upholding prohibition on congregating within 500 feet of a foreign embassy and refusing to disperse when ordered to do so by police).
97. Justice Souter, dissenting in Cohen v. Cowles Media Company, 501 U.S. 663, 667 (1991), quoting Justice O'Connor, concurring in the result in *Smith,* discussed in Chapter 7.
98. 114 S.Ct. 2481 (1994).
99. Id. 2489–90.
100. 114 S.Ct. 2516 (1994). There were four separate opinions. The majority upheld several portions of the injunction, including a 36-foot buffer zone on a public street near the entrance to the abortion clinic. The Court invalidated several other portions, however, such as including private property within the 36-foot buffer zone, and a 300-foot buffer zone where protests were prohibited around private residences. The Court apparently was quite determined to decide this case, as the justices could have exercised various options to avoid decision. For example, they might have dismissed the writ of *certiorari* as improvidently granted in light of the Court's recent decision in National Organization of Women v. Scheidler, 114 S.Ct. 798 (1994), in which all the justices agreed that civil remedies are available against anti-abortion protesters under Sect. 1962 (c) of the Racketeer Influenced and Corrupt Organizations (RICO) chapter of the Organized Crime Control Act of 1970. Alternatively, the Court might have deferred decision in light of the new Freedom of Access to Clinic Entrances Act of 1994, signed into law only a little more than a month earlier, providing criminal penalties and civil

remedies for interference with access to reproductive health services.

101. Id. 2530.

102. Here is one example from Scalia's dissent and accompanying appendix: "Mr. Lacy, I understand that those on the other side of the issue [abortion-rights supporters] were also in the area. If you are referring to them, the Injunction did not pertain to those on the other side of the issue, because *the word in concert with means in concert with those who had taken a certain position in respect to the clinic, adverse to the clinic. If you are saying that is the selective basis, that is, the pro-choice were not arrested when pro-life was arrested, that's the basis of the selection.*" Tr.104–105 (Apr. 12, 1993, Appearance Hearings Held Before Judge McGregor, Eighteenth Judicial Circuit, Seminole County, Florida (emphasis added), quoted 114 S.Ct. 2516, 2540. Scalia's dissent was joined by Justices Kennedy and Thomas. Justice Stevens also dissented in part, but he argued that more of the injunction should have been upheld. Justice Souter concurred separately and sought to narrow the sweep of the majority's rejection of the freedom of association claim.

103. Id. 2535. Scalia's rhetorical overkill seems particularly ironic here: he seems to view the damage done to human lives or even potential lives by the constitutional abortion controversy to be less than the damage the First Amendment suffers in *Madsen.*

104. Id. 2543–44, quoting NAACP v. Claiborne Hardware Co., 458 U.S. 886, 925–26 (1982).

105. See Melville B. Nimmer Symposium, 34 *U.C.L.A. L. Rev.* 1331 (1987); David Anderson,"Media Success in the Supreme Court," Gannett Center for Media Studies Working Paper (1987); Steve Shiffrin, "The First Amendment and Economic Regulation: Away from a General Theory of the First Amendment," 78 *Nw. U. L. Rev.* 1212 (1983).

106. Victor Blasi, "The Checking Value in First Amendment Theory," 1977 *Am. B. Found. Res. J.* 523. Perhaps Eric Fromm overstated this important point when he said, "[G]roups which represent an idea in its purity and without compromise are the seedbeds of liberty; they keep the idea alive, regardless of the rate of progress it makes among the majority." Erich Fromm, *The Revolution of Hope: Toward A Humanized Technology* (New York: Harper and Row, 1968), 160.

107. In University of Pennsylvania v. E.E.O.C., 493 U.S. 182 (1990), for example, the decision of the unanimous Court to enforce a discovery order in a Title VII suit challenging a denial of tenure is surely reasonable and probably right. But the repeated use of slippery slope arguments in Justice Blackmun's opinion for the Court is striking. The Court rejected evidentiary privilege claims and constitutional claims premised on academic freedom on such grounds as the need to "stand behind the breakwater Congress has established" (194), and to avoid "'a long and

difficult journey to . . . an uncertain destination'" (201) (quoting Bran-
zburg v. Hayes, 408 U.S. 665, 703 [1972]). A more sensitive approach
to associational rights is in J. Peter Byrne, "Academic Freedom: A 'Special Concern of the First Amendment,'" 99 *Yale L. J.* 251 (1989), though
Rosalie Tung's pursuit of her claim against the Wharton School might
trump academic freedom anyway in the discovery context of her Title
VII suit. (I ought to note that as a member of "Committee W" I partic-
ipated in some of the discussion within the American Association of
University Professors about what position if any the AAUP ought to
have taken in this case.)

108. Federal Election Commission v. Massachusetts Citizens for Life, 479
U.S. 238 (1986), as discussed in Chapter 2. Though I reject Justice
Brennan's effort to lump all union activities with all corporate activities, some union activities properly are classified as economic and
therefore not protected, and other union activities are not purely economic and should be protected. This distinction resonates with the
long history of workers' efforts to combat the notion that a person's
labor is simply a commodity to be sold for the best price. It also helps
explain the difficult but important line-drawing task in decisions such
as Abood v. Detroit Bd. of Education, 431 U.S. 209 (1977) and Ellis
v. Railway Clerks, 466 U.S. 435 (1984) and their progeny, in which
the distinction between economic and political, ideological, and other
activities is crucial.

109. Robert Cover, "Violence and the Word," 95 *Yale L. J.* 1601 (1986). It
is important to recognize, however, that such use of the state's violence
is not always to be condemned and may be necessary in a good cause.

110. Scholem is quoted in Rothstein, "A Fateful Intellectual Friendship," 84
Commentary 41, 44 n.6 (1987).

6. Faulkner, Fealty, and Communal Obligations

1. Shalom Spiegel discussed the "epoch-making impact" of this confrontation and described the central message of Amos as "the choice of jus-
tice as the constitutive element of all law"; see Spiegel, "Amos vs.
Amaziah" in *The Jewish Expression,* Judah Goldin, ed. (New Haven:
Yale University Press, 1976), 38, 61. Edith Hamilton described the meeting between Amos and Amaziah as "the first time on record [when]
ritual and righteousness confronted each other" in "Amos: Humanity
Versus Form," in Edith Hamilton, *Spokesmen for God: The Great
Teachers of the Old Testament* (New York: W. W. Norton, 1962), 75.
Hamilton argued that Amos was the first to distinguish the essential
from the inessential; to separate "the vital and the trivial in conduct";
and that the importance of this "can hardly be overestimated" (79).

2. See Joseph Blenkinsopp, *A History of Prophecy in Israel* (Philadelphia: Westminster Press, 1983); Johannes Lindblom, *Prophecy in Ancient Israel* (Oxford: Basil Blackwell, 1962). What we generally ascribe to Homer or Amos may well have been the product of many minds, of course. To comment on the intricate scholarly debates about authorship is far beyond my competence. The translation of Amos I use is from *The Twelve Prophets,* A. Cohen, ed. and trans. (London: Soncino Press, 1969).

3. Michael Walzer describes Amos as the founder of social criticism, though I believe that Walzer overstates Amos's "insider" status as crucial to his prophetic role. "The Prophet as Social Critic" in Michael Walzer, *Interpretation and Social Criticism,* (Cambridge, Mass.: Harvard University Press, 1987), 69–94. See Abraham Heschel, *The Prophets* (New York: HarperCollins, 1969).

    In its final verses, the Book of Amos seems to have a happy ending, a return from exile and rebuilding. But this jarring finale, which many scholars believe to have been added at a later time—see Herbert Marks, "The Twelve Prophets," in *The Literary Guide to the Bible,* Robert Alter and Frank Kermode, eds. (Cambridge, Mass.: Harvard University Press, 1987), 210—hardly undercuts the horrific force of the book as a whole.

4. Amos said that the Lord spoke through him to the children of Israel— "the whole family which I brought out of the land of Egypt" (3:1)—with the following chilling words: "You only have I known of all the families of the earth; Therefore I will visit upon you all your iniquities" (3:2).

5. "The Bear" in William Faulkner, *Go Down, Moses* (New York: The Modern Library, 1955), 291.

6. Fletcher v. Peck, 10 U.S. (6 Cranch) 87 (1810). For many readers, the opinion is probably most readily available in the Appendix in C. Peter Magrath, *Yazoo—Law and Politics in the New Republic* (New York: W. W. Norton, 1967), 187–204.

7. See Pacific Mutual Life Insurance Co. v. Haslip, 499 U.S. 1, 25, 26 (1991) (upholding punitive damage award by jury as not violative of due process). Justice Scalia concurred only in the majority's judgment in favor of Cleopatra Haslip—a woman with a Faulknerian name who had been defrauded by an insurance company agent—and took the majority to task for examining due process rights beyond what could be found in "history" and "tradition." See also Cruzan v. Director, Missouri Dept. of Health, 497 U.S. 261, 294 (1990) (Scalia, concurring, rejected a constitutional "right to die" claim because "no 'substantive due process' claim can be maintained unless the claimant demonstrates that the State has deprived him of a right historically and traditionally protected against state interference.")

8. The justices have battled repeatedly in recent years over whether substan-

tive rights are limited to those either explicit in the Constitution or traditional in some long-established, formal sense of what constitutes "tradition." The leading protagonists have been Justice Scalia, who advocates an exceptionally narrow approach to tradition, and Justice Stevens, who disputes both the invocation and the application of tradition as the definitive criteria for discerning fundamental rights. Noteworthy battles have erupted over these matters, particularly in the realm of privacy and family law claims. See Cruzan v. Director, Missouri Department of Health, 497 U.S. 261 (1990) (upholding Missouri restriction of withdrawal of life-support systems to those who signed living wills or where there was clear and convincing evidence of such a desire when patient was competent); Michael H. v. Gerald D., 491 U.S. 110 (1989) (discussed below).

There also have been repeated skirmishes and sustained clashes ranging from the constitutionality of political patronage systems, Rutan v. Republican Party of Illinois, 497 U.S. 62 (1990) (invalidating traditional political patronage system on First Amendment grounds) to imposition of the death penalty, Walton v. Arizona, 497 U.S. 639 (1990) (upholding death penalty, despite point by Stevens, dissenting, that common law tradition and history both mitigated against Scalia's claims, in a concurrence, regarding traditional forms of punishment). For an example even before Scalia joined the Court, see Bowers v. Hardwick, 478 U.S. 186 (1986) (rejecting challenge to Georgia law criminalizing adult consensual homosexual sodomy on grounds of purported "very long" traditional prohibition).

9. As Tom Grey's recent book made crisply and elegantly clear, Wallace Stevens may be read as a poetic pragmatist. Stevens offered one answer to the dilemma posed if all things are equally subjective: "The final belief is to believe in a fiction, which you know to be a fiction, there being nothing else. The exquisite truth is to know that it is a fiction and that you believe in it willingly." Thomas C. Grey, *The Wallace Stevens Case: Law and the Practice of Poetry* (Cambridge, Mass.: Harvard University Press, 1991), 76, quoting "Adagia" and exploring ways in which "fiction" was "a crucially multivocal term" for Stevens.

10. The leading modern source for a cavalier use of "history and tradition," as if the phrase entailed a single concept, was Justice Powell's plurality opinion in Moore v. East Cleveland, 431 U.S. 494, 503 (1977) (holding by a vote of 4–1–4 that a grandmother could not be jailed for allowing two of her grandchildren who were cousins to live with her in violation of a local zoning ordinance). That Scalia's use of tradition as a limiting concept sharply conflicts with the use of history as a source for determining the weight of precedent and principle in constitutional law became abundantly clear in the abortion decision at the end of the Court's 1991

Term. The dispute was particularly vituperative between Justice Scalia, joined by Chief Justice Rehnquist and Justices White and Thomas (concurring in part and dissenting in part), and Justices O'Connor, Kennedy, and Souter, who delivered an unusual Joint Opinion of the Court in Planned Parenthood of Southeastern Pennsylvania v. Casey, 112 S.Ct. 2791 (1992).

Scalia repeatedly invoked "unquestionable constitutional tradition" in his assault on, the "outrageous arguments" of his fellow justices and their "Nietzschean vision" demonstrating that "the Imperial Judiciary lives" (2876, 2875, 2882). The four justices indulged in such rhetoric because their three conservative colleagues had decided not to overrule Roe v. Wade, though the lengthy Joint Opinion surely weakened the precedent whose "central holding" the trio claimed to follow for reasons of *stare decisis* in a regime premised on the Rule of Law. Scalia directed much of his anger at a concept summed up in the Joint Opinion with a telling quotation from Charles Black about the crucial importance of history and context. Black had answered the question of whether segregation ought to have been struck down in Brown v. Board of Education: "That question has meaning and can find an answer only on the ground of history and of common knowledge about the facts of life in [segregated states]" (2813), quoting Charles Black, "The Lawfulness of the Segregation Decisions," 69 *Yale L. J.* 421, 427 (1960).

11. Holmes called history "the first step toward an enlightened skepticism," while he termed it "revolting" to follow tradition for no better reason than its longevity, and particularly revolting "if the grounds upon which it was laid down have vanished long since, and the rule simply persists from blind imitation of the past." Oliver Wendell Holmes, Jr., "The Path of the Law," 10 *Harv. L. Rev.* 457, 469 (1897). See J. Willard Hurst, *Justice Holmes on Legal History* (New York: Macmillan, 1964).

12. Quoted in Thurman W. Arnold, "Criminal Attempts—The Rise and Fall of an Abstraction," 40 *Yale L. J.* 53, 58 (1930). See Courtland H. Peterson, "Particularism in the Conflict of Laws," 10 *Hofstra L. Rev.* 973, 977 n.8 (1982).

13. Aviam Soifer, "Reviewing Legal Fictions," 20 Ga. L. Rev. 871 (1986). See also Lon Fuller, *Legal Fictions* (Stanford: Stanford University Press, 1967); and Kim Lane Scheppele, "Foreword: Telling Stories," 87 *Mich. L. Rev.* 2073 (1989).

14. Faulkner, supra n.5, 327.

15. A popular introduction to the art of literary criticism, itself by now an old stand-by, is *Bear, Man, and God: Seven Approaches to William Faulkner's "The Bear,"* Francis Lee Utley et al., eds. (New York: Random House, 1964). A flood of additional criticism has been published since, much of it debating Faulkner's approach to racial matters. On the

encumbered hero as a prevalent literary device, see Hanna Wirth-Nesher, "The Literary Orphan as Natural Hero: Huck and Pip," 15 *Dickens Stud. Ann.* 259 (1989).

16. Faulkner, supra n.5, 326.

17. Influences on or intended allusions by Faulkner remain uncertain, of course, but Keats may well have been one of them ("Thou foster-child of silence and slow time, / Sylvan historian, who canst thus express / A flowery tale more sweetly than our rhyme." And "What men or gods are these? . . . What mad pursuit? / What struggle to escape?" John Keats, "Ode on a Grecian Urn", lines 2–4 and 8–9.

18. Thus in the wilderness Boon, considered a white man despite his claim of varying degrees of Indian blood depending upon how drunk he is, is clearly subordinate to Sam Fathers, who wears "the frayed five-cent straw hat which had been the badge of the negro's slavery and was now the regalia of his freedom". Faulkner, supra n.5, 206; henceforth cited by page number only.

    I read Boon as quite complex and subversive. Even Boon's maddened last stand at the old tree deserves more sympathy than most critics accord it. A useful article on the role of authority in the story, reflecting the mainstream interpretation of Boon, is John H. Schaar, "Community or Contract? William Faulkner and the Dual Legacy," in *The Problem of Authority in America*, John P. Diggins and Mark E. Kann, eds. (Philadelphia: Temple University Press, 1981), 93.

19. Early in the story, railroad tracks link the wilderness to Memphis and its crucial liquor supply. By the end, a little engine that reminds Isaac of the courageous but foolhardy little dog that played a key role in the pursuit of Old Ben carries Isaac back to what is the end of the line for the forest. He passes the lumber company's planing-mill, still half-finished but already surrounded by stacked steel rails and piled crossties. A young bear, made frantic by the coming of the railroad, finally runs with "two sets of feet, front and back, tracking two separate though parallel courses" (320). In fact, Old Ben is described more than once as "locomotive-like" (193, 211, and 238).

20. As McCaslin Edmonds, Isaac's older cousin, debates with Isaac throughout section 4 of "The Bear," he tries to put the best face possible on Carothers McCaslin, but the best McCaslin can do is to describe Carothers as "him who saw the opportunity and took it, bought the land, took the land, got the land no matter how, held it to bequeath, no matter how, out of the old grant, the first patent, when it was a wilderness of wild beasts and wilder men, and cleared it, translated it into something to bequeath to his children, worthy of bequeathment for his descendants' ease and security and pride and to perpetuate his name and accomplishments" (256). To Isaac, Carothers's ruthlessness as slave owner and

exploiter (including incest with his own slave daughter) is more pertinent in deciding what to do.

21. Isaac acts "not in mere static and hopeful emulation of the Nazarene," but simply because he is good with his hands and he is willing to make a huge, mixed-motive leap of faith that remains, despite apparent clarity, "always incomprehensible to him" (309–10).

22. Id. 310.

23. From the opening 'comic' scenes in "Was," about a cornered pet fox and the hunt for a slave who ran away (only to see his lover, however), through Isaac's final hunt in "Delta Dawn," dogs and legal authorities bark at the heels of every character. There is no escaping old patterns. Yet individual characters constantly challenge the intermingling of blood and human concerns, confrontation and predestination, that bind them all across the conflated generations.

    For example, in the dramatic face-off in "The Fire and the Hearth" between a former slave and his contemporary, the son of his former owner, the impact of their common ancestor, Carothers McCaslin, is inescapable. So are the contemporary forces of legal hierarchy and potential vigilantism. Throughout the book, moonshiners and treasure hunters, slaves and indentured servants, even Samuel Worsham Beauchamp—executed for killing a Chicago policeman, but who still must "come home right" (383)—constantly bounce up against what is restricted, permitted, and expected according to both law and community customs and usages. Isaac's understanding of unwritten rules of skill and fairness pervades "The Bear." It therefore seems fitting that a recent Mississippi Supreme Court decision invoked "The Bear" as it upheld a conviction for "most unsportsmanlike conduct" while hunting deer. Pharr v. Mississippi, 465 So.2d 294, 298 (1984).

24. Faulkner, 254–56.

25. Id. 298.

26. Id.

27. Id. 262–63.

28. Id. 266.

29. In a sense, section 4 is a primer describing the dark side, or the far side, of a law course in trusts and estates. For example, there is a recurrent theme of failed attempts to buy rather than to ask for forgiveness. This is juxtaposed with the emptiness of physical legacies. Thus Isaac has a great deal of trouble delivering Carothers's thousand-dollar legacy to the old man's Negro son and his descendants, and Isaac himself is left only his Uncle Hubert's rustling stack of I.O.U.'s instead of his own "Legacy, a Thing, possessing weight to the hand and bulk to the eye and even audible: a silver cup filled with gold pieces and wrapped in burlap and sealed with his godfather's ring in hot wax" (301). Section 4 also portrays the

limits a black man faces even when he is well-dressed and educated, owns a farm, has faith in the new era, and believes that the country will be a New Canaan.

30. Id. 257.
31. Id. 3.
32. Id. 364.
33. Id. 363.
34. See Julius Getman, "Voices," 66 *Tex. L. Rev.* 577 (1988); Julius Getman and Jacqueline Mintz, "Foreword: Academic Freedom in a Changing Society," 66 *Tex. L. Rev.* 1247 (1988); Mark Yudof, "'Tea at the Palaz of Hoon': The Human Voice in Legal Rules," 66 *Tex. L. Rev.* 589 (1988). For feminist claims about giving voice to the voiceless, see Martha Minow, *Making All the Difference* (Ithaca: Cornell University Press, 1990); Carol Weisbrod, "Images of the Woman Juror," 9 *Harv. Women's L. J.* 59 (1986). See Symposium, "Feminist Jurisprudence," 24 *Ga. L. Rev.* 759 (1990). For my own initial stab at some of these themes and Faulkner, see Aviam Soifer, "Listening and the Voiceless," 4 *Miss. C. L. Rev.* 319 (1984) (part of a "Law and Southern Literature" Symposium).
35. *Faulkner in the University,* Joseph L. Blotner and Frederick L. Gwynn, eds. (New York: Vintage Books, 1965), 84. Holmes said "it ought always to be remembered that historic continuity with the past is not a duty, it is only a necessity." "Learning and Science" in Oliver Wendell Holmes, Jr., *Collected Legal Papers* (New York: Harcourt, Brace, 1920), 139.
36. Faulkner, 4.
37. Id. 327.
38. Magrath, supra n.6, 7, quoting Albert J. Beveridge, *The Life of John Marshall* (Houghton Mifflin, 1916–1919), III, 551.
39. Magrath, supra n.6, 10 (quoting Jackson).
40. This story about Luther Martin apparently did not appear in print until Beveridge, supra n.38, 586 n.1. Consideration of the intricate, heated politics of the various land manipulations in the early Republic is beyond the scope of this chapter, as is the fascinating tale of the involvement of seemingly every leading lawyer and politician of the era including, of course, John Marshall himself.
41. Fletcher v. Peck, 10 U.S. (6 Cranch) 87, 139.
42. Id. 131.
43. Id. 132.
44. Id.
45. Id. 133.
46. Id. 134–35.
47. Id. 133.
48. Id.
49. Id. 134.

50. Id. 135.
51. Id. 136.
52. Id. 137–38.
53. James B. White, *When Words Lose Their Meaning: Constitutions and Reconstitutions of Language, Character, and Community,* (Chicago: University of Chicago Press, 1984), 263–64. For my earlier appreciation and critique of White's reading of Marshall, see Aviam Soifer, "Reviewing Legal Fictions," 20 *Ga. L. Rev.* 871, 893–909 (1986).
54. Faulkner, 192.
55. Fletcher v. Peck, 10 U.S. (6 Cranch) 135.
56. Id.
57. Id. 139.
58. Id. 142.
59. Id.
60. Id. 142–143.
61. Milner Ball, "Constitution, Court, Indian Tribes," *Am. B. Found. Res. J.* 3 (1987); Petra T. Shattuck and Jill Norgren, *Partial Justice* (New York: Berg, 1991); Robert A. Williams, Jr., *The American Indian in Western Legal Thought* (New York: Oxford University Press, 1990).
62. All the quotations in this paragraph are from a single characteristic paragraph in Holmes's famous "The Path of the Law" speech, published originally in 10 *Harv. L. Rev.* 457, 477 (1897). Upon reflection, Holmes's explanation for why the active entrepreneur ought to win in the prescription example he presents as paradigmatic cracks apart badly. "The Path of the Law" contains a number of Holmes's most famous declarations of the need to cleanse legal discourse of moral rhetoric and of how it is "revolting" to follow settled practices simply because they are old (469). Yet in this example he resorts to "the deepest instincts of man," linked mystically to a time before recorded history and to a concept that "takes root in your being" (477). Holmes then makes a great leap of teleological faith. A vague territorial imperative both depends on longstanding expectation and is allowed to upset it. Legal force simply embraces the winners of private struggles over turf, and Holmes, of all people, resorts to what can be done "in justice" as the criterion for judgment.
63. The fealty oath language was quoted in a paper delivered by Paul Hyams at the 1992 Annual Meeting of the Law and Society Association entitled, "Feud Questions and Myth Stories in the Origins Of Common-Law Trespass" (on file with author). This paper added to extensive scholarship in English legal history discussing fealty and the roots of holding property in fee.

A fine, barbed American example of a contrasting approach to property and to freedom, which backfires in ways that parallel Faulkner, is that of Huck Finn. Having escaped to Jackson's Island, "the next day I went exploring around down through the island. I was boss of it; it all belonged to me, so to say, and I wanted to know all about it; but mainly I wanted to put in time." Mark Twain, *The Adventures of Tom Sawyer and The Adventures of Huckleberry Finn* (Modern Lib. ed., n.d.), 299. Huck was neither boss nor alone for long, of course, and Jim eventually was freed only by the *deus ex machina* of a legal will, rather than the actions of Huck or Jim himself. Bennett Kravitz has commented on this passage insightfully in "More Twain Than One: Dreams of Democracy, Domination, and Damnation in the Work of Mark Twain" (Ph.D. thesis draft, Haifa University; on file with author).

There is a large and growing body of work on lawyers and law in Twain and Faulkner. Good recent works include Barry Schaller, "Faulkner's Law: An Analysis of the Interaction of Law and Private Codes in William Faulkner's Short Fiction," 12 Bridgeport L. Rev. 715 (1992), and Robin West, "Communities, Texts and Law: Reflections on the Law and Literature Movement," 1 *Yale J. L. and Human.* 129 (1988).

64. Fletcher v. Peck, 10 U.S. (6 Cranch) 143 (Johnson, dissenting).
65. Id.
66. Id.
67. In West Coast Hotel v. Parrish, 300 U.S. 379 (1937), Chief Justice Hughes wrote, "The Constitution does not speak of freedom of contract. It speaks of liberty and prohibits the deprivation of liberty without due process of law. . . . But the liberty safeguarded is liberty in a social organization which requires the protection of law against the evils which menace the health, safety, morals and welfare of the people" (391). This move, or return, to judicial deference to commonweal notions marked a turning point in constitutional law. See Peter H. Irons, *The New Deal Lawyers,* (Princeton: Princeton University Press, 1982), 272–89; Bruce A. Ackerman, *We The People* (Cambridge, Mass.: Harvard University Press, 1991).
68. Johnson suggested that "a magnanimous and just government" would never exercise such a right without amply indemnifying the individual, but that very way of putting it suggested that such magnanimous policy was not mandated by the Constitution or general principles. Fletcher v. Peck, 10 U.S. (6 Cranch) 145. He went on to suggest that this power "perhaps amounts to nothing more" than obliging a person to sell and convey, when public necessities so require, but again this way of stating the matter undercuts the notion of fundamental restrictions to be imposed by courts.
69. Colfax at the time was a small village consisting of "four or five dwelling houses, two or three stores, and a brick building which had formerly been a stable" but was now the courthouse. Manie White Johnson, "The Colfax Riot of April, 1873," 13 *La. Hist. Q.* 391, 398 (1930).

70. Id. 411, quoting statement by a survivor, Rev. Mike Smith, Feb. 6, 1929; H. Oscar Lestage, Jr., "The White League in Louisiana and Its Participation in Reconstruction Riots," 18 *La. Hist. Q.* 617, 635–40 (1935) (sympathetically describing the role of the Colfax Riot in the organizing of the White League, because "If unorganized rebellion could gain such sweeping results, then organization would surely improve conditions").

71. Johnson, supra n.69, 413, 416 (quoting the *Colfax Chronicle*, April 9, 1921).

72. Id. 418. Congress investigated the chaotic situation in Louisiana, but split bitterly about the legitimacy of the Kellogg government and about how horrific events such as the Colfax Riot ought to be described. Reports of Committees, House of Representatives, 43rd Cong., 2nd Sess., vol. V, no. 261 (1875). A recent, restrained account by Joe Gray Taylor, a modern historian of Louisiana, states that "at least sixty-nine blacks and perhaps as many as a hundred were killed, some twenty being executed after surrendering." Joe Gray Taylor, *Louisiana* 110–11 (New York: W. W. Norton, 1976). Taylor describes the 1872 Louisiana election as "almost Byzantine" and Governor Kellogg's years in office as "almost a period of guerilla warfare in Louisiana."

73. Johnson, supra n.69, 416–17 (quoting a conversation with C. A. Duplissey, on Dec. 27, 1928). From today's perspective, Manie White Johnson's celebration of the bona fides of the white rioters and her deprecation of the blacks is remarkable, as is her compilation of the participants' proud accounts. Johnson's article recalls numerous painful scenes in Faulkner's work.

    Consider, for example, the sheriff's response after the murder of Miss Burden in William Faulkner, *Light in August* (1932, rpt. New York: Garland, 1987), 319, 51, 81, 131, 376: "'Get me a nigger,' the sheriff said. The deputy and two or three others got him a nigger." As in *Go Down, Moses,* the burden of interlinked racial history is palpable throughout the book: "But it is there: the descendants of both in their relationship to one another's ghosts, with between them the phantom of the old spilled blood and old horror and anger and fear." And "it's the dead ones that lay quiet in one place and don't try to hold him, that he can't escape from." A constant theme in Faulkner is the linkage between races across nature and nurture, time and place. Yet simultaneously Faulkner emphasizes the crucial normative distinctions that are constantly tied directly to race.

74. United States v. Cruikshank, 25 F. Cas. 707, 708–11 (D. La. 1874) (No. 14,897).

75. Id. 712. The key issue in this murky area is still to determine what if anything Congress has done to supplement constitutional protections. Today, in fact, there is a clearer difference between constitutional and statutory protection than there was in the wake of Civil War. See also

Fred Lawrence, "Civil Rights and Criminal Wrongs: The *Mens Rea* of Federal Civil Rights Crimes," 67 *Tulane L. Rev.* 2113 (1993); Fitzpatrick v. Bitzer, 427 U.S. 445 (1976) (unanimous opinion by then-Associate Justice Rehnquist emphasizing that Congress has broad power to override constitutional barriers such as federalism if the legislature explicitly chooses to do so to protect national civil rights).

76. *Slaughter-House Cases,* 83 U.S. (16 Wall.) 36 (1873) (5–4 vote held Fourteenth Amendment merely reiterated limited rights of national citizenship, leaving states to determine rights of their own citizens). The *Slaughter-House Cases* arose out of the same tangled world of Reconstruction Louisiana as did *Cruikshank,* and in fact the Court issued the opinion the very week the Colfax Riot occurred. The *Slaughter-House Cases* is much better known than *Cruikshank;* many scholars have explored its importance and its context. See Robert McCloskey, *American Conservatism in the Age of Enterprise, 1865–1910* (Cambridge, Mass.: Harvard University Press, 1951); Charles Fairman, "Does the Fourteenth Amendment Incorporate the Bill of Rights?," 2 *Stan. L. Rev.* 5 (1949); Charles Fairman, *Reconstruction and Reunion, 1864–1888, Part Two* (New York: Macmillan, 1987); Charles Warren, "New Light on the History of the Federal Judiciary Act of 1789," 37 *Harv. L. Rev.* 49 (1923).

77. Robert C. Palmer, "The Parameters of Constitutional Reconstruction: *Slaughter-House, Cruikshank,* and the Fourteenth Amendment," 1984 *U. Ill. L. Rev.* 739.

78. United States v. Cruikshank, 92 U.S. 542, 553 (1876).

79. Id. 551.

80. Id. 553.

81. Id. 551. The *Cruikshank* decision, handed down in March 1876, stands as an ironic Centennial response to the natural rights basis of the Declaration of Independence, which postulated a direct relation between denial of those rights and the obligation to throw off a government that failed to protect them. The appropriate date to mark the end of Reconstruction has been much debated, but is usually associated with the resolution of the 1876 presidential election controversy that took place in early 1877. Yet the Colfax Riot, and the cramped judicial response to federal efforts to do something about it, in conjunction with the inward turn across the nation occasioned by the Panic of 1873, surely serve to mark the end of that era. Nevertheless, in the Court's first construction of the Civil War Amendments in the *Slaughter-House Cases,* Justice Miller's crabbed opinion for a 5–4 majority described "[t]he right to peaceably assemble and petition for redress of grievances" as one of the "rights of the citizen guaranteed by the Federal Constitution." 83 U.S. (16 Wall.) 36, 79.

82. The story is never so simple as good guys and bad guys, and Faulkner

sometimes uses a stiletto to make this point. He mentions in passing, for example, that tribes such as the Chickasaw were themselves slaveowners and traders. Carothers McCaslin acquired Sam Fathers when he swapped an underbred trotting gelding with Ikkemotbbe, the Chickasaw chief, for Sam and Sam's mother. In fact, the Chickasaw fought alongside General Andrew Jackson against the Red Stick Creeks during the War of 1812. This hardly helped the tribe, however, as Jackson and his fellow United States commissioners colluded with tribal leaders and forced the tribe to cede nearly 20 million acres to the United States. See Arrell Gibson, *The Chickasaws* (Norman: University of Oklahoma Press, 1971), 97–105.

83. In the exceptionally rare situation when someone did seek to rely on the "custom and usage" language, the Court firmly rejected the effort, holding that "a 'custom or usage' for purposes of Sec. 1983 requires state involvement and is not simply a practice that reflects longstanding social habits, generally observed by the people in a locality." Adickes v. S. H. Kress and Co., 398 U.S. 144, 166 (1970). In *Adickes,* Justice Harlan's opinion for the Court rejected a civil rights claim by a white schoolteacher from New York who was refused service at a lunch counter in Hattiesburg, Mississippi, when she accompanied six black students. The teacher had not proved the requisite involvement of store personnel with state officials before she was arrested for vagrancy upon leaving the store.

84. Faulkner, 281.

85. Reprinted in Lenwood G. Davis, *I Have a Dream: The Life and Times of Martin Luther King, Jr.* (Westport: Negro Universities Press, 1969), App. V, 261–63.

86. Justice Holmes is said to have been approached by a young man who called out: "Do justice, sir!" to which Holmes replied, "I am not here to do justice. I am here to play the game according to the rules." Elizabeth Shepley Sergeant, "Justice Touched with Fire," in *Mr. Justice Holmes,* Felix Frankfurter, ed. (New York: Coward-McCann, 1931), 183, 206; DeShaney v. Winnebago County Department of Social Services, 489 U.S. 189 (1989).

87. Robert Cover, "The Folktales of Justice: Tales of Jurisdiction," 14 *Cap. U. L. Rev.* 179, 190 (1985).

7. Involuntary Groups and the Role of History in American Law

1. Alexander Pope, "Essay on Man," quoted on the title page of John Adams, "Defense of the Constitutions of Government of the United States of America, against the attack of M. Turgot in his Letter to Dr. Price, dated the Twenty-second Day of March, 1778."

2. Herman Melville, *Pierre or, The Ambiguities,* Henry Murray, ed. (New York: Farrar Straus, 1949).

3. The first elaboration of specific protection for the rights of minorities as minorities occurred in treaties, international law instruments, and court opinions following World War I. For some of the leading discussions that underscore the importance of history and tradition in definitions of group rights, see Natan Lerner, *Group Rights and Discrimination in International Law* (Boston: Kluwer Academic, 1991), chap. 2; Yoram Dinstein, "Discrimination and International Human Rights," 15 *Is. Yrbk. Human Rights* 11 (1985), and Dinstein, "Collective Human Rights of Peoples and Minorities," 25 *Intl. and Comp. Law Q.* 102 (1976). For specific background, see also Fritz Redlich, "Sovereignty, Democracy, and the Rights of Minorities," in Morton Carlisle et al., *Harvard Legal Essays Written in Honor of and Presented to Joseph Henry Beale and Samuel Williston* (Cambridge, Mass.: Harvard University Press, 1934), 377, and a number of essays collected in *Rights of Peoples,* James Crawford, ed. (Oxford: Clarendon Press, 1988) and in 1 *Is. Yrbk. Human Rights* (1971).

4. See Charles Miller, *The Supreme Court and the Uses of History* (Cambridge, Mass.: Harvard University Press, 1969); William Wiecek, "Clio as Hostage: The United States Supreme Court and the Uses of History," 24 *Cal. W. L. Rev.* 227 (1988); Alfred Kelly, "Clio and the Court: An Illicit Love Affair," 1965 *Sup. Ct. Rev.* 119.

5. Bowers v. Hardwick, 478 U.S. 186 (1986) (asserts ancient roots for laws proscribing homosexual acts to justify ban on consensual adult homosexual sodomy).

6. In international law, as in the American constitutional law cases discussed above, today as in 1971 it still seems to be the case—despite frequent references to freedom of peaceful assembly and to freedom of association—that these rights "have yet to attain any meaningful concretization." Dinstein, "Human Rights," 20. But see Lerner, supra n.3.

   Contemporary legal scholars have paid even less attention to so-called involuntary associations, an inartful designation for the groups we are born into and which we may not be able to leave even if we wish to do so. But see Kathleen Sullivan, "Rainbow Republicanism," 97 *Yale L. J.* 1713, 1714 (1988).

7. Civil Rights Cases, 109 U.S. 3, 25 (1883) (invalidating Civil Rights Act of 1875 that prohibited racial discrimination in public accommodations). For a historical discussion of this decision and less well-known decisions in the wake of the Civil War, see Aviam Soifer, "Status, Contract, and Promises Unkept," 96 *Yale L. J.* 1916 (1987).

8. Constitutional decisions legitimating the entire apparatus of racism are legion. The classic survey is Loren Miller, *The Petitioners: The Story of the Supreme Court of the United States and the Negro* (New York: Pantheon Books, 1966). Helpful recent accounts of specific decisions that

upheld, and even required segregation, such as Berea College v. Kentucky, 211 U.S. 45 (1908), include Charles Lofgren, *The Plessy Case: A Legal Historical Interpretation* (New York: Oxford University Press, 1987); Randall Kennedy, "Race Relations Law and the Tradition of Celebration: The Case of Professor Schmidt," 86 *Colum. L. Rev.* 1622 (1986).

9. Frederic W. Maitland, *Selected Historical Essays of F. W. Maitland,* H. M. Cam, ed. (Cambridge: Cambridge University Press, 1957), 126. Maitland referred to English law developing into an occult science "under the fostering care" of the Inns of Court in the late Middle Ages, when "[n]ovel principles could not be admitted until they were disguised in some antique garb."

10. 274 U.S. 200 (1927). Justice Brandeis joined the majority; only Justice Butler dissented, without opinion.

11. Carrie Buck was an 18-year-old white inmate of Virginia's Colony for Epileptics and Feeble Minded. She was already the mother of an illegitimate child when Superintendent Bell began proceedings to have her sterilized. Stephen Jay Gould discussed this case and the eugenics movement generally in *The Mismeasure of Man* (New York: W. W. Norton, 1981). He also detailed the research conducted nearly 50 years later, finding that there were no imbeciles in Carrie Buck's family. Stephen Jay Gould, "Carrie Buck's Daughter," 2 *Const. Commentary* 331 (1985).

12. 274 U.S. at 207. Holmes asserted that "experience has shown that heredity plays an important part in the transmission of insanity, imbecility, etc." (206). The particular form of the greater-includes-the-lesser-power argument Holmes favored was: if "the public welfare may call upon the best citizens for their lives," it would be "strange if it could not call upon those who already sap the strength of the state for lesser sacrifices," particularly if the public wished to "prevent being swamped with incompetence" by those "manifestly unfit" (207). For Holmes's similar argument to validate martial law, see Chapter 3.

13. Id. 208.

14. Their famous dissents are collected and discussed in many places. The best sources include Felix Frankfurter, *Mr. Justice Holmes and the Supreme Court* (Cambridge, Mass.: Harvard University Press, 1938), and Samuel Konefsky, *The Legacy of Holmes and Brandeis* (New York: Macmillan, 1956). But Holmes and Brandeis did not always dissent from the Court's invocations of substantive due process. For example, both joined in striking down the Kansas Industrial Court Act, which provided for mandatory arbitration in labor disputes, Charles Wolff Packing Co. v. Court of Indus. Relations, 262 U.S. 522 (1922) and Charles Wolff Packing Co. v. Court of Indus. Relations, 267 U.S. 552 (1925). Both agreed as well to the Court's use of substantive due process to invalidate Oregon's

attack on private schools, in Pierce v. Society of Sisters, 268 U.S. 510 (1925).

15. 257 U.S. 312 (1921).

16. The crucial decision in the Arizona Supreme Court was Truax v. Bisbee Local No. 380, Cooks' and Waiters' Union, 171 P. 121 (1918). Justice Cunningham proclaimed that William Truax had no vested property right in doing his normal amount of business and that he could not get an injunction against the boycott that union members urged through peaceful picketing and leafletting. Moreover, the Court held, even if the union defendants were insolvent as Truax alleged, and a damages remedy therefore was not a realistic option, "the matter of financial worth does not limit the [Arizona] constitutional right to speak, write, and publish on all subjects" (127). In Truax v. Corrigan, 20 Ariz. 7, 176 P. 570 (1918), the Arizona Court held that its decision in *Bisbee Local No. 380* did not contravene the Fourteenth Amendment of the federal Constitution.

17. This was Truax's second notable trip to the United States Supreme Court. In 1915, the Court upheld his standing as an employer of aliens and used his case to strike down an Arizona constitutional initiative that had required all employers of more than five workers to employ at least 80 percent "qualified electors or native-born citizens of the United States or some sub-division thereof." Truax v. Raich, 239 U.S. 33 (1915). One wonders if William Truax had secret backing for his legal journeys from his *English Kitchen* eatery in Bisbee to Washington, D.C., but it is hardly surprising that nativism permeated the union's subsequent claim that Truax was unfair to labor. See the pamphlet vilifying Truax in the 1916 labor dispute, reprinted in Truax v. Bisbee Local No. 380, Cooks' and Waiters' Union, 171 P. 121, 122 (1918). It would probably be illuminating to trace the roles of the actors in the two *Truax* decisions in the infamous Bisbee deportation of miners in July 1917. Federal courts held that this vigilante action did not constitute a federal crime, U.S. v. Wheeler, 254 Fed. 611 (9th Cir. 1918), *aff'd.*, 254 U.S. 281 (1920).

18. 257 U.S. at 333. Justices Holmes, Pitney, Clarke and Brandeis dissented. Taft's view of equal protection included an affirmative obligation of the state to provide protection: "It emphasizes the additional sanctity of a right which the clause has confirmed beyond the requirement of due process." And equal protection would be denied by "[i]mmunity granted to a class, however limited, having the effect to deprive another class however limited of a personal or property right" just as clearly "as if the immunity were in favor of, or the deprivation of right permitted worked against, a larger class." Holmes attacked the majority for falling prey to "the dangers of a delusive exactness in the application of the Fourteenth

Amendment" (342), and explained, "There is nothing that I more deprecate than the use of the Fourteenth Amendment to prevent the making of social experiments that an important part of the community desires" (344). Brandeis's lengthy dissent offered an essay on the history of labor relations and pointed out, "It is of the nature of our law that it has not dealt with man in general, but with him in relationships" (355).

19. Id. 333. Both the Bisbee deportations and Truax v. Corrigan contributed to the Arizona reality experienced by Chief Justice Rehnquist and Justice O'Connor—a world, as we will see, they tend to perceive as natural, neutral, and fair.

20. In Gulf, Colorado and Sante Fe Railway v. Ellis, 165 U.S. 150, 154, 165 (1897), for example, Justice Brewer invalidated a Texas statute that allowed claimants against railroads up to $10 in attorneys fees, since to single out railroad corporations was to "make the protecting clauses of the Fourteenth Amendment a mere rope of sand" and to fail "the constitutional obligation of equal protection." For further examples and an insightful discussion of early equal protection doctrine, see Richard Kay, "The Equal Protection Clause in the Supreme Court, 1883–1903," 29 *Buff. L. Rev.* 667 (1980).

21. 347 U.S. 483 (1954).

22. I have found no contemporaneous mention at all of the *Carolene Products* decision in leading newspapers and little coverage of the *Erie* decision. See Tony Freyer, *Harmony and Dissonance: The "Swift" and "Erie" Cases in American Federalism* (New York: New York University Press, 1981).

23. 304 U.S. 64 (1938). For a useful discussion of the importance of this decision and its historic context, see Freyer, supra n.22.

24. In Erie Railroad v. Tompkins, Justice Brandeis reformulated the relationship between federal and state law and between federal and state courts. The constitutional basis of Brandeis's decision on federalism is hard to locate. Yet this decision about diversity jurisdiction was the culmination of a campaign he and Holmes had orchestrated for decades to try to halt freewheeling federal court intervention against the progressive possibilities Brandeis and Holmes saw in social experimentation in the individual states. Yet *Erie* rejected an older diversity doctrine that proclaimed that outsiders needed protection from the manipulation of state law by state courts in the interests of local insiders. *Erie*, in this sense, refused to continue to view out-of-state legal claimants as a group in need of special federal court protection.

25. 304 U.S. 144 (1938). Actually, only three justices joined that part of Stone's opinion which contained the famous footnote: Chief Justice Hughes, Justice Brandeis, and Justice Roberts. Justice Black refused to agree to that part of Stone's opinion, since Black wished to go further

than Stone in proclaiming deference to legislative judgments. Justice Butler concurred only in the result; Justice McReynolds dissented; and Justices Cardozo and Reed did not take part in the decision.

26. Even former Justice Powell, who helped lead the recent retrenchment from the footnote 4 approach, acknowledged that this footnote contained "perhaps the most far-sighted dictum in our modern judicial heritage." Lewis Powell, "*Carolene Products* Revisited," 82 *Colum. L. Rev.* 1087 (1982). Numerous other commentators, most notably John Hart Ely in his influential book, *Democracy and Distrust: A Theory of Judicial Review* (Cambridge, Mass.: Harvard University Press, 1980), celebrate and elaborate constitutional norms as extrapolations from the famous footnote. For further discussion, see J. M. Balkin, Symposium: "Law and Social Theory: The Footnote," 83 *Nw. U. L. Rev.* 275 (1989); Bruce Ackerman, "Beyond Carolene Products," 98 *Harv. L. Rev.* 713 (1985); Louis Lusky, "Footnote Redux: A Carolene Products Reminiscence," 82 *Colum. L. Rev.* 1093 (1982); Milner Ball, "Don't Die Don Quixote: A Response and Alternative to Tushnet, Bobbit, and the Revised Texas Version of Constitutional Law," 59 *Tex. L. Rev.* 787 (1981).

27. West Coast Hotel Co. v. Parrish, 300 U.S. 379 (1937) symbolized the new trend. In this decision upholding state minimum wage legislation, the Court reversed itself dramatically and abandoned the individualistic, substantive due process approach generally connected to Lochner v. New York, 198 U.S. 45 (1905) and its progeny. This change, cleverly albeit inaccurately dubbed the "switch in time that saved nine," is often invoked to describe a constitutional revolution associated with President Franklin Roosevelt's New Deal. See Bruce Ackerman, "Discovering the Constitution," 93 *Yale L. J.* 1013 (1984) (identifying self-government on a national level during three "constitutional moments").

28. Stone's opinion upheld a 1923 federal ban on the interstate shipment of filled milk. The Court reversed a lower federal court and, indirectly, the Illinois Supreme Court. It held that Congress had power to label as adulterated "Milnut," a form of skimmed milk in which butterfat was replaced by cheaper, less wholesome coconut fat. This now seems unremarkable. At the time, however, not only was the result in *Carolene Products* somewhat innovative, but the theory of special judicial scrutiny in footnote 4 was new and even daring.

29. All of the decisions Stone cited are at least partially First Amendment decisions, with the exception of two "right to vote" cases: Nixon v. Herndon, 273 U.S. 536 (1927) and Nixon v. Condon, 286 U.S. 73 (1932). These invalidated attempts to exclude blacks entirely from voting in Democratic Party primaries in Texas. Ironically, *Herndon* was written by Justice Holmes, who found it "hard to imagine a more direct and obvious infringement of the Fourteenth Amendment," though his vilification of

equality claims in Buck v. Bell came less than two months later, discussed supra n.12.

30. For this crucial proposition Stone cited two Commerce Clause decisions, as well as First Amendment decisions that invalidated laws held to be discriminatory on the grounds of religion and national origin, and the racial discrimination in voting cases he had also cited in the previous paragraph.

31. The Court did not immediately or fully adopt the activist, strict scrutiny approach suggested by footnote 4. This was underscored quickly in Missouri *ex rel.* Gaines v. Canada, 305 U.S. 337 (1938), the Court's first great step toward Brown v. Board of Education, 347 U.S. 483 (1954). In holding that the exclusion of a black man from the University of Missouri Law School was unconstitutional, the Court made no mention of footnote 4 nor did the decision reflect the footnote's proposed approach. Chief Justice Hughes's majority opinion stressed only that separate had to be equal. Therefore, Missouri's offer to pay tuition for Gaines to attend an integrated law school in a neighboring state did not satisfy his personal right. "It was as an individual that he was entitled to the equal protection of the laws," Hughes stated, and Missouri was bound to afford him substantially equal legal education, "whether or not other negroes sought the same opportunity." 305 U.S. at 351. By 1954, however, such insistent individualism seemed to disappear as the Court proclaimed that an entire class of black students, with hearts and minds ineluctably assaulted by official segregation, could not be equal so long as the law kept them separate.

32. During World War II the Court for the first time stated explicitly that racial discrimination should trigger strict judicial scrutiny, while at the same time a majority of the justices failed to discern racial discrimination in a series of cases arising out of the internment of the Japanese-Americans living on the West Coast. The Court in Korematsu v. United States, 323 U.S. 214 (1944) found a compelling government interest sufficient to override the claims of the interned Japanese. For a lucid historical treatment of the wartime litigation, see Peter Irons, *Justice at War* (New York: Oxford University Press, 1983), which includes a discussion of reparations for historic wrongs and the launching of successful *coram nobis* cases brought, decades later, to vacate the sentences of Japanese convicted for curfew and internment order violations.

After the war, however, the Court refused California the power to deny commercial fishing licenses to Japanese aliens. Takahashi v. Fish and Game Commission, 334 U.S. 410, 420 (1948) (even if legitimate state objectives were assumed, the California statute that barred persons "ineligible for citizenship"—such as the Japanese—from commercial fishing licenses was held to violate federal statutory and constitutional guarantees that "protect 'all persons' against state legislation bearing unequally upon them either because of alienage or color"). Justice Black wrote for the majority; Justice Murphy, joined by Justice Rutledge, concurred separately, emphasizing the extent to which the 1943 California statute was a direct outgrowth of anti-Japanese antagonism; and Justice Reed dissented. Ironically, the precedent Black and Reed most directly relied on was Truax v. Raich, 239 U.S. 33 (1915), discussed supra n.17. See also Oyama v. California, 332 U.S. 633, 646 (1948) (invalidating escheat of land to California when held by interned Japanese alien as guardian for son because "only the most exceptional circumstances can excuse [racial] discrimination").

33. Robert Cover, "The Origins of Judicial Activism in the Protection of Minorities," 91 *Yale L. J.* 1287, 1292 n.14 (1982).

34. D. Thomson, *Europe Since Napoleon,* rev. ed. (Harmondsworth, Eng.: Penguin Books, 1966), 711–30. For a succinct description of the *Anschluss,* which brought forms of anti-Semitism more virulent than anything until then practiced in Germany, see Peter Gay, *Freud: A Life for Our Times* (New York: Norton, 1989), 622–28 (including direct harassment of the aged Sigmund Freud and his family, despite personal efforts by Roosevelt and others on their behalf).

35. In hindsight, the explosive sit-in strikes in 1937 and the labor violence that followed suggested that "the American labor movement has been the most violent nonrevolutionary movement in the world; but the middle-class character of labor's goals could have been doubted then." J. Woodford Howard, *Mr. Justice Murphy: A Political Biography* (Princeton: Princeton University Press, 1968), 157. As economic recession worsened in early 1938, the CIO formally broke away from the AFL and Congress, worried about internal threats, created the forerunner of the House Un-American Activities Committee, chaired by Representative Martin Dies. The deteriorating economic situation; vigorous, even violent, domestic conflict triggered by events in Europe, such as violence surrounding meetings of the German-American Bund in New York City; and obvious, massive cracks in the reigning Democratic Party coalition made it seem in the Spring of 1938 that the New Deal, and perhaps the nation, might be in danger of collapse.

36. Cover, supra n.33, 1294. Cover made it clear that he referred only to American law and assigned pride of place to international law for recognizing and attempting to do something to protect minorities in the wake of World War I. (1297).

37. Martha Minow, "The Supreme Court, 1986 Term—Foreword: Justice Engendered," 101 *Harv. L. Rev.* 10 (1987) provides a summary of cases and a provocative discussion of the "difference dilemma."

38. Geduldig v. Aiello, 417 U.S. 484, 496–97 n.20 (1974). Although the issue

of gender difference is beyond the scope of this essay, issues of sameness and difference are crucial to much contemporary feminist discourse.

39. There has been considerable discussion of this trend. For criticism of its beginnings, see Aviam Soifer, "Complacency and Constitutional Law," 41 *Ohio St. L. J.* 383 (1981); a careful dissection of the crucial middle stage is available in Kathleen Sullivan, "Sins of Discrimination: Last Term's Affirmative Action Cases," 100 *Harv. L. Rev.* 78 (1986); more recent aspects were unpacked skillfully in Michel Rosenfeld, "Decoding *Richmond:* Affirmative Action and the Elusive Meaning of Constitutional Equality," 87 *Mich. L. Rev.* 1729 (1989).

40. 485 U.S. 617 (1988). The lower court had decided that the 1866 Civil Rights Act did not protect a black plaintiff from racial harassment in the workplace. The Court's April 25th order introduced the question: "Whether or not the interpretation of 42 U.S.C. § 1981 adopted by this Court in Runyon v. McCrary, 427 U.S. 160 (1976), should be reconsidered?"

41. Runyon v. McCrary, 427 U.S. 160 (1976), determined by a 7–2 vote that the 1866 Civil Rights Act could reach private acts of racial discrimination. Justice Stewart's majority opinion held that a private school that advertised widely and otherwise comported itself as a business could be held liable under the statute for overt racial discrimination. In an important separate concurring opinion, however, Justice Powell emphasized the particular commercial aspects of the school at issue, and argued that the result might well be different in the case, for example, of a private tutor. Justice White, joined by then-Justice Rehnquist, dissented, arguing that section 1981 dealing with contracts ought not to be read as broadly as section 1982 dealing with property rights. Justices Stevens and Powell concurred separately. Both stated that they would have decided otherwise if the case had posed a new question, but that *stare decisis* required them to agree with the majority, though they cautioned against a broad reading of its holding.

42. Justice Blackmun, joined by Justices Brennan, Marshall, and Stevens, objected to the majority's decision to reach out "to reconsider an interpretation of a civil rights statute that so clearly reflects our society's earnest commitment to ending racial discrimination." 485 U.S. at 621. Justice Stevens, joined by the three other dissenters, wrote a separate dissent in which he decried the majority's decision because it "replace[s] what is ideally a sense of guaranteed right with the uneasiness of unsecured privilege" (622). Stevens also noted the deleterious impact of the decision not only on faith in law maintained by victims of discrimination, but also on public perceptions of the Court as impartial and restrained.

43. Id. 619, quoting 28 U.S.C. Sec. 453.

44. *Winthrop Papers,* (Boston: Massachusetts Historical Society, 1944), IV,

349, 351–52; cf. William Blake in "The Marriage of Heaven and Hell," stating that "One Law for the Lion and Ox is Oppression." Cf. Plato, *The Republic,* P. Shorey, trans. (New York: G. P. Putnam, 1956), vol. 2, VIII, Sec. 558 at 291 (describing democracy as "anarchic and motley, assigning a kind of equality indiscriminately to equals and unequals alike").

45. Shelley v. Kraemer, 334 U.S. 1, 22 (1948). Philip Kurland aptly termed Chief Justice Vinson's *Shelley* opinion "the *Finnegans Wake* of constitutional law." Philip Kurland, "Foreword: Equal in Origin and Equal in Title to the Legislative and Executive Branches of the Government," 78 *Harv. L. Rev.* 143, 148 (1964). Still, some structure emerges. Vinson emphasized that "equality in the enjoyment of property rights" was "an essential pre-condition" of other basic civil rights and civil liberties "guaranteed to the individual" by the Fourteenth Amendment (10, 22). He wished to undermine a defense of the restrictive covenants that claimed that because the restrictions affected white as well as black citizens, they did not deny equal protection. *Shelley*'s emphasis on positive as well as negative aspects of equal protection may be read as a direct repudiation of the formal equality approach of Truax v. Corrigan, discussed supra n.17. In Hurd v. Hodge, 334 U.S. 24 (1948), the companion case that extended *Shelley* to federal as well as state law, the trial court found the petitioner to be a Negro, though "James M. Hurd maintained that he is not a Negro but a Mohawk Indian" (27, n.2).

By the time of Brown v. Board of Education in 1954, *Shelley*'s insistent individualism seemed to disappear, see discussion supra n.32. Cf. Beauharnais v. Illinois, 343 U.S. 250, 263 (1952) (upholding Illinois' group libel statute punishing expression "directed at groups with whose position and esteem in society the affiliated individual may be inextricably involved").

46. The oath is discussed in more detail in Chapter 8.

47. Patterson v. McLean Credit Union, 491 U.S. 164 (1989). The Justices unanimously joined Justice Kennedy's opinion on the *stare decisis* point, but Justice Brennan, joined by Justices Marshall, Blackmun and, in part, Justice Stevens, dissented from the racial harassment aspect of the majority's opinion. Stevens also wrote separately in dissent.

48. 491 U.S. at 177. The majority's remarkably pinched lexicographic approach was evident from the start of its discussion of the statute at issue. Justice Kennedy began by quoting section 1981, the relevant remnant of the 1866 Civil Rights Act: "All persons within the jurisdiction of the United States shall have the same right in every State and Territory to make and enforce contracts, to sue, be parties, give evidence, *and to the full and equal benefit of all laws and proceedings for the security of persons and property as is enjoyed by white citizens, and shall be subject to like punishment, pains, penalties, taxes, licenses, and exactions of every*

kind, and to no other" (emphasis added). Remarkably, however, he then asserted, "The most obvious feature of the provision is the restriction of its scope to forbidding discrimination in the 'mak[ing] and enforce[ment]' of contracts alone." 491 U.S. at 176. This is "the most obvious feature" only if one stops reading at the word "contract." To read the final part of the section, italicized above, is to be forced at least to wonder at the meaning of the clear textual effort to guarantee "full" as well as "equal" benefit of "all laws and proceedings" to "all persons." Congress attempted to ensure that no person in the nation would suffer any pain, penalty, or exaction different from that which all fully protected citizens might suffer.

49. The majority seemed certain of the "plain and common sense meaning" of the statutory terms "make" and "enforce" and therefore did not deign to consider the debates or political context surrounding passage of the 1866 Civil Rights Act. Yet even a most conservative contemporaneous reading of the Civil War Amendments would conclude that their primary purpose was to afford federal protection from "discrimination against the newly emancipated negroes . . . as a class." Slaughter-House Cases, 83 U.S. (16 Wall.) 36, 81 (1873). Moreover, close attention to the congressional debates, President Johnson's blundering, and the highly publicized harshness of the end of slavery suggests that racial harassment was a serious problem, clearly targeted by Congress in 1866. See Eric Foner, *Reconstruction—America's Unfinished Revolution, 1863–1877* (New York: Harper and Row, 1988); Leon Litwack, *Been in the Storm So Long* (New York: Knopf, 1979); Aviam Soifer, "Protecting Civil Rights: A Critique of Raoul Berger's History," 54 *N.Y.U. L. Rev.* 651 (1979).

50. 488 U.S. 469 (1989). A sharply divided majority endorsed Sect. III-B of Justice O'Connor's lead opinion. Marshall and Blackmun wrote searing dissents. The two other most notable decisions sharply restricting civil rights claims that same Term were: Wards Cove Packing Co. v. Atonio, 490 U.S. 642 (1989) (civil rights plaintiff has burden of proving employer has no business reason for practice even if it has dramatic discriminatory effects) and Martin v. Wilks, 490 U.S. 755 (1989) (new group of white firefighters allowed to intervene to challenge 1981 Birmingham, Alabama, consent decree alleged to be reverse discrimination). Such decisions led Justice Marshall to suggest "a deliberate retrenchment of the civil rights agenda" by the Court which put the nation "back where we started" at the time of Brown v. Board of Education. Greenhouse, "Marshall Says Court's Rulings Imperil Rights," *New York Times,* Sept. 9, 1989, at 6. Congress responded by attempting to narrow or overrule these decisions in the Civil Rights Act of 1991, 105 Stat. 1071.

51. 488 U.S. 505–06.

52. Id. 510. O'Connor's fear did not reflect the terms of the actual political

situation that led to Richmond's affirmative action program; it also simply ignored Richmond's blatantly racial political history. Moreover, she stated her discovery of racial politics at the state and local level in a manner insulting to black officeholders, as Marshall forcefully pointed out. For excellent, detailed discussion of *Croson* and its rhetoric, see Thomas Ross, "The Richmond Narratives," 68 *Tex. L. Rev.* 381 (1989); Rosenfeld, supra n.39.

53. Marshall, dissenting, 488 U.S. 551–52. It is not entirely clear what test the majority agreed to apply in applying "strict scrutiny" to a claim of discrimination by a white contractor. Scalia expressed an even narrower idea of what might satisfy the test than the four justices who joined in this section of O'Connor's plurality opinion. Stevens voted with them, but did not accept the "strict scrutiny" test.

54. Id. 558.

55. Id. 528. Scalia conceded that "It is plainly true that in our society blacks have suffered discrimination immeasurably greater than any directed at other racial groups," but he considered this fact constitutionally irrelevant. It is particularly ironic, in light of the judicial approach in *Croson*, that Justice Stevens, who concurred in part and concurred in the judgment, argued that while race is not always irrelevant, "It is the judicial system, rather than the legislative process, that is best equipped to identify past wrongdoers and to fashion remedies that will create the conditions that presumably would have existed had no wrong been committed" (513–14).

56. In a symbolic valedictory, Justice Brennan managed to cobble together a 5–4 majority to uphold affirmative action in Metro Broadcasting v. Federal Communications Commission, 497 U.S. 547 (1990). The Court distinguished sharply between congressional and state power. The majority held that because Congress has much greater constitutional leeway, it could give the FCC power to establish a plan to enhance minority ownership of broadcast licenses. Under *Croson*, a state government could not enact similar plans. There were vigorous dissents, however, and both Brennan and Justice Marshall, who joined his opinion, are no longer on the Court.

57. Frederic W. Maitland, "Introduction" to Otto Gierke, *Political Theories of the Middle Ages,* F. W. Maitland, trans., (Cambridge: Cambridge University Press, 1900), i–xiv; Martha Minow, *Making All the Difference: Inclusion, Exclusion, and American Law* (Ithaca: Cornell University Press, 1990).

In 1900, a leading reformer at the annual Lake Mohonk Conference devoted to helping the American Indian celebrated the General Allotment Act (Dawes Act) of 1887 as "a mighty pulverizing engine for breaking up the tribal mass," quoted in Francis Paul Prucha, *American Indian Policy in Crisis: Christian Reformers and the Indian, 1865–1900* (Norman: University of Oklahoma Press, 1976), 257. Cf. "To a Steam Roller," in Marianne Moore, *Collected Poems* (New York: Macmillan, 1951), 90 ("You crush all particles down/ into close conformity, and then walk back and forth/ on them.")

58. Dennis Curtis and Judith Resnik, "Images of Justice," 96 *Yale L. J.* 1727 (1987).

59. To have legal standing, for example, "at an irreducible minimum, Article III requires the party who invokes the court's authority to 'show that he personally has suffered some actual or threatened injury.'" Valley Forge College v. Americans United, 454 U.S. 464, 472 (1982)(citations omitted). See also Allen v. Wright, 468 U.S. 737, 753–56 (1984). For discussion of the Court's unwillingness to use statistics alone in equal protection claims of discrimination in death penalty cases, see discussion of McCleskey v. Kemp, 481 U.S. 279, 292 (1987). But cf. United States v. Sokolow, 490 U.S. 1 (1989) ("probabilistic" factors have probative value and together amount to reasonable suspicion sufficient to support the Drug Enforcement Agency's authority to stop a suspected drug smuggler at the airport).

60. Milner Ball and Robert Williams provide powerful elaborations of the impact of the multitude of ways in which "[t]he American story of origins fundamentally excludes tribes and denies them voice." Milner Ball, "Stories of Origin and Constitutional Possibilities," 87 Mich. L. Rev. 2280, 2300 (1989); Robert Williams, Jr., *The American Indian in Western Legal Thought: The Discourses of Conquest* (New York: Oxford University Press, 1990).

61. Michael H. v. Gerald D., 491 U.S. 110, 123 (1989). The justices were sharply divided and unusually vitriolic, even judged by the quite embittered standards of the current Court. Justice Scalia wrote for himself and Chief Justice Rehnquist. They were joined in all but footnote 6 by Justices O'Connor and Kennedy. Justice Stevens concurred only in the judgment; he disagreed with Scalia's position, which Stevens took to be a rejection of the possibility that a biological father could ever have a constitutionally protected interest in his relationship with his child when the mother was married to another man and cohabiting with him at the time of the child's conception and birth. Stevens cast his decisive vote with Scalia, however, because Stevens read California law to afford the natural father an opportunity to be heard. Justice Brennan, joined by Justices Marshall and Blackmun, dissented from what he saw as the "make-believe" atmosphere of the plurality opinion (156). Justice White, joined by Brennan, also wrote a dissent.

62. The common law presumption could be rebutted only by proof that the husband was incapable of procreation or by his total lack of access to the

wife, and the grounds for rebuttal of the presumption were strictly construed (124–25).

63. Id. 113.

64. Id. 118.

65. In dismissing an equal protection claim raised on behalf of the daughter,
Scalia explicitly hid behind a legal fiction. Victoria D.'s lawyer made the
unusual argument that equal protection required that Victoria have an
opportunity to rebut her presumed legitimacy. California law provided
an exception to the presumption of legitimacy, allowing Victoria's mother—and perhaps also her presumed father—a chance to rebut the presumption. But, Scalia argued, "Illegitimacy is a legal construct, not a
natural trait" (131). Enthusiastic deference to this "legal construct" then
led Scalia to the extremely deferential "rational relationship" equal protection test and to rejection of Victoria's claim.

66. Id. 124. Scalia said, "The family unit accorded traditional respect in our
society, which we have referred to as the 'unitary family,' is typified, of
course, by the marital family, but also includes the household of unmarried parents and their children" (124 n.3). He did not explain why this
was his family limit, though in Moore v. City of East Cleveland, 431 U.S.
494, 504 (1977) (plurality opinion) Justice Powell said the "tradition of
uncles, aunts, cousins, and especially grandparents sharing a household"
had "roots equally venerable and equally deserving of constitutional recognition" as the traditions protecting the nuclear family. Instead Scalia
resorted to the 'slippery slope argument' and claimed that the logic of
Brennan's dissenting position would lead to the conclusion that if Michael
had begotten Victoria by rape, he might assert the same liberty interest in
his relationship with her that he did here. 491 U.S. 124 n.4.

67. Scalia claimed that judges should discover "the most specific level at
which a relevant tradition protecting, or denying protection to, the
asserted right can be identified" (127 n.6). It is noteworthy that only
Chief Justice Rehnquist agreed to accompany Scalia in this excursion to
seek a rule as to the appropriate level of historical abstraction.

68. It was thus unnecessary to consider more complex, nuanced family narratives. For good introductions to the relevant historical work, see Herbert G. Gutman, *The Black Family in Slavery and Freedom, 1750–1925*
(New York: Pantheon, 1976); Gary Nash, *Red, White, and Black: The
Peoples of Early America* (Englewood Cliffs: Prentice Hall, 1974); Marshall Sahlins, *Islands of History* (Chicago: University of Chicago Press,
1985).

69. 491 U.S. 141.

70. Id. 137.

71. 490 U.S. 30 (1989). Justice Brennan wrote the majority opinion, which
turned on the technical question of the meaning of 'domicile' for juris-

dictional purposes within the Indian Child Welfare Act of 1978, 92 Stat. 3069, 25 U.S.C. sects. 1901–1963; Justice Stevens, joined by Chief Justice Rehnquist and Justice Kennedy, dissented. The Court did not consider any constitutional issues.

72. Brennan acknowledged that this result might undermine the important relationships already formed by the twins with their adoptive parents, but asserted that the tribal court was simply being given jurisdiction, and that it might take such factors into account in making its ultimate decision about where the twins should wind up.

73. This has been true for a long time, of course, as the Mormon polygamy decisions in the nineteenth century make clear, culminating in Reynolds v. United States, 98 U.S. 145 (1878) (upholding federal law making bigamy a crime against freedom of religion claim). What is remarkable, however, is that with the notable exception of the Mormons, other groups with unusual family practices were treated with considerably more sympathy than the current Supreme Court's approach suggests. See Carol Weisbrod, *The Boundaries of Utopia* (New York: Pantheon Books, 1980). Another way in which government traditionally and directly affected how American families were constituted was through laws forbidding miscegenation. These laws finally were invalidated on individual liberty and group equal protection grounds in Loving v. Virginia, 388 U.S. 1 (1967), but it is hard to see how a majority of the current Court could reach that result today, given its willingness to defer to states in *Michael H.* and its requirement of specific discriminatory intent in *Croson* and similar decisions. Laws against miscegenation, after all, treat different races with formal equality.

74. See Lehr v. Robertson, 463 U.S. 248 (1983) (functional definition of paternity from context of father's acts); Wisconsin v. Yoder, 406 U.S. 205 (1972) (right of Amish parents not to send children to school after eighth grade); Stanley v. Illinois, 405 U.S. 645 (1972) (natural father's right to raise illegitimate children). But see Bowen v. Gilliard, 483 U.S. 589 (1987) (Congress could require family receiving AFDC to include payments from noncustodial parents earmarked for individual children in calculating family income). Other courts, of course, have begun to wrestle with the breakdown of definitions of "natural" families in cases involving surrogate mothers and biogenetics generally.

75. DeShaney v. Winnebago County Department of Social Services, 489 U.S. 189 (1989).

76. For a description of the background, and a critique of the majority opinion, see Aviam Soifer, "Moral Ambition, Formalism, and the 'Free World' of *DeShaney*," 57 Geo. Wash. L. Rev. 1513 (1989).

77. 489 U.S. 201. Here, Rehnquist responded to a specific event: Wisconsin's Child Protection Team, which was regularly involved with Joshua, had

once taken temporary legal custody of him. Compare Schall v. Martin, 467 U.S. 253, 265 (1984), in which then-Justice Rehnquist wrote for the Court that children are "always in some form of custody" so that "if parental control falters, the State must play its part as parens patriae."

78. 481 U.S. 704 (1987).

79. 494 U.S. 872 (1990) (holding Oregon not obliged to pay unemployment benefits to members of Native American Church who lost their jobs for using peyote in religious ritual). In an earlier round, the Court rather inexplicably had remanded the case to the Oregon Supreme Court for clarification of the status of peyote use under Oregon's criminal law. Employment Div. v. Smith, 485 U.S. 660 (1988). In the end the case presented only the issue of free exercise of religion. The litigants were two men—one a Native American, one not—who were denied unemployment benefits by the state after they had been fired from their jobs as counsellors in a drug rehabilitation center for their use of peyote in religious rituals. (I ought to disclose here that I co-authored the amicus curiae brief filed by the American Civil Liberties Union in this case).

80. The decision was a shock that touched off an unprecedented, but unsuccessful, petition by over 50 law school deans and professors and by a broad array of religious groups seeking a rehearing. See James E. Ryan, "*Smith* and the Religious Freedom Restoration Act: An Iconoclastic Assessment," 78 *Va. L. Rev.* 1407, 1411 n.25 (1992). Since then, a torrent of articles and scholarly symposia have commented upon, and for the most part severely criticized, the Court's decision in *Smith*. See James Gordon, "Free Exercise on the Mountaintop," 79 *Cal. L. Rev.* 91 (1991); Douglas Laycock, "The Remnants of Free Exercise," 1990 Sup. Ct. 1; Ira C. Lupu, "The Trouble with Accommodation," 60 *Geo. Wash. L. Rev.* 743 (1992), and sources collected therein at 754–58, as well as other articles in the same symposium.

81. 494 U.S. at 882. Here he cited Roberts v. United States Jaycees, which recognized the "correlative group effect" of individuals' freedom to act together: "An individual's freedom to speak, to worship, and to petition the government for the redress of grievances could not be vigorously protected from interference by the state [if] a correlative freedom to engage in group effort toward those ends were not also guaranteed," quoting 468 U.S. 609, 622.

82. 494 U.S. at 886 (rejecting the approach established in Sherbert v. Verner, 374 U.S. 398 (1963) and followed in dozens of Supreme Court decisions, and countless lower court cases).

83. 494 U.S. 890.

84. Id.

85. Id. 888, 890. As Justice Blackmun pointed out in his vigorous dissent, slippery slope arguments are particularly facile in the realm of free exer-

cise of religion claims, because "Behind every free exercise claim is a spectral march; grant this one, a voice whispers to each judge, and you will be confronted with an endless chain of exemption demands from religious deviants of every stripe." Id. 917, quoting Ira C. Lupu, "Where Rights Begin: the Problem of Burdens on the Free Exercise of Religion," 102 *Harv. L. Rev.* 933, 947 (1989).

86. Frazee v. Illinois Dep't of Employment Security, 489 U.S. 829 (1989). Justice White wrote the brief, unanimous opinion.

87. Bowen v. Roy, 476 U.S. 693, 727 (1986) (Justice O'Connor, joined by Justices Brennan and Marshall, concurring in part and dissenting in part).

88. In Bowen v. Roy, for example, the Court rejected a Native American father's claim that to be required to furnish a social security number for his daughter, Little Bird of the Snow, as a condition of receiving federal aid and food stamps, conflicted with his family's religious beliefs. See also Goldman v. Weinberger, 475 U.S. 503 (1986) (Orthodox Jew could be forbidden to wear skullcap while in military service).

89. Minersville School Dist. Bd. of Educ. v. Gobitis, 310 U.S. 586 (1940).

90. West Virginia State Bd. of Educ. v. Barnette, 319 U.S. 624, 642 (1943) ("If there is any fixed star in our constitutional constellation, it is that no official, high or petty, can prescribe what shall be orthodox in politics, nationalism, religion or other matters of opinion or force citizens to confess by word or act their faith therein.")

91. Santa Clara Pueblo v. Martinez, 436 U.S. 49 (1978) (no implied right of action in federal court to challenge alleged gender discrimination by tribe); Attorney-General of Canada v. Lavell; Isaac v. Bedard, 38 DLR (3rd) 481 (1973) (upholding exclusion of Indian women who married outside the tribe). But Canada's law allowing revocation of a woman's Indian status for marrying a non-Indian was said to violate the right to freedom of association, protected in Article 27 of the International Covenant on Civil and Political Rights. Matter of Lovelace v. Canada, Communication No. R/24 (July 31, 1981), U.N. Doc. CCPR/c/DR(XIII) R,6/24. For a useful discussion of international law in the context of sovereignty claims by North American Indians, see Note, "Toward Consent and Cooperation: Reconsidering the Political Status of Indian Nations," 22 *Harv. C.R.-C.L. L. Rev.* 507 (1987). For a devastating critique of the decision in *Santa Clara Pueblo,* including historical information on that tribe's much more complex treatment of gender, see Judith Resnik, "Dependent Sovereigns: Indian Tribes, States, and the Federal Courts," 56 *U. Chi. L. Rev.* 671 (1989).

92. 481 U.S. 604 (1987).

93. Id. 615.

94. Id. 607. Section 1981 contains that remnant of the original 1866 Civil Rights Act dealing with contracts that was also at issue in *Patterson.*

Though the statute does not use the word "race," precedents such as Runyon v. McCrary, 427 U.S. 160 (1976), have made it clear that racial discrimination is prohibited by section 1981 in private as well as public contracts. The Court also dealt in *Saint Francis College* with a statute of limitations issue not relevant here.

95. In an important footnote, White criticized popular understanding that there are three major human races—Caucasoid, Mongoloid, and Negroid—from the perspective of modern biologists and anthropologists. He noted that some but not all scientists have concluded that "racial classifications are for the most part sociopolitical, rather than biological, in nature," and that "[c]lear-cut categories do not exist." 481 U.S. 610 n.4.

96. Id. 610.

97. Id. 610–13.

98. 481 U.S. at 613. The Court thus approved the Court of Appeals holding that being "genetically part of an ethnically and physiognomically distinctive subgrouping" would be sufficient, but held such a showing not necessary to establish a discrimination claim under the statute. Justice Brennan concurred separately and argued that any line separating ancestry and ethnic characteristics from place or nation of origin could hardly offer a bright line test (614).

99. Shaare Tefila Congregation v. Cobb, 481 U.S. 615, 616 (1987). Justice White again wrote for the unanimous Court.

100. Id. 617–18.

101. 784 F.2d 505, 517 (3rd Cir. 1986), quoted with approval, 481 U.S. at 607. For historical sources that support the important point that this statement describes only the bare minimum of the coverage of the 1866 Civil Rights Act, see supra, n.49.

102. Thus White relied on comments made by Representative Bingham when the 1866 Act was repassed in 1870. Bingham claimed that the Act provided "that the States shall not hereafter discriminate against the immigrant from China and in favor of the immigrant from Prussia, nor against the immigrant from France and in favor of the immigrant from Ireland." Cong. Globe, 41st Cong., 2d Sess, 3871 (1870). Precisely the examples White used by way of illustration—as well as many others he might have invoked, particularly references to discrimination against "Celtic Irishmen"—undercut the distinction White advanced in *Saint Francis.*

103. In summarizing recent studies of Southerners, for example, C. Vann Woodward wrote, "Whites identify themselves with the South more than Catholics with their religion, more than union members with other unionists, and at about the same levels as blacks and Jews with other members of their race [sic]." *New York Review of Books,* Oct. 26, 1989,

13, 16. A much-publicized historical example occurred in a colloquy between Senator Henry Cabot Lodge and Julian Mack before the United States Immigration Commission in 1909. When Senator Lodge, citing Cyrus Adler, referred to "the Jewish race," Mack responded, "I do not recognize the Jewish race." Quoted in chap. 13, "What Is a Jew?" in H. Barnard, *The Forging of the American Jew: The Life and Times of Judge Julian W. Mack* (New York: Herzl Press, 1974), 93–100. Mack had a distinguished career as chief lieutenant to Louis D. Brandeis in the Zionist cause and as a federal judge; it was thus somewhat ironic that Mack headed the separate Committee of Jewish Delegates in Versailles in 1919. Like Brandeis, Mack had come to believe in hyphenated American Judaism. As Harold Laski observed in 1916, however, "Whether we will or no, we are bundles of hyphens. When the central linkages conflict, a choice must be made." Laski,"The Personality of Associations," 29 *Harv. L. Rev.* 404, 425 (1916).

104. Ho Ah Kow v. Nunan, 12 F. Cas. 252, 255 (C.C.D. Cal. 1879) (No. 6546). For Field's views generally, see Carl Swisher, *Stephen J. Field: Craftsman of the Law* (Chicago: University of Chicago Press, 1930); Charles McCurdy, "Justice Field and the Jurisprudence of Government-Business Relations: Some Parameters of Laissez-Faire Constitutionalism, 1863–1897," 61 *J. Am. Hist.* 970 (1975).

105. 12 F. Cas. at 255. Justice Field's realistic approach was echoed directly in Justice Harlan's famous dissent in Plessy v. Ferguson, 163 U.S. 537 (1896). Harlan attacked the idea that separate railroad facilities might be equal, because "Every one knows" that the statute's primary purpose was discrimination, thereby violating the principle that "Our Constitution is color-blind" (557, 559). Realistic perception by judges is often problematic, however, as is suggested by Harlan's assertions elsewhere in his dissent that the white race was and would remain superior in fact. Moreover, an aged Justice Field joined Justice Brown's infamous majority opinion in *Plessy.*

106. Id. 255. Justice Field, sitting as a single justice, actually based his decision on the Eighth Amendment's prohibition against "cruel and unusual punishment," without indicating any concern about how it might apply to state, rather than federal, action. To illustrate further how laws "general in their terms, would operate only upon a special class, or upon a class, with exceptional severity," and thus would be unconstitutional, Field mentioned "a large number of Jews" in San Francisco, "a highly intellectual race . . . generally obedient to the laws of the country." He suggested that should there be Jewish prisoners, their "peculiar opinions with respect to the use of certain articles of food" would make it unconstitutional to impose the same prison diet of pork upon them as might be imposed on everyone else.

107. The Court's most famous statement about unconstitutional discriminatory motive occurred a few years later in another case of the discriminatory application of law to Chinese aliens in San Francisco, Yick Wo v. Hopkins, 118 U.S. 356, 373–74 (1886) (when law "fair on its face and impartial in appearance . . . is applied and administered by public authority with an evil eye and an unequal hand," it is unconstitutional). For a careful study of the Chinese as subjects and shapers of a great deal of constitutional litigation in California in the late nineteenth century, see Charles J. McClain, *In Search of Equality: The Chinese Struggle against Discrimination in Nineteenth-Century America* (Berkeley: University of California Press, 1994).

108. William Wiecek, "Preface to the Historical Race Relations Symposium," 17 *Rutgers L. J.* 407, 412 (1986). Or as Ernest Renan noted a century ago, "[P]eoplehood is cemented by shared memories of common suffering," quoted in Dinstein, "Collective Human Rights," supra n.3, at 103. For a forceful elaboration in the context of descendants of slaves in the United States, see Patricia Williams, "Alchemical Notes: Reconstructing Ideal from Deconstructed Rights," 22 *Harv. C.R.-C.L. L. Rev.* 401 (1987).

109. Marc Galanter, "Review Essay: Outside, Inside: Jewish Justices in the Homeless Society," 14 *Law and Social Inquiry* 507, 522 (1989) (discussing C. Wright Mills's sense of "sociological imagination").

110. Minow, supra n.37; William Graham Sumner, *Folkways* 12–13 (New York: Gunn, 1906). The decisions discussed above may demonstrate that "it is a happy faculty of the mind to slough that which conscience refuses to assimilate." William Faulkner, *Light in August* 376 (New York: Garland, 1987).

111. For a recent study and collection of empirical work on the ability of courts in the United States to elicit acceptance of public policies unpopular with the mass public, see James L. Gibson, "Understandings of Justice: Institutional Legitimacy, Procedural Justice, and Political Tolerance," 23 *Law and Society Rev.* 469 (1989).

112. In contrast to recent ahistoricism, the United States Supreme Court insisted immediately after the Civil War, "[W]e cannot shut our eyes to the public history." Sparrow v. Strong, 70 U.S.(3 Wall.) 97, 104 (1866). Chief Justice Chase seemed unconcerned about neutrality in his opinion for a unanimous Court, maintaining that judicial notice of public history was particularly appropriate because the future of "vast mining interests . . . contributing largely to the prosperity and improvement of the whole country" turned on the particular question at issue.

113. This was part of Dinstein's explanation for initiating publication of the Israeli Yearbook of Human Rights, 1 *Is. Ybk. Human Rights* 14

(1971). Such realism seems particularly appropriate for academic critics lounging in easy chairs, watching the fray.

114. Discussed above in the context of the two *Patterson* decisions and the decisions in *Saint Francis College* and *Shaare Tefilla Synagogue,* supra ns.40–49, 92–102.

115. This trend is evident in disparate legal realms such as criminal law, torts, and even the First Amendment. See Brent Fisse, "Reconstructing Corporate Criminal Law: Deterrence, Retribution, Fault, and Sanctions," *56 S. Cal. L. Rev.* 1141 (1983); Robert Rabin, "The Historical Development of the Fault Principle: A Reinterpretation," 15 *Ga. L. Rev.* 925 (1981); Board of Education v. Pico, 457 U.S. 853 (1982) (plurality opinion) (focus on group's motivation for removal of books from public school library).

116. See Minow, supra, n.37; James Clifford, *The Predicament of Culture* (Cambridge, Mass.: Harvard University Press, 1988); Derrick Bell, "Serving Two Masters: Integration Ideals and Client Interests in School Desegregation Litigation," 85 *Yale L. J.* 470 (1976).

117. "Every Man His Own Historian," Presidential Address delivered before the American Historical Association, 1931, reprinted in C. Becker, *Everyman His Own Historian: Essays on History and Politics* 233, 234 (New York: 1935).

118. Id. 249.

119. This is true even when judges allow professional historians to testify as expert witnesses. For a fine study of the ebb and flow of attempts by American historians to achieve objectivity, see Peter Novick, *That Noble Dream: The 'Objectivity Question' and the American Historical Profession* (Cambridge, England: Cambridge University Press, 1988).

120. See Bernard Lewis, *History: Remembered, Recovered, Invented* (Princeton: Princeton University Press, 1975) (distinguishing recovery of forgotten history from illusion, and detailing changing attitudes toward history in Jewish and Islamic traditions).

121. This statement by the Baal Shem Tov is used as the motto of Yad Vashem, the Holocaust memorial in Jerusalem.

8. Judges and Identity Problems

1. President Woodrow Wilson, addressing a group of immigrants in Philadelphia in May, 1915, three days after the sinking of the *Lusitania,* quoted in Arthur M. Schlesinger, Jr., *The Disuniting of America: Reflections on a Multicultural Society* (New York: Norton, 1992), 35.

2. Judith Resnik, "On the Bias: Feminist Reconsiderations of the Aspirations of Our Judges," 61 *S. Cal. L. Rev.* 1877, 1921 (1988) (assessing implications of claim that "The language of the law of judges and the

language of feminism have virtually no convergences"); John Leubsdorf, "Theories of Judging and Judge Disqualification," 62 *N.Y.U. L. Rev.* 237 (1987); John Noonan, *Persons and Masks in the Law* (New York: Farrar, Straus and Giroux, 1976).

3. Felix Frankfurter, quoted in Richard Danzig, "Justice Frankfurter's Opinions in the Flag Salute Cases: Blending Logic and Psychologic in Constitutional Decisionmaking," 36 *Stan. L. Rev.* 675, 696 (1984).

4. Robert Cover, "Obligation: A Jewish Jurisprudence of the Social Order," 5 *J. L. and Relig.* 65, 72 (1987).

5. Reprinted in *From the Diaries of Felix Frankfurter,* Joseph P. Lash, ed. (New York: Norton, 1975), 254.

6. 319 U.S. 624, 646. Although some fancy steps might be fun about how the "one" in the minority leaps in a single "not insensible" bound to become keeper of "our Constitution," that approach sounds a bit too voguish.

7. Felix Frankfurter, "Personal Ambitions of Judges: Should a Judge 'Think Beyond the Judicial?'" 34 *A.B.A. J.* 656, 747 (1948). This speech of Frankfurter's at the 25th anniversary dinner of the American Law Institute was mainly a scarcely veiled attack on Justice William O. Douglas for his alleged presidential ambitions. It also contains a telling portrait of the judicial role, quoting former Chief Justice Hughes's image of "a weighing of evidence in scales with which prejudice has not tampered, of reasoned conclusions satisfying a sensitive conscience, of firmness in resisting both solicitation and clamor" (749).

8. Leonard Baker, *Brandeis and Frankfurter: A Dual Biography* (New York: Harper and Row, 1984), 394. Baker is not specific about the date of this exchange, and seems to imply the conversation took place in 1942, the date Robert Burt assigns to it. Robert Burt, *Two Jewish Justices: Outcasts in a Promised Land* (Berkeley: University of California Press, 1988), 102. Karski's account is that he saw President Roosevelt, Justice Frankfurter, and various government officials and religious leaders on a secret mission that began in August 1943. Jan Karski, *The Great Powers and Poland, 1919–1945* 461 (Lanham, Md.: University Press of America, 1985); Jan Karski, *Story of a Secret State* (1944, rpt. New York: Popular Library, 1965), 377.

9. Baker, supra n.8, Burt, supra n.8, 102. With this dissent, Frankfurter even alienated many of his old friends such as Morris Raphael Cohen and his namesake, Felix Cohen, as well as his Supreme Court colleagues. Joseph P. Lash, "A Brahmin of the Law: A Biographical Essay," in Lash, supra n.5, 71–72.

10. Lash, supra n.5, 254.

11. Id. The reference to anti-Catholicism suggests the intriguing possibility of an additional factor in Frankfurter's passionate *Barnette* dissent. It is well

known that *Barnette* overruled what had been Frankfurter's first major constitutional opinion, Minersville School Dist. Bd. of Ed. v. Gobitis, 310 U.S. 586 (1940), an opinion apparently known around the Court as "'Felix's Fall-of-France' Opinion." It is less well known that Jehovah's Witnesses often were vehemently anti-Catholic in their proselytizing; that the population of Minersville, Pennsylvania, was approximately 80 percent Catholic; and that the father of the Gobitis children was a recent convert from Catholicism who had become the local Jehovah's Witnesses leader. Danzig, supra n.3, quoting sources at 712 n.111, 717. Viewed from this perspective, *Gobitis* seems a bit closer to Frankfurter's concern about group hate in his majority opinion in *Beauharnais,* discussed infra, n.36–42. Relative degrees of concern about anti-Catholicism may help illuminate the vigorously contrasting sides finally taken by Frankfurter and Black in Martin v. Struthers, 319 U.S. 141 (1943) (Black switched sides) and similar cases. It may also help explain Justice Scalia's remarkably cavalier treatment of the *Barnette* precedent, and his preference for Frankfurter's *Gobitis* opinion, in Employment Division v. Smith, 494 U.S. 872 (1990), discussed in Chapter 7.

12. Danzig, supra n.3, 692, quoting Harlan B. Phillips, *Felix Frankfurter Reminisces* 36 (New York: Reynal, 1960).

13. Id.

14. Id. 19.

15. In re J. P. Linahan, 138 F.2d 650, 652–653 (1943). Judges Learned Hand and Swan joined Frank's opinion.

16. Id. 653.

17. Id. 654.

18. Id. As if setting out to twit Frankfurter for his Anglophilic tendencies, Frank's opinion was festooned with classical allusions and with long footnotes quoting English commentators ranging from Herbert Spencer to Macaulay.

19. Id. The controversy between Frankfurter and Frank was often described as a Harvard-Yale Law School contest and as a battle between the legal process and legal realist modes of legal analysis. See David A. Hollinger, *Morris R. Cohen and the Scientific Ideal* (Cambridge, Mass.: M.I.T. Press, 1975).

20. Louisiana ex rel. Francis v. Resweber, 329 U.S. 459, 471 (1947). That *Francis* was decided the day that Adamson v. California, 332 U.S. 46 (1947) was argued before the Court may help explain some of the vehemence in the famous clash in *Adamson* between Frankfurter and Hugo Black. Frankfurter's acknowledgment in *Francis* that his vision of due process involved "a demand for civilized standards which are not defined by specifically enumerated guarantees of the Bill of Rights . . . nor are they confined by them," "the application of standards of fairness and justice

very broadly conceived," and, quoting Holmes, "differences of degree" (329 U.S. 468, 470, 471), could hardly have reassured either a textualist such as Black was fast becoming nor others who feared that a justice's individual views might be imported into a decision, notwithstanding Frankfurter's vigorous protests to the contrary.

21. Arthur Miller and Jeffrey H. Bowman, *Death by Installments: The Ordeal of Willie Francis* (New York: Greenwood Press, 1988), 110, quoting Max Freedman, William Beaney and Eugene Rostow, *Perspectives on the Court* (Evanston, Ill.: Northwestern University Press, 1967), 15. This discussion of the details of the Willie Francis case relies heavily on the Miller and Bowman book.

22. Public Utilities Commission v. Pollak, 343 U.S. 451, 466 (1952) (unsuccessful challenge to radio broadcasts played on public buses, claiming unconstitutional intrusion upon "captive audience.")

23. Id. 467. It is not clear whether Frankfurter was concerned about being able to control his strong feelings, or about the appearance that he might not be disinterested. This is in sharp contrast with his convoluted judicial stance in *Barnette* and *Francis*. As John Leubsdorf has demonstrated, Frankfurter was not alone in agonizing about his feelings and his role, but he was particularly emphatic as he tied himself in knots in the course of his vigorous attempts to articulate the appropriately detached role for judges and other public officials. Leubsdorf, *supra,* n.2, at 244 n.44 and at 264 n.134. For example, Frankfurter insisted that Cabinet officials were not "flabby creatures" and ought not to be disqualified because of their previous expressions of views because, like judges, they were "men of . . . intellectual discipline." United States v. Morgan, 313 U.S. 409, 421 (1941). In Bridges v. California, 314 U.S. 252, 289, 292, 299 (1941), however, Frankfurter's dissent argued that although judges are entitled to "no greater immunity from criticism than other persons or institutions," they are more susceptible to "coercive interference with their work"; therefore, California ought to be permitted to ban critical publications that were a "threat to impartial adjudication."

24. Public Utilities v. Pollak, 343 U.S. 466.

25. Id.

26. See Dennis v. United States, 341 U.S. 494, 517 (1951) (concurring in decision upholding conviction of Communist Party leaders based on judicial notice of clear and present danger they posed); Communist Party v. Subversive Activities Control Board, 367 U.S. 1 (1961) (upholding requirement that Communist Party reveal its membership, because Board rationally concluded Party constituted clear and present danger); Lerner v. Casey, 357 U.S. 468 (1958) and Beilan v. Board of Public Education, 357 U.S. 399, 409 (1958) (concurring in decisions upholding dismissals

of subway conductor and teacher for refusal to answer questions about their possible Communist pasts).

27. 347 U.S. 483 (1954). For details about Frankfurter's extraordinary efforts to build unanimity, see Dennis J. Hutchinson, "Unanimity and Desegregation: Decisionmaking in the Supreme Court, 1948–1958," 68 *Geo. L. J.* 1 (1979). The year before the decision, Frankfurter had said of the death of Chief Justice Vinson just before reargument in *Brown,* "This is the first indication I have ever had that there is a God," quoted in Richard Kluger, *Simple Justice* (New York: Knopf, 1976), 656.

28. See *The Rosenbergs: Collected Visions of Artists and Writers,* Rob A. Okun, ed., (New York: Universe Books, 1988); Robert Coover, *The Public Burning* (New York: Viking Press, 1977); E. L. Doctorow, *The Book of Daniel* (New York: Random House, 1971).

29. Michael Walzer, *Exodus and Revolution* (New York: Basic Books, 1985), 7. Walzer describes the Exodus story as such a story and—perhaps for that reason—as a paradigm for revolutionary politics: a big story that makes it possible to tell other stories, yet that somehow remains open to events.

30. Rosenberg v. United States, 346 U.S. 273, 310 (1953). See Michael Parrish, "Cold War Justice: The Supreme Court and the Rosenbergs," 82 *Am. Hist. Rev.* 805 (1977), a careful study of the complicated procedural wrangling leading to the final decision to dissolve the stay that Justice Douglas had issued after the formal adjournment of the Court. Parrish suggests that despite Douglas's dramatic public gesture, Douglas earlier refused to use several opportunities he had to cast a decisive vote that would have delayed the executions. In earlier rounds, Frankfurter found himself entangled by his own "unbroken practice" of never commenting on the denial of a petition for certiorari, yet anxious to telegraph that the formal record "does not present an accurate picture of what took place," 346 U.S. 281 n.8.

31. Jerold Auerbach, *Rabbis and Lawyers: The Journey from Torah to Constitution* (Bloomington: Indiana University Press, 1990), 164.

32. For a fine essay about the impact of the case on the Jewish community, see Deborah Dash Moore, "Reconsidering the Rosenbergs: Symbol and Substance in Second Generation American Jewish Consciousness," 8 *J. Am. Ethnic Hist.* 21 (1988).

33. 343 U.S. 1 (1952).

34. Id., 34, 42. Frankfurter analogized the role of a judge in a criminal trial to that of a surgeon, and said the courtroom "should have the atmosphere of the operating room" (38). Not only did Frankfurter celebrate the detachment of a judge; he also proclaimed, "If he is adequate to his functions, the moral authority which he radiates will impose the indispensable standards of dignity and austerity upon all who participate in a criminal trial."

In a sense, Frankfurter here was carrying on his dispute with Frank, who in the *Sacher* case had reluctantly changed his vote and joined Learned Hand's opinion upholding the contempt citations, over a dissent by Judge Charles Clark, 182 F.2d 416 (2d Cir. 1950). For an excellent description of this case and of the general persecution of the few lawyers who dared to represent Communist defendants, see Stanley Kutler, *The American Inquisition: Justice and Injustice in the Cold War* (New York: Hill and Wang, 1982), 152–82.

35. Auerbach, supra n.31, 164.
36. 343 U.S. 250, 263 (1952).
37. Id. 261.
38. Id. 273. Black was joined by Justice William O. Douglas in his vigorous dissent, and Justices Douglas, Stanley F. Reed, and Robert H. Jackson all filed additional dissents.
39. Id. 275.
40. Id.
41. Id. 255–256. Frankfurter here quoted and relied upon dictum in the unanimous decision written by the liberal Justice Frank Murphy in Chaplinsky v. New Hampshire, 315 U.S. 568, 571–72 (1942) (defining this "narrow category" to except "insulting or 'fighting words,'" as well as "the lewd and obscene, the profane, [and] the libelous," from First Amendment protection).
42. Id. 263. While he was thus directly anticipating the unanimous Court's concern about the damage wrought by segregation to the "hearts and minds" of black schoolchildren, Brown v. Board of Education, 347 U.S. 483 (1954), Frankfurter also was quite cagey. He repeatedly alluded to the social sciences but argued that the "science of government"—which he said was perhaps not a science at all but rather an experiment—need not be in "the vanguard of science—especially sciences as young as human ecology and cultural anthropology." 343 U.S. at 262. Moreover, Frankfurter insisted that neither the Court's role nor its competence ought to let it try "to confirm or deny claims of social scientists as to the dependence of the individual on the position of his racial or religious group in the community" (263).
43. Benjamin Cardozo, *The Nature of the Judicial Process* (New Haven: Yale University Press, 1921), 13. At the time Cardozo's point was quite controversial, and some people used it to oppose the judge's appointment to the United States Supreme Court.
44. Among the best articles are those in a symposium published in the 1990 *Duke Law Journal,* in particular Charles R. Lawrence III's "If He Hollers Let Him Go: Regulating Racist Speech on Campus," 1990 *Duke L. J.* 431. See also Martha Minow, "Looking Ahead to the 1990s," 19 *C. L. Dig.* 293 (1989); Thomas Grey, "Civil Rights vs. Civil Liberties: The

Case of Discriminatory Verbal Harassment," 8 *Social Phil. and Policy* 81 (1991); Mari Matsuda, "Public Response to Racist Speech: Considering the Victim's Story," 87 *Mich. L. Rev.* 2320 (1989); Robert Sedler, "Doe v. University of Michigan and Campus Bans on 'Racist Speech': The View from Within," 37 *Wayne L. Rev.* 1325 (1991).

45. R.A.V. v. St. Paul, 112 S.Ct. 2538, 2541 (1992), quoting the St. Paul Bias-Motivated Crime Ordinance, St. Paul, Minn. Legis. Code Sec. 292.02 (1990).

46. Justice Scalia wrote for the majority, holding the ordinance to be facially unconstitutional in that it prohibits otherwise permitted speech solely on the basis of the subjects that the speech addresses; Justice White wrote, concurring only in the judgment, in which Justices Blackmun and O'Connor joined, and in which Justice Stevens joined, except for Part 1-A. Blackmun wrote separately, concurring in the judgment. So did Justice Stevens, also concurring only in the judgment, this time joined except for Part I by Justices White and Blackmun.

47. 112 S.Ct. at 2545.

48. Id. 2548.

49. Id. 2549.

50. 315 U.S. 568 (1942).

51. Id. 569.

52. See Batson v. Kentucky, 476 U.S. 79 (1986); Edmonson v. Leesville Concrete Co., 500 U.S. 614 (1991).

53. 500 U.S. 352 (1991).

54. The phrase is Robert Nozick's and its implications are developed in Michael Sandel, *Liberalism and the Limits of Justice* (Cambridge, England: Cambridge University Press, 1982), 100.

55. Doctorow, supra n.28, 132–33.

56. It is hard to be sure, but Jerold Auerbach, who uses Ascher beautifully to set up his richly detailed study of Rabbis and Judges, seems to be among the mockers.

57. Doctorow describes Ascher as a religious man whose honor was unquestionable. Ascher considered witchhunting, paganism, and irrationality as sins. Though he was not politically minded and, "if anything, conservative," Ascher agreed to represent accused Communist spies at the height of the Red Scare when no one else would do so. Ascher could easily condone what was simultaneously pathetic and gutsy in his clients. He "understood how someone could foreswear his Jewish heritage and take for his own the perfectionist dream of heaven on earth, and in spite of that, or perhaps because of it, still consider himself a Jew" (119).

58. Mark DeWolfe Howe and Louis F. Eaton, Jr., "The Supreme Judicial Power in the Colony of Massachusetts Bay," 20 *New Eng. Q.* 291, 294–95 (1947), quoting John Winthrop in *Winthrop Papers* (Boston:

Massachusetts Historical Society, 1944), IV, 383, and 46 *Proceedings of the Massachusetts Historical Society* 280 (Boston: Massachusetts Historical Society, 1913) (explaining the problem of "a meere democratie" to be that it "in effect puts out one of the eyes (if not the right one) of the common wealth," 282).

59. Howe and Eaton, supra n.58, at 304–05.
60. Noonan, supra n.2, 18.
61. German judges and law professors during the Third Reich, for example, used theories of invisible tradition, *lacunae* in the law, and the overarching importance of the *Volk* and the state to ignore or overrule positive law in their campaign against individual and group rights. Ingo Müller, *Hitler's Justice: The Courts of the Third Reich,* Deborah Lucas Schneider, trans. (Cambridge, Mass.: Harvard University Press, 1991), 47–49, 206–09, 219–39.
62. Oliver Sacks reports the case of a judge who suffered frontal-lobe damage from shell fragments. Thereafter, he was totally deprived of emotion. Though in a basic sense impartial, the judge resigned his judgeship "saying that he could no longer enter sympathetically into the motives of anyone concerned, and that since justice involved feeling, and not merely thinking, he felt that his injury totally disqualified him." Oliver Sacks, "An Anthropologist on Mars," *The New Yorker,* (Dec. 27, 1993), 106, 123.

9. Oaths and the Communities of Judges

1. Lysander Spooner, *The Unconstitutionality of Slavery* (1860, rpt. New York: Burt Franklin, 1965), 152. Lysander Spooner was an antislavery activist and an early and eccentric American anarchist.
2. Linda Greenhouse, "In Trying to Clarify What He Is Not, Thomas Opens Question of What He Is," *New York Times,* Sept. 13, 1991, A19, col 1. For a perceptive discussion of this image, and of the difference between prior knowledge and prejudice, see Martha Minow, "Stripped Down Like a Runner or Enriched by Experience: Bias and Impartiality of Judges and Jurors," 33 *Wm. and Mary L. Rev.* 1201 (1992).
3. In a famous essay published simultaneously in three "leading" law reviews, Judge Learned Hand memorialized Justice Cardozo as a judge even more neutral than "the detached man." According to Hand, Cardozo was uniquely not a creature of the past—thus he escaped "all sorts of frustrated ambitions with their envies, and hopes of preferment with their corruptions, which, long since forgotten, still determine our conclusions." Summing up his encomium, Hand proclaimed Cardozo a "wise man," that is, "he is a runner stripped for the race; he can weigh the conflicting factors of his problem without always finding himself in one

scale or the other." Learned Hand, "Mr. Justice Cardozo," 34 *Col. L. Rev.* 9, 10, 11; *52 Harv. L. Rev.* 361, 362, 363; 48 *Yale L. J.* 379, 381 (1939). For a detailed, critical view of Cardozo's detachment, see John Noonan, *Persons and Masks in the Law* (New York: Farrar, Straus and Giroux, 1976).

4. This essay is not the place either to bury or to praise Justice Thomas. But after Anita Hill's accusations riveted attention on the confirmation hearings, the *entendre* of the "stripped down runner" seems at least double, particularly as compounded by John Doggett's vivid self-image of a scantily clad jogger, anxious to move on but held back by an amorous Anita Hill on the streets of Washington, D.C. Judge-as-stripped-down-runner approaches one edge on a spectrum of encumbered judges, perhaps not far from that of an imperial judiciary with no clothes. Felix Frankfurter's reverence for the judicial robes of the Supreme Court, and for what he considered its institutional constraints, might be placed toward the other end of the spectrum. For a poignant, but funny description of Felix Frankfurter's mortification when he felt he was not properly attired, see Robert Burt, *Two Jewish Justices: Outcasts in the Promised Land* (Berkeley: University of California Press, 1988).

   Cf. "Innocence" in Thom Gunn, *Selected Poems, 1950–1975* (New York: Farrar, Straus and Giroux, 1979), 40. This chilling poem, brought to my attention by John Leubsdorf, describes the "egotism of a healthy body" of a runner "ignorant of the past / Culture of guilt and guilt's vague heritage."

5. Laird v. Tatum, 409 U.S. 824, 835 (1972) (explaining decision to deny a motion that Rehnquist recuse himself *nunc pro tunc* in a case that involved government surveillance in which Rehnquist cast the deciding vote). Prior to his Supreme Court appointment, Rehnquist had testified as an expert witness about related matters on behalf of the Department of Justice before congressional committees, expressed his opinion about the law involved in speeches, and supervised preparation of a Justice Department memorandum of law dealing with the lower court opinion in that case and with other "applicable precedents" (826–28).

6. Id. 838, 839. For an outstanding discussion of Rehnquist's position in this case and of judicial disqualification generally, noting that we lack a theory of recusal because we lack a theory of judging and vice versa, see John Leubsdorf, "Theories of Judging and Judge Disqualification," 62 *N.Y.U. L. Rev.* 237 (1987).

7. Michael Sandel, "The Procedural Republic and the Unencumbered Self," 13 (draft article on file with author).

8. Sanford Levinson, *Constitutional Faith* (Princeton: Princeton University Press, 1988), 56 (concentrating on the tension, which all citizens experience, between secular religion of state and competing faiths). For elabo-

ration of this argument about judges, and consideration of the claim that such an obligation might be a form of idolatry, see Sanford Levinson, "The Confrontation of Religious Faith and Civil Religion: Catholics Becoming Justices," 39 DePaul L. Rev. 1047, 1061–71 (1990). See also Kent Greenawalt, *Religious Convictions and Political Choice* (New York: Oxford University Press, 1988), 239–41; Stephen L. Carter, "The Religiously Devout Judge," 64 *Notre Dame L. Rev.* 932 (1989).

9. 485 U.S. 617, 619 (1988).

10. After the controversial amendment of Fed. R. Civ. P. 11 in 1983, costs now could be assessed in all such suits against either parties or attorneys, but parties filing *in forma pauperis* presumably would be judgment-proof.

11. In re Amendment to Rule 39, 500 U.S. 13, 15 (1991).

12. Id. 15 (emphasis in original).

13. Id. Justices Stevens and Blackmun also dissented, finding it "neither necessary nor advisable" to promulgate the new rule.

The Court soon seized the opportunity to invoke the amended Rule 39 against two petitioners whose pattern of repetitious filing "resulted in an extreme abuse of the system." Zatko v. California, 112 S.Ct. 355, 356 (1991). Justice Stevens, joined by Justice Blackmun in dissent, pointed out that the usual procedures that were in effect for years before the amendment assured that the "integrity of our process" was not compromised "in the slightest" (357), and probably saved time now spent deciding when to enforce the new rule against indigent petitioners. Stevens argued that the amendment, and the Court's invocation of the new Rule, were for "symbolic effect," actually conveying a message that "the Court does not have an overriding concern about equal access to justice for both the rich and the poor."

14. 28 U.S.C. sect. 453, derived from sect. 8 of the Judiciary Act of 1789, 1 Stat. 76 (1789). A federal judge also swears or affirms that she or he will "faithfully and impartially discharge and perform all the duties incumbent upon me . . . according to the best of my abilities and understanding, agreeably to the Constitution and laws of the United States. So help me God." Some state judges, such as those in Massachusetts and Tennessee, swear or affirm similarly; most state judges undertake an obligation simply to uphold the federal Constitution and the constitution and laws of their respective states.

15. To be sure, it is possible that the oath simply seeks to be triply certain by repeating the obligation to be impartial three different ways. To interpret the oath to include such an effusion of repetition, however, is peculiar as a matter of construction. Moreover, such redundancy is not supported by the origins or plain meaning of two key phrases—to administer justice "without respect to persons" and "do equal right to the poor and to the rich."

16. Ronald Dworkin, for example, has insisted for many years that persons are obliged to treat others "with equal concern and respect," and the phrase has entered legal discourse, primarily in the context of assessing the requirements imposed by the Equal Protection Clause of the Fourteenth Amendment. See James O'Fallon, "Adjudication and Contested Concepts: The Case of Equal Protection," 54 *N.Y.U. L. Rev.* 19, 34 (1979). The Oxford English Dictionary offers seventeen definitions of "respect," starting with "to have regard or relation to, or connexion with, something" and "to give heed, attention, or consideration to something." To pay attention to the biblical context from which we derive the phrase "without respect to persons" seems to complicate rather than simplify its meaning.

17. Hannah Arendt uses this Kafka parable, briefly paraphrased here, to set the stage for her collection of essays, *Between Past and Future* (New York: Penguin, 1977), 7. The parable itself is available in Franz Kafka, *The Great Wall of China,* Willa and Edwin Muir, trans. (New York: Schocken Books, 1946). For an excellent review and critique of the important current debate among political theorists that may boil down to Kafka's parable, see "Communitarianism and the Self" in Will Kymlicka, *Liberalism, Community, and Culture* (New York: Oxford University Press, 1989), 47–73.

18. Noonan, supra n.3, at 29–31. For further discussion by Judge Noonan of the origins and possible implications of the federal judicial oath, see John Noonan, *Bribes* (New York: Macmillan, 1984), 16, 69, 428; John Noonan, "Judicial Impartiality and the Judiciary Act of 1789," 14 *Nova L. Rev.* 123 (1989).

19. Martha Minow, *Making All the Difference: Inclusion, Exclusion, and American Law* (Ithaca: Cornell University Press, 1990), 65.

20. Judith Shklar, *The Faces of Injustice* (New Haven: Yale University Press, 1990), 124–25.

21. Albert Camus, *The Fall,* J. O'Brien, trans. (New York: Knopf, 1956).

22. Justice Holmes described a "whole proceeding [that] is a mask—[when] counsel, jury and judge were swept to the fatal end by an irresistible wave of public passion" in Moore v. Dempsey, 261 U.S. 86, 91 (1923). His majority opinion sustained Judge Trieber's grant of a writ of federal habeas corpus to save the lives of six black men sentenced to death in a forty-five minute trial, dominated by a lynch mob, following the bloody Elaine (Arkansas) Race Riots of 1919.

23. See Lynne N. Henderson, "Legality and Empathy," 85 *Mich. L. Rev.* 1574, 1584–87 (1987) and sources cited therein, discussing people with whom we cannot empathize and people who abuse empathy.

24. 2 Chron. 19: 6. Yet to be impartial was considered so exceptionally difficult that "Every judge who judges a case with complete fairness even for

a single hour is credited by the Torah as though he had become a partner to the Holy One, blessed be He, in the work of creation." Babylonian Talmud, Tractate Shabbat 10a, quoted in Emanuel B. Quint and Neil S. Hecht, *Jewish Jurisprudence* (New York: Harwood Academic Publishers, 1980), 6. A judge is supposed to be so conscientious about treating equally those who come to be judged that "The judge should feel as though a sword were suspended above his head throughout the time he sits in judgment." Talmud, quoted in *The Pentateuch and Haftorahs*, 2nd ed., J. H. Hertz, ed. (London: Soncino Press, 1960), 500. For further sources discussing "the precariousness of impartiality," see Leubsdorf, supra n.6, at 248.

25. The Hebrew is more directly translated as not "to know" the faces of persons one judges; the word for "know" here is the same word used for sexual knowledge, as applied to Adam and Eve, for example.

26. In Solomon's dream prior to his famous judgment, the Lord offers Solomon anything he asks. Solomon requests "an understanding heart to judge your people." The Lord is pleased and responds: "I have given you a wise and understanding heart; so that there were none like you before, nor shall any like you arise after you." 1 Kings 3: 5–12.

27. My friend Fred Lawrence points out that the Talmud's paradigmatic example is the obligation not to offer wine to a Nazir, because the Nazir has taken an oath not to drink alcohol. This emphasizes the need to consider character in everyday life, as well as in the process of judging. The Talmud's disapproval of a judge who receives equal favors from both sides to a dispute makes a similar point about the judge.

28. Consider, for example, the *sedrah* (Torah portion) concerning Jacob's trickery of a blind judge—his own father, Isaac—to procure his father's blessing. Jacob's uncle, in turn, commits fraud against his nephew, so that Jacob ends up working 14 years and marrying both Leah and Rachel. The *sedrah* includes Jacob's extended trickery in pursuit of a scheme to wrest away his Uncle Laban's flocks, and Rachel's successful lie to hide evidence that she has stolen her father's (Laban's) household icons.

29. Perhaps it is significant that this reference to God's justice is *mishpat*, not *tzedek*. It is instructive that it must be said that, in executing justice, God is no regarder of persons—the translator seems to use "regard" and "respect" interchangeably for the same Hebrew root word—nor taker of bribes. But solicitude for orphans and widows implies that attention must be paid to a person's family situation, much as the distinction among cities to be smashed and cities to be extirpated implies judgment based on group behavior.

30. In *Persons and Masks in the Law*, John Noonan wrestles with what he terms "the central problem . . . of the legal enterprise . . . [which is] the relation of love to power," supra n.3, xii. He argues that rules and per-

sons ought to be seen as "equally essential components" of the legal process (18), and seeks to distinguish roles from masks. He concludes with the aspiration that "Persons speak to persons; heart unmasked to heart" (167).

Noonan interprets the Deuteronomic command of judging "without respect to persons" simply to require impartiality. While the New Testament and Thomas Aquinas continued—perhaps even rigidified—the perception of "respect for persons" as a sin, Augustine supplied the necessary corrective in defining justice as "an active service to another, who is loved" (16, 18). I have tried to suggest that the Old Testament story itself is more complicated, particularly as it anticipates not only the passage in Isaiah discussed above but also Isaiah 1, 17, as well as Psalms 72 and 82, and the words of Zechariah, Amos, and Jeremiah.

31. Code of Maimonides (Mishneh Torah), Book XIV (Judges, Laws of Sanhedrin), c. xxi.

32. Moshe Silberg, "Laws and Morals in Jewish Jurisprudence," 75 *Harv. L. Rev.* 306, 326 (1961).

33. Haim Cohn, "Beit Din" in *The Principles of Jewish Law,* Menachem Elon, ed. (Jerusalem: Encyclopedia Judaica, 1975), 561, 564.

34. Sanford Levinson, *Constitutional Faith* (Princeton: Princeton University Press, 1988), 23, quoting Moses ben Nahman [Nachmanides], *Commentary on the Torah,* Charles B. Chavel, trans. (New York: Shilo Pub. House, 1976), vol. V, 206–07.

35. *Arkansas Gazette,* Sept. 18, 1927, 1, 19 (emphasis added). An article by Judge Gerald W. Heaney of the Eighth Circuit Court of Appeals is a fine and accessible source for background material on Trieber. See Gerald W. Heaney, "Jacob Trieber: Lawyer, Politician, Judge," 8 *U. Ark. Little Rock L. J.* 421 (1985–86).

36. In October 1993 Rayman Solomon took me to visit the small Jewish cemetery in Judge Trieber's hometown of Helena, Arkansas, which dates back to the mid-nineteenth century. I found members of the Trieber family buried there, but no marker for Jacob Trieber.

37. "Trieber for Judge," *Arkansas Gazette,* July 14, 1900.

38. Eli Evans, *Judah P. Benjamin, the Jewish Confederate* (New York: Free Press, 1988).

39. Rayman Solomon, "The Appointment of Judge Jacob Trieber," Paper presented at Conference of Jews and the Law, University of Wisconsin, November 1991.

40. *Jonesboro Daily Tribune,* September 9, 1925, reprinting *New York Times* Editorial. Trieber's 1914 finding of the unconstitutionality of the existing federal statute led to a treaty with Great Britain and a new statute, which Trieber then upheld, as did the Supreme Court in a famous Holmes opinion that stressed how the Constitution must adapt to changing times.

Missouri v. Holland, 252 U.S. 416 (1920). Trieber also presided, by designation, over the very lengthy trial in the key antitrust case against the United Shoe Machinery Company (with which Brandeis had been involved in earlier controversy). Trieber's opinion in that case has remained an important antitrust precedent. United States v. United Shoe Machinery Co., 264 F. 138 (E.D. Mo. 1920), *aff'd,* 258 U.S. 451 (1922).

41. 261 U.S. 86 (1923). "By all accounts, Moore was a watershed," according to Larry Yackle, because it held that "the federal court must determine the facts for itself because, if true, they entitled the petitioner to relief." Larry Yackle, *Post-Conviction Remedies* (Rochester: Lawyers Co-operative Publishing Company, 1981), 88–89.

42. In writing for the majority in *Moore,* Holmes held that habeas corpus might be used in the manner he had suggested in his *Frank v. Mangum* dissent: a writ that "comes in from the outside, not in subordination to the proceedings, and although every form may have been preserved, opens the inquiry whether they have been more than an empty shell." 237 U.S. 309, 346 (1915).

43. 125 F. 322 (1903).

44. See Wyn Craig Wade, *The Fiery Cross: The Ku Klux Klan in America,* (New York: Simon and Schuster, 1987), 114–15; William F. Holmes, "Whitecapping: Anti-Semitism in the Populist Era," 63 *Am. Jewish Hist. Q.* 244 (1974) (focusing on whitecapping in southwestern Mississippi in the early 1890s).

45. 92 U.S. 542 (1876) (invalidating federal indictment after the Colfax Riot of 1873, discussed above).

46. 392 U.S. 409 (1968) (holding that 1866 Civil Rights Act, grounded on the Thirteenth Amendment, applied to private racial discrimination in housing).

47. See Aviam Soifer, "Status, Contract, and Promises Unkept," 96 *Yale L. J.* 1916 (1987); Aviam Soifer, "Protecting Civil Rights: A Critique of Raoul Berger's History," 54 *N.Y.U. L. Rev.* 651 (1979).

48. 125 F. at 325.

49. Id. 327.

50. Id. 330.

51. 203 U.S. 1 (1906).

52. Id. 16.

53. Id. 19.

54. Id. 20.

55. Id.

56. For an extraordinary study of images of justice, suggesting that the blindfold was not part of justice's iconography until quite recently, see Dennis Curtis and Judith Resnik, "Images of Justice," 96 *Yale L. J.* 1727 (1987).

57. United States v. Morris, 125 F. 324.

58. Martha Minow, "The Judgment of Solomon and the Experience of Justice," in Robert Cover and Owen Fiss, *The Structure of Procedure* (Mineola: Foundation Press, 1979), 447.

59. Scalia, J., dissenting, in South Carolina v. Gathers. 490 U.S. 805, 824 (1989), arguing that Booth v. Maryland, 482 U.S. 496 (1987) ought to be overruled. *Booth* had prohibited a prosecutor at the jury sentencing phase of a murder case from supporting a plea for the death penalty with testimony about the impact of the murder on the victim's family. Within two more years, after further personnel changes on the Court, Scalia prevailed and the Court overruled both *Booth* and *Gathers* in Payne v. Tennessee, 501 U.S. 808 (1991).

60. Herrera v. Collins, 113 S.Ct. 853 (1993).

61. John Rawls, "The Idea of an Overlapping Consensus," 7 *Oxford J. Legal Stud.* 1, 4 (1987).

62. Id. 12–13. For an excellent critique of Rawls's approach, and a counter-proposal that argues for "a more capacious understanding of what public life is, or at least should be," see David Hollenbach, S.J. "Contexts of the Political Role of Religion: Civil Society and Culture," 30 *San Diego L. Rev.* 877, 880 (1993).

Conclusion

1. "Letter to Dr. John C. H. Wu, July 1, 1929," reprinted in *Justice Holmes to Doctor Wu, An Intimate Correspondence, 1921–1932* (New York: Central Book, 1947), 53.

2. "Learning and Science" in Oliver Wendell Holmes, Jr., *Collected Legal Papers* (New York: Harcourt, Brace, 1920), 139.

3. Lester Thurow, "A Theory of Groups and Economic Redistribution," 9 *Phil. and Pub. Affairs* 26, 35 (1979). Thurow also pointed out that "[d]iscrimination affects individuals, but it can only be identified at the level of the group" and developed an argument that "[o]nly groups can be treated equally" (29).

4. Shalom Spiegel, "Amos vs. Amaziah" in Judah Goldin, ed., *The Jewish Expression* (New Haven: Yale University Press, 1976), 62. Spiegel observed that "The mischievous subtlety of the law can frustrate the very ends of law. The sheer inertia of outlived tradition, the dead weight of knowledge of the past, may stifle the living flame of justice" (57). Yet he also forcefully developed the idea that reasoned justice is an inescapable obligation or commandment, indeed, the supreme obligation for any community (54–55).

5. Alexis de Tocqueville, *Democracy in America,* J. P. Mayer, ed., George Lawrence, trans. (Garden City: Anchor Books, 1969), 705.

6. Id. 50.

7. I supplied more details about "Casablanca," and attempted to link it more extensively to constitutional law, in my "Complacency and Constitutional Law," 42 *Ohio St. L. Rev.* 383 (1981).

8. Hillel's cryptic questions have been discussed for centuries. For a modern application, see Kenneth Arrow, *The Limits of Organization* (New York: W. W. Norton, 1974).

Acknowledgments

There is not sufficient time, space, or memory to thank all the people who aided me and are partially responsible for this book. I am very grateful to my friends and former colleagues at Boston University School of Law and to the alumni, students, staff, and faculty at Boston College who taught me much about how mutual support still exists in some communities. They have my gratitude and deepest affection.

I also benefited from opportunities to give conference papers or endowed lectures at Amherst College, the University of Connecticut, the University of Maryland, Stanford University, Tel Aviv University, Washington and Lee University, the University of Wisconsin, and Yale University. Faculty workshops at Cardozo Law School, the University of Georgia, the University of Iowa, Louisiana State University, the State University of New York at Buffalo, the University of Texas, and my home institutions allowed me to float and to retract ideas and gave me new insights to ponder.

Two anonymous readers for Harvard University Press read perceptively and made helpful suggestions, and it has been a pleasure to work with Michael Aronson and to get excellent editing help from Anita Safran. Several libraries and many wonderful librarians quietly aided this project, especially Dan Freehling, Marlene Alderman, Sharon Hamby O'Connor, and their first-rate staffs.

Other remarkable people also helped me greatly. I am grateful in particular to Kathy Abrams, Victor Brudney, Marc Galanter, Mary Ann Glendon, Arnon Gutfeld, Haggai Hurvitz, Stanley Kutler, Fred Lawrence, John Leubsdorf, Hugh Macgill, Tracey Maclin, Jim Malley, S.J., Maeva Marcus, David Seipp, Steve Wizner, and Larry Yackle for extended discussions, close readings, and friendship. I could not have written this book without terrific research assistants, including Leiv Blad, Lisamichelle Davis, Steve Lincoln, Linda Love Mesler, Ken Rivlin, and, in particular, Janet Judge and Barbara Moreira, as well as

Brad Steiner, Anne Stuart, and Dan Trinkle. Linda Glennon and Ken Westhassel provided invaluable aid, comfort, and organization.

Milner Ball urged me on and Carol Weisbrod slowed me down at precisely the right moments—each also read and thought along with me. Ken Karst, whom I have never met, demonstrated that a sense of community does not require face-to-face communication. He carefully and constructively commented on the entire manuscript. Martha Minow repeatedly provided encouragement, criticism, and clear thinking, as well as her customary astute reading of my work.

Ahuva Woll Soifer and Samuel Soifer always have given me more than I can say, and they did not stint in their meticulous attention to the style and substance of this book; Amira and Rafi Soifer were always delightfully with me and their ability to distract me for more important things gave the book time to mature; and Marlene Booth prodded, loved, laughed, and helped with everything.

Earlier versions of parts of chapters 1–5 and 7 appeared as:

"Assaying Communities: Notes from *The Tempest*," *Connecticut Law Review* (1989): 871–897.

" 'Toward a Generalized Notion of the Right to Form or Join an Association': An Essay for Tom Emerson," *Case Western Law Review* (1987–88): 641–670.

"Freedom of Association: Indian Tribes, Workers, and Communal Ghosts," *Maryland Law Review* (1989): 350–383.

"Objects in the Mirror Are Closer Than They Appear," *Georgia Law Review* (1994): 533–553.

"On Being Overly Discrete and Insular: Involuntary Groups and the Anglo-American Judicial Tradition," *Washington and Lee Law Review* (1991): 381–418.

Index